Rude Pravo

Soviet and East European Studies

THE CZECHOSLOVAK REFORM MOVEMENT
COMMUNISM IN CRISIS 1962–1968

Soviet and East European Studies

EDITORIAL BOARD

FIRST BOOKS IN THE SERIES

THE CZECHOSLOVAK REFORM MOVEMENT

COMMUNISM IN CRISIS
1962–1968

BY

GALIA GOLAN

*Lecturer in Political Science and
Russian Studies at the
Hebrew University of Jerusalem*

CAMBRIDGE

AT THE UNIVERSITY PRESS

1971

Published by the Syndics of the Cambridge University Press
Bentley House, 200 Euston Road, London NW1 2DB
American Branch: 32 East 57th Street, New York, N.Y.10022

© Cambridge University Press 1971

Library of Congress Catalogue Card Number: 76–163059

ISBN: 0 521 8246 3

Printed in Great Britain by
Alden & Mowbray Ltd
at the Alden Press, Oxford

CONTENTS

Contents

ACKNOWLEDGEMENTS

A number of persons have graciously given of their time and abilities to help me in the preparation of this work. I am particularly grateful to Leonard Schapiro and Shlomo Avineri for reading the manuscript and advising me throughout the preparation for publication. I am also grateful to Ruth Klinov and Michael Keren for their laborious efforts in helping me prepare the economic chapters. The excellent Czechoslovak research unit of Radio Free Europe was invaluable in supplying both source material and analyses. I am similarly indebted to my friend Yehuda Lahav. I wish also to thank my assistant Michael Shafir for his preparation of the index, and Mrs Malka Kroll and Naomi Meyuchaas for their devoted help in typing and administration of the technical side of this study. The Eliezer Kaplan School of Economics and Social Sciences of the Hebrew University generously provided me with the grant for the research.

I am especially indebted to a large number of Czechs and Slovaks who were willing to give me long hours of their time and information regarding their roles in the Czechoslovak reform movement. It is to them, their courage, and their hopes that I would like to dedicate this book.

GALIA GOLAN

Jerusalem 1971

NOTE ON TRANSLITERATION

All Czech and Slovak names and titles throughout the text, footnotes, and bibliography have been anglicized.

INTRODUCTION: 1956 TO 1962

As the only East European country with a democratic tradition centuries old and a newer albeit brief parliamentary heritage, Czechoslovakia has often been considered somewhat exceptional for that part of the world. So too the communist movement in Czechoslovakia has often stood out as somewhat unique in Eastern Europe. Yet this distinction has, at varying times, been achieved for what would appear to be contradictory characteristics: the movement's liberal, humanistic, democratic nature – at times *and*, at other times, the movement's dogmatism, cruelty, and docility. Both in the 1920s and in the 1940s, the Communist Party of Czechoslovakia found itself at odds with the international communist movement because of its apparent lack of revolutionary fervor, its tendencies towards a peaceful, parliamentary, and perhaps evolutionary road to socialism. In both periods, however, it accepted the will of the international movement, in the 1920s by undergoing 'Bolshevization' through purges, in 1948, by staging a coup d'etat. Yet, after coming to power, the party demonstrated its obedience by undertaking the most extensive and ruthless series of trials and purges known to Eastern Europe; and it became known as the most dogmatic, imitative, and loyal servant of Moscow in Eastern Europe.

It may be said that this conservatism was, in fact, because of the party and the country's democratic background, i.e. that the ruling hand had to be all the more firm. Czech communists themselves have explained the phenomenon as the logical outcome of the very use of terror whereby a dependence upon these methods becomes ingrained and the regime built on insecurity and police methods falls servant to both this insecurity and these police methods. Thus Czechoslovakia was even the last, or among the last, communist regime in Eastern Europe to respond to the process of liberalization begun after Stalin's death, and known in the West as de-Stalinization.

It is customary to date de-Stalinization from the year 1956, be it in the Soviet Union or Eastern Europe, and to trace its origins to Malenkov's 'New Course.' In Czechoslovakia, however, this process all but did not take place. The pressures for a thaw were present in Czechoslovakia as in the other East European countries, but the party was wary of both the New Course and the discrediting of Stalin. It made every effort, therefore, to reduce the pressures to a minimum and to prevent the type of situation which had resulted from the New Course and rising expectations in Poland and Hungary. It was only after the Twenty-Second CPSU Congress in 1961 and, more directly, the Twelfth Congress of the Czechoslovak Communist Party in December 1962, that de-Stalinization began in earnest in Czechoslovakia. Begun belatedly, as a result of a variety of pressures and circumstances, Czechoslovak de-Stalinization was destined, however, to be of deep significance, for the Czech and Slovak de-Stalinizers had the benefit of their own traditions, as well as the experience of earlier 'de-Stalinizers' (Poland and Hungary). The result was an effort for a thoroughgoing, genuine, and lasting transformation of the institutions of Czechoslovak society rather than a superficial, precarious thaw.

The Prague regime more or less ignored Malenkov's New Course as a temporary phenomenon that they could safely 'wait out.' After the popular outburst in reaction to the 1953 currency reform, the party was aware of the dangers of a relaxation of controls. The political trials, begun in 1949, continued into 1953 and 1954, even after Gottwald's death and the replacement of the deceased leader by Antonin Novotny in 1953. One of the few concessions, if not the only one, the Prague regime made towards the new line from Moscow at this time was a pause in the till then intensive drive for collectivization. The regime did not, however, abandon the idea, nor did it look favorably, in public pronouncements, upon the exodus from the collectives which took place in response to the change in Moscow's line. Indeed by 1955 the regime reintroduced its harsh collectivization drive. Other than the short-lived thaw in agriculture, the New Course could be felt only in the regime's formal emphasis upon collective leadership (not an unwelcomed concept given the fact that Gottwald's death meant changes in the highest constellations of the Czechoslovak party) and a certain restraint in public mention or praise of Stalin.

The Czechoslovak party was not, however, interested in a downgrading of Stalin or an attack on Stalinism. The main reason for this, true in the 1960s as well as in 1956, and an important factor in the delay of de-Stalinization in Czechoslovakia, was that the party's leadership was intimately involved with the phenomenon of Stalinism. Novotny, who had come to power only after Stalin's death, was tainted both by his active contribution to the trials while working his way up in the *apparat* prior to 1953 and by his continuation of Stalinist methods after

1953. If a relaxation of rigid controls was dangerous for the party insofar as its continued rule was concerned, de-Stalinization was dangerous for the individuals occupying the leading positions in both the Czechoslovak and Slovak parties. As a result as little as possible was instigated by the regime in the name of de-Stalinization. What little did lead to what might be called a thaw was the result of a minimum of obedience to Moscow and the initiative taken by certain dissidents: the intellectuals and the students. It is important to note two things in this connection, however. The New Course having failed to find strong (enough) adherents high in the party ranks, there was missing the figure of a dissident leader such as existed in Poland and Hungary. Moreover, the workers, for a variety of reasons, did not join the intellectuals and students in their protest, so that the worker–intellectual alliance which played an important role in the Hungarian and Polish events was also absent in Czechoslovakia. This is not to say that there were no pressures or disagreement within the party with regard to the response to be taken to Khrushchev's policy. There were indeed sharp differences of opinion expressed in the party's central committee meeting of March 1956, and it may be said that 1956 laid the seeds for personnel changes and reappraisals which facilitated the later rise of the liberals. However, the line which predominated both at the above meeting and at the special party conference called in June attested to the victory of the Stalinists in 1956.

There was to be no new Czechoslovak scapegoat or 'native Stalin.' Gottwald's memory was left almost entirely unscathed; there were no 'revelations' or purges. The only victim was Gottwald's son-in-law, First Deputy Premier and Minister of Defense, Alexej Cepicka, who was relieved of his party and government functions in April 1956. An unpopular figure, albeit a member of the politburo, his demise was not the cause of much concern or material for any break-down in discipline. It was only much later, in response to the Twenty-Second CPSU Congress in 1961 that Gottwald (and Zapotocky) was tentatively criticized – he was reburied and the statue of Stalin was ordered dismantled. By the same token 1956 saw no rehabilitations or renunciations of the political trials. The only revision of the trials was the dropping of the charge of Titoism – in keeping with Moscow's entente with Yugoslavia. The anti-Yugoslav allegations were declared fabrications created by Beria and Slansky. Slansky, executed in 1952, was thus represented as Czechoslovakia's major Stalinist. A commission for the review of the trials was created but no official action was taken. The

3

only positive result of all this was that, without rehabilitation or publicity, many of the imprisoned victims of the 1949–54 trials were released in 1956 and 1957.

As elsewhere the greatest pressures for de-Stalinization came from intellectuals and the students who took advantage of the new policy in Moscow to press their demands for their own country. A minor thaw did take place in the cultural world, primarily as a result of a certain hesitancy on the part of the party as to how to handle this initiative from below. Thus briefly, in the spring of 1956, numerous bold and critical articles began to appear, a number of previously suppressed manuscripts were published, and demands for a change in cultural policies could be heard. All this reached a climax in the Second Writers Congress of April 1956 when such writers as Ladislav Mnacko and poets Hrubin and Seifert criticized Stalinist cultural practices and demanded change. The dissident writers even managed to gain control of the union and elect a liberal presidium. This outburst was followed and taken up by the students, whose own campaign climaxed in their traditional Majales Festival on May Day 1956. In their parades both in Bratislava and Prague, the students unfurled anti-regime slogans and demands for liberalization, such as freedom of speech, access to western press, contacts with the West, and so forth.

The party's response to these actions was relatively swift and by 1957 the brief thaw was over. The students were forbidden to hold their festival again and the liberal writers were castigated at both the party national conference in June 1956 and at the plenary session of the Czechoslovak Writers Union in June 1957. In January 1957, according to *Rude Pravo* of 29 January 1957, Novotny condemned 'the ambiguous word "de-Stalinization" ' as standing 'only for the idea of weakening and giving way to the forces of reaction.' Prague's continued loyalty to the memory of Stalin was oft repeated and the policy of 'neo-Stalinism,' as some observers choose to call it, was enshrined. The 1958 Party Congress formalized the open continuation of Stalinism, sharply criticizing the writers for their earlier deviations; and the 1959 Conference of the Czechoslovak Writers Union returned the conservatives to the union's leadership. With the re-introduction of accelerated collectivization, the clamp-down on the writers and students, and the hard line declared at the 1958 Party Congress a period of harsh repression set in in Czechoslovakia. While this could by no means be expected to solve or eliminate the potential for dissidence within the party, a period of political stability and economic progress followed. Indeed a slight liberalization, the tentative agreement to a limited amount of decentralization of the economy, was wrested from Novotny but its genuine implementation was never permitted.

The Czechoslovak party affirmed the legitimacy and victory of its conservative policies with the 1960 Constitution and the declaration that Czechoslovakia had reached socialism, soon to be followed by the transition to Communism. Czechoslovakia was thus the first of the People's Democracies officially to reach socialism. This presumably was the result of Czechoslovakia's advanced economic position as compared with the other East European countries. The Constitution was to reflect more accurately this new reality in Czechoslovakia, replacing the former relatively parliamentary–democratic Constitution with a 'socialist' one resembling more the Soviet model. In addition to the need for a document more suitable to reality, it was revealed by a Czech theoretician in 1968 that there was a connection between this and the USSR's declaration in 1959 of the completion of the stage of socialism and the beginning of the transition to Communism in the USSR. The intention was a general step upward for the whole bloc on its way to Communism and, specifically, a recognition of the large role Czechoslovakia was to play in the expected 'overcoming of the West.' The Constitution was a centralist document in which the party and the government were more intimately drawn together and the party declared 'the leading force in society and in the State.' The conservative nature and purpose of the new constitution was confirmed by Novotny, as quoted in *Rude Pravo* of 17 April 1960: the Constitution was to 'cleanse our State of various "marks of birth" of the past, comprehensible in a transitional period.' By way of example he cited as such 'marks of birth,' 'liberal pseudo-democratic principles of the division of power.'

The declaration of Czechoslovakia as a socialist state was a high point for the regime, one marked by optimism and confidence in its chosen methods. The threat of de-Stalinization seemed a thing of the past, the party's central role both vis-a-vis the government and Slovakia ensured. Circumstances swiftly changed, however, and with these changes came new irresistible pressures which launched a drive for reform. Until 1968 this was a drive basically within the party, conducted by party members motivated by varying views of socialism – including the nationalist view of many Slovaks – but more or less agreed on the idea that the then present system did not provide the proper framework for socialist society as each understood it. This drive was of particular

5

significance, not only for Czechoslovakia, because the reformers sought fundamental, institutional changes. In effect they sought to adjust Marxism–Leninism to the realities of a twentieth-century, advanced, industrialized country which would not accept a contradiction between the concepts of socialism and democracy. This book attempts to trace this drive for reform, the factors and ideas involved, and its results.

The major part of this text was prepared before January 1968 and, therefore, was based on published sources only. Interviews were possible only after January 1968 and served primarily for confirmation rather than as primary sources. I have made an effort to preserve the spirit of this period and its discussions through a frequent use of the participants' own terminology and words wherever possible. The classifications 'liberal' and 'conservative' are mine, although one prominent liberal described it thus:

> One group wished to preserve the old, i.e., to conserve the old style and method of work; therefore one cannot but describe it as conservative. The others believed that the methods of work must be fundamentally changed. The important thing is that the progressive forces proved to be the more powerful.[1]

These are nonetheless loose terms used for convenience to characterize, generally, the forces involved. These terms do not mark fixed factions for indeed these were amorphous groupings with many persons changing their views, many revealing certain tendencies only as a result of events. These reservations about the terms 'liberal' and 'conservative' may also be applied to the term 'de-Stalinization.' One might use this term for the first stage of the process, using the term 'liberalization' for a later (post-Novotny) stage; one might use the term 'liberalization' instead of 'de-Stalinization' altogether, and use the term 'democratization' for the later stage. Indeed all three words have been used more or less interchangeably in the literature on the subject, each often being a mere euphemism for the others. While there are essential differences between the three terms, the use of any one of them is a mere convenience to characterize a process of fundamental change. The basic elements or nature of the process, as well as of the terms 'liberal' and 'conservative' will, I hope, become more clearly understandable from the text than from the single one-word term used to describe this process.

[1] Ota Sik in *Kulturni Noviny* interview, 29 March 1968.

6

1

THE TWELFTH PARTY CONGRESS
AND ITS BACKGROUND

The Twelfth Party Congress of the Communist Party of Czechoslovakia which took place from 2 until 8 December 1962 was to most observers a disappointing testament to continued dogmatism in Czechoslovakia.[1] The rumored instability of party first secretary Antonin Novotny – attributed to Czechoslovakia's failure to respond sufficiently to the CPSU Twenty-Second Congress, the Barak affair, the deteriorating economic situation and growing popular discontent, combined with the postponement of the congress from October to December – had led to expectations that startling changes would be forthcoming at the congress.[2] At the very least, some liberalization such as had been expressed by the Hungarians at their congress a month earlier was expected. Given these expectations many observers were disappointed by the endless stream of phrases at the congress on the need to improve the economy (by the conservative method of tightening centralized planning). Indeed, the single most 'startling' event of the congress appeared to be the intensification of open polemics against the Chinese which came with the speeches of Soviet representative Leonid Brezhnev and of Novotny himself.

It was probably not an accident, however, that the congress destined to become a major turning point for the Czechoslovak party, perhaps the most important meeting since the historic 1929 Fifth Congress, was outwardly drab, doctrinaire, and uninteresting. It may be that just this impression was intended and achieved by the skillful handling of the congress by party first secretary Novotny. As we shall see, forces at play within the Czechoslovak party at that time presented a threat to continued stability, and Novotny most likely hoped to keep these forces under tight rein, conceding and compromising only where necessary, without undue publicity or drama. Liberal elements within the party central committee had been gaining in influence and, together with their Slovak colleagues, had been pressing for reform in Czechoslovakia.

[1] See for example, *The Economist*, 15 December 1962; Adam Bromke, *The Communist States at the Crossroads* (New York, 1965), pp. 96–7.
[2] See below for details.

Events of 1963: The Decision to De-Stalinize

The first, but symbolically significant, step for which the liberals were pressing was a review of the purge trials of 1949–54 which had marked the height of Stalinist terror in Czechoslovakia. This was not a new demand but one which had gained momentum since the Twenty-Second CPSU Congress and particularly since the Hungarians and Bulgarians revised their past records prior to the Czechoslovak congress. Evidence that such demands had been felt in Czechoslovakia was presented by Novotny himself when, in a speech to the central committee at the end of 1961, he dismissed demands for review and revision of the trials as 'irresponsible and unjustified.'[1] The party leader had good reason to fight the demands, however, for he was faced with a three-fold problem. First, such a review was bitterly opposed by party 'conservatives' (basically the *apparatchiks*) who risked unpleasant publicity – perhaps even dire repercussions – if the injustice of these events and their own contributions to them were revealed. This group formed the backbone of Novotny's support, support he could hardly afford to jeopardize in the atmosphere of division and factionalism then current in the party. Secondly, Novotny himself, along with many of his top associates in the party, had been intimately involved in the perpetration of the 1949–54 injustices and had come to power as a result of the massive purges.[2] He too was an *apparatchik*, whose major qualification like those of his *apparatchik* supporters was his unimaginative but dutiful loyalty to the system. A true redress of past errors would inevitably lead to questions about Novotny's own qualifications or right to rule the party. Thirdly, Novotny as well as the rest of the party most likely realized that it would be difficult to restrict such a review solely to the trials, especially since not only many of the persons responsible for the 1949–54 events but also the malpractices themselves continued to function in the Czechoslovakia of 1962. Any rehabilitations or public redress of errors was likely to lead to a more general questioning of the atmosphere, conditions, policies, and organization that had permitted these malpractices *and* their continuation. Thus the opening of the whole issue was like the opening of a Pandora's box, given the situation in Czechoslovakia in 1962, fraught with potentially uncontrollable repercussions.

[1] Cited in Victor Velen, 'Czech Stalinists Die Hard,' *Foreign Affairs*, 43:1 (1964), 322; *The New Leader*, 24 December 1962.
[2] See the then security chief Bacilek's praise for Novotny's role, *Rude Pravo*, 18 December 1952; Karel Kaplan, 'Deliberations about Political Trials,' *Nova Mysl*, XXII:8 (1968), 1058.

Novotny was justified in almost all his fears, as was later borne out, but forces within the party, coupled with pressure from Moscow that Prague fall in line with the more liberal posture of the Soviet bloc, brought Novotny quietly to concede to a review of the trials. This concession, almost buried in the verbiage of the congress speeches, was apparently made grudgingly and most cautiously – which accounted for the outwardly uneventful course of the Twelfth Party Congress. However cautiously tucked between phrases of dogmatic rhetoric and exhortation the decision to review the 1949–54 trials (taken by the central committee three months earlier) was nonetheless revealed and adopted as a congress resolution. Following references to the Twenty-Second CPSU Congress Novotny, in his accountability report, admitted that 'anti-party methods' had crept into the life of the Czecho-slovak party too and revealed that the party had decided that 'socialist legality' had also been violated in most of the 1949–54 trials. Anxious to find a scapegoat and to further discredit his former rival, Novotny claimed that Interior Minister Rudolf Barak, chairman of the committee set up in January 1955 to investigate certain trials, had withheld information from the politburo, with the intention of using it to his own advantage later, rather than see that justice was done.[1] Novotny then announced:

> The central committee has decided once more to investigate in detail the political trials from 1949–54, to draw fundamental conclusions from them and write a definite conclusion to the matter ... a commission of the central committee is studying in detail all materials from the archives of that time and is drawing conclusions chiefly regarding party activity, the activity of leading party and state organs, and also conclusions regarding individual cases ... we propose to the twelfth congress that it instruct the new central committee within four months to deal with and conclude all remaining instances of political trials of the period of the personality cult.[2]

The political trials of 1949–54 actually had been composed of several sets of trials of two categories: the trials of 'bourgeois nationalists' directed against the wartime leadership of the Slovak party, and the trials of 'Titoist-cosmopolitans' which resembled the anti-semitic

---

[1] Presumably a reference to material Barak discovered about Novotny. After Barak's arrest Novotny confiscated certain of Barak's files, presumably those containing this information (*Reporter*, 5 June 1968).

[2] *Rude Pravo*, 5 December 1962.

purges throughout Eastern Europe and were climaxed by the execution of the Secretary-General of the Czechoslovak Communist Party, Rudolf Slansky. As a nod to de-Stalinization the Barak committee had been set up by the party in January 1955 for the purpose of reviewing the trials of the 1949–51 period, i.e. the period under Slansky's rule. In 1956 this period was extended to include 1952 as well, but only with the Twelfth Party Congress was the period extended to include 1954, i.e. the period of the trials of Slovaks, and others, when Novotny himself was party first secretary. Moreover, neither of the earlier reviews had produced rehabilitations as such and had merely confirmed Slansky's responsibility for Stalinism in Czechoslovakia.[1] Novotny made no reference in his speech to specific victims nor to which set of charges were now considered spurious. Politburo member Jiri Hendrych filled this gap somewhat, however, by the statement in his speech to the congress that 'nothing needs to be changed with regard to the guilt of Slansky and certain others.'[2] First secretary of the Slovak party Karol Bacilek, long-time Stalinist intimately connected with the trials and indeed destined to become the first victim of the redressment of errors, made no reference in his own remarks to the injustices suffered by his fellow Slovaks. Rather, he squarely placed the blame for all the purges – indeed for the entire personality cult – on the shoulders of Slansky.[3] Nonetheless the congress confirmed the central committee's establishment of a committee in 30 August 1962 chaired by a then Novotny man, Drahomir Kolder, to investigate the cases of leading communists prosecuted in the 1949–54 period.[4]

The liberals in the party could garner little else of comfort from this congress. A few promising cliches were uttered about the need to increase socialist democracy by giving greater power to the elected organs, but this generally was to be at the price of increased control by these organs over the lives of the people. One significant step forward was Novotny's pronouncement that 'in the stage for proposing candidates for deputies [to the local government organs, National Committees], it will be right to take into consideration several candidates and let the workers decide on the most appropriate one for a particular election.'[5] This was still a long way from having a choice on the ballot

---

[1] For details on the trials and reviews, see Kaplan, *Nova Mysl*, XXII:6–8 (1968).

[2] *Rude Pravo*, 9 December 1962. The name politburo was changed to presidium at the Twelfth Congress in accordance with the Soviet change.

[3] *Ibid.*

[4] *Rude Pravo*, 6 April 1968 (Kolder speech).   [5] *Rude Pravo*, 5 December 1962.

itself, but nonetheless a step in the right direction. Moreover, in a still more promising statement, Novotny said that 'with increasing socialist consciousness of the broadest masses, the activity of security police, courts, and the Prosecutor's Office will decrease naturally, compared with the present state of affairs.'

The basic tone and thrust of the congress, however, was decidedly conservative and best summed up by Novotny's unbudging position on the authority and role of the party. Despite the problematic state of the economy, which he blamed principally on poor management, Novotny declared that 'the basic viewpoint' for the selection and distribution of cadres 'must continue to be their political awareness and loyalty to the cause of socialism ... we have to oppose a non-political attitude toward the needs of society.'

ECONOMIC BACKGROUND

There were a number of forces at play which led to Novotny's tentative concession at the congress and to the radical interpretation of this concession responsible for the beginning of thoroughgoing de-Stalinization in Czechoslovakia. One of the most important of these factors was the deteriorating economic situation. As early as mid-1961 there had been signs that the Third Five-Year Plan (adopted in January 1961) was not going as smoothly as might have been wished. The six-month status report presented by the State Planning Commission to the government showed overall fulfillment of the plan but also significant shortcomings in foundries and hard coal mines – the backbone of industrial production – as well as below quota production in the chemical industry.[1] The industrial growth rate showed a drop from the average 11 per cent in the years 1958–60 to 8·9 per cent in 1961 and, for the first time since 1953, gross industrial output failed to reach the planned target.[2] Agricultural production was in a still more serious state and food accounted for nearly one-fifth of all imports, at a cost of $390 million.[3] This in turn placed a strain on an already serious balance of payments problem.

The directives for the 1962 plan already included major revisions of the planned targets for that year contained in the Third Five-Year Plan.[4]

[1] Prague radio, 1 September 1961.
[2] *The Economist*, 27 October 1962; 'Results of Plan Fulfillment,' *Statisticke Zpravy*, 1 (1962) and 2 (1962), 47.   [3] *The Economist*, 27 October 1962.
[4] See J. M. Montias, 'The Evolution of the Czech Economic Model,' Unpublished paper (Yale University, 1962), 100–10.

In spite of these changes (or in some ways because of them) the early months saw the problems of 1961 turn into an economic crisis. Czechoslovakia's economic difficulties became the most severe in the entire Soviet bloc. By mid-1962 Czechoslovakia's industrial growth rate was the lowest in Eastern Europe, standing at 6·7 per cent instead of the planned 9·4 per cent. Productivity showed only a 3·2 per cent rise as against the planned 7 to 8 per cent.[1] Agriculture, which had been showing a downward trend since the late 1950s, also registered setbacks. In the first three-quarters of 1962, planned deliveries of meat fell short by 20000 tons, of poultry by 3000 tons, of eggs by 163 million and of milk by 55 million gallons.[2] The average age in agriculture was fifty and was rising. The increased importation of food strained still further the balance of payments – already aggravated by serious short-comings in such key industries as metallurgy, heavy engineering, and building. Meanwhile, capital investments were steadily declining.[3]

Admitting the gravity of the situation, *Rude Pravo* of 14 August 1962 made public a party central committee document entitled 'On the Outlook for the Further Development of the Czechoslovak Socialist Society,' which revealed that 'in the past year and especially in the first months of this year difficulties and shortcomings have arisen, the main reasons for which lie in the disruption of proportionality and inadequate efficiency.' These in turn were said to stem from 'a low level of leadership and of planning and from the non-fulfillment of plan tasks.' The central committee therefore recommended that the present plan (Third Five-Year Plan, 1961–5) be dropped, without further effort to correct it. In its stead a seven-year plan (1964–70) was to be elaborated.

Left to trickle to a close, 1962 ended with only a 2 per cent increase in industrial production (instead of the projected 9·4 per cent) and a 7·6 per cent *decline* in agricultural production. 1963 was intended to be a year of retrenchment – a breathing spell – and the planned growth rate of production was put at a safe all-time low of 1 per cent.[4] Nonetheless, production continued to decline and Czechoslovakia actually saw its rate of industrial production regress by 0·4 per cent.[5] Agricultural production showed a slight improvement but still remained below the 1961 level; food shortages, particularly of meat, but also of dairy goods, were widespread. Long queues before butchers and grocers

[1] *New York Times* news service, Vienna, 19 January 1963.
[2] *The Economist*, 27 October 1962.
[3] Montias, 'Czech Economic Model,' 104–5; *Zemedelske Noviny*, 7 August 1964.
[4] *Rude Pravo*, 5 January 1963.   [5] *Rude Pravo*, 11 February 1964.

became a familiar sight throughout Czechoslovakia in 1962 and 1963. The shortage of meat was such that the government ordered one meatless day a week for restaurants. Shortage of fuel and electric power caused the regime to 'turn off the lights' in streets in the evenings.

The breakdown of a once prosperous economy – one that had once been the most productive in Central Europe – in times of world prosperity (as distinct from world-wide recession or depression) was not easy to explain. Outside observers maintained that one of the main factors contributing to this breakdown was the general failure of agriculture. Whereas food consumption had been rising sharply since the war years agricultural production had failed to show any progress after 1958. Indeed in 1962 it was admitted that agricultural production was only at the same level – if not lower – as 1938 production.[1] This stagnation of agricultural production stemmed from disproportionately small investments compared with the other branches of the economy, inefficient use of the investments made, uneconomic price structures, and ruthless collectivization which had led to peasant hostility and passive resistance. With labor shortages in industry and collective farm incomes reaching less than one-half of industrial wages, large-scale migration from the countryside to the towns had occurred, with the resulting rise in the average age of workers in agriculture. As we have mentioned, failure in agriculture necessitated an unplanned increase in food importation, placing an unexpected strain on the already strained balance of payments.

Reserves of productive capacity in industry and transportation were exhausted. Industries producing finished goods, which accounted for the great bulk of Czechoslovak exports, became increasingly obsolete because of inadequate technological progress and the high concentration of investments during most of the post-war period in industries producing basic materials. Large funds often became frozen in accumulated stocks and large unfinished investment projects. Moreover, despite the acute labor shortage, the ponderous bureaucratic apparatus encouraged labor hoarding and stimulated the drive for 'global fulfillment' of the planned targets, regardless of quality. The latter, for example, caused a loss in 1962 of 1 million kcs. in metallurgical rejects.[2] Foreign and domestic customers became less willing to accept products of low quality.

Also responsible for the crisis were a number of 'external' factors:

[1] *Rude Pravo*, 5 December 1962.
[2] *The Economist*, 27 October 1962. Official exchange rate was 7 kcs. to $1.

costly military build-up at the time of the 1961 Berlin crisis; the collapse of trade with China, from exports totaling $110 million in 1960 to $12 million in 1962; an unusually severe winter in 1962–3, a shortage of electric power (partially a result of poor planning), and costly economic rivalry instead of the hoped-for cooperation within the Council for Mutual Economic Aid (CEMA). Moreover, unable to secure Soviet credits, the regime was forced to draw on its own reserves to the order of approximately $60 million.[1] In addition, the USSR failed to honor its contractual obligations to deliver railroad equipment critically needed to ease the transportation bottleneck and, as Novotny himself admitted, the USSR failed to meet its grain delivery commitments to Czechoslovakia.[2]

Prior to the Twelfth Party Congress, Czechoslovak economists were most cautious in pointing out the then existing problems and defects in the economy. Domestic literature did, however, produce some criticism of measures then current in agriculture, and a number of economists were relatively candid in pointing out the shortcomings in the system of planning, including only thinly veiled criticism of the government and practices inherent to the Soviet type of economy.[3] Although public pressures on the regime on the part of liberal or reform-minded economists had to wait until 1963, there is much evidence that a struggle over the causes and solutions of the economic crisis was already being waged within the party as early as the first few months of 1962.[4]

The principle at issue was centralization: how much. Many party economists, including central committee member Ota Sik, who was later to become the author and architect of economic reform in Czechoslovakia, argued that decentralization of planning and control was essential to recovery, and that the faults of the present crisis lay in the fact that the 1958 decentralization had not been permitted to go far enough. More conservative party economists argued, on the contrary, that the 1958 decentralization was to blame for the crisis, and that the only logical solution was strengthened central planning and control. In

---

[1] See J. M. Montias, 'Uniformity and Diversity in the East European Future,' Unpublished paper (Yale University, 1965), 17; Velen, *Foreign Affairs*, 43:1 (1964), 322–3.

[2] Prague radio, 23 March 1962; Novotny speech, *Usneseni a Dokumenty Ustredniho Vyboru KSC: Od Celostatni Konference KSC 1960 do XII Sjezdu KSC*, II (Praha, 1963), 232.

[3] For example in *Hospodarske Noviny*, 1 and 22 December 1961, 9 March 1962.

[4] J. M. Montias, 'Communist Rule in Eastern Europe,' *Foreign Affairs*, 44:1 (1965), 345–6; J. F. Brown, *The New Eastern Europe* (London, 1966), 81–7.

1962, as demonstrated by the party statement issued at the time of the abandonment of the Third Five-Year Plan and by the party congress, the exponents of the conservative approach still had the upper hand. Novotny declared to the congress that 'the most serious fault in the practical application of the managerial system was the violation of the principles of democratic centralism through a weakening of central direction.'

Although the congress did sanction a committee to investigate economic reforms, the actual measures adopted by the congress to solve the economic crisis were conservative and, characteristically, sought organizational–administrative rather than substantive–qualitative solutions. Several ministries were to be split and new 'central authorities' created including a Commission for the Development and Coordination of Scientific and Technological Research. A State Price Commission was to be established to formalize and strengthen the regime's control of prices. A large number of ministerial employees were to be released. To help strengthen the authority and control of the plan a pyramid of Peoples Control Commissions was to be established so that an 'elected' body at each level, from the local enterprise to the district and regional level up to the Central Office of Peoples Control, could check on plan fulfillment and efficiency. A similar unit was to be created for agriculture, known as the Agriculture Production Administrations. In addition to control functions, however, these Administrations were to contain experts who could offer practical advice on the local level. The failure of these and various belt-tightening measures adopted in the course of 1963 and early 1964 was clearly demonstrated by the unprecedentedly poor performance of the economy in 1963 and the continued deterioration of the economic situation.

POLITICAL BACKGROUND

The abandonment of the Third Five-Year Plan was a serious blow to the regime's prestige – and particularly to that of Novotny. Although the population's grievances were not limited to the economic sphere, the economic crisis served as both a catalyst and a focal point of their opposition. The Czech and Slovak populations at large cannot be said to have been enthusiastic supporters of Novotny or even of the communist regime after the 1940s, but their relatively high standard of living had gone far towards keeping them amenable. By 1962, however, the population had apparently become indignant over the shortage of

consumer goods, the long queues for and shortages of basic com-
modities such as meat and dairy products, and the poor quality of the
manufactured goods they did secure.[1] It may be argued that by East
European standards the Czechs and Slovaks were accustomed to such
a high standard of living (in diet for example) that the shortages were
only relative. Nonetheless, discontent was rising among the population
because of the sudden come-down.

The population generally blamed the situation on communist
bureaucracy and bungling. More specifically, however, people felt that
two of the regime's policies were ruining the economy and causing their
material discomfort: the close cooperation with the Soviet bloc through
CEMA and the allocation of aid to underdeveloped countries. The fact
that the regime was under pressure on these issues could be seen in the
numerous articles and speeches defending both policies. There was
also a report in the West that in the important Tatra works in Northern
Bohemia 'critics demanded a thorough review of intra-bloc trade under
CEMA [*sic*] auspices which was said to be conducted on unequal terms,
and also a review of the country's overseas technical assistance activities.'[2] Once again it is immaterial if the population was right or wrong
in its assessment of the causes of the problems. People believed that the
regime was permitting the economy to be drained by commitments to
the other, less developed East European countries. By the same token
they believed that the shortages were a result of goods being shipped
to underdeveloped countries (especially Cuba) for political reasons and
that home needs were suffering from Czechoslovakia's heavy commitment to the underdeveloped countries on behalf of the Soviet bloc.
Included in this was bitter resentment against the large number of
foreign students studying in Czechoslovakia. Students resented the
larger scholarships and preferential treatment that foreign students
received from the Czechoslovak government.[3] As with the population
at large these specific grievances of the students aggravated already deep
frustrations and promised to bring the situation to a dangerous point.

The stop-gap administrative measures attempted by the regime not
only did little to help the economic situation but often further antagon-
ized the workers, including party rank and file. For example, with the

[1] See Velen, *Foreign Affairs*, 43:1 (1964), 323: *The Economist*, 27 October 1962;
New Statesman, 27 September 1963.
[2] *Christian Science Monitor*, 20 April 1963.
[3] See *Kulturni Tvorba*, 14 November 1963, or 'Those Foreign Students,' *East
Europe*, XI:3 (1963), 5.

reshuffling of manpower and the dislocation of output attendant upon the economic slow-down, superfluous workers were dismissed and often arbitrarily transferred to labor-short sectors such as construction, mining, and agriculture. The procedures used were often antagonizing as well, for strict adherence to the cadre system was generally maintained, i.e. the first to go were those with relatives who owned private plots while failing to meet their regular quotas. The last to go were loyal party members with no blemishes on their cadre records.[1] Slovaks in particular felt that they were being discriminated against in the reshuffling. Party and population alike felt that the 'Prague' ministries discriminated against Slovak plants in distributing scarce materials and in ordering shut-downs. In addition party rank and file were losing respect for the higher planning organs of the party. The inability of the regime to find a solution, the reversal of the early decentralization policy, and the accompanying debates contributed to factionalization of the party even down to the rank and file.

Other factors were also at play in this process of factionalization, however, and internal party pressures were assuming a serious aspect by 1962. The CPSU Twenty-Second Party Congress and its renewed attack on Stalinism had come at a most inopportune time for the Prague party. Although Novotny, upon his return from the Moscow congress and in obedience to the Soviet example, criticized the era of the cult, he did so by placing all the blame for the past errors on Slansky and the last stages of Gottwald's rule.[2] Due to the confluence of circumstances and pressures, however, the matter could not be so easily dismissed. The Soviet congress had come at a time when the Prague party stood weakened by what appeared to be a power struggle in the top ranks. The number two man in the party and most likely successor to Novotny, Rudolf Barak, had apparently made an attempt to build a power base for himself with the intention of usurping Novotny's position. The facts remain far from clear on the Barak case, but it is known that as Interior Minister Barak had had an excellent opportunity to build a power base of his own, to collect incriminating material on his adversaries, and to wield an independent power similar to that which Tito accused his number two man Rankovic of having wielded prior to his purge in 1966. More specifically, Barak headed an earlier committee created by the party to review the 1949–52 purge trials. In this capacity Barak presumably had uncovered much material of

[1] *Kulturny Zivot*, 1 June 1963 (Roman Kalisky).
[2] *Rude Pravo*, 21 November 1961.

potential use against Novotny himself. Moreover, Barak was a slightly younger, more popular man (despite his onerous job as Interior Minister) than Novotny. Known for his interest in modern art, the outgoing and sociable Barak was believed to be a more attractive, though not a more liberal leader than the colorless *apparatchik* Novotny.

In June 1961 Novotny began his move against Barak by transferring him from the Interior Ministry to the job of Deputy Premier. Although Novotny probably hoped in this way to cut Barak off from his base of power, there is reason to believe that Barak had already gained sufficient support to cause dissension in the party itself over this demotion. In this atmosphere came the CPSU Twenty-Second Congress and the attendant pressures upon Moscow's satellites to undertake more significant de-Stalinization. There were younger or at least more liberal men in the Czechoslovak and Slovak parties who wanted to see their own parties put their houses in order in the manner of the Soviet party. Indeed, the *apparat* itself had become increasingly dotted with reform-minded individuals since 1956. The deteriorating economic situation prompted many to think in the direction of reform. Aware of this incipient corrosion of the *apparat* and perhaps fearful that Barak might exploit these elements within the party, Novotny decided to wage a full-scale purge against him. Barak was stripped of all his positions and arrested in February 1962. The nucleus of the charges Novotny intended to bring against him were contained in a speech Novotny delivered in Bratislava on 22 February 1962, in which he said that Barak had aimed at 'seizing political power.'[1] Significantly this charge was never formally brought against Barak, perhaps because too many party members opposed such an extreme accusation or perhaps because Moscow would not tolerate a Stalinist-type trial in 1962, or perhaps for both reasons. There have long been rumors that Moscow had even played some role in the bolstering of Barak against Novotny in the interests of seeing the somewhat more popular Interior Minister assume the party leadership. This was directly implied in an Albanian attack on Barak in 1961 which predicted his arrest and trial.[2] Barak's close relationship with Soviet ambassador to Prague, Zimyanin, was

---

[1] This statement was deleted from the 23 February 1962 *Rude Pravo* version, though included in the Prague and Bratislava radio versions. At the Twelfth Congress both Novotny and Barak's successor, Strougal, confirmed that these were the real charges against Barak. (*Rude Pravo*, 8 December 1962.) See also *Reporter*, 5 June and 31 July 1968; *Kulturni Noviny*, 29 March and 5 April 1968.
[2] Cited in W. Griffith, *Albania and the Sino–Soviet Dispute* (Cambridge, Mass., 1963), 74.

often cited as proof of this, although given the nature of Barak's job it was natural that the Soviets should maintain close contact with him. Barak did, however, send a letter to Khrushchev expressing his opposition to Novotny's policy prior to his arrest.[1] While the point has remained a most difficult one to clarify, at least for outside investigators, it does appear that pressures were brought to bear upon Novotny to abandon the political charge and his plans for a show trial. Barak was tried in secret from 17 to 20 April 1962 on charges of embezzlement, misuse of party funds, and conspicuous consumption. He was given a fifteen-year sentence.

Although the case of Rudolf Barak ended with his imprisonment (no further purges were undertaken in connection with the 'case'), rather than consolidate Novotny's position it in fact led to a further deterioration. Barak's supporters inside and outside the party seem to have resented the high-handed treatment of the relatively popular figure, while reform-minded party members may have seen this as Novotny's unacceptable answer to demands for de-Stalinization of some kind in Czechoslovakia. In his speech to the central committee plenum of 12 April 1962 Novotny actually mentioned that an 'insignificant minority' of party organizations had dissented in the decision against Barak, demonstrating that Barak's support did not end with his arrest.[2] In effect, the Barak affair, coming as it did in the atmosphere of the Twenty-Second CPSU Congress, tended to solidify until then merely amorphous factionalism within the party and to incite rather than quell demands for a new line in Prague.

All this must be viewed with reference also to the incipient economic crisis and the outside pressures brought to bear by the Soviet Union. The Russians were anxious to have the East European parties follow their lead in denouncing the errors of the Stalin era and to rehabilitate selected victims of the past terror. Thus Bulgaria and Hungary made their concessions. In addition, Moscow was once again engaged in the pursuit of rapprochement with Yugoslavia and embarrassed by the refusal of some of its disciples to recognize the invalidity of charges of 'Titoism' used in the past. Here too Novotny was found wanting, for as late as 1961 he had conducted party proceedings against several intellectuals for advocating a pro-Yugoslav policy.[3] As the situation deteriorated in Czechoslovakia Moscow's interest became more pressing. She was disturbed by the economic crisis and the attendant

[1] *Reporter*, 31 July 1968.   [2] *Usneseni a Dokumenty*, 244–5.
[3] J. Pelikan, *Potlacena Zprava* (Wien, 1970), xxxii–xxxiii.

inability of Czechoslovakia to meet her bloc commitments, and by the demands the Czechoslovaks were beginning to make for Soviet economic help or concessions. There is reason to believe that Moscow also became increasingly concerned with the political problems – and line – within the Czechoslovak party. CPSU ideology chief, Ilyichev, visited Prague in May 1962, one month after the Barak trial, and shortly thereafter the decision to postpone the Czechoslovak party congress was announced. The reason given was that the basic program had not yet been completed, but it has been reputed that in fact the postponement was due to strong disagreements within the party.[1]

Another important source of pressure upon Novotny, one which may actually have been the decisive one, was that of the Slovaks, both inside and outside the party. Some observers attribute Slovak pressures to the general renascence of nationalist sentiment in East Europe which had begun to be felt at about that time.[2] Although it is true that nationalism was a strong factor in Slovak demands, this nationalism could hardly be described as part of a renascence since Slovak nationalism had in fact never been quiescent but merely contained through very tight controls. The confluence of all the aforementioned circumstances and forces at play weakened these controls, with the result that Slovak demands became open, vocal and, as it turned out, crucial in the struggle for reform or liberalization.

From its inception the Czechoslovak state had suffered from serious minority problems; particularly that of large German and Hungarian populations, far from satisfied with their position (or even inclusion) in the Czechoslovak Republic created from the break-up of the Austro–Hungarian empire in 1918. There was no minority problem so great, however, as that of the Slovaks in their unequal union with the Czechs. The numerous divisive factors in this union not only failed to be eliminated by the establishment of communist rule in Czechoslovakia, but, in fact, were aggravated by the addition of some specifically Slovak communist grievances.

The Slovak communists of the war years had cherished a dream of Slovak statehood under the Soviets, but such a policy was abandoned by Stalin towards the end of the war (if indeed it had ever been entertained by him). Disappointed Slovak communists tried to content themselves with the idea of a federation with the Czechs which would accord them equality and independent status as a party, the way they had operated

[1] See for example, *The Economist*, 24 July 1962.
[2] See for example, Bromke, *Communist States* or Velen, *Foreign Affairs*, 43:1 (1964).

during the war. Prague (and Moscow) had still other plans; after the 1948 communist takeover of Czechoslovakia a rigidly centralized regime was established in Prague which exhibited even less concern for Slovak rights than the pre-war regimes. To eliminate the possibility of rival authority outside that of Prague, the new communist regime quickly emasculated the existing separate Slovak political institutions such as the Slovak Board of Commissioners, the Slovak National Council, and the Slovak communist Party itself. Although there was probably some element of anti-Slovak prejudice in this policy, Prague was basically following the Soviet model for dealing with nationalities problems in its treatment of the Slovaks.

Mindful of the ever-present dangers of the strong nationalist feelings of the Slovak communists, Prague next sought to discredit and finally to eliminate those leaders of the Slovak Communist Party most closely associated with Slovak national aspirations. This it did first by condemning Slovak communist participation in the wartime Slovak National Council and by discrediting the Slovak party's wartime resistance, particularly the 1944 Slovak National Uprising against the Nazis which had been the result of an alliance between Slovak communists and non-communists.[1] Next, in 1951, it attacked the heart of the Slovak communist intelligentsia, the editors and contributors to the pre-war Slovak journal *Dav* (which included the most appealing, outstanding, and nationalistic leaders of the Slovak party). This process climaxed in the final action taken: the trials, purges, and execution or imprisonment of most of the pre-1948 Slovak party leadership, on charges of 'bourgeois nationalism.' The most notable victim was the well-known and respected communist Foreign Minister Vladimir Clementis, executed in 1952. To ensure Prague's will in Slovakia there were sycophants like Karol Bacilek and Viliam Siroky.

In the early 1960s Slovak communist intellectuals seized upon the settling of accounts at the CPSU congress to press their own demands for rehabilitation of their maligned former leaders. Rehabilitation could mean anything from admission that the charges were unjustified to reinstatement in the party or even to their former positions for those still living.[2] They used this opportunity to press other demands as well, as we shall see below, but their campaign for rehabilitations significantly contributed to the pressures on Novotny to permit a review of the trials in general – the concession announced at the Twelfth Party Congress and which, in fact, marked the beginning of de-Stalinization in Czechoslovakia.

---

[1] See chapter 14 below.   [2] Most were quietly released in 1955 and 1956.

2

REVOLT OF THE INTELLECTUALS

The revolt of the intellectuals with which the year 1963 and the real de-Stalinization process in Czechoslovakia got under way was both the manifestation and the expression of all the pressures mentioned in the foregoing pages. In addition, more general complaints of the population at large found their expression in the efforts of the intellectuals in the course of the year. The continuation of the pressures and circumstances, constantly publicized by the intelligentsia against a party leadership increasingly fearful of losing control, forced concession after concession from Novotny. A great part of the intellectuals' strength lay in the fact that most of those engaged in the battle with the party leadership were themselves party members, and they voiced the grievances of many elements of the party. Moreover, try though he did, Novotny was never quite able to find a way effectively to silence the critics even with concessions. In the post-Twenty-Second CPSU Congress period he was hesitant to resort to the out-and-out repressive measures (generally referred to as administrative methods) to which he had been accustomed. Mindful of the events in Hungary, and to some degree of those in Poland, that had resulted from an open alliance between dissident intellectuals and the population at large, Novotny probably was anxious to avoid creating heroes or popular martyrs of the intellectuals. As we have seen, Novotny's own position was not too secure, denying him the power to act from a position of strength. Even given these elements, however, it is unlikely that the intellectuals could have succeeded in publishing (or producing on the stage or screen) their increasingly bold criticism without support from within the highest ranks of the party.

As we have seen, the Slovaks in the party provided a strong source of pressure on Novotny, and the Slovak party itself was often at odds with Prague. Thus the intellectuals were able to carry their criticism even to the pages of the official Slovak party organ, *Bratislava Pravda*, lending great force to their arguments. The Slovaks decidedly were in the vanguard of the intellectuals' campaign, partially perhaps because they were temperamentally bolder than their Czech counterparts, partially because the nationalist aspect of their grievances gave them the appeal and unity of a 'wronged minority.' Thus they had relatively

popular albeit communist heroes such as Vladimir Clementis, Gustav Husak, and Laco Novomesky to avenge while the Czechs could hardly rally much excitement over the hated Rudolf Slansky. Nonetheless, it must not be construed from this that the intellectuals' demands were delineated along strictly national lines nor that the Slovaks acted entirely alone or separately from the Czechs. Anxious to induce a national awakening such as had occurred so much earlier in Poland and Hungary, and desirous of obtaining sweeping changes, the Slovaks sought and received Czech support for their specifically Slovak grievances. During at least part of the struggle for liberalization, they campaigned together with Czech liberals for bold reforms and redress of errors in all areas of Czechoslovak life and society.[1]

The intellectuals' campaign got fully under way almost simultaneously with the party's Twelfth Congress in December 1962. In its December issue, the Czechoslovak Writers Union monthly *Plamen* carried an article in which its editor Jiri Hajek implicitly challenged the party to fulfill its oft-repeated promises to de-Stalinize. Thus he boldly claimed:

> The instances when we have solemnly renounced dogmatism are numerous, and we are nearly the world champions as regards the number of proclamations against it ... yet dogmatism still exists ... I could provide further concrete evidence to the effect that our specifically Czech (and Slovak) dogmatism not only goes on living and in security, but that it has recently been flourishing more than ever before.[2]

In this early appeal, however, Hajek limited himself to a demand for an end to 'unhealthy' trends in literature. In its 5 January issue the union's weekly *Literarni Noviny* went slightly further when it prophetically declared that 1963 would be 'historical' in the struggle against the 'non-personality cult.'[3] It was a call for respect for the individual and the need for individual initiative and courage, condemning the collective approach to everything. In these early days only oblique attacks were made – and the union weekly when it said that 'no one will be able to hide behind a collective view' was indirectly referring to party secretary Jiri Hendrych's speech to the party congress in which he had said that everybody, collectively, had been more or less under

[1] See for example, Jiri Hajek's speech to Slovak Writers Union Conference, *Kulturny Zivot*, 4 May 1963 or *Kulturny Zivot*, 1 June and 6 July 1963.
[2] Jiri Hajek, 'For and Against,' *Plamen*, 4:12 (1962), 130.
[3] *Literarni Noviny*, 5 January 1963 (Milan Schulz, 'The Non-Personality Cult').

the influence of the methods of the personality cult.[1] This theme was to be used repeatedly, more and more openly, as the year progressed.

On the same day the Slovak Writers Union weekly *Kulturny Zivot* came out with an article by Slovak writer Ladislav Mnacko calling for a rehabilitation of the word 'conscience.' Basically an appeal to stand up and protest according to the dictates of one's conscience, it also made an attack on the practice of ignoring or misusing laws. Thus Mnacko argued that the 'conscience,' a term banned in the period of the cult, should again be raised to the strength of law. This was perhaps the boldest article that had appeared in print in Czechoslovakia in years, for it defended morality, i.e. a code higher than the arbitrary dictates of the party. A few days later, on 11 January, the Slovak party daily *Bratislava Pravda* struck another note in an article by Slovak academician Ladislav Szanto. He presented the idea that 'non-party workers are just as much members of the working class as are the party people' and that, therefore, it would be illogical to bar non-party people from leading positions in the economy. The value of non-communists in the building of Czechoslovak socialism was later honored by the party theoretical journal *Nova Mysl*, edited at the time by party secretary Cestmir Cisar.[2]

The regime's first official reaction to these early signs of protest on the part of the intellectuals was cautious and defensive. Slovak party first secretary Karol Bacilek, who was deeply disliked in Slovakia and had reason to be defensive because of his own major role in the Stalinist abuses, exhibited this reaction in a speech to cultural workers in Bratislava on 14 January. He admitted that 'many cases of interference in the creative questions of art and culture during the era of the cult of the personality and from the positions of this cult were wrong, schematic, and dogmatic. More than once it struck hard and by administrative means many honorable artists. It was damaging to our culture.'[3] On 20 February the party daily *Rude Pravo* backed up this admission with an editorial in which it was stated that Czechoslovak art was beset with 'mediocrity, eclecticism, and lack of courage to burn one's fingers.' The editorial did not go into the reasons for this situation; the intellectuals were not so negligent, however, as we shall see below.

From 10 to 12 January 1963 the journals *Plamen* and *Slovenske*

[1] *Rude Pravo*, 6 December 1962.
[2] F. Hajek and A. Svarovska, 'Communists and Non-Communists,' *Nova Mysl*, XVII:3 (1963), 296–304.
[3] Cited in *Literarni Noviny*, 2 February 1964.

Pohlady (the Slovak Writers Union monthly) organized a symposium on the problems of contemporary prose with the participation of East European (including Yugoslav) and Soviet writers. The Czechoslovak contributions to this symposium reflected the atmosphere in Czechoslovakia: Jarmila Glazarova attacked the corruption of prose by the permeation of political jargon and urged a return to aesthetics. Milan Kundera complained about Czechoslovak literature's isolation from the outside world; he also attacked the sacred concept of socialist realism, adding a veiled defense of art for art's sake. Karel Kosik in a speech on the underestimation of Jaroslav Hasek and Franz Kafka used the works of these writers to argue against present-day corruption and bureaucracy. Several writers, including the Czech Milan Jungmann, referred to the young Soviet writers and poets as a sign of the recovery of creative ideas. For this they were attacked at the symposium, however, by the Soviet participant, Dementyev. He argued that they failed to see the 'literary whole' which existed in the USSR, including writers who 'have already matured.'[1]

The day after the close of the symposium Czechoslovakia published its own Yevtushenko: a poem by Jiri Sotola entitled 'The Death of Stalin.'[2] The satirical poem, carried in the cultural weekly *Kulturni Tvorba* was a symbolically Soviet representation of Czechoslovak events, especially as seen in the climate of January 1963. Thus Sotola spoke of the doctors' plot (the anti-semitic trials in Czechoslovakia), the thaw, the hope, the casting of blame for the past on everybody, and a final question mark as to what the future would bring.

A few days later from an unlikely quarter, the illustrated weekly of the Committee of Czechoslovak Women *Vlasta*, Dr Oldrich Mandak continued the refrain that dogmatism was far from dead in Czechoslovakia and that 'authoritarianism' had led to fear and passivity.[3] Slightly more explicit than preceding articles, he spoke of the need for intellectuals to lead a 'double life.' He added that the matter could not end with a review of the political trials, and he closed by acknowledging the difficulties that were surely to be encountered in overcoming the still powerful dogmatists.

It is interesting to note that the January issue of the party theoretical

[1] *Literarni Noviny*, 26 January and 2 February 1963; 'International on Prose,' *Slovenske Pohlady*, 79:5 (1963), 29–30.
[2] *Kulturni Tvorba*, 17 January 1963. The journal explained that the poem had been written in 1961, before Yevtushenko's poem, but not allowed to be published.
[3] *Vlasta*, 23 January 1963.

journal *NovaMysl* joined the intellectuals' drive for criticism. One of two significant articles was by Karel Kaplan, historian and member of the central committee agitation–propaganda department. Kaplan called for the rewriting of history free of self-satisfying fabrications, with a new look especially at the periods 1929, 1938, and post-1948. The second article was written by a member of the editorial board, Jiri Sekera, and advocated a fight against conservatism, in ideology, and the need for creative writers to assume responsibility and creatively examine problems with an eye towards new approaches. This last was a central theme in the first step that had to be taken in order to overcome the habit of fear and to bring about the assumption of individual initiative and responsibility. The liberals were in pursuit of an awakening. In a *Literarni Noviny* editorial, for example, Milan Jungmann criticized the timidity and fear of writers to touch on unpleasant or controversial issues. He also criticized, however, the above-cited *Rude Pravo* editorial for having condemned this timidity without having made any reference to the cause for it, i.e. the repressive atmosphere which had prevailed. In summary, he said that the issue was 'bringing about an atmosphere in which boldness is honored, understanding is shown for failures, and stubborn rigidity is condemned.'[1]

The party apparently became concerned about this outburst from the intellectuals and, in the hope of at least inhibiting the public from joining forces with the intellectuals, *Rude Pravo* of 10 February published an article entitled 'What the Just Ones See and What They Don't See.' Rather than respond to the intellectuals' attacks, the party daily addressed itself to dissatisfied elements of the public, reducing all criticism to the more vulgar 'things were better under the capitalists' and 'today's difficulties are only because of the communists,' cries of anti-communists. Thus it was able to ask: 'is it suppression of criticism if we tell a person he is wrong . . . and if we show him by means of facts that . . . we are able to cope with them [the 'temporary difficulties'] for the most part better than other countries.'

Almost simultaneously with this party effort, there appeared an article in *Kulturni Tvorba*, the organ of the Committee for Socialist Culture, which shocked the party and precipitated a debate that was to continue for two years until the announcement of a sweeping reform of the economy. In this article the party economist Radoslav Selucky coined a new phrase long to haunt the party: 'the cult of the plan.'[2]

---

[1] *Literarni Noviny*, 2 February 1963. [2] *Kulturni Tvorba*, 7 February 1963.

Selucky held that one of the major reasons for the crisis in the economy was the existence, side by side with the cult of the personality, of a cult of the plan. Where the Twelfth Party Congress had called for the strengthening of the role of the plan as a solution to the current problems, Selucky attacked this sacred cow and argued for a reform along the lines advocated by Soviet liberal economist Liberman. The party reacted almost immediately in a 23 February *Rude Pravo* article entitled 'Phrases will not Improve our Planning,' and a debate was begun. The extent of interest in this issue was evidenced in a *Hospodarske Noviny* article which remarked that the *Rude Pravo* attack on Selucky had occasioned a two-hour debate in one factory of which the writer was aware.[1]

At about the same time, a significant break-through for the cultural world was made. On 16 February Professor Eduard Goldstuecker, himself quietly rehabilitated, began his campaign for the rehabilitation of Franz Kafka in a *Literarni Noviny* article. Goldstuecker described Kafka as a victim of the cult of the personality, condemned in his own country (though extolled abroad) because of the oversimplified view of things held by the party, which saw Kafka as a decadent bourgeois. Kafka suffered from what Goldstuecker described as the party's replacement of discussion by administrative measures. He added: 'limiting scientific work by unnecessary restrictions, this [*sic*] condemnation to hopeless provincialism is harmful, objectively socially harmful, for it brings to life exactly the thing it intended to prevent.' Goldstuecker bemoaned the fact that one might speak of Kafka even at the time only because an outsider, Sartre, had opened the subject (at the Moscow Peace Congress of 1962). He called for writers to replace this meekness with social responsibility, which in turn 'will be . . . of extraordinary importance, for upon it will depend in what manner the critics (and the creators) treat the enlarged horizon of freedom, the features of which are beginning to emerge from the mist.' In the spring, on 27 and 28 May, Goldstuecker chaired a symposium in Liblice on Kafka which opened the issue for all East Europe.[2]

---

[1] *Hospodarske Noviny*, 15 March 1963. See also Josef Toman in *Kulturni Tvorba*, 28 February 1963. Selucky was informally black-listed by the party after this and reportedly saved from a perhaps more serious fate only by the protection of a very highly placed party official.

[2] The East German representative objected to the tenor of the symposium, returning home in disgust. The majority of the delegates, however, supported Goldstuecker's efforts. See Brown, *The New Eastern Europe*, 154; *Franz Kafka – Liblicka Konference 1963* (Praha, 1963).

Two weeks later there appeared an article by a third intellectual destined to cause the regime much trouble, even unto the toppling of the government. This was Miroslav Hysko, a former editor of *Bratislava Pravda*, then professor of journalism at the University of Bratislava. In the pages of the official Slovak party daily of 28 February, Hysko argued that the party was not infallible. In a plea for truth – objective, scientific truth – Hysko said that in the era of the cult 'we felt as if we became some sort of religious sect convened to confirm the correctness of the belief.' In this context he criticized the prohibition on doubt and creative discussion.

The journals kept up the barrage in March, demonstrating not only the growing courage of the writers and an increase in the number of journals and writers involved, but also the broadening of the revolt to include the most varied aspects of society. Among the monthlies, *Nova Mysl* spoke in favor of non-communists and made an appeal for freedom to travel; *Slovenske Pohlady* continued the protest against fetters and taboos on literature, and against the physical and spiritual isolation from the West; *Plamen* hit out against the restrictions placed on the radio (condemning the radio for its failure to be sufficiently critical, informative or truthful, partially because it was not permitted access to many things or, if given access, forbidden to report shortcomings or national disasters).[1] In the same vein a *Kulturni Tvorba* article attacked Czechoslovak documentary films as propagandistic.[2] *Plamen* gently hinted that another shortcoming of the radio might be too much worship of the USSR – a most delicate point raised also in a *Bratislava Pravda* article by Szanto on 1 March. Protesting the fabrications existing in current textbooks, *Plamen* also commented that youth would not tolerate 'the big lie.'[3] This point had been made earlier, in *Kulturny Zivot*, by a teacher who complained of the impossibility of teaching a new line every day, and the damage being caused the youth because 'we tore down old morality and left the youth a vacuum.'[4] *Plamen* also attacked the party's practice of removing dogmatists from office without ever acknowledging, publicly, the reason for the removals.[5] Although this last may have been published too early

[1] Hajek and Svarovska, *Nova Mysl*, XVII:3 (1963), 296–304; Dominik Tatarka, 'A Cautious Note on the Writers Congress,' *Slovenske Pohlady*, 79:3 (1963), 1–5; Jiri Lederer, 'We Expect Prompt Reaction and Truth on the Air,' *Plamen*, 5:3 (1963), 135–6.

[2] *Kulturni Tvorba*, 14 March 1963.

[3] Vaclav Zygmunt, 'Dogmatism, Youth, and Textbooks,' *Plamen*, 5:3 (1963), 134.

[4] *Kulturny Zivot*, 7 (1963).   [5] Zygmunt, *Plamen*, 5:3 (1963), 134.

to have been an intended reference to the 1 March 'retirement' of Supreme Court chairman Josef Urvalek, chief prosecutor in the Slansky trials, it was at the least timely.[1]

This first stage of open criticism was climaxed on 16 March with the beginning of publication in *Kulturny Zivot* of Evgeny Yevtushenko's autobiography, copyrighted in Slovak by the journal. This was the first publication of Yevtushenko's controversial work outside of France – one week after Yevtushenko began to come under fire in Russia for having published his autobiography in Paris. This was the only publication of this work in East Europe.

NOVOTNY'S ANSWER

The party – or at least the still predominant conservatives – were not willing to permit this accumulating disregard for basic principles of party solidarity and discipline to go unchecked. While it had not as yet announced the results of its review of the political trials, the situation seemed already to be getting out of hand. Novotny expressed his and the regime's position at the industrial coal district of Ostrava on 21 March.[2] Apparently anxious to prevent any worker–intellectual alliance Novotny chose to deliver his attack on the intellectuals among workers, playing on the latter's prejudices and disdain for intellectuals. Novotny devoted much of this Ostrava speech to criticism of economic performance and the lack of managerial foresight. In this connection he made a mild concession by saying that political considerations need not be the only criterion for selection of cadres in the economic sphere – a slight retreat from his congress position on the subject. He defended the policy of cooperation with CEMA, saying that this cooperation and the specialization it would bring would not hurt the Czechoslovak economy as some people feared. He attacked the apathy of the youth, calling for greater numbers to go into agriculture. Fearful that the youth, if left unattended, would 'break away from us and make wrong demands on life,' Novotny said: 'All right, let them dance, but we will not permit these modern dances to degenerate into vulgarisms and thus actually cultivate dark lusts in our people.'

[1] Prague radio, 6 March 1963. The announcement said only that Urvalek had requested to be relieved of his duties in order 'to devote himself to theoretical questions in justice.' He did indeed go to work in the research institute of the Prosecutor-General's office (*Rolnicky Noviny*, 24 February 1968).

[2] *Rude Pravo*, 24 March 1963.

The most important part of the speech, however, was Novotny's presentation of the party's view on criticism; how much and what kind it would tolerate. Novotny struck directly and by name at Selucky, accusing him of trying to introduce chaos and anarchy 'into the Czechoslovak economy, under the guise of criticism of past short-comings' by the use of the phrase 'the cult of the plan.' Novotny was distressed not only about the attention (and anti-regime criticism) this phrase had attracted, but also about certain other statements of Selucky's. He quoted Selucky as having told a question–answer discussion group that organized recruitment of youth into agriculture should not be approved ' "because the way in which it is done is similar to the situation existing in feudal times when serfs had to await approval from their masters before leaving the village." ' Referring to Selucky and, more generally, to the articles of the preceding three months, Novotny said that the idea of freedom was being abused by certain people who were seeking to 'make prevail chaos and anarchy in the life of society.' He accused them of not recognizing the principle of socialist society (he did not specify which principle) but rather conceived of Czechoslovak society 'as some sort of free rally.' Having said this Novotny made the party's position clear:

In no way do we restrict the freedom of any man ... but in no case can we or will we agree with some people smuggling into our life, particularly in our culture, under the cloak of their subjective notion of freedom, the trends of the decadent capitalist society. We will not allow this decadent capitalist culture to be propagated in our society, and we will not allow the socialist system, won in hard struggles, to be attacked in various ambiguous terms in the television and often also in the theatre. We will also not permit wrong conclusions to be drawn against socialist society as a whole from individual cases, shortcomings, and errors of individuals.

Allowing that some criticism was permissible if it were 'correct criticism,' even if it pricked a little, Novotny laid down the criteria thus:

at least everybody will realize that he is constantly under a certain control ... To criticize everything, however, to make criticism a fashion, to criticize socialist society – that we will not permit. We need criticism ... but let no one dare touch our Communist party, its program, or our socialist system. This must be sacred, and it must stay sacred for all. You can criticize this or that person, please yourself; you can also criticize organs – you have the right to criticize. We do not want to wrap up our cultural life into restricted boxes . . . we also do not want to prescribe to this or that writer how to write, create, and so forth. This is really his own affair. However, the party maintains the right to direct cultural activity, the same as it directs and manages the entire life of the country.

Novotny continued at greater length with subtle remarks linking the workers with the party against the criticism of the intellectuals. The speech was designed not only to clarify the limits beyond which the party would not tolerate intellectuals to go, but also to serve notice on the writers, mainly, that the decision to de-Stalinize did not mean that the party intended to give up its control – in any sphere. The intellectuals did not, however, heed this warning. They not only continued but even stepped up their assault, becoming an integrally woven part of the fabric of the political developments which followed.

3

REGIME RESPONSE AND CRISIS

REHABILITATIONS AND PURGES

Aside from the quiet resignation of the former chief prosecutor Urvalek, the first significant actions were not taken until the 3–4 April central committee plenum received and acted upon the review of the trials. Although the events of this historic plenum and of its no less important counterpart in Slovakia on 7–8 April were not made public for some time, the news was quietly filtered to party rank and file (and later piecemeal to the public) in a series of meetings throughout the country. Removed from their party offices were Slovak party first secretary and Czechoslovak party presidium member Karol Bacilek[1] and Czechoslovak party secretary Bruno Koehler, both among the founding members of the party and both old Stalinists. Bacilek had once been Minister of State Control (1951–2) and of National Security (1952–3), while Koehler had once been in charge of party cadres, positions which had accorded them both central roles in the 1949–54 trials. It was also decided at these plena that Pavol David would be dropped from the Slovak party presidium. He had been number two man in the Slovak party under Bacilek in 1953. These men were not, however, expelled from the party, nor were any public accusations or charges brought against them. There were rumors that others were also to be purged – indeed the failure of the party ever fully to reveal the conclusions of that plenum encouraged such rumors and speculation. Reports appearing in the western press claimed that Premier Siroky too had come under attack at the meeting for 'violations of legality.'[2] It was later revealed that Novotny had done his utmost to protect both Siroky and Bacilek, particularly at the Slovak plenum which he himself attended. Indeed he left the meeting, apparently angry, without awaiting the

---

[1] Bacilek became head of the Slovak party in 1953 when Siroky was made Premier and Novotny first secretary of the Czechoslovak party after the death of Klement Gottwald. These promotions all preceded the trials of the Slovak 'bourgeois nationalists' by one year.

[2] See *The Economist*, 11 May 1963; the *Guardian*, 26 April 1963. The liberal Vaclav Slavik was also demoted but this apparently was a personal action of Novotny's against Slavik, who had been responsible for agit–prop matters. He remained in the secretariat.

election of Bacilek's successor Alexander Dubcek. It is difficult to determine if this action was part of a personal or specific opposition by Novotny to Dubcek or if it was merely a sign of Novotny's dissatisfaction with the ouster of Bacilek. He did not, however, deign to attend a Slovak plenum after that and it is known that he did try later to replace Dubcek. Over the latter's opposition Novotny appointed Siroky to officiate over the meetings in Slovakia designed to explain the changes.[1]

Replacing these old Stalinists were generally younger men who, if not all liberals, at least were untainted by their past. In addition to Alexander Dubcek, who took Bacilek's place as head of the Slovak party and the latter's seat on the Czechoslovak party presidium, Frantisek Penc, an industrial administrator, replaced Koehler in the Czechoslovak party secretariat; and liberal *Nova Mysl* editor Cestmir Cisar, not yet a central committee member, was named party secretary.[2] Although he was not to stay there long, Cisar's promotion to the secretariat, along with the promotion of Alexander Dubcek, was among the most promising and fruitful developments of the early days of Czechoslovak de-Stalinization.

The April central committee session also decided on the basic questions of rehabilitations, although the fact of this decision was not announced to the general public until a *Rude Pravo* announcement on 14 May, and the details had to wait until the following August for publication (which even then omitted points to be decided or admitted only later). The regime's intention, as was later revealed, was to avoid arousing public opinion or wide discussion; revealing the admission of past errors piecemeal, and in many cases ambiguously, was designed to muffle the impact and dilute the reaction so as to protect Novotny and his closest collaborators from demands for their ouster as well.[3] This policy may have been sound in theory but it was not wholly successful, as we shall see.

The plenum apparently decided that the criminal indictment against

---

[1] *Bratislava Pravda*, 14 April 1968; *Kulturni Tvorba*, 11 April 1968 ('Documents from Barnabitky').

[2] At the time of Cisar's promotion, *Nova Mysl* carried an article in which Cisar said that as the party had committed errors in the past (which due to the all-pervasiveness of the party had led to 'unfortunate consequences'), the party must take an honest look at itself. The central committee must, he said, study the role of the party in society and correct itself. (Cestmir Cisar, 'The Clean Shield of Communism,' *Nova Mysl*, XVII:4 (1963), 385–97.)

[3] *Bratislava Pravda*, 4 April 1968.

Slansky and his alleged accomplices (forming an 'anti-state' conspiracy) was invalid, but that Slansky (and a few others) had nonetheless been guilty of violations of legality and 'gross violations of the organizational statutes and principles of party work.'[1] Thus the execution of Slansky and others was invalidated, but their expulsion from the party was upheld. In fact the party intended to continue to place the guilt of the evils of the Stalin era in Czechoslovakia on the shoulders of Slansky, claiming that he later fell victim to his own apparatus. It thus became clear that there would be no real rehabilitation for Slansky, for upon whom could the blame be placed for the whole era and wrongdoings if Slansky were completely absolved?[2] The 'bourgeois nationalists' were also absolved on all points of the criminal indictment but the question of their rehabilitation was left for settlement until a central committee plenum the following December. The 14 May announcement of the 3–4 April plenum merely said that the question of rehabilitations (in all cases) had been discussed and that the prosecutor-general had submitted proposals to the Supreme Court for the 'civil and legal rehabilitation of leading party and state functionaries who had been unjustly condemned in the political trials in the years 1949–54.'

As news of these party measures reached the rank and file party members and leaked out to the public, Novotny's critics were encouraged. While the campaign for greater freedom continued stronger than ever in the press, the grievances of the Slovak communists found public expression. *Kulturny Zivot*, as early as 23 March, published an article by Slovak party historian Samo Faltan demanding a place of honor in history for the Slovak National Uprising and the Slovak National Council, retraction of the past accusations of 'bourgeois nationalism,' and recognition of the wartime role played by the London-directed Czechoslovak army units in Slovakia. Faltan criticized the party censorship and falsification, even in his own past works, of the history of the anti-fascist battle in Slovakia and the immediate post-war period there. The April issue of *Slovenske Pohlady* contained an even more direct attack on the persecution of Slovak communists under the charges of 'bourgeois nationalism.' Slovak communist Zora Jesenska published 'Two Chapters of My Memoirs' in which she described the 1951 party *aktiv* organized against the journal *Dav* and

[1] Prague radio, 22 August 1963.
[2] The minor attempt in 1961 to discredit Gottwald as the Stalin of Czechoslovakia was not taken seriously enough nor sufficiently supported within the party to provide the needed scapegoat.

those who had purportedly fallen under its 'bourgeois nationalist' influence. She also described the 1953 application of the Zhdanov line against the very perpetrators of the *aktiv*, on charges of cosmopolitanism, Zionism, and collaboration with Slansky. The significance of her article was not so much in the details she provided but rather in her description of the hysterical atmosphere of the trials period and the total absence of foundation to the charges.

On 13 April the Slovak party daily published a poem by Laco Novomesky, former *Dav* collaborator and former communist Education and Culture Minister of Slovakia tried, imprisoned, and quietly released in the 1950s, but at the time still unrehabilitated. The poem was an ode to the executed Clementis, sharply attacking those who had refused to stand by him or to speak up in those days. In the poem Novomesky also pointed out the damage done by the dogmatists – damage which had led to such things as the Hungarian revolution, he claimed. With the publication of this poem the Slovak party organ made clear its position on the victims of the false charges, thus paving the way for the unofficial rehabilitation of the victims which occurred long before the party settled the matter officially. Although not necessarily an act of defiance, since party policy was often subtly to prepare the public for forthcoming announcements, there is reason to believe that the Prague party had not yet finally decided on the future of the Slovak victims.[1] At the very least, the contribution the Slovak party paper thus made in the form of the Novomesky poem itself to the campaign for public rectification of all past errors – including those in which present leaders had been involved – was of little help to Novotny's struggle to keep criticism and demands under control.

At their 22 April congress the Slovak Writers Union anticipated party action by readmitting Novomesky to the ranks of the union, electing him to the union's committee, and rescinding the order by which he had been expelled from the union twelve years earlier. The union, charging its weekly organ *Kulturny Zivot* to publish the proceedings, sought in every way possible to make this a complete rehabilitation. To this end one speaker analyzed the history of *Dav* and categorically declared that there never had been any substance to the charges of 'bourgeois nationalism.'[2] Novomesky himself made a moving

[1] *Rude Pravo*, 29 January 1964, revealed that it had taken a decision on the 'bourgeois nationalist' charges only in December 1963.

[2] *Kulturny Zivot*, 4 May 1963 (Michal Chorvath). In his 23 April 1963 Lenin Day speech, the then liberally inclined Slovak Jozef Lenart *condemned* the phenomenon

appeal to the writers to remember the greater tragedy of the 1950s and, specifically, their 'mutual friend and comrade' Vladimir Clementis.[1] The conference itself had an importance beyond the purely Slovak issue, however. A number of writers criticized the general lack of morality or personal sense of ethics among intellectuals – a weakness that, many argued, had led almost everyone to comply with distortions and injustices or to withdraw from artistic pursuits in favor of materially worthwhile ones. Not only the intellectuals' having given in to party pressures was criticized, but these pressures themselves, i.e. the political – administrative control of the cultural sphere, were also criticized. Writers called for a genuine return to 'Leninist norms,' not merely controlled, measured out adjustments, and an elimination of the party-imposed criterion of political 'functionality' in culture. The newly elected chairman of the union, Karol Rosenbaum, summed up these speeches with the declaration that 'the past few days have been charged with events which are of inestimable importance for the future moral health of society and literature. They again have character and, let us not be afraid to say so, a revolutionary aspect.[2] Commenting that the conference had taken a positive stand towards the elimination of the results of the personality cult, he said that he considered this proof that there was sufficient strength to prevent a return not only to the cult but to the 'reasons and conditions from which the cult and its inhuman and anti-party methods sprang.'

In these same days the Congress of Czechoslovak Composers too prompted critical discussions on socialist realism and party meddling in the arts; the Congress of Czechoslovak Journalists occasioned some strong comments on freedom of the press (including once again outspoken contributions in the pages of the Slovak party daily); and the Congress of the Czechoslovak Youth Union (CSM) revealed a rift in that organization over the role of CSM and over the liberal tendencies of the organization's publications. These numerous congresses and conferences, long scheduled for the spring of 1963, provided semi-public platforms for the heated debates and recriminations. Outside these meetings the campaign continued with articles demanding respect for the law, open criticism of public officials, freedom of discussion,

---

of 'bourgeois nationalism', thus suggesting that the party still considered the charges valid in principle. (*Rude Pravo*, 23 April 1963.) See preceeding note.

[1] *Kulturny Zivot*, 4 May 1963.

[2] *Ibid.* (Speech of Karol Rosenbaum.) See also speeches of Matuska, Hrusovsky, Karvas and Plavka in *Kulturny Zivot*, 27 April and 4 May 1963.

and greater contact with the West.[1] Slovak party theoretician Szanto even pointed out the distortion of 'democratic centralism' that had occurred over the years, resulting in 'excessive centralism' with criticism from above but only 'self criticism' from below.[2] Also at this time appeared the first open reference to Hungary as a possible model for the liberal rule of a communist regime.[3] This was followed by an article in May on Poland's liberalization and another on 'The Hungarian Miracle.'[4] By way of encouragement *Literarni Noviny* of 25 May also published favorable Polish comments on the Czechoslovak intellectuals' struggle from an article originally carried by the Polish journal *Nowa Kultura*.

The regime did not permit everything to appear, however. It suppressed an issue of *Kulturny Zivot* and called back an issue of *Kulturni Tvorba*, releasing it again only after deleting certain portions of an article by Miroslav Filip. It was indicative of the liberals' gains and the erosion of party control that these issues had originally made it through the censors, with censorship coming only after publication, reportedly only upon direct intervention by Novotny.[5]

Popular discontent was increasingly a factor in the mounting tension of the spring of 1963. Public interest in the debates of the writers was demonstrated by the almost immediate sale of all copies of the 4 May issue of *Kulturny Zivot* containing the Slovak Writers Conference speeches.[6] Western travelers to Czechoslovakia in those days brought back reports that the lively discussions on the pages of this journal were indeed attracting wide readership, even among the workers. The population found in the journals not only, apparently, the expression of many of their own frustrations and grievances, but also some indication of the party's till then secret decisions and plans for de-Stalinization. The general public's interest in the events of the spring must not be exaggerated, for only the more politically oriented citizens saw in these inner-party struggles the groundwork for changes which would be of great significance to the general public as well. At the very least, how-

---

[1] See *Rude Pravo*, 10 April 1963; *Bratislava Pravda*, 12, 14 April 1963; *Kulturni Tvorba*, 25 April 1963 (Zdenek Mlynar); Mlynar, 'Socialist Democracy and the Citizen,' *Osvetova Prace*, XVII:8 (1963), 104-5; and *Kulturni Tvorba*, 30 April 1963 (Jiri Cerny).

[2] *Bratislava Pravda*, 2 and 4 April 1963.

[3] *Kulturny Zivot*, 6 April 1963.

[4] *Kulturny Zivot*, 18 May 1963; *Kulturni Tvorba*, 23 May 1963.

[5] Anthony Buzek, *How the Communist Press Works* (London, 1964), 148.

[6] *Bratislava Pravda*, 6 May 1963.

ever, the public enjoyed the entertaining spectacle of party members openly fighting with party members, but this breakdown in party discipline could hardly occur without some attendant effect on public discipline – particularly in view of the already wide discontent over economic conditions.

On 1 May the traditional student poetry reading session around the statue of the Czech poet Karel Hynek Macha in a park in Prague erupted into an anti-regime demonstration of students and young workers. Although the police relatively quickly dispersed the crowds (demonstrators had been joined by spectators in the shouting of anti-regime slogans) and made some arrests, the following two weeks were dotted with other outbursts on the Prague and Bratislava streets. These later 'riots' were often prompted by attacks on Africans whose presence in large numbers as students in Czechoslovakia not only evoked racist sentiments but also was resented because of the money and preferential treatment these students received from the authorities. The party press treated these events as mere outbreaks of 'hooliganism,' but even denying the political nature of some of the demonstrations any breach of public order was a danger to leaders struggling to maintain themselves without resorting to past terror tactics.[1]

Although the public still had to wait for announcement of any party action on the trials' report, a 29 April Prague radio foreign broadcast beamed to Africa said that the central committee had made 'certain recommendations to the Supreme Court and the Prosecutor's Office.' On 9 May Novotny prepared the public for the imminent announcement of at least some of the party's decision by a cryptic impromptu comment at the end of his Liberation Day speech, saying, 'people come and go, but the party is eternal.'[2] Finally, on 14 May, the removal of Bacilek and Koehler and the promotions of Dubcek, Penc, and Cisar were announced. The announcement did not, however, offer any explanation for the changes. Only a *Rude Pravo* editorial accompanying the announcement referred indirectly to these measures as the results of investigations, announcing for the first time that the question of rehabilitations had been submitted to the Supreme Court. The following week a 21 May *Rude Pravo* article by Czechoslovak party presidium

---

[1] There were many reports in the spring and summer of 1963 of the discovery and apprehension of anti-state youth groups or 'provocateurs,' such as the group of youngsters called 'The Bloody Hand,' operating in Slovakia. (*Praca*, 18 April 1963.)

[2] *Rude Pravo*, 11 May 1963.

member Drahomir Kolder (head of the committee designated by the Twelfth Party Congress to review the trials) insisted that the shuffle had not been for political or disciplinary reasons, but that the 'changes in positions' merely reflected the fact that 'work in the central organs is not a life time job.' Such a denial apparently was necessitated by the fact that the men being purged were hardly any more guilty in connection with the trials than Siroky or Novotny or others still in high positions. Public admission of the connection (clearly understood in any case by those interested in the affair) risked opening the door to demands for more dismissals. It was a tactic which in fact had little chance of succeeding in the climate of 1963. Sensitive to outside pressures upon him to de-Stalinize, however, Novotny did permit the drawing of a direct connection between the ousters and the 1949–54 trials, in a Prague radio broadcast to Yugoslavia on 24 May.

Anticipating announcements that were still to be a long time coming, a Slovak agricultural paper, *Rolnicke Noviny*, reported the following on 28 May:

As is well known by now, the special commission of the Czecho-slovak Communist Party Central Committee has established that neither the anti-state conspiratorial center nor the specific group of bourgeois nationalists ever existed, and that the charges on the basis of which the purported members of these so-called groups were tried and sentenced were fabricated.

Indeed Novotny had not yet officially decided anything of the kind. It would appear, therefore, that the Slovak paper was taking matters into its own hands, on whose authority one can only guess, in an effort to force the issue, much the way the Slovak writers had been doing.

The Congress of the Czechoslovak Writers Union from 22 to 24 May was an historic occasion and an apt follow-up to the Slovak Writers Conference. Czech as well as Slovak writers strongly and mercilessly attacked the cult, the evils which had been perpetrated and to some degree continued, the lack of courage on the part of every one, the irreparable damage done, particularly to Slovak literature, by the unjustified campaign against *Dav* and the Slovak communists (Clementis and Novomesky were mentioned by name), and the damage done all Czechoslovak society, particularly the youth, by dogmatism and the delay until the present of de-Stalinization.[1] Speeches were also heard calling for greater contact with the West, freedom to travel, and freedom

---

[1] Unless otherwise stated, sources for the congress were the proceedings carried by *Kulturny Zivot*, 1 June 1963 and *Literarni Noviny*, 1 June 1963.

to write without 'directives' or threats. The congress was by no means a uniform and orderly stream of criticism, however. There was much dissension within the union itself (especially since much of the leadership of the union was in Stalinist hands as a result of the aftermath of the brief 1956 thaw), and there were arguments and accusations in addition to the self-criticism.[1] Two of the most outstanding speeches (for their political potential) made at the congress were by Miroslav Valek and Zora Jesenska. The latter mentioned Premier Siroky by name, implying his involvement in the trials against the 'bourgeois nationalists.' Valek was the strongest – though by no means the only – speaker to attack the continued presence of dogmatists when he said:

> Many functionaries who were bearers of the cult still hold their positions, and have hardly changed in their thinking. Perhaps they stand up and cry, 'Away with the cult?' They raise a strict and critical finger and say 'Comrades, we have lived through a terrible time, in which you, too, have your share.' And in doing this, they think: 'I shall get out of this somehow.' In short, they act in accordance with the well-known Slovak proverb: Talk or be talked about.[2]

The congress resolution called for a discussion with the Ministry of Education and Culture on 'the necessity of amending and completing the school curriculum so as to guarantee an historically correct and scientifically objective teaching of the new and up-to-date history of Czechoslovak literature. Chiefly concerned is the period of the last twenty to thirty years if we think of the Czech vanguard and the *Dav* group in Slovakia.' The writers also resolved to make every effort 'to ensure that writers are properly informed about literary developments abroad, to import foreign books and periodicals.' Moreover, they resolved to pay more attention to 'national' literature and writers in Czechoslovakia, i.e. Hungarian, Ukrainian, and Polish. The literary journals thoroughly publicized the congress materials, but before discussion could die down (and some of it had criticized the congress for having been too political) still another congress took place which was to have far-reaching consequences: the 27–28 May Slovak Journalists Union Congress at Bratislava. On 3 June the Slovak party daily *Bratislava Pravda* published the speech delivered to the congress by the paper's former editor Miroslav Hysko, in which the regime and

[1] See *Rude Pravo*, 24–26 May 1963; *Bratislava Pravda*, 23 May 1963; *Prace*, 24 May 1963; *Kulturni Tvorba*, 16 May 1963; and Prague radio, 28 May 1963.
[2] Cited by Skilling in Bromke, *Communist States*, 119.

specifically Premier Siroky came under sharp, direct attack. The direct language of Hysko's speech was as important as the content itself; for this reason the following excerpts are best directly cited. Hysko first explained that the current 'struggle for the revival of Leninist norms' must address itself to the past, for this struggle had been carried out only 'inconsistently and more or less by declarations' since the Twentieth CPSU Congress. 'Thus,' Hysko asserted, 'basic questions which should have been settled as long ago as 1956 are now confronting us again.' Important for Hysko, however, was the period that should be reviewed, so that the regime might not withhold reform on the grounds that dogmatism was a matter of the past only. 'This period lasted from 1949 to 1962, approximately,' he said:

The issue is not only the responsibility for the violation of legality and Leninist norms before 1956, but also the responsibility for the continuation of the methods of the personality cult, particularly the raising of obstacles to the thorough realization of the conclusions of the Twentieth CPSU Congress in our country.

Addressing himself to the Slovak issue, Hysko said:

all those conclusions of the [1950 Ninth Slovak party] congress which dealt with the so-called exposure of the so-called group of bourgeois nationalist deviationists – comrades Clementis, Smidke, Husak and Novomesky – were a typical consequence of the personality cult; it is evident that from this viewpoint the Ninth Congress itself can be considered the real beginning of the well-known repressions directed against outstanding communist officials throughout the Republic . . . *Comrade Siroky's report to the Slovak Communist Party was not* – with regard to the so-called exposure of the bourgeois nationalists in our party – *the result of an objective analysis*, but – as was then characteristic of our entire propaganda – quite the other way around: he followed the *a priori* thesis on the inevitability of the bourgeois nationalist danger in our party and all facts had to be marshalled according to this thesis. This report was and *still is* being used as a basis for an unobjective assessment of an entire era – it looked for dangers where there were none and guided in this false direction not merely propaganda organs, but in its objective consequences also the security organs, which based their drastic so-called convictions of so-called bourgeois nationalists for imaginary crimes on it. Other reports delivered after the incriminated comrades were arrested in the spring of 1951 – *the reports of Siroky*, Slansky,

Kopecky, and Bastovansky, merely gave a more profound formulation of the theses formulated at the Ninth Congress . . .[1]

It was not by chance court indictments used the formulations
of the congress report verbatim. This connection, allegedly a
'natural law' by which a deviation changed into a desertion to
the side of the class enemy, was also intimated at the Ninth Congress in comrade Siroky's concluding speech, in which he said
among other things: 'With the bourgeois nationalist deviation,
everyone of us gives a finger to the class enemy; and you know
that the class enemy will grasp the whole hand.'

Hysko then made the point that the responsibility for the whole 'shame-
ful' purge must rest on those who prepared the reports upon which the
party decisions to act were based. In this connection he attacked also
Koehler and Gustav Bares and especially Kopecky. Support for Hysko's
explosive remarks was evidenced by his unanimous election to the
union's committee.[2]

Not only was this speech the most incriminating accusation levied
against the regime in the course of the intellectuals' revolt, implicating
the ruling Premier by name, but it was pronounced by an upstanding
party member and published, without comment, in the official organ of
the Slovak party. Novotny could not be expected to tolerate the criticism of the number two man in his administration, but the publication
of this criticism in the Slovak party organ indicated the existence of an
opposition which would probably (and did) lead to the removal of
Siroky. Novotny's principal decision had to be not how best to save
his Premier but how best to handle the whole affair and save his own
position, given the implied criticism of himself in both the speech and
the fact of its 'official' publication.

POLITICAL CRISIS

The events of the spring of 1963 apparently put Novotny on the
defensive; his position was threatened and his ability to remain in
power was seriously challenged. He struck out at his critics in an
angry speech to party members in the East Slovak town of Kosice on
12 June.[3] Showing his sensitivity to charges even by 'some comrades'

---

[1] Emphasis mine.

[2] The congress also observed a minute's silence to honor the memory of Clementis,
Andre Simone, and Ivan Horvath. Ladislav Holdos, Slovak writer purged with
Novomesky, Husak, Horvath, and Okali, addressed the congress 'after an enforced
interval of twelve years.' (*Kulturny Zivot*, 1 June 1963; *Prace*, 28 May 1963.)

[3] *Rude Pravo*, 13 June 1963.

of continued dogmatism, Novotny insisted that the party had been de-Stalinizing since 1956, and that the rectification of past errors was a purely internal party matter not subject to non-party comment or interference. Unwilling fully to acknowledge the past 'mistakes,' Novotny explained that 'the party also judges offenses from the political aspects' so that 'legally' innocent people might and indeed were still considered guilty of violations against the party. This as we have noted was the line to be used in dealing with Slansky when publication of the party decisions finally came in August 1963. Novotny's explanation of the 'mistakes' was an interesting Stalinistic convolution of theories: the struggle against remnants of bourgeois ideology and against 'the imminent threat of imperialist aggression ... created a fertile ground for the application of wrong forms of the personality cult. The struggle of the party was right and inevitable, but it was distorted by wrong methods inside the party, particularly by seeking the enemy primarily inside the party.' This Novotny blamed on 'petit bourgeois elements' which had infiltrated the party and gradually distorted its policy. The critical and disciplinary role of the party was thus 'paralyzed and actually handed over to the security authorities.' Continuing this line of reasoning Novotny concluded that the greatest guilt was, therefore, that the trials resulted from a violation of party principles since those tried should have undergone party investigation prior to any court verdict. Referring to Slansky and others by name, Novotny claimed that those who started the whole process then fell victim to it but certainly were to be held responsible (and guilty) for violation of party principles.[1]

This then was the first public exegesis of the line adopted by the party with regard to the 1949–54 trials. Despite the pressures and, specifically, despite Hysko's attack, Novotny strove to maintain the innocence of his regime. Indeed he directly met the Slovak challenge by upholding the charges of 'bourgeois nationalism' levied at the 1950 Slovak Party Congress and the condemnations that followed from these charges. Although he praised the Slovak National Uprising, Novotny also upheld the charge that participation in the Slovak National Council in 1944 was a sign of 'bourgeois nationalism,' and that

[1] In an interview to the London *Times* Novotny also mentioned the party's continued consideration of Slansky as guilty. In this interview too he demonstrated his sensitivity to charges of having failed to de-Stalinize; he stated categorically that there were no differences of opinion between him and Khrushchev on this issue. (*The Times*, 12 June 1963.)

Husak and Novomesky had been guilty of offenses against the party.

Thus Novotny upheld his Premier; he angrily attacked the Slovak party daily for allowing itself to become 'a platform for the sounding of wrong views and for a compilation of hysterical sallies against the party.' He served notice on both *Pravda* and *Kulturny Zivot*, warning writers and editors alike that they were following a dangerous road. He demanded to know where they stood. Again denying any desire to stifle criticism, Novotny asserted that the critics were aiding the interests of the imperialists. He reiterated the Ostrava line: criticism must remain 'within the intentions of party policy.' Novotny criticized the intellectuals, and particularly the Slovaks, at great length, both angrily and defensively,[1] but one of the most significant aspects of the speech was the repeated reference to disunity within the party and the lack of traditional party discipline. Indeed, even his effort to present his remarks as 'the views of the party presidium and the whole central committee' was deleted from the speech as carried by *Rude Pravo*.[2] The speech, albeit strong and vituperative, revealed the impotence and frustration Novotny must have felt at the time as he intoned almost every possible argument, slogan, and sentiment to regain a measure of solidarity and unity within the party.

Novotny's entreaty–ultimatum went all but ignored. A few days after the speech *Kulturny Zivot* carried a very favorable account of a Husak speech on the Slovak National Uprising and the Slovak National Council delivered to a meeting of the Slovak Historical Society.[3] The Bratislava trade union daily, *Praca*, on 16 June unequivocally declared worker support for the intellectuals. Shortly thereafter the Slovak Union of Motion Picture Artists associated itself with the discussions of the Slovak Journalists Union congress.[4] The 29 June issue of *Kulturny Zivot* praised the readmission of Clementis' nephew to the Komensky University Law School after his expulsion twelve years earlier; it also carried a favorable review of a book by trial victim Artur London praising purge victims Sling, Svermova, Clementis, Husak, and Novomesky

---

[1] He took the line: Could you be publishing all these things if there were not freedom under my regime? Novotny specifically took to task Roman Kalisky for his article 'How to Kill Flies' (*Kulturny Zivot*, 1 June 1963), accusing him of Slovak nationalism. Kalisky's article was widely debated but *Kulturny Zivot's* publication of this debate (and the popular support of Kalisky) was in itself an answer to Novotny's remarks.

[2] Carried originally by Prague radio, 12 June 1963.

[3] *Kulturny Zivot*, 15 June 1963.

[4] *Kulturny Zivot*, 29 June and 6 July 1963.

and Czechoslovak communist contributions to the Spanish civil war (till then a taboo subject).

The regime tried once again to make its point at the end of June when party number two man Jiri Hendrych wrote in *Rude Pravo* against bourgeois nationalism.[1] He charged that the culprits even if rehabilitated would never be readmitted to the central committee. Nonetheless, the critics continued. A 28–29 June plenary session of the Slovak Writers Union committee resolved to continue the struggle against dogmatism and against the 1951 *aktiv* against *Dav*, to support *Kulturny Zivot*'s efforts in the political sphere, to rehabilitate *Dav* and to encourage public debate.[2] The Slovak Writers thus answered Novotny, and *Kulturny Zivot* published the union's decision that the journal 'remain political' and critical. Although *Bratislava Pravda* had acquiesced somewhat by publishing some articles critical of Hysko, its continued liberal sympathies were demonstrated by a favorable review of London's book and a call for recognition of wartime Czechoslovak underground activities in the West.[3]

The struggle was by no means limited to Slovak intellectuals at this stage. The Slovak Writers Union had made a point of the fact that Czechs were as much involved in the campaign as Slovaks,[4] while *Praca* had urged the participation and support of the workers and the peasants. There were reports of worker demonstrations (over meat shortages) in Brno and Hradec Kralove, while demonstrators in Pardubice were reported to have carried placards complaining of police brutality.[5] The 17 August issue of *Praca* actually reported – sympathetically – a strike in a carpentry plant in which the workers charged the management and trade union bureaucracy with responsibility for lowering wages and for poor relations with workers.

While the country may not have been on the brink of revolution, the situation had nonetheless gotten out of hand. Public interest was increasing at a time when regime admonitions to party faithful were being ignored. Western travelers reported cases of local party leaders authorizing events or exhibitions vetoed by Prague. Bratislava television reportedly refused to televise Novotny's Kosice speech – some say on

---

[1] *Rude Pravo*, 29 June 1963. [2] *Kulturny Zivot*, 6 July 1963.
[3] *Bratislava Pravda*, 14 June 1963.
[4] Indeed *Literarni Noviny* and *Kulturni Tvorba* were almost as active and critical as the Slovak weekly. To curb this the party central committee took over *Kulturni Tvorba* in August 1964, firing its chief editor Miroslav Galuska.
[5] *Paris-Presse*, 4 June 1963.

the authority of Cisar – despite orders from Prague to do so. Although nothing as bold as the Hysko attack on Siroky appeared again, the pressures, now more public than during the winter, continued to build within the party and between the Slovak and the Czechoslovak parties. It was difficult to delineate fixed factions within the Czechoslovak party or inside the central committee; rather, various individuals took various positions depending upon the issue. In the central committee and its various departments the liberals sought to influence or at least neutralize the conservative *apparatchiks*, in hopes of introducing reforms both in party activity and party policy. There the list of progressives is a long one, including such old-timers as Vodslon and Kriegel, as well as Sik and Martin Vaculik, given the specific issue. In the presidium and secretariat it was difficult to determine just who was sanctioning the activity of the liberals or advocating change, though in the secretariat Cisar was a champion of reform. Lenart was considered sympathetic and reform-minded, at least in the early stages, while others, such as Kolder and even Koucky and Hendrych, upon occasion opportunistically took the liberals' side on specific issues.[1] While it is difficult to say what influence if any Alexander Dubcek tried or was able to wield in Prague, his leadership of the Slovak party was most likely a factor in the greater liberties taken by dissidents in Slovakia than in the Czech lands. A loyal Slovak, his political position became clear and of importance only in the course of events. As noted earlier, a certain battle between Dubcek and Novotny did apparently begin, however, over Bacilek and Siroky as early as April 1963.

Not only were the positions of many people ambiguous, determined often only by the issue at hand, but many advocated change only because they saw this as the politically expedient road, i.e. given Moscow's position and the problems within Czechoslovakia, liberalization, though perhaps only limited, was the path of the future. This would perhaps explain the fluctuations of such people as Martin Vaculik or Jozef Lenart, promising younger men who nonetheless eventually abandoned the reformers. As we shall see below, the position of the Slovaks too became ambiguous as their interests and those of the reformers appeared to diverge in the following years. While one must, therefore, be cautious about conceiving of a united bloc of liberals relentlessly pressing their demands, serious divisions did exist within the party which at the least provoked discussions and disputes often unfavorable to Novotny at the top levels of the party, and provided a sympathetic ear or even protection for dissidents at lower levels.

[1] See for example, 'Current Developments,' *East Europe*, XI:11 (1963), 34–6.

On 22 August the party finally published its verdict on the principal cases of the 1949–54 trials, but the details did not vary from the line already gradually revealed and, therefore, did little to relieve the situation. More drastic measures were called for if Novotny wanted to keep his position. The party central committee met on 20 September and agreed upon a government and party reshuffle at the top levels. The following day it was announced that Siroky was relieved of his duties as Premier and party presidium member 'for shortcomings in his work, for inadequate implementation of the party line in directing government activity, for certain mistakes in his past political activity, and in view of bad health.'[1] Jozef Lenart was named as his replacement, with Michal Chudik replacing Lenart as chairman of the Slovak National Council. Numerous other changes were made in both parties and in the government, but the most significant aspect of the reshuffle was the elevation of younger, more qualified men, the removal of some hard-liners, and the generally more liberal profile of the new regime – despite the continued presence of Novotny at the top. The only serious casualty – possibly agreed upon to offset the liberal gains – was the removal of Cisar as party secretary. He was made Minister of Education and Culture, a position from which he could (and did) continue his efforts for reform. Another significant action taken by the party at this juncture was the creation of four central committee commissions to direct matters concerning ideology (chaired by Koucky), the economy (chaired by Kolder), agriculture (chaired by Hendrych), and standard of living (chaired by Dolansky[2]). Despite their conservative chiefs the composition of these commissions, announced only later, bore out the liberal nature suggested by the pressures attendant upon their creation.

Moscow responded immediately to this attempt by Novotny to stabilize the situation. Khrushchev sent Lenart a telegram of congratulations within twenty-four hours. Moscow undoubtedly welcomed and may even have advised the line now adopted by Novotny. In a speech of 22 September Novotny calmly and confidently referred to the changes as part of the process begun by the party in 1956 to strengthen the principle of collective leadership.[3] Novotny apparently hoped by this new emphasis upon collective decision-making – and by the concessions just made – to continue in power. This did in fact

[1] Bratislava radio, 21 September 1963.
[2] Dolansky nonetheless lost his seat on the Czechoslovak party presidium in this reshuffle, presumably because of his involvement in the Slansky purges.
[3] *Rude Pravo*, 23 September 1963.

47

mark the beginning of the solution to the power crisis in Prague, although Novotny still had many more concessions to make. In this speech Novotny still criticized his critics and asserted the 'correctness' of party policies. That he was still sensitive to charges of his own complicity in the Slansky trials was apparent in an interview he gave to the West German magazine *Der Stern* in early October.[1] In response to a question on his role in the trials Novotny said that he himself had almost been a victim; he claimed to have discovered in the Prague district headquarters (of which he was the chief in that period) voluminous files 'exposing' himself as an American spy. Although this tale was not likely to deceive very many, it was evidence that Novotny still felt it necessary to defend himself. Apparently there were still many in the party who would be satisfied only when the party was truly clear of old Stalinists. More dominant, however, were those who felt that personnel changes were only a first, not a last, step to be followed by policy changes of a similar liberal hue. The intellectuals and the Slovaks kept up the pressure while the party itself continued to struggle with the issues.

On 25 November Novotny led a party–state delegation to Moscow without prior announcement. In Moscow Khrushchev gave him personal VIP treatment and, in moves most likely designed to bolster Novotny's position, praised him generously.[2] It appeared from this trip that Khrushchev, interested in maintaining Novotny's active support in the Sino–Soviet dispute – and stability in Prague – was basically satisfied that Novotny could continue in power with certain de-Stalinization. Brezhnev was dispatched to Prague two weeks later for the renewal of the Czechoslovak–Soviet treaty of mutual friendship and assistance, at which time Moscow demonstrated to the Czechs and Slovaks its support for Novotny. Brezhnev's speeches and activities in Czechoslovakia at this time suggested, however, that he was also commissioned to reassure the liberals that Khrushchev favored orderly de-Stalinization, and that the continuation of Novotny's rule with Soviet backing did not mean an end to their gains.[3] Subsequent developments, the full-scale de-Stalinization that did indeed follow, attest to the compromise Novotny was forced to make to maintain his position. For the next

[1] *Der Stern*, 10 October 1963. The *Rude Pravo* version of this interview consisted of Novotny's comments regarding Germany *only*. (*Rude Pravo*, 5 November 1963.)
[2] *Pravda* (Moscow), 26, 27 November 1963.
[3] See Brezhnev's speech at a Prague rally, Prague radio, 12 December 1963; his trip to Slovakia accompanied by Kolder, Prague radio, 12 December 1963; and Brezhnev's speech, *Rude Pravo*, 15 December 1963.

several months Novotny remained very much in the background and collective leadership did in fact seem to be the ruling principle. The December plenum of the central committee reversed the party's earlier position on 'bourgeois nationalism' – a reversal which may have been ordered by Moscow to placate the still angry Slovaks.

In reviewing the year's developments *Kulturny Zivot* editor Pavol Stevcek called 1963 a 'remarkable year,' one of 'rebirth,' of 'anti-dogmatism' and of 'truth,' of the 'humanization of socialism;' Slovak writer Mnacko called it a year of 'frank discussions, ideas and acts' which should never cease, as a safeguard against 'new deformations in all branches of our life.'[1] Stevcek concluded that 1963 'should stay in history, in our consciousness, in our tasks of tomorrow, and in our newspapers.' It is true that a great deal was accomplished in 1963, but most of the gains were still elusive, fragile, and liable to reversal or distortion as had occurred to many of the gains of 1956 in Poland. Keenly aware of this, Czechoslovak liberals kept up their pressures and continued their campaign, directing it towards formal, legal changes, hoping to assure permanence through institutionalized reforms.

[1] *Kulturny Zivot*, 21 December 1963.

4

PRINCIPLES OF THE NEW SYSTEM

THE DEBATE FOR REFORM

While the Czechoslovak economy stagnated during 1963, growing criticism of the centralized command–economy system seemed to indicate that only radical measures would solve the problems at hand. *Kulturny Zivot*, unwilling to limit its attack on dogmatism to purely political matters, printed what may have been the most extreme of the economic analyses of this period: a series of articles by the rehabilitated Slovak economist Eugen Loebl.[1]

Loebl maintained that the advent of socialist society had brought a fundamentally new economic system, qualitatively different from anything accounted for by Marxist concepts. Therefore new concepts were necessary to take into consideration the new factors. The problem as Loebl saw it was that Stalin had understood the economy of socialism with the concepts Marx applied to capitalist economy. From this there came opinions drawn not from reality but from Marx's basic thesis. This method of thinking or 'rule of opinion over reality' was the root of Stalinist dogma, according to Loebl's analysis. For example, Loebl explained, with the advent of socialist society there was much discussion as to how to direct a socialist economy, and it was agreed that planning would be preferable to the anarchy and competition of capitalism. Planning was not, however, the only possible form of direction. It was merely the one considered to be the best and most progressive. It was not a 'law' inherent to socialist society itself in the way that competition and anarchy, for example, were intrinsic elements of capitalism. There were two possible attitudes towards socialist society. There was the view that laws objectively determined things, i.e. that laws were not a direct reflection of phenomena but rather determined all phenomena, and there was the view that socialism offered human beings the possibility to change things. In the second case, the task was to achieve optimal production; one must decide, scientifically, how best to do this, and a plan might well be one such way. Adherents to the first view believed that since laws determined economic facts socialist society must be a planned society. Stalin made

[1] *Kulturny Zivot*, 28 September, 5 and 12 October 1963.

planning itself a 'law' of socialism and arbitrarily directed socialist society on the basis of this law. Stalin thus could say that any disregard for or distortion of the plan would lead to confusion and chaos. Loebl pointed out, however, that 'to plan the production of automobiles without planning the production of spare parts does not violate the law of planned development; it violates the most basic principle of common sense.'

The natural consequence of this system, Loebl maintained, was a stifling of creative economic thinking; instead of science, there came to the fore subjectivism and 'most of all, cliches.' While the 1956 Twentieth CPSU Congress denounced dogmatism, this phenomenon continued to exist in the Czechoslovak economy. This was due both to the persistence of 'neo-dogmatists' (in whose ranks Loebl included Ota Sik, the architect of the future reforms) and to the lack of experience or training of Czechoslovak economists in any other methods.

Loebl maintained that the only way to overcome this was to adopt a dialectic, as distinct from a dogmatic, understanding of Marxist or economic laws. Economic laws were not natural laws; social and economic laws did not operate independently of human existence and activity but rather assumed them, he argued. Loebl pointed out that Marx himself asserted that even his laws of capitalist society, e.g. the law of accumulation, were subject to modification by varied circumstances. The dialectic approach took these varied circumstances into consideration, grasping the moment when quantitative changes, in reality, have led to qualitative changes demanding new concepts.

Loebl also addressed himself to the influence of dogmatic thinking upon Czechoslovakia's economy, offering by way of example the concept of labor productivity. After 1948 labor productivity in industry was four times that in agriculture. The regime, therefore, decided to effect a mass transfer of farm labor into industry. While Czechoslovakia should have been trying to curb the tendency of farm labor leaving for industry, it not only supported this tendency but actually 'forced' the people into this transfer. This, Loebl argued, had been because of a failure to change the conceptual understanding of this phenomenon to one which conformed more closely to reality. The dogmatic approach saw only the outdated concept which considered manual labor or the efforts of the worker the major factor in labor productivity; the role of machines and of scientific knowledge as factors more important than the role of the worker himself in the enhancing of labor productivity was not recognized. This failure in conceptualizing, or the use of the old concept, had led to millions of korunas worth of expenditures without any significant results in industrial production. Moreover, agricultural production had declined, increasing the need for imports (with the additional costs therein implied).

Loebl argued that the primary role of economics should be to establish realistically the possible economic optimum and to make provisions for realizing this optimum. The economy, he maintained, was in fact dependent upon the level of technology plus the organization of enterprises as well as the administration and organization of the entire economic structure and, therefore, upon the intellectual level upon which this last factor was built. Therefore, one must have economists educated in independent, creative thinking, able to judge critically rather than become mere 'yes-men'. Such persons should have the opportunity to implement their capabilities, instead of being shifted or undercut by red tape and bureaucracy.

While Loebl's ideas were received critically and considered radical to the extreme, they in fact paved the way for much that was to follow. Subsequent discussions and even the accepted reforms reflected much of his thesis. The party's economic weekly, *Hospodarske Noviny*, together with the Czechoslovak Society for the Propagation of Political and Scientific Knowledge, sponsored a conference in Prague on economic problems, and the former explicitly identified itself with the contributions, which it promptly published.[1] In this discussion the head of the Department of Political Economy of Bratislava University Zdenek Haba, as well as Milan Plachky, of the Prague Technical Institute, argued that the only way to prevent a return of dogmatism was to subject everything to a critical approach 'down to the underlying principle' (Plachky), including 'socialism as a social order' (Haba). Haba argued that to improve the conditions of the economy one must realize one's subjective limitations and face all the problems of the society, including such hitherto forbidden ones as the conflict between the workers and the peasantry. Like Loebl, Haba pointed out that the way chosen had been chosen not because it was the only way but because it appeared to be the best way. However, methods, such as collectivization and nationalization, for example, had come to be viewed as ends in themselves, synonymous with socialism. This consideration of the realm of production relations as decisive for socialism was basically incorrect, Haba said. In fact the whole point was not that things would be free once socialism was achieved but that they would be

[1] *Hospodarske Noviny*, 8 November, 1963.

free for all, and that there would be enough to satisfy the needs and demands of all. Thus, he claimed, it was the content not just the form of socialism which was of importance.

Another contributor, Korda, blamed not just dogmatism and misconceptions but also a total lack of any conception of economics or economic methods. Economic education tended to ignore reality and shied away from logic, he said. Selucky attributed some of these conceptual shortcomings to gaps in Marxism. For example, he said, the Marxist theory of value did not provide a basis for a policy of foreign currency and foreign exchange relations; for reasons connected with this, no price system with a justified economic relationship had been set up in Czechoslovakia. Echoing Loebl's criticism of outdated concepts, he said existing economic problems might be promisingly tackled if, for example, it were clear to the specialist or the manager that the 'law of supply and demand must be decisive for the structure of the consumer industries and that, in the long run, it should be decisive for the structure of the whole economy.' Thus, almost as an aside, to support the general argument for the need for economists to provide a set of concepts to shape economic policy in accordance with reality, Selucky introduced the principle which was to provide the basis for the reform of the Czechoslovak economy.

PRINCIPLES OF REFORM

These discussions, as well as those conducted privately within the party, led to the foundation in 1963 of a 'working group of experts,' led by Ota Sik, head of the Czechoslovak Academy of Sciences (CSAV) Institute of Economics, to work out a new system of management and planning. On 14 September 1964 the party presidium and the government approved basic principles drawn up by this group; and on 17 October 1964 *Rude Pravo* published the recommended principles for economic reform. By way of introduction, the 'Principles' explained that most experts agreed that a permanent solution to such objective problems in the economy as unsatisfactory industrial structure, insufficient resources for increasing labor productivity, inability to satisfy the purchasing capacity of the population, difficulties with foreign trade, and so forth, was handicapped by serious defects in planning management and incentives to production. What was needed, therefore, was a revaluation of the socialist system of the planned economy and an effort towards the improvement of planned management principles. The planning system should be based on economic cost accounting (*khozraschot*) in relations between enterprises; material incentives, wages, and salaries should become more directly related to the economic success of the enterprises, the efficiency of their operation, and the quality and usefulness of their products; commercial, fiscal, and credit policies should play a greater role. The goal was to use economic instruments to adjust output more closely to the expanding demand.

The 'Principles' explained that the reforms were to introduce a second (intensive) stage in the economic development of Czechoslovakia. The prior stage had been one of extensive development aimed at rapidly expanding the industrial potential of the whole of Czechoslovakia. The existing system of economic management had, however, become outdated. As the productive potential of the country expanded, factors conducive to the overall economic growth gradually weakened and internal defects in the planned management system became increasingly evident. The planned management system could not 'impart sufficient impulse to accelerate the rise in labor productivity or open new growth resources.' It did not provide for the required technical advances or modernization nor for a 'renewal' and 'modernization' of the labor force in order to release those required for transfer to the most vital sectors of the economy. Such problems as quality of manufactured goods were unsolved by the old system.

Sik maintained that the present economic problems were the result of applying the methods of the extensive stage of development to the second, intensive, stage of development.[1] This two-stage view was contested by a number of liberal economists, for example B. Korda, who argued that Czechoslovakia was already an intensively industrialized country prior to World War II. The centrally controlled economic management system imposed by the communists had in fact been unnecessary and harmful, and it had caused severe and chronic dislocation in the Czechoslovak economy.[2] Nonetheless, the two-stage view was the one adopted by the party, probably because it offered a rationalization for past actions despite the admissions of the liabilities of the previous system.

[1] Ota Sik, 'A Contribution to the Analysis of Czechoslovak Economic Development,' *Politicke Ekonomie*, XI:1 (1963), 1–33; Sik, 'Das Neue Verhaltnis Zwischen Wirtschaftsplanung und Market–Mechanismus in Der CSSR,' Unpublished paper (Goesing, Austria, 1965), 1–3.

[2] B. Korda, 'Comments on J. Goldmann's Study on the Rate of Growth,' *Planovane Hospodarstvi*, XIII:2 (1965), 41–5.

The 'Principles' pointed out that the criterion of gross output had neglected such things as efficiency in production and distribution. Plans were based on simple percentage indicators and the mere quantity of increases in production. Moreover, plants were forced to exaggerate their needs for investment funds and labor while struggling to have their output goals reduced. Production planning had failed to take into consideration costs of production, return on investments, future costs due to poor construction or low quality production, costs due to shortage of raw materials, and so forth. Planning, according to the 'Principles,' should be based on a rational calculation of profitability of investment projects. An objective unit of measure must be found so as to compare results of enterprises with each other and with the foreign market with regard both to cost and to quality. Not only would enterprises no longer be guided solely by the principle of plan fulfill- ment but the accompanying interference and direction from the state in the interests of plan fulfillment, assigning quotas, publishing and basing computations on percentage increases of gross output, were to be eliminated. An enterprise's real interest in improving quality, market- ing a greater variety of goods, and optimal utilization of all resources was to be stimulated. Therefore, enterprises were to be permitted to decide, themselves, how best to operate and how best to utilize the resources available to them.

With regard to stimulating worker interest in production, the 'Principles' asserted: 'The tremendous advantages of socialism, beginning with the worker's understanding that he is not working for a capitalist but for society, are fully effective only if both material and political stimuli also operate in the same direction and strengthen each other.' The worker must be made to feel that his share in the national wealth was dependent upon his own efforts. A decline in technical quality or a drop in profits would mean a drop in earnings just as rapid economic progress would be reflected in the earnings of those who contributed to this rise.

Prices determined by supply and demand were intended to tie the enterprise to the market. Thus the ultimate criterion should be profitability, based on such parameters as prices, wages, and interest rates. These parameters or economic levers should be effectively applied within each enterprise so as to expand production of goods which were in demand, to introduce new goods, and to restrict production of goods for which there was diminishing or no demand. Thus producers would have a real interest in long-range plans which foresaw markets trends, and in adjusting their production to these probable trends. The profitability criterion should, therefore, be used in central planning and create conditions which would promote plans which were in line with the people's interests.

This general presentation of the basic principles was intended to introduce Sik's proposal that the old centralized–directive planning system be abandoned. Under the old system every detail was centrally planned; production plans stipulated overall volume, assortment, costs, labor force, and so on. Sik wanted greater independence for the enterprises, with the plant manager deciding on the assortment and production volume, assessing costs and being held responsible for the technical level. Most of all Sik wanted the plant manager to be responsible to the customer through his dependence upon the market for profitability.[1]

Stating that the reforms were to affect every aspect of the national economy, from the compiling of the plans to worker earnings, the 'Principles' outlined the ideas to be introduced, the details of which we shall see below. The timetable for the proposed reforms, which were described by the 'Principles' as the most 'deep and fundamental changes' the Czechoslovak national economy had undergone since nationalization, was to be the following: debate and approval of the 'Principles' by the end of 1964; implementation to be begun in 1965, with total implementation as of January 1966 simultaneously with the beginning of the 1966–70 plan.

Top party leaders (as well as middle-level functionaries) apparently were concerned about this nod in the direction of apparently capitalist measures and sought to supply various explanations. Hendrych almost apologetically argued that the time had come when Czechoslovakia was no longer in the 'fortunate position' of 'being able to draw from the experience of the Soviet Union.'[2] Czechoslovakia had reached a stage, he said, wherein many problems would have to be solved simultaneously with the Soviet Union and other socialist countries, while there were even spheres in which Czechoslovakia would have to act as a pioneer. In the same vein a later article in the party daily painstakingly explained that the new system was not, like the NEP of Lenin or the 1956 de-collectivization in Polish agriculture, a temporary step backward from the point of view of political aims in order to achieve a certain advance economically. The new principles were *not* a return in

[1] See Ota Sik, 'Problems of the New System of Planned Management,' *Nova Mysl*, XVIII:10 (1964), 1165–80.

[2] *Rude Pravo*, 2 February 1965 (speech to January 1965 central committee plenum).

any way towards capitalism but rather a step forward to communism, for a communist system could not be achieved by an authoritative system of administration.[1] Using a political argument the author echoed Sik's thesis that the former methods may have been necessary during the first phase of development, during the struggle for power against the capitalists, but they had now lost their value. A new path, not a return to capitalism, was needed for the development of socialist economic and social relations. This path was to lead to the communist goal of satisfying the demands of the people in accordance with their needs, and the freeing of the creative forces of labor.

There were, however, many economists who argued that there was much worth copying in the advanced capitalist system. Agreeing with Hendrych's idea that there was no longer a socialist model to follow, one Slovak economist argued that capitalism might well be a 'prototype of advanced socialism in many respects.'[2] Capitalism could not provide a model for distribution of income or unemployment or social services, he said, but it could provide one for the operation of production and commercial enterprises, including a place for efficient private tradesmen and farmers, even in advanced socialism. Indeed, a study of conditions in the U.S., Canada, Sweden, and Switzerland might, he argued, help Czechoslovakia formulate a theoretical concept of advanced socialist society.

The discussions of how best to characterize the economic reforms were by no means a matter of semantics but a sign of the opposition to the system. Sik himself had foreseen opposition both from dogmatists and from managers and functionaries who owed their positions to the goodwill of the party, since their knowledge and training were far below the standard required by the new system.[3] It was just these elements of society which tried to discredit the 'Principles' with cries of 'capitalism,' and, as Sik had warned, they tried to neutralize the changes by demanding compromises of the principles upon which the reforms were based. The 'Principles' were, however, tentative. Many points demanded clarification and refinement, many led to problems, many were distorted, and many underwent changes as the effort to implement them got under way. The most comprehensive pronouncement was the 'General Conditions of Enterprise Management

---

[1] *Rude Pravo*, 16 February 1966.
[2] Jozef Ceconik, 'The Advanced Socialist Society,' *Kulturny Zivot*, 9 September 1966; *Bratislava Pravda*, 21 September 1966.
[3] Sik, *Nova Mysl*, XVIII:10 (1964), 1170.

Effective on 1 January 1967,'[1] which accompanied the beginning of at least partial implementation. It is to the details of the reform as they emerged, with their modifications, distortions, problems, and arguments, that we shall now turn.

[1] *Hospodarske Noviny*, 29 July 1966.

5

PLANNING AND ORGANIZATION OF INDUSTRIAL PRODUCTION

PLANNING

One of the goals of the new system was 'to strive for integrated functioning of social planning generally and to make use of market relations'[1] or, as Sik put it, a tying of planning to the market mechanism. This meant a rejection of the former planning system of directives (which Premier Lenart once described as a 'Procrustean bed') to which each enterprise had to shape its production schedule.[2] The *function* of the plan was to serve as an instrument for long-term optimization of economic development. Enterprises would be accorded greater opportunity to decide such things as the structure, delivery times, and quality of their production, for quantitative indices would be reduced considerably to serve, principally, as a set of orientation figures.[3] Commercial relations rather than detailed targets would govern relations between enterprises. Therefore, there would have to be direct contact between the supplier and the customer, with the latter free to choose his own supplier and to purchase according to the range and quantity he wished.[4] Economic levers would replace directives for the realization of the overall objectives of the planned structure of the economy. As envisaged by Sik, central directives would be used only if and when planned objectives could not be ensured by the use of economic stimuli and only if and when optimal economic development would be impossible without 'highly circumscribed' central directives.[5]

Central planning was to remain responsible for certain national matters, including: first, the basic structure and pattern of production, i.e. the apportionment of national income between investment and consumption, the relationship between personal and social consumption, and the general progress of living standards; secondly, the main

[1] *Main Reports and Documents Concerning the New System of Management of the National Economy in Czechoslovakia*, 5 (1965 central committee resolution on the new system) (Prague, 1965), 93.

[2] *Rude Pravo*, 10 November 1965 (speech to November 1965 central committee plenum).

[3] Jan Sekera, 'Interview with the Premier,' *Nova Mysl*, xx:1 (1966), 5–6.

[4] *Main Reports and Documents*, 5 (Prague, 1965), 117–18.

[5] Ota Sik, 'Market–Mechanismus in Der CSSR' (Goesing, 1965), 2–3.

lines of development of productive industry, i.e. scientific long-term planning of crucial capital investment projects, long-term provisions for improving workers' qualifications, determination of vital needs for technical and scientific progress, responsibility for international agreements and trade, and maintenance of balanced economic development in all parts of the country; thirdly, the way in which economic incentives were applied in management; fourthly, basic price and wage policies; and fifthly, financial and credit policy to ensure that social (welfare) needs could be met by the state by means of payments to the state treasury (taxes, interest) and to stimulate interest in foreign currency earnings.[1]

Not only the role of the plan was redefined but also its formulation. Instead of the former practice of formulating plans according to purely quantitative considerations the plan was to base its calculations on the economic effectiveness of considered projects. This would be judged from the point of view of world standards of quality, technical specifications, and costs; and from the point of view of capital investment and operational costs. In keeping with Sik's proposals, projects were to be accepted only if they would serve production growth while maximizing returns on investment. If a plant failed to produce at world standards and competitive costs, it would have to be decided if it would pay to continue.[2]

There were to be three types of plans, the first of which was to be long-range (ten to fifteen years), for overall state economic development. This plan was to forecast market trends, scientific progress, and international developments. A shorter but still long-range (five-year) plan was to be the basic instrument of economic management. Compiled in cooperation with the enterprises, the task of the five-year plan was to integrate long-range forecasts and developments (capital construction, investments, technological development, etc.) to ensure economic continuity. In conjunction with the five-year plan the central authorities would issue basic regulations governing such matters as economic incentives, taxes, reserve funds, and financing of capital construction. Enterprises, for their part, were to take the initiative in drafting their own long-range plans. Within the context of the five-year plan, shorter one- to three-year implementation or operational plans would be drawn up.[3]

---

[1] *Main Reports and Documents*, 5 (Prague, 1965), 96–100.
[2] *Rude Pravo*, 17 October 1964.
[3] *Main Reports and Documents*, 5 (Prague, 1965), 97–9. The party resolution, unlike the 'Principles,' did not specify if these were to be compiled by the enterprises.

THE GOVERNMENT

To accommodate the new system certain changes would be required in the methods and working style of the government. The main purpose of the specialized government agencies would be to submit to the government detailed proposals for solutions of pending economic and social problems.[1] The most important of these agencies was to be the State Planning Commission, to be composed of government ministers, experts, academy members and university personnel, and superior (as previously) to government ministries. It was to meet more regularly than in the past and work as a collective organ responsible to the government, although the party presidium might intervene in preparatory stages of their work 'and give them the right direction.'[2] It was to submit periodic solutions to basic questions. A State Commission for Finance, Prices, and Wages was to submit proposals, in cooperation with the State Bank, on credit policy, prices, wages, levies, and economic regulations. It was, however, to be independent of and refrain from interfering in the Ministry of Finance, the State Bank (which itself was separated from the Finance Ministry), and the State Office for Social Security.[3]

The Commission for Capital Investment was merged with the Commission for Scientific and Technical Development to form a Commission for Technology in the interests of a single policy for technological progress. A Commission for Economic and Scientific Technological Cooperation was to be responsible for foreign economic relations and cooperation (principally with CEMA). It would not have the authority of a ministry, however, nor of the other relevant organs carrying out foreign cooperation and trade.[4] A Commission for Management and Organization, established earlier in the year, was to be concerned with problems of central management, of organization, of enterprises, and the management of economic relations, as well as training of management cadres.

The role of the production ministries was redefined to accord with the new system's decentralization of decision-making, and the substitution of economic for administrative levers of control. The ministries were to guide capital investment and technological development as well as the application of economic regulations and incentives. Many of the

---

[1] *Rude Pravo*, 4 November 1965.
[2] *Rude Pravo*, 10 November 1965 (Lenart speech).
[3] *Rude Pravo*, 4 November 1965.   *Ibid.*

tasks formerly in the hands of the ministries were to be assumed by the branch directorates, and there was to be a reduction in the number of personnel in the central management organs.[1] Moreover, the minister, who formerly looked upon his task as that of administering a government department and section of industry, would have to take a more active role in the collective organs of the government.

With regard to changes in the style of government work, alternative suggestions were to be submitted with each proposal, and the method of opposing proposals with the varying viewpoints of different departmental organs was to be used. Thus each department of the government would be responsible for compiling proposals for its area; the specialized agencies would submit their proposals; the State Planning Commission would coordinate the process of working out a plan; and the highest state and party organs would make the decision on the key issues on the basis of the various proposals presented.[2] With these changes it would be essential that the quality of personnel in all management capacities be improved. While political maturity would remain the primary requirement, also required would be a high degree of specialized knowledge, practical experience, organizational talent and ability, determination, and a sense for enterprise and technical progress. Persons in executive positions who did not possess sufficient knowledge or ability would have to be replaced. More responsibility was to be delegated to the branch and enterprise organs for the selection, training, and placement of cadres. Outside experts and advisors were to be used systematically as a basic working method of the apparatus.[3]

ORGANIZATION OF INDUSTRY

In July 1965 the industrial base of the economy was reorganized.[4] There were to be two types of production or management units: 'associations' with subordinate enterprises, and trusts. This was in fact a dual grouping, along vertical lines in the 'association' and along horizontal lines in the trust. The 'association' would consist of enterprises in various or specialized phases of the industry, from raw materials up to the finished product, interrelated through production and technology. The trust would be used for organization of enterprises engaged in the

[1] *Rude Pravo*, 10 November 1965.   [2] *Bratislava Pravda*, 11 November 1965.
[3] *Rude Pravo*, 2 February, 4 and 10 November 1965.
[4] See Frantisek Vlasak, 'Czechoslovak Industry under the New System,' *Czechoslovak Foreign Trade*, 6:1 (1966), 6–10.

production of essentially the same items. Together the associations and trusts were referred to as branches.

To provide the branches the independence promised by the new system of planning, indices within the state plan were to be severely reduced – from 1200 to 67 – and branches were to set their own production targets. The branches were to be subject to the economic regulations of the state which would stipulate such things as levies to be paid to the state budget, payments to certain enterprise funds, credit terms, wage and salary categories, and price rules. They would also be subject to the overall central planning targets. The new method of plan compilation provided, however, for cooperation between the central and branch authorities. For their part the branches were to operate on the *khozraschot* principle, as independent business units, comparing earnings and costs and striving for the profitability of their enterprises.

Branch management was to be in the hands of a branch directorate. The directors of the subordinate sectors or enterprises were to be subordinate to this board, though originally they were to select the branch general director. In December 1966, however, the party decided that the general director would be appointed by the state. These boards would be the link between the central organs and the enterprises, for the central organs could give tasks only to these boards. The directorates were to be responsible for the effective management of their branches, without interfering unduly with the independence of the subordinate enterprises. Their control was to be primarily through economic levers.

The branch directorates were to take the necessary steps for the *long-term* development of the enterprises subordinate to them. This implied market research as well as the introduction of technologically progressive processes. In this connection they might be responsible for purchase and sales. The directorate was also to work out an efficient system of management. Specifically, it was to work out the rules for the distribution of the enterprise income, adjustments of prices and wages in the enterprises, investments and incentives. There was to be an interlocking of the results of the individual enterprises so that at least a part of the profits would be at the disposal of the branch as a whole. Finally, the directorates were to coordinate the subordinate enterprises regarding deliveries, technical development, and supplies, for example. The enterprise remained the basic unit of production, however, and after fulfilling its duties to the state budget and branch directorate it would allocate its profits to its own 'funds' (investment, workers', reserve and cultural–social funds), which it alone would control. Enterprises in trusts would maintain their legal identity as independent organizations.

SHORTCOMINGS AND CRITICISMS

In 1965, there were experiments with the new system in some 450 organizations and, as of 1 July, the above reorganization of the industrial base was introduced. Problems and opposition were encountered, however, and 1966 was to see only partial introduction of the new system.[1] Aside from political opposition by conservatives and by unqualified functionaries who feared for their positions,[2] there were substantive complaints about the organization and planning aspects of the new system. A repeated complaint was that the number of indices had not been reduced as promised, mainly because of the persistence of old habits but also because of branch directorate interference.[3] Sik urged that branch directorates take note of the distinction between guidance and directive indices. He said that while there had been an overall reduction in indices, some central organs and branch directorates had actually augmented the number of plan indices or the required documentation for the plans required of the enterprises. Enterprises did *not* have a greater feeling of independence, and they lacked sufficient security with regard to future obligations and levies. Long-range obligations had to be made clear so that an enterprise would know where it stood and could chance business risks with a certain amount of confidence. In some cases, according to Sik, branch directorates had actually taken over the management of production and marketing. They thereby undermined the spirit of competition within the branch, instead of concentrating on long-range problems and use of economic levers. Branch directorates' responsibility for the actual course of production should be limited 'to an absolute minimum,' he warned.[4]

Many critics were willing to admit that this branch directorate interference might be a temporary phenomenon particular to the 'transition period' and, therefore, not the fault of the new system itself.[5]

[1] See M. Sokol, 'Changes in Economic Management in Czechoslovakia,' *Czechoslovak Economic Papers*, 8 (1967), 7–8.
[2] See for example, *Rude Pravo*, 23 December 1965.
[3] See for example, *Hospodarske Noviny*, 11 March 1966.
[4] *Praca*, 7 December 1966; *Rude Pravo*, 18, 22, and 23 February 1966.
[5] For example *Hospodarske Noviny*, 10 December 1965 (Josef Toman).

There were others, however, who saw enterprise independence limited by the subordination of enterprise managers to superior (branch) organs rather than to their own production collectives.[1] Still others pointed out that one flaw of the previous economic system was actually rendered more serious by the reforms: the domination by monopolies. Sik understandably did not believe that the reforms themselves but rather the way in which they were implemented augmented the problem of monopolization. Thus, he argued that one of the tasks of the branch directorate was to devise anti-monopolistic policies, through the use of enterprise independence, competition, and economic values. Implicitly recognizing the existence of the problem even within the scope of the reforms, Sik believed that since there was a sellers' market it was desirable to make use of foreign competition by way of imports to combat the market monopoly power of domestic enterprises. Structurally this was provided for by the new system, Sik would argue, although in many sectors the monopolistic position of producers had been organizationally and administratively strengthened due to faulty implementation.[2]

The practical aspect of this problem was demonstrated by one economist who claimed that the reforms strengthened the monopolies of the suppliers and sales organizations.[3] While the new system called for contracts, it did not make them obligatory, and penalties for non-fulfillment rarely provided full compensation. In fact, the position of the supplier had actually been strengthened by the relaxation of the distribution function of the plan, and the centralization of sales and supply operations at the branch directorate level merely strengthened the monopolistic position of the suppliers. If market relations were to influence production, the mutual relationship between enterprises would have to be based on a free choice of supplier and customer in domestic trade and on mutual agreements regarding orders. This principle was not fully adopted by the new system.

Under the new system eighty per cent of the branches were to be of the trust type. While this type of branch was more favorable to production freedom for the individual enterprises, it nonetheless represented monopolies of whole types of production since it was based on horizontal organization and consisted of one managerial organ for the whole industry. Thus there would be a disproportionate centralization

[1] See *Kulturny Zivot*, 14 January 1966 (Eugen Loebl); *Rude Pravo*, 6 July 1967.
[2] *Rude Pravo*, 18, 22, and 23 February 1966; *Praca*, 7 December 1966.
[3] *Lud*, 4 March 1966.

in the organization of production, for there were no small or medium sized enterprises. While America too has a high rate of concentration, it was argued, more than fifty per cent of its total production is produced by tens of thousands of medium and small-sized firms. This phenomenon proved that there are 'rational techno–economic limits to concentration of production.' In the Czechoslovak 'concentration-mania' such basic considerations as transportation costs, location of resources and markets, and suitability of size to task were completely overlooked. Further, the diversification of production should be closely connected with management methods within a monopoly. Under the new system the management within the branch was the same whether a single product, such as coal, or thousands of varied products, as in the chemical industry, were involved. The internal organization of each branch directorate ought to be different, but the new system tended towards uniformity and centralization in the organization of the branch directorate.[1]

Some economists believed that the organization of production according to the branch principle 'is still largely the result of deliberations in the spirit of the old system of management.'[2] The branch rendered planning and central management easier than would a system of numerous, small, independent enterprises with varied production programs. In fact, it was argued, conditions should be established whereby enterprises themselves might transfer factories or plants on the basis of mutual agreements, whereby enterprises might merge with or dissociate themselves from a branch, and whereby enterprises might join other types of organization than the current type of branch administration.[3] One economist proposed that individuals be permitted to form a cooperative enterprise, with the help of bank credits. This would provide an opportunity for competition within the branch enterprises and a brake on monopolistic means.[4] Addressing themselves to the solutions offered by Sik, these experts argued that if foreign trade were to be used to combat the monopoly of domestic enterprises on the market there must be competition in the conduct of foreign trade as well.

[1] For above arguments see *Reporter*, 10 December 1966 (interviews with leading economists). See also Zdenek Vergner, 'The Paths of the Czechoslovak Economy,' *Ekonomicka Revue*, 5 (1966), 214.
[2] *Reporter*, 10 December 1966.   [3] Vergner, *Ekonomicka Revue*, 5 (1966), 213.
[4] *Ibid.*

6

ECONOMIC LEVERS IN THE
INDUSTRIAL SECTOR

A basic feature of the reforms was the encouragement of the profitability principle instead of the state-supported and, if necessary, state-subsidized system. Enterprises were to cover their operating costs from their own income, contributing to the state budget through a system of levies, and negotiating with the State Bank for credits. As explained by the 'Principles,' all enterprise or branch calculations were to be based on gross income. Increased production, savings in material costs, and increased quality of production in accordance with flexible prices would all increase the gross income and, therefore, the size of the funds (after levies to the state budget). Wages per capita would also increase with increased labor productivity and the division of the wage fund among fewer workers. Thus the workers (and the enterprise) would have a material interest in greater efficiency and productivity.

REMUNERATION OF WORKERS

The wage and premium fund was to be derived from the gross income, the actual amount depending upon the sum earned by the enterprise for this purpose. There were to be no state subsidies to cover even wages. Enterprise reserve funds were to be rapidly built up to provide contingency funds to cover instances when expected economic results were not achieved. A significant part of the worker's wages was to depend upon the individual results of his work and, through premiums and bonuses, of the earnings of the plant. As dependence of remuneration upon results was to be 'direct and immediate,'[1] there would have to be a differentiation instead of the former equalization of wages. Those with greater responsibility in production (managers, foremen, etc.) were to be remunerated in proportion to this responsibility and according to the satisfactory or unsatisfactory results of their efforts. For all workers, wages and premiums would also be tied to the quality of the goods they produced, with direct penalties for poor-quality work.[2]

[1] *Main Reports and Documents*, 4 (Prague, 1965), 18 (Lenart report to January 1965 central committee plenum).
[2] *Rude Pravo*, 2 February 1965.

Although wages were to be flexible they were not to be entirely free. Trends in wage scales, piece-wage rates, and basic salaries were to be fixed centrally. To further assure overall wage stability, a so-called stabilization levy was to be inserted into the new system as of December 1967.[1] The purpose of this levy was two-fold: first, to create funds in the state budget which could be used to raise wages in the government administration and non-profit services in proportion to wage rises in the 'productive' spheres; and secondly, to ensure that wages would not be raised at the expense of investments, or more workers hired at the expense of labor productivity. The rate of the levy was to be thirty per cent of the volume of wages paid in excess of a certain minimum and was to be raised in proportion to the increase in the number of workers per year. Thus for every one per cent increase in the number of workers over a year the levy would be raised by one per cent of the total wages paid.

INVESTMENTS

Serious problems of investments under the former system were the volume of projects under construction, the length of time taken to complete projects, the low technical standards of the projects, and rising costs. It was found that financing of investments from the state budget did not guarantee an economically justifiable return on investments. The new system, therefore, was to introduce economic levers in the area of investment financing. Gradually the role of the central budget in this area was to be replaced by negotiated bank loans. The overall volume of capital investment was to be planned centrally, with the most significant projects stipulated by the five-year plan.[2] Approximately fifteen per cent of the volume of investments was to be financed by the state budget through non-repayable funds. Included in this fifteen per cent figure were projects such as independent water and air depollution systems for factories; new constructions to serve area purposes, presumably public services; certain unfinished or newly started investments considered economically indispensable but which were not in harmony with the direct interests and possibilities of the relevant enterprise.[3] The enterprises or branches were to finance some centrally ordered significant projects, modernization and reconstruction projects, and smaller projects. These investments were to be financed

[1] *Hospodarske Noviny*, 29 July 1966 ('General Conditions').
[2] See Sokol, *Czechoslovak Economic Papers*, 8 (1967), 16.
[3] *Hospodarske Noviny*, 29 July 1966 ('General Conditions').

by repayable loans from the State Bank or self-financed by the enterprise or branch. Rough proportions of resources for financing capital investments were to be: twenty per cent from enterprise funds, sixty per cent from bank credits, fifteen per cent from state subsidies, one per cent from 'other' sources.[1] The central authorities would have the right to approve or disapprove all investments over a given sum (before credit was requested from the bank). All investments, however financed, were to be judged on the basis of profitability and the principle of recoupment of invested funds. Foreign advisors would be consulted on state-supported projects and construction efficiency would be judged according to world standards.[2]

With these changes in the system of financing capital construction the role of the State Bank was also to be altered. In effect the Bank would be changed from an accounting institute to a commercial–financial agency. The large share of investment funds going through the banks would ensure mobility of capital funds. Enterprises would have to demonstrate that they had instituted conditions consistent with the policy of accountability and increased productivity before loans would be granted.[3] Preference would be given to investors making greater use of profits for a faster amortization of the credit. In addition, enterprises would be penalized by higher interest rates if their own reserves were not employed before applying for a loan.[4] Basically, however, interest rates were to be uniform (six per cent for investment, four per cent for operational capital, as of 1966). During the transition period, however, flexible credit policy would be used also to eliminate imbalances.

Investment in accord with the principle of 'territorial equalization' was introduced by the 'General Conditions,' primarily to ensure development of Slovakia. There were to be state subsidies and a reduction of certain levies to encourage investments in under developed areas. On the other hand, surcharges and higher levies were to be used to discourage investments in 'overdeveloped' areas.

LEVIES

Formerly the amounts paid by enterprises to the state budget were decided arbitrarily by the central authorities. Enterprises were obliged

[1] *Ibid.*
[2] *Rude Pravo*, 2 February 1965.   [3] Sekera, *Nova Mysl*, xx:1 (1966), 6.
[4] *Bratislava Pravda*, 11 November 1965. See also Leopold Ler, 'The State Budget in 1966,' *Finance a Uver*, 16:1 (1966), 1–9.

to pay into the state budget their plan-determined profits. This, however, had led to hiding of reserves, changing of types of goods produced to make 'speculative' profits, struggling to get low targets in the plan, lowering the quality and technical level of goods, and so forth.[1] There was also an attempt to set payments to the budget on a long-term planned profit basis rather than year-by-year planned returns.

Under a system of uniform rates of taxes trends in enterprise income would not be determined by an arbitrary estimate of the possibilities for increasing profits but rather by an objective criterion. The principle of uniform levies was not wholly instituted in the transition stage of the new system, however. In 1966 a differentiated system was used in the interests of stabilization and altering the imbalances between enterprises. Thus the tax system for 1966 was composed of a basic levy on the gross income of enterprises and a tax on the increase in gross income. In addition to this there was to be a capital use charge or 'fixed capital levy' and wider use of the already existing turnover tax.[2] The gross income of an enterprise would be distributed as shown in table 1.

TABLE 1[3]

Transfers of revenue to state budget = 26% of gross income		
of this:		
basic levy	55%	
levy on increase in gross income	14%	
fixed capital tax	31%	
total	100%	
'Non-productive' outlays (insurance, interest, fees, etc.)		= 13%
Allotments to funds (reserve fund and investment fund)		= 2%
Allotment to workers fund (for wages, premiums and bonuses)		= 59%
Total		100%

[1] Sokol, *Czechoslovak Economic Papers*, 8 (1967), 13.
[2] Ler, *Finance a Uver*, 16:1 (1966), 2.
[3] *Ibid*. The chart pertains to a break-down before the introduction of a stabilization tax and depreciation payments provisions of late 1966.

The transitional 'differentiated' levy was abandoned in the plans for full implementation by 1967 of the new system. A uniform levy on gross income was to be introduced at a rate of eighteen per cent for industry and construction. To cope with the inequalities that existed, nonetheless, enterprises which were unable to comply with the generally applicable rate could apply to the branch directorate for a temporary subsidy. To cover these subsidies the branch directorate would extend levies upon the more successful enterprises in the branch, but the enterprise financing the subsidy would be given a certain degree of control over the subsidized enterprise.[1] In addition to these special levies, levies were to be paid to the branch directorate by *all* its member enterprises to cover the costs of the management of branch affairs and to establish reserves for the needs of the branch.

The fixed capital tax introduced in 1965 was in essence a charge for capital funds tied up by a specific enterprise. This levy was to be based on the net worth of fixed assets, i.e. the value of investments after deduction of depreciation allowances, at the rate of six per cent annually, and paid in addition to interest on bank credits. Together with the levy on gross income this tax was meant to replace, eventually, the turnover tax,[2] but this eventuality depended upon a reform of the wholesale price system. A two per cent levy on stocks was also added, in 1966.

PRICES

The new system was to eliminate what Lenart called the 'petrified concept of stability of wholesale prices in the practice of planning and creation of prices.'[3] Prices were to be adjusted as much as possible to the real development of production conditions, resources, and needs; criteria for prices would be socially necessary production costs, supply and demand as determined by the market, and world prices. Pressures, nonetheless, for the maintenance of price stability were reflected in the proposals for three categories of prices (fixed, partially fixed, and free) and a central price policy, and later by actual price subsidies. From the beginning it was decided that the central organs would determine overall price policy. This would mean, primarily, long-range definitions of the levels and relationship of prices of the most important products of a branch or sector. Thus the central authorities would set or modify

---

[1] *Hospodarske Noviny*, 29 July 1966 ('General Conditions').
[2] Ler, *Finance a Uver*, 16:1 (1966), 7.   [3] *Rude Pravo*, 2 February 1965.

the prices of the 'fixed price' category; this was to include only the most important items, having stable production conditions and a limited and stable assortment and for which stability of prices was important, e.g. raw materials and the basic necessities of life.[1]

Central authorities would also have a share in setting the margins for the limited or partially fixed prices. These were to be applied primarily to products or services of a seasonal nature. The exact price, however, was to be a function of the economic conditions, to be decided by the producer in agreement with the customer. The free price category would, as the name implied, not be set by the central authorities even insofar as limits of flexibility. Such prices should be used for competitive products, products produced in small series, products of exceptional quality, and products of an essentially luxury nature. For 1966 the categories were as noted in table 2.

TABLE 2[2]

	Percentage of industrial production
Fixed prices	64·0
Maximum limit prices	14·7
Maximum and minimum limit prices	14·1
Free prices	7·2
Total	100·0

The new function of prices required a reorganization of price fixing and a general adjustment of wholesale prices, but in this area serious difficulties were encountered. The reform of the wholesale prices was not included in the partial implementation, although some adjustments were made then and even in 1965.[3] This delay, due mainly to a failure to work out new prices in time, severely curtailed the efficiency of the measures that were introduced. Almost all the economic levers depended upon the reform of the wholesale prices and as a result of this delay a need for subsidies and other transitional compensatory measures, and a general deformation of the system resulted. Thus

[1] 'An up-to-date Economic Vocabulary,' *Zivot Strany*, 1 (1965), 37.
[2] *Sbirka Zakonu* Ordinance No. 8/1966.
[3] See *Rude Pravo*, 24 August 1965; *Zemedelske Noviny*, 11 March 1966; and Sokol, *Czechoslovak Economic Papers*, 8 (1967), 8.

'temporary' price subsidies were introduced in 1966. They were to be dispensed from the central budget through the branch directorate to the enterprises, but they would *not* be granted if the branch as a whole were earning enough resources to cover costs.[1] Price subsidies were available only for products of the fixed or limited price categories, and would not apply to those products for which the wholesale prices had already been reformed.

It was generally accepted that the wholesale price reforms would not be introduced before 1968, at the earliest. In February 1966, however, the party central committee approved a plan devised by Sik which would permit a speedier two-step introduction of wholesale price reforms. Instead of waiting until data could be processed for the adjustment of several million individual prices adjustment was to be made according to some twenty-odd thousand groups of products. These reforms by groups were introduced in 1967, while the specific changes of each and every price, adjusted properly, was to follow in 1968.[2]

CRITICISM AND DISCUSSION

The delineation of the economic levers and their use were by no means to the satisfaction of everyone, particularly the authors of the principles of the new system. Despite the fact that a number of the 'transition' measures were explained by the fact that the system of economic levers could not work freely until wholesale prices were reformed, these features were generally retained even after the price reforms. While it is true that these controls were economic and not administrative levers, this use even of economic levers to interfere in the market was the subject of some debate.

Sik attributed the delays and compromises the reforms were encountering to two subjective factors: persons of faint heart who, through pessimism, exaggerated the difficulties encountered by the new system; and persons who were out and out opponents to the new system out of fear of losing their perhaps undeserved or easy jobs, who purposely exaggerated and even created difficulties in the hopes of causing delays or compromises which would render the new system ineffective. He pointed out that certain solutions had been prematurely

[1] Josef Soucek, 'Price Subsidies and Reductions in Transfers of Revenues on Fixed Capital,' *Finance a Uver*, 16:1 (1966), 26.
[2] Sokol, *Czechoslovak Economic Papers*, 8 (1967), 2; *Praca*, 22 March 1966.

rejected, the most important of these being the one-time wholesale price reform which he had originally advocated.

A second compromise which Sik saw as a 'serious error limiting the efficiency of the new system' was the interpretation of the price categories in such a way that only limited and free prices were flexible, with the fixed prices considered unchangeable and unmovable. All prices must to some degree be flexible, he believed. Towards this end the differentiated turnover tax should be eliminated, for the differences in this tax created anomalies. Sik also sought elimination of the limitations placed upon wage increases. He advocated faster growth of nominal wages so as to create greater wage differentiation within professions and between good and poor workers. Higher wages need not lead to higher prices; they could and should be paid for out of higher productivity. Sik pointed out that dogmatic obstruction could destroy this mechanism.[1]

Sik consistently opposed the delays in the full implementation of the new system, pointing out that any attempt to work out a new five-year plan by the old methods would necessarily harm the effectiveness of the proposed changes.[2] Premier Lenart was an ally of Sik on this point, and in time the regime agreed to the speeding up of the implementation.[3] Thus Novotny himself called for a speeding up at the Thirteenth Party Congress, as did Slovak party first secretary Dubcek at the Slovak Congress and central committee economic commission chief Kolder.[4] This speed-up did not necessarily effect the compromises, however, nor the problems inherent in the new system.

One government economist, Hvezdon Koctuch, pointed out that the problems involved could be overcome only if the final goals were quite clear. The ultimate criterion must be a maximized difference between input and output. To accomplish this one must have a bi-polar economic mechanism, which could not be based upon profits alone. It must also be based upon economizing on the costs of work. The market price would be the basis for this economic mechanism. This was not merely a redistribution of the national income on the basis of production costs in the various branches, but the creation of conditions

---

[1] See *Rude Pravo*, 18, 22, and 23 February 1966; *Praca*, 25 February and 7 December 1966.

[2] Indeed the five-year plan was delayed numerous times, and from 1963 until this writing (1971) Czechoslovakia has been operating on one-year interim plans.

[3] See *Rude Pravo*, 22 April 1966.

[4] *Rude Pravo*, 1 June 1966; *Bratislava Pravda*, 13 May 1966; *Hospodarske Noviny*, 14 October 1966.

permitting a more realistic basis for the foreign exchange rate of the koruna – preparing the way for convertibility. A realistically based exchange rate would not only permit the application of world prices to the domestic market; it would also disclose the micro-structural and macro-structural changes required by the economy. As a second step, the central organs should be removed from the determination of investment; and the third step should be a freeing of the labor market. Workers should be free of administrative transfers dictated by the so-called 'different social importance of work.' A labor market should be created to provide an economic mechanism whereby a worker might try his luck in another sector of activity.[1]

According to other critics, the system of subsidies was a foreign body in the reformed system and was bound to create difficulties.[2] Subsidies tended to promote the type of production which requires maximum state intervention rather than the opposite and desired effect of the new system, argued still another economist.[3] They also disturbed relations between the producers and consumers, which were to be based on value. There was also criticism with regard to the levies and funds available for investments. A State Bank employee from Ceske Budejovice pointed out that the overall levies did not leave sufficient room for enterprise incentive. Only seven to eight per cent of profits were left to pay fixed capital levies, interest payments on circulating capital, and the funds of the enterprise, including the investment as well as the reserve and social funds.[4] Loebl pointed out that whereas formerly the enterprise had floating capital, it was now forced to apply for credit. While he agreed that this was not undesirable in itself, it nonetheless did constitute a violation of the principle of enterprise independence. The enterprise was not permitted to own what it had produced, he claimed, and a prosperous enterprise was 'deprived of the fruits of its work,' for under the 'transition' system a redistribution would take place to finance the less successful enterprises.[5]

The Ceske Budejovice bank employee also pointed out that according to the principles of the new system capital levies were to be determined on a long-term basis in the five-year plan. Instead, however, branches assessed the amounts of enterprise capital levies on a yearly basis,

[1] *Hospodarske Noviny*, 18 March 1966.
[2] J. Typolt and O. Novak, 'The Principles for the Overhauling of the Wholesale Price,' *Planovane Hospodarstvi*, XIX:2 (1966), 68.
[3] *Hospodarske Noviny*, 10 December 1965 (Toman).
[4] *Rude Pravo*, 17 February 1966.   [5] *Kulturny Zivot*, 14 January 1966.

separately for each year. Owing to this practice, enterprises lacked a reliable basis upon which to project for the future and compile a plan in which they themselves were interested. This might, the critic concluded, easily lead to the malpractice of plants concealing reserves even in the planning work.

The wage system also came under fire both from economists and from workers. Loebl criticized the fact that the extent of remuneration would be limited by the state and by branch directorates in their fixing of general wage policy and by the categories of fixed and limited prices. The stabilization tax too, Loebl argued, might encourage a hiding of reserves and encourage low wages at the expense of greater efficiency; it was in fact a brake on increased productivity.

Workers had shown signs of resentment of the new use of economic levers, particularly the penalties for poor-quality work. They also resented wage de-equalization and feared unemployment as a result not only of the stabilization levy and linking of salaries to the wage bill but also of the introduction of economic criteria which demanded the closing of inefficient plants. Work stoppages were reported in connection with the settlement of wage disputes, and workers even refused to pay their union dues, threatening to quit, in protest against penalities for poor-quality work.[1] The Slovak trade union organ *Praca* reported numerous worker complaints against de-equalization of wages, e.g. that of a worker who questioned why he, 'a rank and file worker,' should receive only 200 korunas while the deputy director, 'a scamp who does nothing apart from walking around the factory,' received 1500 korunas.[2]

While *Praca* tended to express worker dissatisfaction with rather banal examples which hardly seriously placed in doubt the principle of wage de-equalization, Sik did not so lightly dismiss this problem. He admitted that conservative opposition to and obstruction of the implementation of the new system was reinforced by the opposition of many workers to the new system.[3] The latter was a result of the demoralizing effects of the old system. The purely quantitative development of production; the 'enormous underestimation' of highly qualified workers and work of high quality, the disregard for demand; the frequent 'subjectivistic' changes in assignments, tasks, or promises; the inefficiency and frequent interruptions in production leading to idle waiting; the rigid, formal control of the results of labor, and the exag-

---

[1] *Kulturni Tvorba*, 26 May 1966 (J. Kanturek). [2] *Praca*, 8 January 1967.
[3] *Rude Pravo*, 18, 22, and 23 February 1966.

gerated limitation of piece rates; the frequently oversimplified (i.e.
political) criteria governing choice of executive cadres, promotions, and
premium pay; the false 'social' viewpoints of many leading workers
and organizations in the factories, according to which any strict or
demanding executive was almost regarded as an anti-social element –
all these had led to worker demoralization, according to Sik. Many
workers feared the more exacting demands of the new system. Others
simply had not yet grasped the magnitude of the economic problems
and the long-range benefits the worker himself would derive from the
new system. To combat this opposition Sik urged greater propaganda
work among the masses.

Two particular ramifications of the economic reforms led to provocative discussions: the possibility of inflation and the desired change in
the structure of the economy. A number of the 'transition' compromises
introduced into the new system or conservative features of the reforms
themselves were due to a fear that free prices or fluctuating wages or
even the regulated price changes themselves would lead to inflation.
The problem of inflation appeared early in the reform stages when
National Assembly vice-president Vaclav Skoda pointed out the
existence of 'unrealized purchasing power' among the population
which would be 'unhealthy for any economy.[1] This excess purchasing
power was basically a potential demand without supply. It was feared
that although a market-based economy might solve the problem of
unusable purchasing power by guiding production away from un-
wanted goods and towards those for which demand existed, it might
in so doing create a still greater potential for inflation. Higher sales,
it was feared, would lead to higher wages and this in turn would bring
inflation if allowed to go uncontrolled. For this reason the wholesale
price reform was delayed; then, to keep wholesale price rises from
affecting retail prices, subsidies were introduced to help enterprises
operating at a loss and to prevent them from raising their prices. At
the same time, price controls were introduced to prevent monopolistic
speculation or control of the market, and the wage controls were
introduced. In effect, economic instruments (as the regime called
them), which were replacing purely administrative instruments, were to
be used 'administratively' in the interests of avoiding the problems of
a free, market economy.

In the debate on these problems of inflation, some argued that a
rise in wages would not be harmful. Indeed, according to Czech

[1] Prague radio, 15 December 1965.

sources, the Czechoslovak rate of wage increase was one of the lowest in Europe.[1] In the period 1961–5 nominal wages had risen by 5·9 per cent but real wages by only 2·3 per cent; in 1966 nominal wages of all workers rose by only 1·3 per cent and those of manual laborers stood still. This stagnation of incentives affected productivity and production expansion was marked by extensive growth only, i.e. increases in numbers employed rather than increased productivity and effectiveness. It was argued that the expected price rises (resulting from the new system) should be accompanied by still faster rising wages so that a rise in standard of living could be maintained. Those who feared a rise in wages, it was argued, simply did not understand that stagnation of wages was no more than a sign that wages were not fulfilling their function as a stimulus of economic growth and labor productivity.

Two colleagues of Sik in the Economic Institute, Klaus and Jezek, argued that inflation was not necessarily such a bad thing.[2] All economic growth, they argued, was accompanied by some degree of inflation, just as stagnation was accompanied by a fall in prices or deflation. Inflation, however, was not only a symptom of but actually fostered growth because in a market economy rising prices were looked upon by enterprises as a favorable sign (of increased demand) and, therefore, had the effect of stimulating increased economic activity. Current economic theory, Klaus and Jezek claimed, holds that inflation is an objective economic process arising from divergent factors and disproportionalities in economic growth. Price increases are merely a sign of and at the same time a corrective for these imbalances. Prices, therefore, must be left free to act as indicators or warning signals pointing to a degree of economic disequilibrium.

In looking to the system in Czechoslovakia prior to the reforms it becomes clear, they said, that prices did not function as the signal of imbalance; they failed to signal the imbalance that existed in the economy and led to the stagnation of 1963–4. Prices had not been permitted to fluctuate and, therefore, were not in line with the real situation. Increased demand resulted, in Czechoslovakia, not in higher prices but in longer queues. Thus while open inflation was objected to because of its effects on redistribution of income (fixed salary earners suffering), the suppressed inflation had a tendency to favor certain parts of society as well: those with luck, speed, stamina, and a large number of acquaintances.

---

[1] See *Zemedelske Noviny*, 23 December 1966 and *Rude Pravo*, 5 October 1966 for these figures.   [2] *Kulturni Tvorba*, 15 December 1966.

One of the chief causes of inflation, according to Jezek and Klaus, was the pressure arising from increases in the wage bill which tended to exceed increases in labor's total product. While wage rates as such had not increased much in Czechoslovakia over the past ten to fifteen years, the wage bill had increased more rapidly than the national income created. This was due to increased employment, which in turn was due to the low price of labor, 'thus one of the strongest inflationary pressures in our economy, represented by the growth of employment, is the result of the policy of cheap labor for the enterprise.'

A faster growth in wage rates reflecting the real gains in productivity curbs demand for labor by making the latter relatively expensive, and induces labor-saving technical devices. Because of the artificially low wage-rates this mechanism for stimulating technical progress was missing. The authors' conclusion was that moderate price increases should be accompanied by faster nominal wage increases, thus raising the standard of living and reflecting the real price of labor relative to capital.

Karel Soska, a member of the State Planning Commission, responded to Klaus and Jezek by arguing that wage and price rises were not indispensable to economic growth, even if they were a sign of growth.[1] Nor were such increases limited to periods of economic growth, for they might appear at other times, such as wartime. However, like Jezek and Klaus he believed that inflation had occurred even in the context of the directive system, despite price controls and reductions coupled with a slow wage or growth rate. It could be seen in the shortage of goods on the market even when prices were not permitted to be the indicator. This suppressed inflation had concealed the imbalance, the full effect of which was felt in 1962 and 1963. Soska pointed out that investments had an effect on inflation by creating more demand for labor and creating more demand for consumer goods. Restriction of demand through controlled wages might curb the problem of supply of consumer goods and help investments, but limiting the volume of investments, alone, would not solve the problem of inflation. Rather, one must change the structure of investment, adapting it to meet demand, and create the conditions for stimulating a higher technical standard of new capital investment.

The redistributive effects of inflation could not be lightly dismissed, Soska argued. Price developments affected all people, while the instruments of the market mechanism affected the income only of persons

[1] *Kulturni Tvorba*, 23 February 1967.

working within the scope of the market and production. Therefore, while the market should influence the development of prices via the incomes of the enterprises, intervention from the center should 'eliminate those aspects of the inflationary process which might lead to a violation of the overall economic balance.' The center should assure the maintenance of certain social services (for which there must be levies to the state budget), and regulate wages in the non-productive organizations upon which the market had only partial effect.

The inflation issue was to some degree a political one, for the opponents of reform tended to refer to the danger of inflation with horror, and as sufficient reason for maintaining central controls. This discussion also raised the traditional – and political – issue of the structure of the economy. While the limitations placed on the use of prices and wages as economic levers were designed as a brake on inflation, this very effort reflected a conservative tendency to divert emphasis away from a consumption-oriented economy to an investment-oriented one by protecting and assuring enterprise investment ability. This tendency basically was opposed to the spirit of the new system insofar as the latter was designed to introduce the market as the determining factor of all economic development. This would place emphasis on consumer goods insofar as this was the area in which unsatisfied demand was most acute. Thus the protagonists on this issue could be divided into two groups, the first of which argued that prices and wages should be controlled in such a way as to limit personal consumption. The second group argued that this would not (and had not in the past) provided sufficient stimulus to labor. Wage and price restrictions should be lifted and demand be met through the directing of resources into the light industries. The worker would thus have a larger pay packet, labor productivity would rise and lead to a subsequent creation of resources for investment.[1]

The conservatives sought to use the new system to make investments more efficient, which in their terms meant to use economic instruments to further investments in heavy industry. Increased investments, they felt, would promote increased production and, eventually, greater consumption. In the short-run wages should be stable so that increased production would not result in increased consumption. This group saw the sources of Czechoslovakia's problem in the past tendency towards greater consumption at the expense of future wealth and

[1] See for this breakdown, Stanley Riveles, 'The Czechoslovak Middle Way,' RFE (1967), 37–40.

accumulation of resources necessary for modernization through re-investment.[1]

The liberal group, represented mainly by Sik, argued that the reason for past problems was not a too-rapid growth of consumption but the old system of planning and management which did not permit efficient production. Josef Goldmann pointed out that even though personal consumption had increased during the difficult years (1961–4), inventories and construction had increased even faster so that one could hardly point to the increase of the former as the cause of the crisis.[2]

Given the exhaustion of the advantages of this extensive development system, financing should be supplied by sales of goods most in demand, the liberals argued. Lenart maintained that the incentives provided by this would lead to greater productivity and therefore greater efficiency. Investments should be concentrated and credits used to promote the production branches offering the greatest promise of rapid return and profitability, i.e. the consumer industries.[3] Higher wages would not only act as incentives to workers but make labor dear, thus forcing the enterprise to seek technical solutions towards increased productivity. Thus the rise in standard of living would itself act as a stimulus to economic growth.

[1] See *Hospodarske Noviny*, 29 April 1966; and V. Rendl and J. Kublik, 'The Development of Our Economy in Recent Years,' *Planovane Hospodarstvi*, XIX:4 (1966), 1–12.

[2] Josef Goldmann, 'The Progressive Consolidation and Growth of the Czechoslovak Economy,' *Ekonomicky Casopis*, XIV:9 (1966), 290–1.

[3] Sekera, *Nova Mysl*, XX:1 (1966), 6–7.

7

REFORMS IN OTHER SPHERES OF THE ECONOMY

The non-industrial spheres of the economy, including foreign trade, retail trade and services, and agriculture, were given less attention than the industrial sphere. What reforms there were in the domestic trade system followed closely those of the industrial sector. This meant market-oriented prices and methods, freed (within certain limits) from central controls and subsidies.[1] Services too were adjusted in a similar direction, the only significant innovation being the 1964 decision to return to 'private enterprise' in certain limited areas. The latter included catering, carpentry, hairdressing, tailoring, etc., but the category and number of persons permitted to engage in private services was greatly limited.[2]

FOREIGN TRADE

Due to its necessary (and to be increased) connection with industry, foreign trade was the major non-industrial sphere subjected to reforms and serious debate. One of the basic goals in the reforms connected with foreign trade was to bring the domestic market in line with the world market. World prices were increasingly to influence the income both of domestic producers and foreign trade organizations. To achieve these goals the structure of foreign trade would have to be redefined. The foreign trade organizations, operating according to the *khozraschot* principle, were to work more closely with the producing enterprises, and a direct economic relationship was to be created between foreign trade and production. Foreign trade enterprises for their part were to be interested not only in the price at which they received their goods from producers, but also in the commercial costs and expenses which they themselves incurred. Premiums for employees in foreign trade organizations were introduced on 1 January 1966.[3]

To further interest the producers in foreign trade the following

---

[1] See *Main Reports and Documents*, 5 (Prague, 1965), 135–49.
[2] See *Rude Pravo*, 25 January and 14 July 1964.
[3] For details see Frantisek Hamouz, 'Czechoslovak Foreign Trade under the New System,' *Czechoslovak Foreign Trade*, 6:1 (1966), 5; *Hospodarske Noviny*, 11 December 1964.

measures were to be gradually introduced for the enterprises: a share of foreign currency earned by their products, unrestricted exchange of foreign currency at fixed rates, foreign currency credits, the possibility of transfer of foreign currency allocations and bonuses from contractor to sub-contractor, and so on.[1] The enterprise itself could seek credits abroad, although it had to bear the exchange risk. The State Bank might grant credits in foreign currency both to foreign trade and production enterprises, and Lenart asserted that local banks should be able to grant such long-term credits directly to enterprises (or at least branch directorates). This would supplement if not replace the former system whereby the State Bank and trade organizations bore all responsibility for foreign currency credits and purchases abroad.[2]

At the end of 1966 Novotny promised that joint stock companies, including the foreign trade enterprises and the producing enterprises, would be formed.[3] This measure was not, in fact, implemented until 1968 when the companies set up divided the interests in the following way: sixty per cent to the producers, thirty per cent to the foreign trade enterprise, and ten per cent to the state.

Certain of these organizational measures were criticized for their basic conservativeness. Even the 'Principles' provided for a maintenance of the state monopoly on trade, and although the foreign trade concerns were to be subjected to the new system of management, they were nonetheless free from competition and retained a large degree of control over the producers for whom they negotiated. Loebl pointed out that although certain enterprises produced for export, they still could not directly contact their foreign buyers.[4]

Premier Lenart pointed out the need for purchasing foreign patents and international cooperation in production in order to raise the level of Czechoslovak technology. In this sphere Czechoslovakia had been extremely weak; in terms of per capita costs, the industrialized countries spent from $1.50 to $3.00 on license royalties while Czechoslovakia spent $0.30, he said.[5] As a start in this direction Czechoslovakia negotiated a number of license agreements in 1966 with companies in Sweden, France, Austria, Holland, Britain, and the U.S.[6]

[1] *Main Reports and Documents*, 5 (Prague, 1965), 102.
[2] *Rude Pravo*, 10 November 1965. [3] *Rude Pravo*, 21 December 1966.
[4] *Kulturny Zivot*, 14 January 1966.
[5] *Bratislava Pravda*, 11 November 1965; Jozef Lenart, 'Economics, Production, Trade, and Management,' *Czechoslovak Foreign Trade*, 7:1 (1967), 6.
[6] 'Trade News,' *Czechoslovak Foreign Trade*, 7:1 (1967), 24.

Lenart condemned the fact that Czechoslovakia's annual per capita exports were fifty per cent less than the per capita exports of comparable western countries. There should be an all-over increase in exchange of goods between Czechoslovakia and the rest of the world, including imports as well as exports, he claimed. Czechoslovakia's trade problem, however, came in part from a dearth of raw materials, combined with the slow rate of national income growth which led to limitations on diverting means to the accumulation as well as consumption funds, resulting in disproportionately high import bills. This was intimately connected with the management–planning system, for the amount of production capacity set aside for trade did not produce the expected values. The technical standard of Czechoslovak production was not up to world standards; Czechoslovak goods were often subject to discounts for inferior quality or added expenses for repairs or refunds for returned goods.[1]

This issue of imports and how to finance them became a controversial one not dissimilar to and connected with the dispute over the structure of the economy. Premier Lenart and the liberal economists including Sik agreed that imports of consumer products or products for the consumer goods industries should be increased if the quality of Czechoslovak goods were to be stimulated and demand met. As Lenart explained it, consumer goods in 1966 accounted for only five to six per cent of imports; such a small amount failed to encourage competition and added little to the range of goods on the market. He was opposed to any type of trade restriction as a restriction on economic growth itself, for Czechoslovakia's resources were not adequate to the needs of her market, i.e. she could not supply sufficient resources for her investments. In fact what was needed was a further growth of imports. If the economy could not pay for imports with exports, the cheapest other source of investment resources would be long-term foreign credits. Lenart pointed out that Czechoslovakia had not been exploiting the opportunities for 'an active credit policy' presented her over the past years.[2]

Czechoslovak trade policy until the economic reforms had been based mainly on the barter system between her and the socialist countries. It included long-term credits granted by Czechoslovakia to the socialist and underdeveloped nations, primarily to finance deliveries of Czechoslovak goods (mainly machines and heavy equipment). They were granted at long-term low interest rates (two and one-half

[1] See *Rude Pravo*, 18 January 1966.　　　　[2] *Predvoj*, 18 August 1966.

per cent) and usually repaid in deliveries of raw material. Although this did ensure the needed supply of raw materials, this was usually at the cost of unfavorable trading or credit conditions.

The liberals were now demanding two things: mutually advantageous trading conditions and a shift from being a creditor nation to a receiver of credits. A *Rude Pravo* article pointed out that Czechoslovakia was not a large power which could afford liberal gestures.[1] More important, one must not be afraid of receiving long-term credits. This 'fear,' it was admitted, tended to come from the fact that it was basically the West which was a source of long-term credits, but, the article asserted, there was no reason to fear a political risk as long as all the rules of business were observed. To demonstrate the legitimacy of long-term credits from the West for a socialist country, the article pointed to the Italian Fiat credit of $300 million granted to the Soviet Union at 5·9 per cent for fifteen years.

The conservatives, in this case including Novotny and State Planning Commission Chief Cernik, favored balanced foreign trade, i.e. a balance of imports and exports through a limitation of imports.[2] Unlike the liberals, the advocates of limited imports believed that the economy did possess sufficient productive resources for investment and therefore did not need the costly imports, nor should it risk the credits needed to cover such imports. There were a number of ways to limit imports, though Cernik's emphasis on 'strong measures' suggested that he advocated the use of administrative rather than economic measures. Certain 'transition' instruments were introduced to curtail imports, e.g. tariffs, exchange surcharges and discounts, price surcharges and discounts, and a limited and controlled market in foreign exchange.[3] Novotny made it quite clear that whatever the instruments, imports would be curtailed: 'we cannot continue the present imbalance of the plan by increasing imports which are not covered by corresponding exports.'[4] At the central committee plenum in December 1966, the party agreed to seek long-term credits, but it maintained the line that these must be self-liquidating, project-linked enterprise credits repayable by the enterprises' own exports.[5]

---

[1] *Rude Pravo*, 31 August 1966.   [2] Cernik in *Rude Pravo*, 3 August 1966.
[3] K. Podlaha and M. Vrskovy, 'Utilizing Economic Instruments in Foreign Trade Relations,' *Finance a Uver*, 15:11 (1965), 674; Ludovit Kovacik, 'Problems of International Payments,' *Finance a Uver*, 16:1 (1966), 16.
[4] Antonin Novotny, 'Contemporary Problems of the Development of Socialist Society,' *Zivot Strany*, 21 (1966), 3.
[5] *Rude Pravo*, 22 December 1966.

Part of the problem in the credit debate was, as we have seen, political. Yet the introduction of a market-oriented economy demanded that foreign trade also be market-oriented, with political considerations giving way to purely economic, business-like considerations, in trade as in internal production. Although this need not (and indeed did not) result in significant territorial reorientation of Czechoslovak trade, it did lead to some changes.

In its efforts to broaden its markets and raise its technological level, Czechoslovakia sought to expand her trade with the West. The major problems here were the lack of hard currency reserves, and the lack of goods able to compete on the western markets. While long-term credits would solve or at least relieve the first problem, this idea was rejected in all but a limited form at the December plenum. Within this limited form (self-liquidating project-linked credits) trade ventures were entered into with the West and Czechoslovakia sought ways of attracting western business. Thus Prague opened, in 1966, two advertising–public relations firms: 'Made in Publicity' and 'Made in Commercial,' to handle foreign advertising in Czechoslovakia. At the same time Czechoslovakia sought to build up its tourist trade as a source of hard currency earnings by simplifying administrative and financial procedures for the entry of western tourists.[1] Hotels and services were improved (to which end private services were expanded), and Prague was cleaned up after having been left to fall into disrepair over the past few years. Prague assured western governments of the safety of their nationals visiting in Czechoslovakia, and it demonstrated this by dealing most leniently with westerners involved in attempts to smuggle persons out of Czechoslovakia.[2] By the same token certain westerners held prisoner in Prague were released as a sign of good faith.

Despite these efforts, which also included exchange of trade or commercial delegations with the West, the West's share of Czechoslovakia's total trade turnover rose only slightly between 1965 and 1966 (from eighteen per cent to twenty per cent). However, trade did increase substantially with certain countries, e.g. Britain, Italy, and the U.S.[3]

Czechoslovakia had two disappointments in its attempts to expand its trade with the West, specifically regarding the U.S. and West Germany. In the case of the U.S., despite an increase in trade, Czecho-

[1] Prague radio, 16 June 1964.
[2] See for example, 'Current Developments,' *East Europe*, XIII:11 (1965), 36.
[3] 'Imports–Exports,' *Statisticke Prehledy*, 4 (1966), 128–9; 'Foreign Trade according to Groups of Countries,' *Statisticke Prehledy*, 2 (1967), 62–3.

slovakia actually met with obstacles to her efforts. Since 1951 the U.S. had denied Czechoslovakia 'most favored nation' (MFN) treatment – to which Czechoslovakia claimed the right as a member of GATT. Czechoslovak goods were therefore at a serious disadvantage because of U.S. tariffs. While President Johnson proclaimed a policy of 'building bridges' to Eastern Europe, especially in trade, there was no congressional reversal of the 1951 MFN decision. U.S.–Czechoslovak relations were further complicated by an old problem of compensation for nationalization claims of U.S. citizens, the payment of a significant part of which the U.S. demands in conjunction with the return to Czechoslovakia of her U.S.-held gold reserves removed from Prague during World War II. While Prague reopened talks with Washington on this subject in 1965, the two nations found themselves far from agreement on the sum to be deducted from the gold in payment of the claims. The conservatives, not without a certain degree of legitimacy, used U.S. recalcitrance on the issues of the gold and MFN as 'proof' of U.S. unwillingness to implement the trade policy proclaimed by the President and sought by the liberals.[1] Indeed U.S. inflexibility apparently continued even in 1968.

The other disappointment was the trade agreement with Bonn. West Germany was Czechoslovakia's largest trading partner in the West, and Prague hoped to stabilize as well as expand her relations with Bonn by the signing of a trade agreement similar to that signed by Warsaw and Bonn in 1964. The trade agreement was intended to raise Prague's commercial mission in Frankfurt to semi-diplomatic status with consular privileges. This was to be the first step towards normal diplomatic relations with West Germany, desired for the economic value stable relations promised.[2] The major obstacle here was purely political. On the surface it hinged on Prague's insistence that Bonn formally declare the 1938 Munich Pact null and void from its inception. While Bonn was often willing to state that the pact was no longer valid, Prague demanded formal admission that it had never been valid. Talks between the two countries went on month after month, encountering obstacles from both sides. The West Germans do not appear to have been too anxious to come to agreement with Czechoslovakia, and Prague was under serious pressure from the Russians, on behalf of the East Germans, to abandon any improvement in relations with Bonn. It was

[1] *Rude Pravo*, 1 June 1967; *Rude Pravo*, 6 January 1967.
[2] See interview with deputy Foreign Minister Otto Klicka, Prague radio, 20 December 1966.

only after two and one-half years that Prague and Bonn finally signed their trade agreement – and then only after Rumania had taken matters a step further and opened diplomatic relations with Bonn.

Czechoslovak trade and cooperation with Yugoslavia also increased with the introduction of the new system. For example, the two countries agreed to create joint firms which would offer their products jointly on the markets of third countries. At the same time the two countries began talks on the possibility of adopting a free financial settlement system and the creation of a common bank, which was in fact created in 1968.[1]

While the total volume of Czechoslovak foreign trade rose by 4·18 per cent in 1966 as compared with 1965 and total trade with the West rose by 20·2 per cent, the volume of trade with the socialist (CEMA) countries actually declined by 3·6 per cent.[2] It would be exaggerated to term this a deliberate territorial reorientation of trade, since the socialist countries did account for 69·12 per cent of Czechoslovak foreign trade (the Soviet Union for 32·87 per cent); more likely this decline was the result (perhaps temporary) of the switch to economic values as criteria for trade. While the Prague regime often reiterated its continued devotion to the goal of cooperation with the socialist bloc – and particularly the Soviet Union – it was explained on a number of occasions that this cooperation would have to be a new type.[3] Adolf Suk of the State Planning Commission explained that Czechoslovakia's economic relations with the bloc would develop simply because they were advantageous to her.[4]

Thus the new system evoked two demands with regard to CEMA: that Czechoslovakia's relations to this body and its members be in the spirit of the new system and that CEMA itself conform to the spirit of Czechoslovakia's new system. Czechoslovakia wanted, first of all, a transferable ruble as an international monetary unit upon which to calculate one world price (for the socialist as well as the capitalist market) and with which to invest and operate as well as trade.[5] By this it was meant that the International Bank for Economic Cooperation (CEMA's bank) become a real bank able to transfer, loan, and invest

[1] PAP (Polish News Agency), 22 June 1967.
[2] Figures from *Statisticke Prehledy*, 4 (1966), 128–9 and 2 (1967), 62–3.
[3] For example Novotny, *Zivot Strany*, 21 (1966), 1, 3.
[4] *Reporter*, 7 January 1967; *Hospodarske Noviny*, 15 October 1965.
[5] See Vera Kyprova, 'World Prices and the New System of Management,' *Plano-vane Hospodarstvi*, XIX:10 (1966), 46–57; *Rude Pravo*, 9 April 1967.

funds rather than act merely as a clearing house with the ruble valid only as an accounting unit. This would also permit the bank to deal outside CEMA, linking the capitalist and socialist markets.[1] Czechoslovakia brought her views to the Moscow debate on CEMA integration in February 1966, urging free market relations within CEMA, direct contacts between enterprises, and plan coordination only for macro-economic relations. These views were neither rejected nor accepted, since the member nations were divided on almost all the suggestions heard in Moscow.[2] Despite the new system, and proclaimed intentions to seek only profitability in trade relations, Czechoslovakia signed a long-term agreement for investment cooperation with the Soviet Union for the development of the West Siberian oil fields.[3] This was, basically, in response to the Soviet announcement that it could not maintain raw materials deliveries as previously and that investment was invited from those who wanted continued delivery.[4] A similar agreement was signed for the mining of Soviet iron ore, despite the low quality of this ore.

AGRICULTURE

Few reforms were provided for agriculture, as this area was left for gradual future adjustment. Nonetheless, certain experiments were introduced in time, and reforms were proposed on the basis of applying the principles of economic effectiveness and profitability to agriculture. Reforms announced in 1966 provided for looser central planning, i.e. long-term government plans; five year plans worked out by the farms and the state; one-year operational plans worked out by the farms themselves.[5] In agriculture too production was to be market-oriented and based on contracts between producers and consumers (rather than the quota system), but the 'consumer' remained the state procurement agencies – which were in effect monopolies. These agencies had the right to reduce prices, which were for the most part set centrally on the basis of average production costs and long-range market developments. Subsidies were to be provided, temporarily, for farms unable to meet

---

[1] Jaroslav Mazal, 'Transferable Ruble—Prospects,' *Noviny Zahranicniho Obchodu*, v:9 (1967), 2. [2] *Rude Pravo*, 12, 24, and 25 February 1966.
[3] Prague radio, 23 September 1966. [4] *Rude Pravo*, 13 June 1966.
[5] For these reforms see *Rude Pravo*, 22, 24, and 25 March 1966; *Hospodarske Noviny*, 29 July 1966; 'Excerpts from the Project on Principles of the Perfected System of Planned Management of Agriculture,' *Socialisticke Zemedelstvi*, 3(xvi):8 (1966).

costs at the new prices. This in part would be provided by a progressive tax system based on the ratio of gross income to number of workers permanently employed. There was also to be a land tax fixed centrally but relative to land values. As in industry wages were to be provided out of a farm's own funds, though the state would provide all-over wage policy and indeed planned to limit wage increases for at least two years so as to encourage investments. For the latter, credits were to be provided from the State Bank.

Reforms announced in 1967 provided for a reorganization of agriculture into branches or associations of farms, both horizontally and vertically, as in industry.[1] These branches were called District Agricultural Associations (DAA), consisting of member but independent farms, the whole unit operating on the *khozraschot* principle and run by a management directorate. The directorate was composed of the managers of the member farms and a chairman elected from among them. DAAs consisting of collective farms were to be subordinate to the District National Committees, although this relationship was not clearly explained. DAAs of state farms were to have somewhat more direct government control. Basically the DAAs had powers – and drawbacks – similar to the branch association in industry. The reforms, on the whole, left most of the basic problems of the use of economic levers in agriculture unsolved, especially the crucial one of prices and the relationship of the producer to the market, given the continued monopolistic interference of the procurement agencies and such things as limited access to foreign currency for direct foreign trade contacts.

THE NEW LABOR CODE

The codification of the various labor laws into one Labor Code in 1965 was intended to accommodate the ideas of the economic reform.[2] The most important aspect was the relative freeing of labor movement, in keeping with the new emphasis upon the market and wage de-equalization. The compulsory labor clause of Decree No. 88 of 1945, with its modifications of 1959 and February 1963, which provided for more or less obligatory placement of young people after their schooling, was finally abrogated. The code provided specifically for mutual consent in

---

[1] *Rude Pravo*, 25 March 1966.
[2] *Sbirka Zakonu* No. 65/1965 (*The Labor Code*, Prague, 1966). Drafted before the reforms, in 1963, it became more controversial as the liberalization got under way. Implementation which was to have begun in 1964 was delayed until 1966.

contracting for labor (exclusive of brigades and campaigns organized by the National Committees), and enumerated the limited conditions in which an employee could be assigned to a task other than that for which he had contracted. More significant perhaps was the fact that an employee could leave his job or contract for work without the previously required approval of the district National Committee and the local trade union committee. This last was combined with a number of other changes designed to facilitate labor movement. For example, the transfer of accrued leave time and welfare benefits was facilitated (for all but agricultural workers for whom greater control over mobility was desired).[1] The conditions for termination of work with and without notice, by the employer and by the employee, were enumerated with the all-over effect of permitting the worker greater freedom. For example, in the case of an employee's request for termination of work, the employer was required to respond within fifteen days. Failure to respond would be construed as consent, thus releasing the employee – and eliminating the former procedure whereby an employer could (and did) hold the employee in suspense indefinitely, often discouraging any further attempts on his part to change jobs. In addition, the institution of the 'transfer card' (the equivalent of the Soviet work book) was abolished, and the employee was accorded the right to inspect, and appeal, the contents of the materials passed on about him from his previous to his future employer, though this last did not apply to the worker's cadre report or security file. The government also decided in December 1966 to require terminating enterprises to pay severance pay and hiring enterprises to pay for retraining as well as partial compensation for lower earnings.[2] An unemployment allowance of sixty per cent of the worker's former average net pay was to be paid by the district National Committees in the cases for which new work could not be found.[3] This last was to facilitate the regime's plans under the economic reforms to close uneconomical concerns or streamline inefficient enterprises. On the other hand, a worker could no longer be dismissed on the former invidious 'loss of confidence' clause.

While all of the above was designed to facilitate labor mobility, it was realized that central control and planning of the labor force might be hampered. Therefore the government, as provided by the code, could

---

[1] Agricultural workers were likewise excluded from improvements in the social insurance workers' compensation benefits provided by the code. They had to wait for a Social Insurance Law of February 1967.

[2] *Prace*, 25 December 1966.   [3] *Lidova Demokracie*, 18 July 1967.

and did place 'temporary' limitations on the clauses concerning worker termination, e.g. a required extended notice period.[1] Nonetheless, *Rude Pravo* observed, the 'labor law opens the door to the gradual process of manpower movement, at first limited to certain fields of work according to the needs of our national economy. This process will not be regulated *administratively* [i.e. there will not be] limitations which make it impossible for individual workers to change their working places.'[2]

The code provided the worker with greater protection of his rights also by providing for easier and earlier recourse to the courts for settling problems; and in the courts themselves, individual and enterprise were to have parity instead of the former law which had given preference to the enterprise.[3] At the same time, the custom, characteristic of Soviet law, of providing by labor law even for the behavior and moral standards of workers was criticized, and the Czechoslovak Labor Code did away with the nearly exhaustive list of legally binding disciplinary actions. According to one commentary, the code overcame the

> tendencies imbedded in the directed management of the national economy toward the most detailed elaboration of labor legal regulations, without respect to whether basic or auxiliary matters are involved. This therefore, narrowed down the initiative of both managers and workers and made it impossible to approach the solution of problems in accordance with local conditions . . . the inherent interest of the labor code is to establish basic rights and obligations . . . [not] highly detailed regulation of behavior . . . [which] exceeds the competence of law.[4]

The new code applied to non-State enterprises as well, thus providing protection for employees in the private sector, while the private sector itself was given a boost by the code's provision for 'Agreement on Work other than within an Employer Contract.'[5] When not performed at the enterprise itself, leisure-time private work was not subject to supervision over hours, work conditions, and the like.

The more liberal aspects of the new Labor Code, like those of the

---

[1] According to *Nova Mysl*, this might be applied only in cases in which an organization would find it difficult 'due to a large labor turnover' to meet plan requirements. (M. Kalenska, 'Czechoslovakia's First Labor Code,' *Nova Mysl*, xix:8 (1965), 998.)

[2] *Rude Pravo*, 18 August 1965.

[3] The previous law was *Sbirka Zakonu* No. 141/1950.

[4] *Hospodarske Noviny*, 18 June 1965.   [5] *Labor Code* (Prague, 1966), 54-5.

economic reforms, were barely implemented or, in fact, impeded by party conservatives. Implied in the principles, for example, of labor mobility, enterprise independence, and the market system as a whole, was the abandonment of strict central control and regulation by the regime. In effect they would mean a severe limitation on the monopoly of power in the hands of the party. Critics of the economic reforms rightly saw these reforms as part and parcel of the interwoven process of de-Stalinization and liberalization – caused by and clearly to affect not only the economic, but also the political, social–cultural, and ideological institutions alike. Sik too saw this, and pointed it out to the 1966 Thirteenth Party Congress, for he realized that there was little hope of a successful operation of the economic reforms without basic political adjustments.

8

MASS ORGANIZATIONS

The mass organizations basically serve a communist state as a means of organizing the people in the interests of channelling their energies to productive activities useful or at least ideologically acceptable to the state. Since membership in these organizations largely is voluntary in theory only, the mass organizations also serve as instruments of indoctrination and control. They are generally organized at the individual's place of work or study so that leisure time as well as work time can be more easily or almost entirely accounted for. With the advent of de-Stalinization, pressures began to build for a reorganization of the mass organizations – pressures which in themselves belied the ability of these organizations satisfactorily to fulfill the function the regime had envisaged for them. The party was interested in improving the effectiveness of the mass organizations – notably a way to get the people interested in them. As candidate party presidium member Martin Vaculik indicated, speaking of recent polls taken: 'The social organizations have shown up very badly in this research . . . They do not satisfy certain interests and they do not even try to do so. Nobody has to campaign among garden enthusiasts, hunters, or fishermen; nobody has to organize them with great difficulty.'[1] He said that the Czechoslovak–Soviet Friendship Association, the Union for Cooperation with the Army (SVAZARM), the Physical Training Union, and the Czechoslovak Youth Union (CSM) should not be for the benefit of conferences or campaigns but rather 'to really satisfy the peoples' interests . . . There was a period when we fought for the power and the sympathies of the people. Many people came near us through these organizations. Today conditions have changed and thus we must seek new methods and possibilities; we must strive to make the social organizations meet the natural needs.'

Thus a debate began to develop on the purpose of such organizations and demands were heard that the social or mass organizations be transformed from the status of puppets to that of real interest groups or even political parties.[2] A very conservative statement of the problem was made by the party's legal commission secretary Zdenek Mlynar:

Very often their [the mass organizations] fundamental function,

[1] *Kulturni Tvorba*, 10 March 1966. [2] See also chapters 12–15 below.

namely to defend certain defined interests and needs of the people (with the aim of achieving harmony between individual and social needs) is overlooked. The essence of their purpose is often seen in their taking over some of the functions of the State . . . thus they become, in a way, 'nationalized.' This happened with physical training . . . In my view, the top problem facing our social organizations is the necessity of strengthening their character as voluntary special interest organizations.[1]

Demands began to be heard for a reorganization of CSM, and workers began to demand genuine trade union representation of their interests, particularly with respect to the introduction of the new economic program and, specifically, the new wage policy. Proposals were even heard for a national union of cooperatives to represent farmers' interests, a proposal which could harken back to the existence of a strong agrarian party.

As early as 1964 Novotny announced that changes would be forthcoming in the mass organizations. To improve socialist democracy, he announced, the role and authority of the elected organs of the social organizations must be raised, with a reduction in the number of paid personnel in the apparatus of these organizations.[2] A year later the 'Theses' for the forthcoming party congress outlined a general policy change whereby the mass organizations were to transfer their organizations and activities from the place of work to the place of residence. Thus the basic unit of most of the mass organizations (with the obvious exception of the trade unions) was moved from the factory, shop, communal service, school, office, or institution to the locale. The measure to a large degree freed the individual from the pressures of participation since supervision was rendered considerably more difficult and a person's job was, therefore, less dependent upon the extent of his activity in the mass organizations. The party officially argued that it was introducing this measure of decentralization in response to the anticipated reduction of working hours and the hoped for increase in leisure time. It was also believed, however, that the organizations might respond more adequately to local needs and interests if attended by persons of the same locale, village, or block. Vaculik had said, for example, that it was senseless to import CSM to organize youth in a village when the local firemen were doing an excellent job of it.[3]

[1] *Praca*, 25 January 1966.　　　　　　　　　　　[2] *Rude Pravo*, 29 May 1964.
[3] *Kulturni Tvorba*, 10 March 1966.

The party was well aware of the dangers of decentralization, i.e. the loss of central control involved and the corresponding increase in local autonomy. Discussing this reform, the party 'Theses' added: 'this has far more persistently confronted Communists and party organizations with the task of uniting the activities of social organizations, of more purposefully and completely influencing the political, public, and cultural life in the villages and towns.'[1] To meet this challenge party units in the locales were also to be created to join the traditional block committees and to be supplemented by an 'aktiv' of party members representing the local units of the mass organizations.

In addition to this general organizational reform for all the mass organizations the two largest and perhaps most important organizations, the trade union movement (ROH) and CSM began to undergo reforms, the former as a particular consequence of the economic reforms, the latter as a particular consequence of the social reforms.

THE TRADE UNION MOVEMENT

The basic issue at stake in the reform of the trade union movement was the extent to which the ROH could act as the independent representative of the interests of its members without infringing upon the 'leading role' of the party. Around this point revolved all such questions as trade union autonomy, participation of workers in management, and the rights and powers of the trade union organizations vis-a-vis the party as well as management. The ROH had indeed acted from its inception in 1952 as an arm of the party or 'transmission belt.' Mention of an independent or autonomous role for the ROH or its affiliates in the past had usually been labeled 'anarcho-syndicalism' and condemned for 'negating the leading role of the party.'[2] Although this position had softened somewhat, especially with the 1958 reorganization of the trade unions, little or no progress had been made towards autonomy or worker self-government. Accordingly, this gap too was criticized in the campaign for de-Stalinization.

The same party central committee plenum which finally approved the adoption of the new economic program in February 1965 foresaw the problems greater enterprise autonomy could create for the strongly centralized trade union movement. It passed a resolution calling for the investigation and reform of the ROH, particularly with regard to the role of the basic or lower level trade union organization. Thus the reso-

[1] *Rude Pravo*, 23 December 1965.   [2] For example *Prace*, 3 July 1954.

lution called for a trade union system corresponding and responsive to the new economic system both in organization and content.

The new role of the ROH was outlined in this resolution and, in the weeks that followed, in the Labor Code and the Fourth Trade Union Conference of May 1965, accompanied by commentaries and critiques in the press and radio. Most parties concerned agreed that effective worker participation in management must somehow be introduced. The Yugoslav system of worker management was frequently mentioned, and an alternative apparently seriously discussed within the party, though clearly rejected, was that of 'autonomy,' i.e. 'that the management of the economy and especially the management of the individual enterprises be entrusted to workers' autonomous bodies, or to bodies elected by the workers collectives and responsible to them and working under the supervision of the trade unions.'[1] It was argued that if the new economic system made the worker's wages dependent upon the performance of the enterprise, then the worker should have a controlling voice in matters connected with this performance, e.g. selection of managerial cadres.[2] A reason given for the rejection of the Yugoslav system, however, was the premature nature of the suggestion. The party maintained that at that particular stage of Czechoslovak development, the economy would best be left in the hands of the state organs 'which are a broader organization than the trade unions, for they are an organization of the whole electorate.'[3]

The system finally adopted, outlined first in the party central committee resolution, was a compromise. A new institution, the production committee, was introduced for all enterprises as a vehicle of worker participation, but the powers of this unit were so limited that it was difficult to see in it even the basis for future 'workers councils.' Subordinate to the trade union organization in the enterprise, and consisting of 'leading workers, technicians, economic executives, and trade union and party functionaries,' the committee's principal tasks were to offer opinions or draft plans, and handle workers' suggestions.[4] The production committee did not have either autonomy or an effective say in the direction of the enterprise, for the decisions of the committee were not binding upon management. The party nonetheless

[1] Margita Piscova, 'About Some Problems of Transferring Certain State Functions to the Trade Union Organizations under the Conditions Created by an Improved Management of the National Economy,' *Pravnicke Studie*, XIII:4 (1965), 608.
[2] Ivan Bystrina in *Literarni Noviny*, 17 December 1966.
[3] Piscova, *Pravnicke Studie*, XIII:4 (1965), 608.   [4] *Rude Pravo*, 4 February 1965.

claimed that the powers of the production committees would be increased with the implementation of the economic reforms.[1]

The system introduced was criticized for its basic conservatism regardless of the potential implied. Critics contended that the workers did not even have the powers and responsibilities with regard to management accorded the workers councils of 1945–8, i.e. the right to supervise the economic activity of the plant or enterprise concerned and the right to participate in the administration of the enterprise as a representative body of a legal character (albeit subject to supervision by the trade unions, which prepared the list of candidates for the workers councils). Many critics also considered the management boards which ran the nationalized enterprises of the pre-communist economy worthy of emulation by the branch management directorates envisaged by the new economic program. It was argued that the branch directorates should include representatives elected from among the workers rather than one trade union representative delegated by the branch itself. Critics wanted such an administrative body, including workers' representatives, at the plant or enterprise level as well.[2] Although it was generally agreed that the pre-communist system of generous worker rights and powers had originally been designed to further communist interests and to counter the rule of the capitalist, critics of the regime argued that these measures were still necessary and referred to them in their demands for greater democracy.[3]

In an effort to improve plant management efficiency and to create a freer flow of labor, the trade unions' functions with regard to day-to-day enterprise activities were limited, ostensibly in exchange for a greater say on the broader issues of gross income distribution, financial administration and investment.[4] Thus management no longer had to consult with the union works committee for hiring, specific wages and hours questions, or disciplinary actions, as under the former 1959 statute, although prior management consultation with the works com-

---

[1] *Rude Pravo*, 11 May 1965. A form of worker self-management was added to the reforms only in 1968.

[2] However, the party ruled in December 1966 that members of the branch directorate would be appointed by higher organs, with trade union representatives to be approved by the party.

[3] Piscova, *Pravnicke Studie*, XIII:4 (1965), 586; *Prace*, 17 August 1966; Karel Kaplan, 'Economic Democracy in the Years 1945–8,' *Ceskoslovensky Casopis Historicky*, XIV:6 (1966), 844–61.

[4] Resolution of the fourth trade union conference, supplemented by the May 1965 trade union conference.

mittee would still be required for termination of employment, given the nearly irrevocable nature of that act. With regard to the government, the ROH was given the right to express an opinion on draft labor legislation as well as to propose new labor regulations, but works committees in government agencies or social organizations could not concern themselves with the activities of those organizations nor the firing of political appointees.

The financial position of the trade unions was also to be altered in keeping with the general policy of making each organization and institution more, if not entirely, self-sufficient and efficient. Works committees would no longer be state-subsidized but would instead receive a grant from the enterprise or organization. This grant would be indirectly linked to the enterprise's earnings. And to improve the political tasks of the union, the party decided that, 'the number of superfluous formal meetings, conferences, and consultations on individual levels of the trade union organization should be limited.'[1]

The most important question with regard to the reforms in this area was, however, to what extent would the trade unions become champions of the workers' interests. As late as May 1965 the National All-Trade Union Conference identified as a task of 'primary importance' for the ROH the improvement of profitability. Ideally, in a communist system in which the worker truly did manage the economy and the enterprises, this would be a perfectly legitimate primary task for the organization of the workers. Given the far from ideal stage of economic management and policy in Czechoslovakia, however, and the still existent dichotomy of interests, liberals believed that the primary task of the trade unions should be to serve, protect, and pursue the interests of the workers in relations with and even in opposition to management or the state.[2] This view was reflected at the November 1966 plenum of the ROH central council which promised that the primary concern of the trade unions would be to take care of the workers. This was not, however, defined as party policy and it appeared that the trade unions would have to try merely to broaden those limited powers granted them by the reforms. There were signs that liberals in the trade union movement grasped this and strove towards this goal. Illegal strikes and work stoppages found a sympathetic ear in the trade union press, especially *Praca*, which was an active exponent of de-Stalinization. Moreover,

[1] *Rude Pravo*, 4 February 1965.
[2] ROH central council secretary Hamernik admitted the existence of such views among workers (*Rude Pravo*, 23 May 1967).

99

workers began putting greater pressure on the trade unions to secure better wages for them and to protect them from dismissal or transfer as a result of the economic reforms. Some unions demanded work-retraining programs and unemployment benefits to cope with the vicissitudes of the new economic program – a demand partially granted in December 1966. Thus in some ways, whether willingly or not, the ROH was forced by worker pressure to undertake the representation of workers' interests beyond the previously dictated confines of the Soviet-type system.

THE CZECHOSLOVAK YOUTH UNION

Demands for a revaluation and reorganization of the Czechoslovak Youth Union (CSM) came both from above and from below. The party was already quite disappointed in the youth, as evidenced by the decision to reform the educational system. Not only had 'hooliganism' become a problem (juvenile delinquency and political demonstrations by young people),[1] but also other pastimes and attitudes incompatible, in the eyes of the party, with socialism had taken root. Young people were increasingly seeking pastimes in groups or individually *outside* the framework of the social organizations, and disinterest in the party and socialism was general. One poll concluded that among students interrogated only some 11·4 per cent considered themselves politically active, while 47 per cent considered themselves politically neutral, 6·6 per cent passive and 35 per cent 'did not know.'[2] Another study showed that only 11·3 per cent of the students who were members of the party joined out of 'inner conviction,' 27·6 per cent joined for material advantage, 4·4 per cent under the influence of their environment, and the remainder for 'other reasons,' of which material motives and environment were predominant.[3] Still another study revealed that Czechoslovak youths were pacifists, uninterested in the army, and so desirous of peace that they 'underestimate' the motives of the enemy. Moreover, an astonishingly high percentage of nineteen-year-old boys were unaware of the existence of the Warsaw Pact.[4]

---

[1] For example the 11 October 1964 riots in Prague and 2 December 1964 riots in Bratislava. A conference on the growing problems of juvenile delinquency was held as early as 1963, a year in which delinquency rose by twelve per cent. (Bratislava radio, 8 March 1964.)

[2] Milan Schneider, 'Students and the Party,' *Zivot Strany*, 6 (1966), 13.

[3] *Student*, 19 January 1966.

[4] *Smena*, 28 December 1965. One may assume this percentage declined after August 1968.

In early 1965, party committees were established at the institutes of higher learning, even though or perhaps because only five per cent of students were members of the party. This move presumably was designed to counter what presidium member Koucky had termed 'petty bourgeois weeds and anti-Marxist attacks . . . new formations of technocratism, managerism, mysticism, pro-Djilas pamphlets, the apotheoses of bourgeois democracy, and philosophical irrationalism' in these institutions. Lest it be thought that the problem was limited to young 'intellectuals,' Koucky pointed out that a poll of a provincial agricultural secondary school had revealed unsatisfactory attitudes to-wards work, lack of drive, and insufficient social responsibility.[1] More-over it was well known that many of the youths involved in the 1963 and later May Day disturbances were apprentices.[2]

Much of the blame for this state of affairs was placed on CSM, the organization designed to stimulate and direct youth. In the former, it had clearly failed as it became increasingly obvious over the years that instead of an organization for and of the youth, CSM was a regime agency over the youth. Because of the fluid nature of its membership and the small number of communist members, CSM, in 1958, had become the only mass organization to be under *direct* party control instead of the usual indirect control exercised through communist members of the organization's leadership. In 1966 it comprised 1 055 000 young people from the ages of fifteen to twenty-six, although only fifty per cent of those eligible were in fact members.[3] Most of these were pupils and students, reflecting, perhaps, the fact that CSM member-ship was a co-decisive factor in admission to higher studies or other educational benefits. Only twenty-five per cent of factory youth were CSM members and the percentage was even smaller from the country-side.[4] Membership in CSM had become a largely formal affair, and many a youth left CSM as soon as he felt that membership was no

[1] *Rude Pravo*, 24 October 1964 (Koucky to central committee).

[2] On May Day 1965 the regime permitted the traditional students' Majales Festival for the first time since 1956. Posters in Prague and Bratislava bore such slogans as 'Whoever Cannot Read or Write Can Always Quote,' 'Criticize Only the Dead Ones' and several too vulgar for reproduction here. In Prague the students elected visiting 'beat' poet Allen Ginsberg Majales King; he was expelled from the country a week later. The 1 May 1966 riots were even larger and evoked severe action by the regime against a number of demonstrators.

[3] Prague radio, 27 May 1966. (Pioneers ages 9–14, Sparks 6–9. In June 1967 the Sparks were abolished and the ages for Pioneers changed to 8–15 and CSM to 15–30.)

[4] *Prace*, 24 April 1966.

longer necessary to his career (a feeling that became increasingly prominent with the reforms of de-Stalinization, when membership fell from 1 418 783 in 1963 to 1 055 000 in 1966).[1] He felt no genuine attraction for an organization which offered him little beyond social obligations, boring meetings, labor brigades, or political indoctrination. Even other mass organizations such as SVAZARM, with its ventures into motoring, radiocommunications, flying and parachuting, were preferable to CSM, although most desirable was no affiliation at all.

CSM itself was dissatisfied with this state of affairs and at least the student element formulated some ideas of its own on the subject of reform. According to remarks by Jiri Hendrych to a central committee plenum in May 1964, both he and ideology chief Koucky had been confronted with student demands for an organization outside the framework of the National Front and outside party influence.[2] At the time Hendrych rejected this notion, as did Koucky six months later, as reflecting a very unsound state of affairs. The latter revealed that student leaders within CSM were agitating for an independent organization of their own – a notion which Koucky dismissed as 'politically untenable.' Koucky did allow, however, that the present system of direct party control of CSM was sometimes 'misunderstood' as an 'authoritarian relationship between superior and subordinate' which often failed to go beyond 'the imposition of tasks, the bearing of reports and criticism of shortcomings,' but he maintained that CSM should be run by young communists.[3] Presumably to eliminate this 'misunderstanding,' the party conducted a long series of meetings under an action called 'Party Speaks with Youth Campaign.' It also permitted certain concessions to make the official organization more attractive. For example, the regime suddenly 'discovered' that the exceedingly popular pastime of camping, which it had formerly condemned as incompatible with the socialist view of life, was a movement with its roots in the proletariat. CSM was, therefore, authorized to join the movement and bring it under its auspices by sponsoring camping trips and similar activities.

The problem was, however, beyond such minor concessions. As with the educational system,[4] the so-called unified approach which precluded any differentiation of methods or activities according to the persons

---

[1] *Mlada Fronta*, 24 April 1963; Prague radio, 27 May 1966.
[2] Hajek and Niznansky, 'Students Demand Right to Political Opposition,' RFE (1966), 2.
[3] *Rude Pravo*, 24 October 1964. [4] See chapter 9 below.

involved, was one reason for the failure of CSM. It was also argued that the ambiguity of the youth organization's real function and authority contributed to its ineffectiveness. Cognizant of the validity of these arguments, the party decided at its January 1965 central committee plenum to instigate a reform of CSM, specifically encouraging the formation of clubs for teenagers along the lines of hobbies and special interests. The CSM, at its October 1965 central committee plenum, followed this with the promise that its activities would take into account age and social characteristics. At this meeting, however, Hendrych ruled out the two extreme positions: that which sought an independent, purely political organization and that which rejected the political content of the mass organization, favoring a pure interest group which would leave indoctrination and political/ideological activities to society and the educational system.[1]

Both the party and the CSM were looking for a better formula and in the course of this search, a possible model was resuscitated: the scout movement of pre-communist Czechoslovakia. An article in the CSM Slovak daily in March 1965 admitted that the Scouts had been a good influence on youngsters and had been condemned only out of a need for a scapegoat. In December 1965 a court quashed the heavy sentences meted out to Scout leaders in 1952 and the way was cleared for emulation of some of that movement's methods (although the movement itself was not to be revived).[2] At the same time, the 'CSM problem' became part of the general discussion on interest groups and the role of criticism or opposition in a socialist society – a discussion which tended to encourage the solution offered by the students.

The student plan was finally revealed in detail at the National Conference of University Students in Prague, 18–19 December 1965. In the presence of Koucky, a representative of a group later known as the 'Prague radicals,' engineering student Jiri Mueller, advocated a thoroughgoing reform of CSM designed to make the organization a genuine independent representative of the youth.[3] Mueller said that CSM had failed to fulfill its role as 'middleman between the youth and the leadership' as disillusionment set in over the contradiction between the 'notions in which we were brought up and reality.' Since the youth organization had been unable to 'work out' the ideals afresh, no solution

---

[1] *Mlada Fronta*, 21 October 1965.
[2] *Literarni Noviny*, 7 January 1967 ('Scouts Again Before the Courts'). They were reinstituted only in 1968.
[3] *Student*, 26 January 1966.

could now be found within the existing framework of the organization. Mueller maintained that the youth organization should be a platform for youth's ideas; it should represent and support these views vis-a-vis the decision-making powers of the country, using whatever means legally or traditionally possible, despite the 'limitations of socialist democracy.' As it was, CSM was a political organization (as the party would have it, serving the latter's interests and preparing youths for the party) 'without any possibility of *acting* as such.' To act as such it must truly express the views of its members even to the extent of opposing the party, if necessary. Concretely, Mueller demanded a representation for the CSM in all state bodies including the National Assembly. In essence he was advocating the formation of a genuine political party.

Mueller did not perceive this new role as feasible without structural changes which would divide CSM into two age groups. The younger group, aged from fifteen to eighteen, would be a special interest group; the older would be 'socially fully engaged' since its interests and needs are 'interwoven with those of society as a whole to such a degree that its organization must necessarily be a political one.' This older group would be a federation of three sub-groups, representing industrial youth, agricultural youth, and university youth, with one central directing body composed of an equal number of representatives from each sub-group.

Koucky took the floor for a second time to respond to the lively discussion which had followed and in large part supported Mueller's proposals. He attacked Mueller's ideas on the grounds that possibilities for opposition through frank discussion already existed within the party and CSM, as well as between them. Koucky said, however, that the matter of organization might be taken up by the next CSM congress. The conference then resolved to form an eleven-man board to prepare a draft on the structure, contents of work, and working conditions of CSM, including a definition of the status of students. This was to be considered by a special CSM conference to be held before the next CSM congress scheduled for June 1967.[1]

The regime attempted to disregard or at least to avoid publicizing this radical call for a 'second party,' but the fourth issue of the new weekly of the university committee of CSM, *Student*, carried Mueller's speech almost in full. At the same time, serving to keep the issue active,

[1] *Mlada Fronta*, 27 January 1966. The eleven-man group quickly split three ways, the Slovaks, the party's sycophants, and the Mueller-radical group. See *Universita Karlova*, 6 March 1968.

a mimeographed student paper; *Elixir*, published a proposal for an independent students' organization entirely free from CSM.

The party press too joined in the discussion, and there were definite signs that party members preferred a relatively liberal solution. Martin Vaculik, then a rising star in the party hierarchy, wrote in the party theoretical journal that 'a youth organization cannot merely imitate the organizations of the adults, but it must find contents and forms of work which correspond to the needs, interests, and thinking of the young.'[1] This, he said, CSM had completely failed to do, although the new tendency toward differentiation and special interests might provide a solution. The more conservative party organization and political department chief Jan Svoboda was quoted by Prague radio on 13 January 1966 as approving the idea that CSM activities be differentiated and organized according to age and social interests, although he considered a unified political organization with a clear 'ideological profile' essential.

Rude Pravo published an article claiming that youth simply did not feel a part of the system they had inherited. This absence of an active political relationship to the system had led to apathy, opposition, and criticism, it was argued. The failure of CSM in this regard 'deprived . . . our young people of their political platform,' and, in the author's opinion, a main reason for this was the fact that the youth union was unsure of its jurisdiction and lacking in authority in areas clearly within its jurisdiction. Due to the fact that CSM was often limited to only boring or 'doubtful' activities and mere formalism, coupled with the fact that usually only officials of the union engaged in even these activities, 'the young people easily get the impression that in a socialist society all people do not have an equal opportunity of sharing in the administration of public affairs, that power is not equally divided in a socialist society and that a socialist society lacks a democratic character.'[2]

Novotny was apparently aware that the reform of CSM was a potentially dangerous issue, especially given the movement towards a second party idea. In view of the concessions he had already made towards the youth in the area of education and the organizational reforms he had ordered for the other mass organizations, Novotny apparently decided to draw a clear line beyond which he was not yet prepared to proceed in the issue of CSM. In a speech to a CSM delegation of young factory workers in the spring of 1966, Novotny warned against any split

[1] Martin Vaculik, 'The Younger Generation,' *Nova Mysl*, XX:1 (1966), 19–21.
[2] *Rude Pravo*, 8 April 1966.

according to the nature of work such as proposed by the students. It was typical of Novotny to deliver this warning to a delegation of workers rather than to the students themselves; he had long played upon the worker distrust of intellectuals in hopes of setting them against each other and thereby defeating the intellectuals' initiatives.

This warning, however, was heeded by the conservative majority in the CSM leadership which condemned the 'centrifugal tendencies' of university students as 'one-sided and politically wrong.'[1] To emphasize their point, the CSM leaders added that direct party guidance was the guarantee of improved CSM work. So the matter stood on the eve of the party congress, which was to enunciate a major new position on youth. The congress did not, however, address itself directly to this issue, but rather left it for the 1967 CSM congress, undoubtedly hoping that the interceding year would operate to divest the issue of some of its inflammability.

The 'Prague radicals' did not, however, succumb to party pressures. Although of his own volition Jiri Mueller took a year's leave of absence from the university, beginning in May 1966, he and the group remained active. In November they gained a majority in CSM's Prague district university committee and, eventually, in that group's presidium.[2] As a result of these activities, Mueller was expelled from the university on 22 December, on 23 December from CSM (by the Prague city CSM committee), and drafted into the army on 27 December. Lubomir Holecek then took over the leadership, organizing a campaign supporting Mueller's appeal. It was this campaign and the group's agitation for its original program which thwarted the regime's hopes of 'defusing' the atmosphere prior to the June 1967 CSM congress.

RELIGIOUS–NATIONAL GROUPS

There was also a change in policy towards religion, specifically the Catholic Church. This came partially as a result of Khrushchev's policy of improving relations with Pope John XXIII, but it also served both to improve the regime's image for its pursuit of increased relations with the West, and, to a lesser degree, to answer internal demands for rectification of past injustices. Thus the ranking Czech prelate, archbishop Josef Beran, was released after twelve years' internment. He was not, however, permitted to resume his church

[1] *Rude Pravo*, 20 May 1966.
[2] *Student*, 13 March 1968, and *Literarni Listy*, 7 March 1968.

duties and an understanding was worked out between the regime and the Vatican whereby Beran, named a Cardinal in 1965, was transferred to Rome (though Beran claims that he was unaware that he would not be returning to Czechoslovakia).[1] A number of other bishops were released with Beran but were not permitted to resume their ecclesiastical functions. Nonetheless, the understanding with the Vatican did lead to the naming of Rome-accepted prelates to high ranking church positions in Czechoslovakia, in the place of regime collaborators, e.g. the replacement of Stehlik by Frantisek Tomasek as apostolic administrator of Prague on 11 March 1965, and an improvement of the position of formerly persecuted bishops.[2]

The regime also revaluated its agit–prop activities with regard to religion and concluded that its vulgar anti-religion campaigns had made martyrs of believers, merely strengthening the appeal of religion among even the basically anti-clerical Czechs. More seriously, perhaps, it was pointed out that the atheistic policy had produced a 'spiritual vacuum' among the young people best seen as indifference.[3] Few solutions other than a more sophisticated approach to religious belief and tolerance for believers were suggested, but the regime did inaugurate regular 'dialogues' between the party and the Catholics (both inside and outside Czechoslovakia).[4] The regime also refrained from interfering in the creation of 'study groups' among Jewish youth and even permitted the training of a new rabbi (in Hungary, since the regime still did not permit rabbinical training in Czechoslovakia). There was also a limited resumption of contacts between the Jewish community and international Jewish groups, but this did not mean a change in the attitude or policy towards Israel or specifically Zionist organizations, for these fell into the category of foreign relations dependent upon an entirely different constellation of events and pressures. As a national (as distinct from religious) minority, the Jews

[1] *Student*, 7 May 1968.
[2] Prague radio, 23 June 1965; *Suddeutsche Zeitung*, 30 June 1965; *Frankfurter Allgemeine Zeitung*, 1 July 1965.
[3] See Viteslav Gardovsky, 'Marxism and Atheism,' *Veda a Zivot*, 2 (1966), 67–70 or J. Krejci, 'Criteria of Scientific–Atheist Education,' *Nova Mysl*, XXI:8 (1967), 17–19.
[4] In addition to bi-weekly meetings between local Catholic and party leaders, the regime permitted participation in Christian–Marxist dialogues abroad and even hosted one such meeting in 1967. The Czechoslovak Society for the Propagation of Political and Scientific Knowledge, which coordinated atheist propaganda, sought to improve its image (and its work) by changing its name in 1965 to the Czechoslovak Socialist Academy.

benefited in another way from de-Stalinization, i.e. from the re-habilitations in connection with the 1950s, for, given the anti-semitic nature of the trials, a disproportionate number of Jews had been affected. Nonetheless this aspect of the trials was never referred to specifically, probably because of Novotny's own role in preparing the anti-semitic materials at the time and because of the international implications.

None of the other religions or national minorities profited notably from the de-Stalinization drive, although Protestant–Catholic dialogues not connected with the regime, were begun. If anything, however, the Hungarian minority suffered, for the upsurge of Slovak nationalism and the granting of more Slovak rights tended to be at the expense of their traditional enemies, the Hungarians. Relations between the two national minorities indeed were aggravated, and the regime even attempted to exploit this in order to limit the Slovaks' demands.

9

EDUCATION

As with the once prosperous, quality-producing economy, the educational system of Czechoslovakia – formerly highly respected internationally – suffered from its albeit gradual conversion to the Soviet-modeled communist system. The 'unified' school system was introduced whereby all education at all schools on all levels was to be based upon identical ideological principles, unified organizationally, politically, and legally under the central authority of the Ministry of Education. In time the Soviet-based system, eliminating the traditional 'gymnasia,' brought in an eleven-year school, with three divisions (ages six to eleven; eleven to fifteen; and fifteen to nineteen) unified into one unit from age six to seventeen, with the last three years reserved for university preparation. Education was compulsory only up to the age of fourteen, thereby shortening the period of obligatory study from nine to eight years. High school was likewise shortened from four to three years, and entrance examinations (formerly required for the gymnasia) were eliminated. Those who did not choose to prepare for university study (the overwhelming majority) could at the age of fourteen seek admission to technical or vocational schools similar to the Soviet *technium* or study while working at State Labor Reserve Schools similar to the Soviet *ucilishcha*, or train as apprentices at factory schools similar to the Soviet FZO (factory–plant institution system). The reduction of basic study time was to be compensated at least in part by the reduction or elimination of the study of material deemed superfluous by the polytechnic-oriented communist educators. Therefore time spent on the humanities, including language training, was severely reduced, and religious instruction was eliminated from the regular curriculum, to be provided outside the regular school hours if specifically requested by the parent.

The brief thaw in 1956 unleashed severe criticism of this system, directed mainly against the reduction of study time and the subsequent overburdening of pupils. The quality of students' work suffered from overburdening due also to requirements to serve in youth work-brigades, extracurricular obligations, meetings, and 'socialist competitions.' Teachers' as well as students' time was filled with bureaucratic and compulsory 'political' tasks. Moreover, the necessity of building a 'communist' system of education required 'properly' oriented teachers, which often meant sacrificing pedagogical substantive skills for political reliability. A rapid turnover of teachers resulted, while the tasks of often unqualified teaching staffs were further complicated by constant party tampering with textbooks, curriculum, and standards.

Despite one concession – the resumption of nine-year rather than eight-year compulsory study – a reform in 1960 brought the Czechoslovak system in line with further developments in the USSR. The major change was a further polytechnicalization of the schools (thirty per cent of weekly class hours devoted to polytechnic subjects), with its introduction of six to eight hours per week of practical work in factories or farms for pupils from ages eleven to fourteen, and eight hours per week for high-school students plus practical work in the summer. High-school students were expected to acquire an apprentice certificate along with their diploma.

Higher education as well suffered from Sovietization, particularly by the elimination of autonomy for the universities and the subordination of higher education to the government. Thus in 1948 all matters of staff, curriculum, and organization, formerly left to the Faculties and their elected administration were turned over to the Minister of Education and a state commission for scientific degrees. Formerly elected administrators such as rectors, pro-rectors, and deans were to be appointed by the state, which would also determine not only curriculum and faculty matters but also content of courses and textbooks. Compulsory military and physical training were introduced as well as the compulsory study of Marxism–Leninism for all students, regardless of field of study. Entrance examinations were eliminated and, in their place, strict adherence to the class principle and cadre system were introduced for entry and scholarship qualifications. Attendance at courses was made compulsory, the course load significantly increased, and frequent examinations introduced. Humanities were downgraded in favor of the sciences (especially the applied sciences) and, in 1959, practical work in factories and farms was introduced for all students at the rate of four months per year. In addition, according to laws introduced in 1952 and 1953, students were required to work three years in a job assigned to them upon graduation.

The problems created by the new system in higher education were much the same as those at the lower levels – the deteriorating quality of which contributed to the deterioration of the universities. The strict adherence to the class and cadre system and the recruitment rather than selection of students for science brought many people to the university who under the old system probably would not have qualified for entrance. Although students with the proper cadre profile were given many concessions, all students suffered from poor preparation received in secondary school and the heavy burden placed upon them at the university of courses, production work, obligatory meetings, and extracurricular functions of a political nature. Another element, that of fear, also impeded maximum performance, for students were conscious of the danger of expulsion or worse if some factor detrimental to their cadre profile should arise or be discovered. As with the lower schools, finding and training politically reliable teachers was a serious problem which led to a lowering of pedagogical standards in favor of political interests.

By the early 1960s the entire lower and higher education system had come under heavy criticism as the poor quality of graduates was comprehended. Some of the strongest of this criticism appeared on the pages of *Kulturny Zivot*, which attacked the cadre system, the preference given to party members for teaching positions, the general lowering of educational standards, and the time wasted on reforms which had been of no practical use. The regime response came in late 1964 when Education and Culture Minister Cisar and party ideology commission chairman Koucky outlined and explained a program of reforms.

PRIMARY AND SECONDARY EDUCATION

In their presentations of the changes both Cisar and Koucky admitted that the previous reforms had been incorrect in many respects. Perhaps mindful of announcing what the public was liable to scorn as 'still another education reform,' neither official called the changes a 'reform.' Rather, Koucky claimed that changes were needed to accommodate the 'qualitatively new economic system' and to prepare for the transition to communism which was still expected for the near future.[1] Nonetheless new measures were announced, the main purpose of which was to undo at least some of the damage wrought by the previous reforms and to raise the standards and quality of Czechoslovak education to the pre-1948 level. Koucky thus characterized the reform and its goals:

to teach people to think independently and to educate themselves

[1] *Rude Pravo*, 24 October 1964 (Koucky to central committee).

systematically in close connection with the acquisition of knowledge and facts on the level of the findings of contemporary science and consciously to devote their abilities to the construction of the new society. The road toward the achievement of this aim lies through the all-round modernization of subject matter and methods of school work and – within their framework – through a correctly understood and differentiated approach which is based on the differences of interests, talents, and leanings of youth.[1]

The reference to independent thinking (Cisar had spoken of independent creative thinking)[2] struck a new note, manifesting the regime's awareness, prompted not in small part by the bold criticism of the previous years, of the regrettable lack of individual initiative, particularly apparent in the economy.

The operative words in Koucky's summary were, however, 'differentiated approach,' for in the program outlined by him there was the admission that the 'unified' approach introduced by the communists had been neither realistic nor effective. As Cisar described it, children begin to decide what they want – by inclination and interest – as early as the age of eleven and usually between the ages of eleven and fourteen. The basic nine-year school as well as the high school provided no leeway for variation and, in fact, leaned too heavily towards polytechnic training for everyone. Koucky asserted that the unified approach had been suitable to the needs of the 1950s when it was introduced, but that it now appeared outdated, as evidenced by the fact that students at age fourteen were not prepared for university-preparatory study. The mistake in past thinking was to ascribe too great an importance to education and environment as contributing factors in the development of character and personality while ascribing too little (in fact none) to inherent characteristics and pre-school influences.

It was therefore decided to return at least somewhat to the pre-communist system by providing a better balance between humanities and natural sciences in the basic schools; to step up demands upon the lower grades, to introduce 'semi-professional' instruction in the fourth or fifth grades, and to introduce specialization by means of elective courses and the grouping of pupils along lines of capabilities. This 'differentiation' was to begin first in the tenth grade and be gradually extended to the eighth and ninth grades. An 'adjustment' of time spent in production work would be made to allow for the additional

[1] *Ibid.*
[2] Cestmir Cisar, 'School and Life,' *Socialisticka Skola*, v:4 (1964), 193–6.

studies. Only qualified teachers would be permitted to teach the ninth graders. This system, already begun on an experimental basis in 1964, sought eventually to reintroduce early specialization in the European sense and modern pedagogical methods of dealing with variations in native ability.

The high schools, according to Cisar, had also suffered from ill-advised reforms which had 'incorrectly' modeled them to resemble technical schools. Koucky pointed out that the high schools had suffered from the unified approach, for all students did not continue on to secondary school as originally envisaged when the unified system was established. The leveling downward of the secondary school had meant that material which should have been presented at the high-school level had to be studied at the universities, e.g. languages, high-school mathematics, and physics. Cisar revealed that 'the goal of the secondary school for general education has now been precisely defined to train graduates who have a general and technical education' from which the universities and institutes of higher learning might draw their candidates. To this end differentiation or specialization was to be reintroduced at the secondary schools as well. Although the length of study would remain three years, students would be divided upon successfully completing entrance examinations (also a return to pre-communist practice) into either natural science studies or humanities with foreign languages and philosophy (including psychology and ethics) equally represented in both areas. Physical training lessons were to be increased at both secondary and basic schools to relieve the necessity of such training at a higher level. Aesthetic instruction was also to be improved to provide students with a basis in music and art. This was introduced to offset the influences of 'immoral' or 'decadent' music and art penetrating from the West, but also, as Koucky admitted, 'to overcome the one-sided opinion that at a time of the upsurge of science and technology the importance of culture and arts recedes into the background.'

The failure of the 'production' training in the general education high schools was admitted by Koucky, although he maintained that the principle was sound. Therefore, student work and brigades would be continued (the latter particularly were necessary to the labor-short economy) but time spent in production work in high school was to be reduced to four hours weekly. In fact, production work was entirely eliminated in the spring of 1965 when it was declared that this training had caused 'serious problems' and that the time would now be used for work in natural sciences, school laboratories and workshops.[1] In an effort to raise teaching standards, more men were to be encouraged to join the profession by way of increased salaries, and 'outside interference' in teachers' tasks was to be eliminated. Efforts were also to be made to increase the number of graduates going on to and succeeding in higher education. For the fifty per cent of the graduates who did not choose to go on to university study, one-year courses were to be introduced in finance, transport, and administration. According to Koucky, abbreviated apprenticeships were also to be offered to provide these more academically trained graduates the wherewithal for entering the economy without the benefit of higher education.

Of greater concern to the regime, however, were those youngsters who chose to abandon their formal studies after the compulsory nine years, i.e. at the age of fifteen. Referring to this, Koucky said to the party central committee 'I should like to point to the grave consequences stemming from the extremely insufficient gradation of compensation for qualified and less qualified work. This induces a number of parents, even in the case of gifted children, to seek immediate transition to jobs for their children after the nine-year school instead of having them study or become apprentices.' Wage equalization not only accounted for youngsters leaving school but also for the large number of good students who chose to continue at technical schools rather than the general-education high schools. The party reported that, according to a recent study,

at the age of forty the college graduate-engineer will have earned 7 per cent less than the secondary school technician and 14 per cent less than the average skilled worker of the same age. Only at age sixty will the lifetime earnings of the engineer college graduate come to 11 per cent more than the earnings of the technician, and his earnings will then still be only 3 per cent above those of a skilled worker.[2]

The wage reform contained in the new economic program was so designed to overcome this problem and a step towards implementation came in June 1965 when the State Wage Commission resolved to give preference by way of higher salaries to 'university and secondary vocational school graduates' in certain fields.[3]

Although the regime thus demonstrated its understanding of and

[1] *Rude Pravo*, 14 April 1965.   [2] *Rude Pravo*, 1 June 1965.
[3] *Kulturni Tvorba*, 24 June 1965.

willingness to remedy at least one aspect of its drop-out problem and the shortage of candidates for higher studies, it still had to address itself to the youths who would nonetheless continue to disregard the opportunity for general secondary education. The standard of technical or vocational schools was to be raised partially by introducing more theoretical subjects, e.g. physics for students in agriculture, chemistry for those in engineering, and partially by improving teaching methods and materials. Here too the unified approach was to be abandoned: duration of studies was to depend on the time needed for the material to be covered, whether it be more or less than the uniform three years. Apprentice schools were to be improved principally by improving the quality of instruction. Koucky underlined the need for this when he said: 'At the secondary schools for general education 5 per cent of the teachers are insufficiently qualified, at the industrial schools 12 per cent, but at the apprentice schools 28 per cent and at the vocational training establishments – including foremen of vocational training – even 41 per cent.' The salaries of apprentice school teachers were the first, therefore, to be raised. Much of the blame for this situation was also placed upon the enterprise managers who misused this training in efforts to bring the apprentices into production as early as possible. The regime decided that apprentice training, also, would no longer be uniform but depend in length upon the requirements of the jobs themselves. Moreover, it would be voluntary, permitting those unwilling or unable to apprentice to obtain on-the-job training. While the regime's wish was to train more – not fewer – people, this measure would release personnel to help fill the gap in the supply of labor (especially in agriculture). It was principally designed, however, to eliminate the misusage of the training by management and to raise incentive by removing the element of compulsion. Thus those who desired and were capable of absorbing more training could receive what was necessary – no more, no less – while the labor-starved economy could earlier draw upon those desirous of work without having to resort to subterfuge or deception, especially for tasks which required little or no training.

Koucky attributed much of the deterioration in the quality of education to budgetary planning which had placed education in the category of consumption, thereby denying it priority status for funds. Equipment, facilities, staff, all suffered because of this. Koucky announced that the public would be called upon to make a greater direct contribution in both money and labor to overcome these shortcomings.

HIGHER EDUCATION

These last measures applied also to the system of higher education, but the reforms in this area presented a problem of their own. Whereas the measures outlined above were to go into effect as early as the school year 1965–6, the reforms for higher education were debated an additional year and one-half. There apparently was considerable dissent within the party as to the degree of autonomy to be accorded the universities – a crucial point for reforms in this sphere. The party made every effort to reach agreement before its Thirteenth Congress in May 1966 and, eventually, the liberals were victorious on the issue: the new universities bill of March 1966 was basically as liberal a document as that originally presented by Koucky to the central committee – and opposed by conservatives within that body – in October 1964.[1]

A major issue was the question of election or appointment of rectors. To accord the faculty a greater say in matters which would rule them, specifically responsibility for the selection of a rector (and pro-rector and deans), would indeed restore to the universities and institutions of higher learning a significant part of their pre-communist independence. A second disputed issue was that of according student representatives the right to participate in the governing councils of the institutions of higher learning. Increased roles of both students and faculty were likely to induce greater responsiveness to the real needs and wishes of the institutions as distinct from those of the party or the regime.

Thus the party was faced with a serious dilemma of relinquishing some of its control in the interests of improving the quality of higher education just at a time when ferment was high among students and professors alike – a fact which seemed to ensure that full advantage would be taken of any freedom granted.[2] As with almost every aspect of de-Stalinization in Czechoslovakia, it was this ferment itself, of which the party was fearful, that brought enough pressure to win the long-term concessions from the regime. Even as party conservatives pointed to the present insolence of the intellectuals and students as arguments against greater freedom in higher education, the liberals, apparently with the support if not the direct leadership of Cisar, intensified their pressures, pressed their already won advantages and achieved most of their aims.

---

[1] *Sbirka Zakonu* No. 19/1966. In the interim the architect of the reforms, Cisar, had been relieved of his post as Education and Culture Minister.

[2] For example the students of the Prague Faculty of Philosophy who protested to the party over Cisar's removal. (*Die Welt*, 27 November and 2 December 1965.)

Education

The 1966 Law on Advanced Schools therefore provided for the three-year presidential appointment of rectors after their election (by secret ballot) from the ranks of the professors by the council of the institution. Pro-rectors, deans, and pro-deans of Faculties were also to be elected from among their colleagues; the Minister of Education and Culture would confirm appointments of the elected pro-rectors. The regime did reserve the right of recall of rectors (by the President), thereby retaining for itself an element of control. An earlier version of the bill had granted the government a veto over the selection of the rector, but opposition had forced the government to drop it in the final version.[1] Rectors and deans were to have greater freedom regarding financial matters and more latitude in contracting and using the proceeds from research projects and in establishing international contacts.

Although the Ministry of Education and Culture would still be responsible for determining entry requirements, curriculum and regulations, the new Minister, Jiri Hajek, said that the bill 'limits central management of higher learning establishments to matters which demand a nationally unified conception. The purpose of the bill is on the one hand to establish the main trends of the network of universities; on the other, it gives maximum independence and authority to them to decide their current affairs.'[2] Students and workers of the institution staffs were to be represented on the councils, although they would not be permitted to vote on appointments or conference of degrees. While the student representatives would come from CSM, this clause established an innovation in principle. Moreover, with the changes advocated for and within CSM this innovation could eventually mean genuine student participation in the direction of the university.

Returning to another pre-communist practice, entrance examinations were to be reintroduced. Moreover, students were to be granted admission 'according to their individual capacities, talents and interests and in harmony with the needs of the society.'[3] This was taken to mean that students could choose their field of study, according to their abilities, rather than be dependent upon the desires or restrictions of their employers and the requirements of their jobs.[4] The law also added that completion of secondary school would be required for entry. This eliminated the 'preparatory students' – party activists who formerly

[1] *Literarni Noviny*, 14 August 1965.   [2] Prague radio, 16 March 1966.
[3] The cadre system had already quietly begun to disappear in 1964.
[4] *Mlada Fronta*, 7 January 1965.

117

were permitted to enter without matriculation and had done so much to lower the standards of the universities. A new scholarship system was introduced which tended to reward students with high academic achievement as well as those who demonstrated need or promised to work in specified areas for five years after graduation.[1] The unified system for higher education was also to be abandoned and length of studies adjusted to the needs of each field. Undergraduate specialization was to be limited to a reduced number of areas, leaving more narrow specialization for post-graduate studies. The Soviet system of academic titles, which had been extremely unpopular, was to be abandoned (because these titles 'didn't take root'[2]) in favor of the pre-communist titles.

The new bill did not go into the question of content of studies, but Koucky's earlier report had indicated that students should have already acquired sufficient knowledge of foreign languages at the secondary school to enable them to study at higher institutions without need of further language training. Military training, although retained, would be shifted mainly to vacations with only a minimum of theoretical instruction during the school year. Physical training would be optional. Production work was also to be retained but would be transferred to the summer holidays and linked with the student's field of study. Moreover, students might choose their jobs instead of being assigned. The Marxism–Leninism courses were to be presented in a more realistic light with reference to actual political and economic problems, in hopes of making the material more relevant and interesting rather then pure indoctrination.[3] Moreover, the 'secondary school type discipline' was to be 'relaxed,' according to the new Minister of Education and Culture.[4]

Although the changes in entrance procedures were designed to raise the level of the quality of students entering higher studies, the success or failure of the reforms depended a great deal upon the quality of instruction and the actual content of the courses at all levels. As early as 1963 the re-rewriting of textbooks began; new methods connected with modern psychology and sociology were gradually being introduced;[5]

[1] See *Lidova Demokracie*, 11 February 1965; *Mlada Fronta*, 26 January 1965.
[2] *Rude Pravo*, 24 October 1964.
[3] The modification of these courses began in 1966–7.
[4] 'New Year's Talk with the Minister of Education and Culture, Jiri Hajek,' *Ucitelske Noviny*, XVI:1 (1966), 1.
[5] See Edward Taborsky, 'Sociology in Eastern Europe,' *Problems of Communism*, XIV:1 (1965), 62–6; Edward Taborsky, 'Where is Czechoslovakia Going?,' *East*

contacts with the West opened and/or expanded in the form of scholar and student exchanges, participation in symposia abroad, and expansion of quantity and accessibility of scientific and other literature received from the West. It remained to be seen just how much independence the newly elected officials actually could or would assert within the framework of the reforms, and how much the party would tolerate. In effect, however, an attempt was being made to retain basic communist goals and party authority while returning to many of the institutional forms and ideas of pre-communist Czechoslovakia in hopes of recovering some of the lively, creative atmosphere and high quality of education of that era. Nominal controls existed within the reforms should the situation get out of hand, but these controls promised to become increasingly difficult to exercise as the institutionalization would take hold.

Europe, xv:2 (1967), 2–12. The first Czechoslovak Sociological Society was founded in April 1964. Efforts were made to write more objective histories of such matters as Czechoslovaks who fought on the western fronts in the last war, the Hungarian revolution, Benes, both Masaryks, and even party history. This trend was sharply criticized by Novotny himself in a speech to factory workers (*Rude Pravo*, 29 May 1964). 28 October was restored as National Independence Day in 1966.

10

THE ARTS

The liberalization in cultural policy was to some degree imposed upon Novotny from below by the liberal party intellectuals. After the high point of activity in 1963 – during which the intellectuals significantly broadened the boundaries within which they could safely operate and in essence launched the de-Stalinization campaign – the cultural scene became a somewhat more settled area of creativity, albeit markedly more free and bold than hitherto. The campaign to achieve greater freedom was combined with an effort to realize and use the newly won freedom, the general purpose being not only to preserve that which had already been gained, but to broaden still further the rights and limits of creative activity. To this the party reacted with sporadic attempts to narrow these limits, if for no other reason than to remind the intellectuals that there were indeed limits, however broad. Its actions came in the form of personnel changes in the ideological bodies of the government and the party (the most significant of which were the assignment of Pavel Auersperg, believed to have been a close ally of Novotny, as head of the party central committee's ideological department in January 1965 and the replacement of Cestmir Cisar as Minister of Education and Culture in November 1965),[1] editorial board shuffles, suppression or censorship of various journals or works of art, and, in some cases, expulsion from the party and persecution of liberal intellectuals. These were generally accompanied by decidedly less effective speeches, resolutions, decisions, and debates. On a day to day basis, the party strove to maintain control over the cultural world through party members themselves within the cultural organizations, in the hopes of eventually being able to rely on self-policing or self-censoring methods.

THEATRE

An area in which the cultural liberalization was most rapidly reflected was the dramatic arts. The technical level of both film and theatre had

---

[1] In a possible reference to Cisar, Novotny told the central committee in October 1966: 'Some work centers whose mission it is to watch over adherence to the norms of socialist life also succumb to political and ideological liberalism and to laxity in the face of anti-social actions and excesses.' (Antonin Novotny, 'Contemporary Problems of the Development of Socialist Society,' *Zivot Strany*, 21 (1966), 4.) Cisar became ambassador to Rumania.

long been of high quality, but the ideological limitations placed upon them greatly restricted subject matter and style, leading to a certain drabness and a propagandistic lack of originality or depth. The Czechoslovak public was doubly deprived, for presentations of foreign works were similarly limited – in films, to a large percentage of Soviet productions; in theatre, to ideologically acceptable foreign authors. This was almost immediately remedied, for the 1963–4 theatre season included a Czech production from the French theatre of the absurd, Eugene Ionescu's *Rhinocerous*, as well as plays by Friedrich Durrenmatt. By the 1964–5 season western plays outnumbered all others in the Czechoslovak theatres and included American playwright Edward Albee's *Who's Afraid of Virginia Woolf* (in Czech entitled *Who's Afraid of Franz Kafka*) and the forerunner of western avant-garde theatre Samuel Beckett's *Waiting for Godot*. The 1965–6 season added even less social conscious playwrights such as Noel Coward and the even more avant-garde Luigi Pirandello and Morris Schisgall.

The real renascence in Czechoslovak theatre came with original productions, however, and with these, two new phenomena: critical/satirical drama and avant-garde theatre of the absurd. The first of these works, which appeared as early as the 1963–4 season, was a political play written by a Slovak playwright Peter Karvas. Entitled *The Scar*, it was privately dedicated to the rehabilitated victim of Stalinist persecution Laco Novomesky. *The Scar* strongly attacked Stalinism, portraying a case of Stalinist persecution of an innocent but nonetheless still convinced communist. This form of protest theatre was imitated around the country in small, provincial theatres, youth theatres, and cabarets which most often presented their own critical, original productions or adaptations of older Czech and Slovak dramas. In Prague the 'Semafor,' 'Na Zabradli,' and 'Paravan,' became exceedingly popular not only for the engaging irreverence of their productions but also for their high level of artistic competence. Provincial party officials were in many cases taken aback by the phenomenon, unequipped to handle the sophisticated criticism and concerned lest their authority be questioned. For example, the district party officials of Usti Nad Orlici complained of the demoralizing effect such productions were having upon the workers and announced that they had barred a number of performers and productions for being 'ideologically and politically unsuitable under the conditions prevailing at the time.'[1] The indignant

---

[1] 'Standpoint of the Party Organization of the District of Usti Nad Orlici Concerning the Situation on the Cultural and Artistic Front,' *Zivot Strany*, 1 (1965), 13.

statement of the Usti Nad Orlici functionaries called for 'party firmness' and cadre action against the perpetrators of these 'insults' to the party and the workers.

At the same time that this form of political drama was getting under way, less political, artistically more adventuresome avant-garde dramas were performed, such as *The End of the Carnival* by Josef Topol and *The Garden Party* by Vaclav Havel, who together with director Jan Grossmann originated theatre of the absurd in Czechoslovakia. Theatre of the absurd represented a revolutionary and highly objectionable artistic trend from the point of view of the party, for even when devoid of political content it rejected, even defied, the dictates of socialist realism and generally concentrated on the problems of the individual and his alienation from society.

From the Czech avant-garde Vaclav Havel emerged as one of the most popular and talented playwrights in East Europe. His works *The Garden Party* and *The Memorandum* were produced throughout East and West Europe, receiving high praise from western critics. *The Memorandum*, which opened in Prague in 1965, caused a political and cultural stir because of its daring subject and style. It was the tale of an official who received a document in a new language for which he was not authorized to order a translation, and the political foibles of the unknown and constantly changing times. In his analysis of the depersonalization or alienation of man in the process of social and political adjustment, Havel presented a startlingly realistic (albeit through the medium of the 'absurd' methods) view of socialist society. One critic called *The Memorandum* 'a satirical picture in which the hyperbole of the vicious circle of organization and ideological somersaults is not an expression of pessimism but simply a warning.'[1] Another emphasized that 'no allegorical drama takes place here ... everything we see on the stage could happen in reality.'[2] The party tried to prevent the play's production, but succeeded only in delaying its opening.[3]

In response to these developments, Jiri Hendrych warned the Third Congress of the Union of Czechoslovak Theatrical and Film Artists that the party was dissatisfied with the weak ideological attitude of many dramatic artists. It objected to the

manner in which works from the West are sometimes presented without due discrimination in this country, works which attempt to suggest to the spectator the feeling of human helplessness, to

---

[1] *Vecerni Praha*, 28 July 1965. [2] *Lidove Demokracie*, 30 July 1965.
[3] *Frankfurter Allgemeine Zeitung*, 5 August 1965.

depict life and all human endeavor as nonsensical, to create a psychosis of skepticism and to convince the spectator that 'life is beyond the powers of man.' And what is more, there are some people who inculcate such views on the public in their own works.[1] Novotny described these developments as 'unhealthy,' with the purpose of injecting

doubts and distrust into the public ... they [various 'cultural actions'] ridicule our life with gross insinuations or various allusions, intentionally distorted examples combined with sneering remarks and unintelligible intellectual airs ... This also applies to various translations of older plays produced in Prague and Bratislava which are full of various symbolisms attacking the principles of socialist life.[2]

In January 1966 Czechoslovak audiences were startled by the adaptation and production of a passion play of the Czech baroque period, *A Comedy of the Crucifixion and Glorious Resurrection of Our Lord and Redeemer Jesus Christ*. While the Polish playwright Dejmek had already adapted and presented two passion plays in Poland, the production of passion plays had been banned in Czechoslovakia since 1948. Moreover, the performances, both in Prague and in Brno were extremely successful, being entirely booked weeks in advance.

In reply to a question, the producer Jan Kopecky found 'nothing surprising' about the fact that the passion play was attracting larger audiences in Brno than the local hockey team. Explaining his motives for producing such a play, he said: 'As a communist, I consider it my duty to look critically and seriously at the heritage of the thousand years of Christian culture. Father Frost is no solution! Only someone who pays mere lip service to the Marxist principle of a faithful and sober analysis of reality can close his eyes to a living problem.'[3]

The liberal Education and Culture Minister Cestmir Cisar apparently played some role in the liberalization which had occurred in the world of dramatic arts. In a report on the theatre, published just a few weeks before he was removed from the ministry, Cisar said that there was a need for new intellectual dynamism among playwrights, who 'only rarely deal with the "microworld" of modern man – which is full of conflicts that society and the social order reflect only indirectly in their

---

[1] *Rude Pravo*, 1 December 1965. Hendrych replaced Koucky as chairman of the ideology commission on 1 April 1965.

[2] *Rude Pravo*, 29 May 1964.

[3] Jan Kopecky, 'Conversation,' *Divadelni a Filmove Noviny*, IX:6 (1966), 10.

overall complexity.'[1] He lamented the fact that Czechoslovak audiences had to look to western playwrights for such themes. In a more practical vein, Cisar reported that actors and theatre personnel were unjustly paid less than the average industrial wage and that theatres were operating at a loss. Therefore the new economic system would be introduced in this area as well, i.e. theatres were to be 'more flexible' in determining ticket prices, based on production costs and the demand of the public, within price limits set by the government.

When the Union of Czechoslovak Theatrical and Film Artists held its congress towards the end of 1965, it drew heavily upon this report, concentrating on the more practical problems not yet settled in the course of the revitalization of the theatre. Among the more notable comments at the conference were those of Darek Vostrel, artistic director of the Rokoko Theatre, who in strong words called for a real union, willing to represent the interests of its members.[2] The congress endorsed the positive trends which had come into Czechoslovak theatre life, particularly the opening to the West and the creative adaptation of the 'impulses' found in western works, despite the warning delivered to the congress by Hendrych.

A major act at the congress was an official split into two independent unions: a Union of Theatrical Artists and a Union of Film and Television artists. The latter promptly elected as its chairman Martin Fric, director of Barrandow Studios, thereby endorsing the new path taken by the Barrandow Studios in film-making.

FILMS

Although Czechoslovak films came to rank with the finest produced anywhere, the ascent was by no means smooth, for the party often felt its tolerance abused or, at other times, believed that what could be used abroad for improving the regime's image in the West might not be suitable for domestic consumption. For their part the film producers, much like their colleagues in the theatre, strove for two things: the possibility of producing films on topics of their own choosing, devoid of propagandistic cliches and the educational–social action duties imposed upon them by socialist realism; and the opportunity to raise their

[1] *Kulturni Tvorba*, 28 October 1965.
[2] 'Congress of the Union of Czechoslovak Theatre and Film Artists,' *Divadelni a Filmove Noviny*, IX:8 (1965), 12. Hendrych's speech: *Rude Pravo*, 1 December 1965.

voice in criticism or protest. Where the avant-garde dramatists sought their vehicle to modernity in the theatre of the absurd, so Czechoslovak film-makers sought to imitate the 'new wave' of West European cinematography, with its negative heroes, themes of individual alienation, and inventive film techniques. One of the earliest successful ventures into protest films was *The Accused* by Jan Kadar and Elmar Klos, the story of wasteful hyprocrisy in officialdom (in this case of a factory). This film won first prize at the 1964 Karlovy Vary Film Festival. Another successful Czech film, which used satire for protest, was Jasny's *The Good Soul*, starring Jan Werich, which won a prize at the Cannes film festival in 1964. The new wave made its real debut in the western world in a highly successful Czechoslovak Film Week held in London from 31 May to 5 June 1965. The highlights of this 'Week' were *Joseph Kilian*, a Kafkaesque film by Juracek and Schmidt, and *The Shop on Main Street*, a non-political tale from the war, by Kadar and Klos, which went on to win numerous international prizes.

Subsequent films combined the 'new wave' technique with criticisms and/or satire, concentrating on present-day Czechoslovakia and becoming increasingly bolder in their absolute new-wave honesty. The best example was the work of Milos Forman, the director of *Peter and Pavla* and *Loves of a Blonde* which appeared in 1964 and 1965 respectively. In both pictures Forman treated the problem of the dissatisfaction and search for identity suffered by only ordinarily intelligent youngsters who find themselves in dull, soul-destroying jobs. He concentrated on their conflict and total lack of communication with the older generation, and their confused encounters with sex and the problem of the amoral attitude towards sex of the modern generation.

Both films were well received by the critics abroad but the same was not entirely the case in Czechoslovakia, at least not for *Loves of a Blonde*, which encountered serious difficulties with the regime. Forman's films were similar in spirit and technique to British film portrayals of working-class youths and families, with very little in them unique to the Czechoslovak scene. The regime, however, was far from accustomed to such a pessimistic, dreary (however humorous) picture of workers' lives. Nor was it accustomed to the free-handed, amoral treatment of sex, the frank, realistic portrayal of alienation demonstrated by the problem of the generations and the total failure at communication, nor to the preoccupation with personal problems devoid of positive political or social content. Evidence of the regime's efforts against the film came in the form of artists' defense of it against 'dogmatic criticism.' The presidium of the Film and Television Artists Union issued a 'Proclamation' on the film answering the film's detractors and defending the 'basic principles' of creative work and the 'very foundations of democratic existence' of citizens with differing views.[1] The Club of Czechoslovak Film Critics followed this up by awarding *Loves of a Blonde* second place to *The Shop on Main Street* for the Czechoslovak Film Critics Award. Nonetheless, the regime apparently was beginning an attempt to bring the Czechoslovak film-makers back within more tolerable bounds.

This affected in particular still a third stream in the Czechoslovak new wave: highly avant-garde, obscure, impressionistic films such as Jan Nemec's *The Celebration and the Guests*, Vera Chytilova's *Daisies*, and Nemec's *Martyrs of Love*. After its first showing Nemec's *The Celebration and the Guests* was immediately withdrawn, reportedly as a result of direct orders from Novotny himself.[2] *The Celebration and the Guests* caricatured contemporary society through a sequence of satirical, highly imaginative scenes much in the style of Fellini. After repeated demands and urgings the film was released under a new name, *Summer Festival*, for limited showings in what were known as cinemas for 'demanding audiences.' Though available for export, it was thus effectively banned in Czechoslovakia. Nemec's *Martyrs of Love* and Chytilova's *Daisies* suffered much the same fate, presumably because they too verged on the abstract and incomprehensible, using fantasy and impressionism familiar to western audiences of Fellini and Antonioni. The suppression of these films, and others, was part of a campaign to discourage the making of such highly intellectual ventures and to return cinematography to the level of mass entertainment. Novotny expressed his own view in October 1966 when he condemned the trend to depict 'the feeling of futility and mental turmoil which beset so-called modern man.' He criticized the use of 'doubtful "heroes" ' who 'often impertinently criticize everything around them [and] show their contempt for the past.'[3]

LITERATURE

As we have seen, the writers at the forefront of the intellectuals played

[1] *Literarni Noviny*, 26 February 1966.
[2] See A. Kratochvil, 'The Literary Scene in Czechoslovakia July–December, 1966,' RFE (1967). Novotny reportedly thought he was being satirized in the film.
[3] Novotny, *Zivot Strany*, 21 (1966), 4.

a larger role, mainly through the literary journals, in bringing about and guiding de-Stalinization than any other group in Czechoslovakia. One of the most important books to come out of this period, one which itself played a role in bringing about a real de-Stalinization, was Ladislav Mnacko's *Delayed Reportages*, published in Slovak in 1963. It was a series of dramatic sketches illustrating various aspects of life under Stalinism, its trials, hardships, and injustices. The party had for years prevented its publication, but on its appearance with the beginning of de-Stalinization the book became an immediate popular success.[1] Mnacko followed this up in 1966 with a still more controversial novel, *The Taste of Power*, which was stronger and more explicit in its critical portrayal of the Stalinist years. After difficulties with the censor the monthly *Plamen* published excerpts from the novel in two installments, but it reportedly aroused the anger and direct intervention of Novotny himself. Originally scheduled for 1967 publication by the Slovak Writers Union publishing house, the book ran into further difficulties, to be published, finally, only abroad – an event which brought disciplinary action against Mnacko.[2]

A second work which achieved prominence in 1963 was the novel *The Cowards* written by Josef Skvorecky. Skvorecky too had written his work some years before, but he had succeeded in having it published in 1958. At that time, however, it had been severely criticized by the party, confiscated, and banned. The story dealt with reactions among young Czechs living in a Bohemian village during the last week of the war. Most notable for its frank style and colorful language, *The Cowards* was not a directly political book in the sense that Mnacko's was, for it was concerned with the political world only insofar as that world impinged upon the more important human and personal considerations. Others who also wrote in this a-political vein were Trefulka (*Twenty-Three Silver Quails*) and Belohradska (*The Wind Blows Southeast*), who tended to concentrate on personal, moral problems.

There was also a group of young writers and poets who dealt with the generation conflict. This included Jan Benes (*As If Shooting Sparrows* and *Situation*) as well as Jaroslava Blazkova, Ivan Klima, Milan Uhde, Ales Haman, and Milan Kundera. The party considered the generation theme dangerous, bordering on an 'anti-state' viewpoint.[3] In addition

---

[1] In its first year the Slovak edition sold 100 000 copies in three printings. (*Smena*, 29 March 1966.)
[2] In 1968 it was finally published in Slovakia.
[3] See *Pravda* (Pilsen), 30 April 1964.

to political poetry such as Jiri Sotola's poem on Stalin, a 'new' poetry was appearing under the influence of the western 'beat' movement. Such young poets as the Slovak Jan Stacho were greatly influenced by the American poet Allen Ginsberg, for example, who visited Czechoslovakia for two months in 1965 until expelled by the regime for having an 'immoral influence on youth.'[1] Poetry reading clubs cropped up all over the country, and the cabaret Viola in Prague became a favorite place for beat-poetry readings (against a background of jazz). The critics generally confessed to total failure to understand these poets, but many argued for their right to express themselves and to try these new methods.[2]

The party's reaction to some of these developments was reflected in an article by Stepan Vlasin defending the social function of literature. Vlasin strongly criticized the purely personal, passive heroes and themes of western literature as distinct from the society-oriented literature that should be produced in a socialist society. Unfortunately, he claimed, one finds 'in some of our current writers' these very trends of 'bourgeois literature' which have 'stepped between reality and creation,' transferring all conflicts to the family and personal life, 'to the image of "naked" man removed from social connections.'[3]

A significant event for the de-Stalinization of literature occurred in late 1964 when the Academy of Sciences' Institute for Czech Literature succeeded in publishing the *Encyclopedia of Czech Writers*. It was published by the Czechoslovak Writers Union rather than the Academy of Sciences itself because of a controversy between liberals and dogmatists within the Academy which almost prevented publication entirely.[4] The *Encyclopedia* applied new criteria of literary criticism,

---

[1] *Rude Pravo*, 17 May 1965 (Novotny at Mnich).

[2] See *Kulturny Zivot*, 6 February 1965.

[3] Stepan Vlasin, 'The Social Function of Literature,' *Nova Mysl*, XVIII:11 (1964), 1352–3.

[4] Ladislav Stoll, the Institute's conservative director, was criticized by a younger member of the Institute Jiri Brabec. A polemic ensued, with the Czechoslovak Writers Union demanding greater freedom for CSAV staff. A still more serious dispute erupted over philosopher Ivan Svitak who was expelled from the CSAV Philosophy Institute – and the party – in 1964. One of the first victims of the regime's efforts to maintain controls on the liberalization, he publicized his case abroad (*Forum*, October 1965 and February 1966). The Institute's party group refused to expel Svitak when ordered to do so, as did the next higher party organ, so the party presidium itself had to take action. As a result, the Institute's party group was also more or less dissolved. Another early victim was Milan Huebl, dismissed the same year as pro-rector of the party higher school.

with the result that a continuous presentation of contemporary literature was finally possible. Political orientation was virtually absent while a purely aesthetic approach and analysis was attempted throughout. As a result, a number of writers were included in the *Encyclopedia* whose names had long been avoided because they were unacceptable to the party, suffered persecution or imprisonment at the hands of the communist regime, or left for the West after 1948.

The appearance of the *Encyclopedia* marked the beginning of a number of quiet rehabilitations in the literary world. Various literary journals followed the *Encyclopedia* with favorable comments on poets in exile, such as Egon Hostovsky, Jiri Voskovec, and Leopold Lahola, while the later-banned *Knizni Kultura* published an article by the formerly imprisoned Josef Palivec. In 1965 *Plamen* published an anthology of the works of poet Jan Zahradnicek, sentenced in 1952 along with fifteen other Czech writers to twelve years' imprisonment for alleged espionage on behalf of the Vatican and the United States. Some of the works of literary spiritualist Jaroslav Durych were reissued, while the historian–essayist Zavis Kalandra was once again mentioned favorably in literary works. Kalandra had been executed as a Trotskyite in 1950, but his rehabilitation was publicly called for in 1964 by Novomesky, himself only recently rehabilitated.[1] Official rehabilitation came for some writers in the summer of 1966 and January 1967 when the courts quashed or reversed the decisions of the 1950s. This official action did not, however, mean full rehabilitation, for most of the rehabilitated writers still living were not permitted to publish. Moreover, the quiet way in which the 'rehabilitation' took place contradicted the principle of rehabilitation, i.e. return of these persons to their rightful place in society and in the minds of the public.

As we have seen, Franz Kafka was one of the first Czech writers rehabilitated in the de-Stalinization campaign,[2] but his rehabilitation had repercussions beyond the borders of Czechoslovakia. Although most of the participants at Goldstuecker's May 1963 colloquium on Kafka agreed with the new, favorable interpretation of this problematic writer, this, together with other cultural–ideological developments in Czechoslovakia greatly disturbed the East German party. Horst Sindermann, a candidate member of the East German party politburo openly accused 'certain Czech artists' of trying to 'revise' Marxism–

[1] *Kulturny Zivot*, 18 July 1964.
[2] Karel Capek was also 'rehabilitated' by another Goldstuecker conference in September 1965.

Leninism, generating a number of exchanges and a good deal of ill-will between the two parties.[1]

Although there had been no Soviet representative at the Liblice colloquium, tacit approval of the rehabilitation of Kafka could be surmised from the publication of two of Kafka's stories in the January issue of the Soviet journal *Innostranaya Literatura*. This was followed, however, by the publication of a Soviet monograph on Kafka which, basically, expounded the conservative view of Kafka as a bourgeois.[2] Czech writers reacted strongly to what they considered a Soviet attempt to reimpose the dogmatic interpretation of Kafka, both in the pages of their own journals and at the International Conference on German Literature held in Prague in November 1965.[3]

A much more serious and politically dangerous dispute erupted between Czechoslovak writers and the Soviet Union over the trial of Soviet writers Sinyavsky and Daniel. Czechoslovak writers were concerned that the trial signified a return to Stalinist repression, and they feared the repercussions this could have on the Czechoslovak party and its still precarious de-Stalinization. The Writers Union presidium drafted a protest to the Soviets which it delivered through a delegation of three that went to Moscow on 15 March 1966. While the union never revealed the nature of the delegation's business and the regime denied the connection with the trial, the Italian Communist Party organ *L'Unita* reported that the delegation went to 'discuss' the trial with the Soviet writers union, as a result of a debate which had taken place in the Czechoslovak union.[4] This direct reaction of the Czechoslovak writers to the Sinyavsky–Daniel trial may have been designed to warn their own regime that it could not expect quiet acquiescence should it attempt to reintroduce such repressive measures in Czechoslovakia. The issue was all the more topical, for there had been rumors in Czechoslovakia that the Soviets were to revise their negative assessment of Stalin at their imminent party congress, and there was the feeling that Novotny intended to present measures of stricter control of the cultural world at the Czechoslovak party's own congress in May.

CONCLUSION

A great deal of progress was made in all the arts as cultural policy was

[1] SED central committee plenum, 3–7 February 1964; J. F. Brown, *The New Eastern Europe* (London, 1966), p. 154.
[2] D. V. Zatonskiy, *Franz Kafka and the Problem of Modernism* (Moscow, 1964).
[3] *Literarni Noviny*, 11 December 1965.   [4] *L'Unita*, 15 March 1966.

affected by de-Stalinization. Contacts with the West were augmented
in the fields of literature, theatre, and films, and controversial exhibits
of avant-garde art work began to appear, sometimes without party
approval.[1] Western jazz became so entrenched that the regime finally
gave it official blessing, inaugurating a bi-annual international jazz
festival in 1965. Nonetheless the party continuously urged caution and
vigilance with regard to the damage that could be caused by too wide
or speedy a liberalization of cultural policy. In setting the stage for its
Thirteenth Congress, the party 'Theses' repeated these warnings,
saying: 'We must take an unequivocal and irreconcilable stand against
all ideological currents alien to the class standpoint and hostile to
socialist ideology, against fashionable slogans of so-called "internationalism," ignoring the existence of two kinds of culture – reactionary and
progressive – in the capitalist world.'[2] And the party ideological journal
reminded its readers in January 1966 of an earlier warning from Hendrych: 'It is inadmissible for any institution of the socialist society and
state to offer a platform for ideologically hostile views.'[3] The congress
resolution on culture was, however, milder than expected, acknowledging the responsibility of publishers for the material published. Nonetheless, although the resolution spoke of 'autonomy' within the cultural
sphere, it qualified this with the words 'within the limits of the Party
line, with full Party and civic responsibility toward Party offices.'[4]
Novotny himself had harsh words for the writers (especially), but the
only action announced by the party in the cultural area was the preparation of a Press (censorship) Law.[5]

The party did, however, take another action in this sphere, designed
presumably to provide a warning example for dissident writers. The
young writer Jan Benes and a film–television student Karel Zamecnik
were arrested in August 1966. Benes was one of the outstanding young
writers of the current period of dissent and he had been involved in a
number of controversial issues, including the writers' protest against
the Sinyavsky–Daniel trial. He was accused of publishing in the
Paris-based Czech language journal *Svedectvi*.[6] The International Pen
Club and Amnesty International took up the case of the two intellec-

[1] For example the number of Western titles imported rose from 1774 in 1958 to
3351 in 1965. The number from communist countries dropped slightly. (*Rude
Pravo*, 19 January 1967.)
[2] *Rude Pravo*, 23 December 1965.
[3] 'Disquieting Trends,' *Zivot Strany*, 1 (1966), 16.
[4] *Rude Pravo*, 8 June 1966,   [5] See chapter 11 below.
[6] *Neue Zurcher Zeitung*, 7 October 1966. For details see chapter 17 below.

tuals but a certain fear persisted among Czechoslovak intellectuals that the regime was preparing a Czechoslovak copy of the Sinyavsky–Daniel affair to bring the cultural scene back under control. Indeed the action against these intellectuals did coincide more or less with a general crack-down in the form of a policy statement on the mass media and a strong speech by Novotny in the fall of 1966.[1]

[1] See *Rude Pravo*, 3 April 1964; Novotny, *Zivot Strany*, 21 (1966), 1–5.

11

MASS COMMUNICATIONS

The instruments of mass communications, radio, television, and the press also took an active part in the de-Stalinization process and underwent a transformation as a result of liberalization of cultural policy. As a consequence of the demands for more prompt, thorough, and truthful reporting, changes began to appear in the public media. Both the radio and television began to organize live panel discussions marked by relative frankness and straightforward criticism, to broadcast letters from discontented listeners, satirical entertainment, and slightly more independent commentaries. The effectiveness of these programs was attested to by Novotny's adverse reaction to them, for in May 1964 he sharply attacked

> certain programs of the radio and television which have been subjected to justified criticism at district and regional conferences. True, a great deal has changed for the better on radio and television, and recently a whole number of artistic programs and newscasts have been well regarded ... [but] certain shows and satirical programs as well as commentaries and their supercilious attitude towards the work of the National Committee functionaries, economic workers, and cooperative farmers have called forth resolute protests from party members and working people.[1]

RADIO

Aware that much of the liberals' criticism of radio programming was justified, the party, in 1965 conducted a revaluation of the communications media. On the basis of a plan approved by the central committee in 1960 (but never implemented) and a new report which reflected some of the liberals' demands, a reorganization of broadcasting was undertaken. Among other things a 'new system of editorials' was introduced, the number of news programs was raised, and several news commentary and discussion programs were added. The party also decided on the following list of priorities: introduction of regular programs in which listeners' letters would be discussed and answered; programs explaining the new economic program; more entertainment

[1] *Rude Pravo*, 29 May 1964.

and musical programs; audience research; distribution of programs to provide everyone with the opportunity to hear the more interesting broadcasts.[1]

By 1965, even without the party's plan for reform, significant changes were already established in the character of radio broadcasting. News and political programs on foreign affairs or events demonstrated a new flexibility, objectivity and promptness. In some cases these programs even took a line independent from Moscow or provided more details than TASS. Karel Kyncl, the radio's New York correspondent even presented occasionally favorable analyses on the Kennedy administration and U.S. aid to underdeveloped countries.

The former uncritical admiration of the Soviet Union began to disappear. Whereas in 1960 an editor of a provincial daily was dismissed for having placed a report on a Soviet space venture on the second page, in 1965 a report from CTK in Moscow actually admitted that all the planned operations of a Soviet space venture (Luna 7) had *not* been successful.[2] At another time Prague quoted a Soviet citizen criticizing the production of automobiles in the Soviet Union and the poor state of Soviet highways.[3] The radio correspondent in Moscow, Jan Petranek, greatly contributed to this new type of reporting on the USSR. Acknowledging this change in policy and admitting its necessity, a Prague youth program read a young worker's letter which criticized Czechoslovak propaganda for uncritical bias, lack of objectivity, distortion of facts, and misleading the public by such things as reporting little of American successes and exaggerating American failures while doing just the opposite regarding the Soviet Union. The editor of the program admitted that it was not easy to reply to this letter, for 'a few years ago our propaganda really was aimed at trying to suppress success of western science under the slogan of "Everything was invented in Russia." ' He then cautiously tried to deny the current accuracy of the listener's charges by citing examples of recent reporting of Soviet failures.[4] In a similar vein, Bratislava radio carried a broadcast criticizing the automatic copying of the USSR in Czechoslovakia, explaining that in the past the slightest critical comment could lead to accusations of anti-socialist attitude or revisionism.[5]

More time was devoted to frank comments on or discussions of

---

[1] 'On the Activity and Current Problems of Czechoslovak Radio,' *Zivot Strany*, 5 (1965), 282–6.
[2] Prague radio, 6 October 1965.   [3] Prague radio, 14 August 1965.
[4] Prague radio, 9 December 1965.   [5] Bratislava radio, 10 December 1965.

domestic matters in which shortcomings, especially of the economy, were often admitted. This was one of the improvements prompted in part by the competition of western radio stations, for the population had often heard of internal Czechoslovak events, tragedies, or developments over the waves of foreign stations because of the regime's severe limitations on information. In conjunction with the new economic system, western economic systems often were referred to favorably, specifically the American marketing system, business administration, and training institutions. Live broadcasts of discussions with government and party officials were introduced. On one such program Premier Lenart spoke with young people in Nitra and was compelled to answer such questions as why is the quality of goods available locally lower than that exported? Why doesn't the government lower automobile prices? Why were some decisions implemented so slowly?[1] Formerly such discussions had been planned carefully, preventing the possibility of such questions arising on the air.

The level of cultural programs was also raised and experts were invited to speak openly, regardless of their background or cadre profile. For example, Eduard Goldstuecker spoke frankly on the suppression of the outstanding Czech writer Karel Capek, saying 'Our intellectual heritage does not consist of material postulates alone; ethical and moral aspects cannot be exempted and they are as important as the material ones. We must not be surprised and morally indignant when our own children present to us a bill for the past.'[2]

Bolder still were the comments of another formerly persecuted expert, Dr Robert Konecny. He prepared a program in which various attitudes of young people were discussed, attesting to the rejection of state and party authority by the youth. One participant was broadcast as saying: 'An ill-considered forcing of authority on young people leads to a negative attitude; if it assumes a permanent character the young people begin to reject authority altogether. Whatever manner of talk you adopt, they will simply reject any state, party, social authority; authority for them does not exist.' Konecny himself closed the program with the statement: 'We must not let ourselves be lulled by what we used to say several years ago, namely that with the change of the economic conditions man will change and a new man will grow. It

---

[1] Bratislava radio, 20 November 1965. See also Prague radio, 13 January 1966.
[2] Prague radio, 12 August 1965, cited in A. Kratochvil, 'The New Look in Czechoslovak Radio,' RFE (1965), 9.

simply is not true. We just do not have a man, and what we want is to have one.'[1]

The radio also sought to appeal to the youth directly and to compete with the highly popular western broadcasts beamed to young people. Thus in 1965 it introduced the program 'Microforum,' geared to young listeners. The CSM monthly carried the following reaction to the new program:

When we heard about the program under preparation for youth, we laughed heartily. We said to ourselves 'a new competition for Radio Free Europe, and a Czech competition at that.' We could presume what it would be like. However, after we listened to the first 'Microforum' programs we were happy to be able to conclude that we had been wrong this time.[2]

In 1966 the standard of broadcasting continued to rise, still greater diversification was introduced, and more programs in Slovak were added. Western-style 'magazine programming' was introduced which alternated topics of the day with music. Questions of aesthetics, philosophy, sociology, and economics were frequently discussed, whereas such topics had formerly been avoided. These even included a bold revelation by a party historian of disunity and disputes within the party over de-Stalinization in 1956. With the beginning of 1967 came an innovation in Czechoslovak radio which went beyond mere 'improved programing,' a VHF series entitled 'Club of Committed Thinking.' This was to be an open club of listeners, intended for the intelligentsia and designed to air questions of interest to such a group. The program was sponsored by the Czechoslovak Socialist Academy, but the contributions demonstrated a decided freedom and absence of party supervision (or at least of conservative supervision). Personalities from the academic and cultural sphere were invited to speak on such topics as political courage, Benes, Masaryk, Czechoslovak participation in the western World War II effort, and so forth. These talks were frank and attracted a great deal of attention, according to the radio itself.

The party by no means gave up or lost all control over the radio. On issues of particular importance to the regime the firm hand of the party could still be felt. Thus Prague radio failed to announce the October 1965 visit of Soviet party first secretary Brezhnev until the day of his

---

[1] Brno radio, 24 November 1965.
[2] Marta Horakova *et al.*, 'It Can Be Tuned in but it Can Also Be Turned Off,' *My 65*, II:11 (1965), 63–4.

departure for home – a demonstration of information suppression which tended to remind one that de-Stalinization did not mean elimination of all restraints or controls.[1] Probably in an effort to reassert its control, the regime named Milos Marko chief of Czechoslovak radio in February 1967, replacing Karel Hoffmann who had become Culture and Information Minister. The change in itself did not, however, cause any significant changes in the direction the radio had already taken.

TELEVISION

Television reaches fewer people in Czechoslovakia than does radio, but together the media occupied one and one-half to three hours of the average Czechoslovak citizen's day.[2] The changes which characterized radio broadcasting with the advent of de-Stalinization were equally perceivable in television transmitting, with greater independence and boldness particularly in telecasting from Slovakia. Unable successfully to compete with foreign telecasts, specifically those from Austria and West Germany, Czechoslovak television began buying programs from the West and producing some programs or tele-films in cooperation with other countries. Director of Czechoslovak television Jiri Pelikan explained that 'Euro-Vision can supply us with topical, prompt, and high quality news coverage while Inter-Vision [the East European television association], on the contrary, is able to give us only stale, low-quality material once a week.'[3] In 1964 the regime established an export agency for television films, Telexport, which within its first four months had contracted to make four co-productions with West German television studios and one with Austrian studios.[4] In this type of venture Czechoslovakia was the most active of the East European countries. At talks between officials of Euro-Vision and Inter-Vision in Prague in January 1966 it was agreed that exchanges of news and documentary programs would be encouraged provided 'all remnants of the cold war' could be avoided.[5] With Austria, Czechoslovakia also engaged in exchanges of artists and experts for live discussion programs – some of which were not always as innocuous or non-political as the regime would have them.

Czechoslovak television also began buying programs from the

[1] Prague radio, 17 October 1965; Kratochvil, RFE (1965), 5.
[2] Rosemary Kavanova, 'The Mass Media Man,' *Czechoslovak Life*, 2 (1967), 6.
[3] Bratislava radio, 14 March 1965.   [4] *Vecerni Praha*, 12 March 1965.
[5] 'Current Developments,' *East Europe*, XIII:8 (1965), 43.

United States. In 1965 and early 1966 Czechoslovak viewers could regularly watch such comedians as Jackie Gleason and Dick Shawn or such classics as the 'Dinah Shore Show' and 'Dr Kildare' plus the detective series '97th Precinct' or nature series 'Wild Kingdom.' The network also bought American television specials on the French Revolution, 'Mark Twain's America,' and 'An Essay on Bridges,' as well as old American movies.

Czechoslovak television, like the radio, established an audience research department. The regime knew, however, that the only way to counter the population's interest in western propaganda and normal television offerings was to improve the quality of home production and to purchase those foreign telecasts of which they approved. Thus it would have some 'control' over the fare offered viewers from foreign sources. The regime by no means, however, gave Czechoslovak television an entirely free hand any more than it did in any other field. The censors suppressed, for example, a New Year's Eve transmission almost at the very last minute on 31 December 1964,[1] and the following month the party ideology commission met to discuss radio and television, issuing a resolution critical of both. Television was specifically attacked for a wrong ideological orientation which was said to be impairing its overall positive effect. Its shortcomings included an 'uncritical, ingratiating attitude' towards youth, political errors and wavering, and 'abstractly conceived notions of "courage," "conscience," "humanity," and "truth" which do not contribute to a healthy development of society,' as well as a tendency to negate creative work of the past and uncritically adopt 'alien fashionable trends and models.' The party approved of the purchase of news films from Euro-Vision but demanded that up-to-date ones be procured from the USSR and the bloc as well.[2]

Despite the party's efforts to control the medium, television continued to improve, introducing a wide range of frank documentaries, relatively bold political commentaries (in which the official hand-outs were largely ignored[3]) and lively discussion shows. By 1966 Prague television became a significant forum for certain controversial views,

[1] Jiri Lederer, 'Let's Abolish New Year's Eve,' *Plamen*, 7:3 (1965), 169–70; 'The Censor Swallowed Up *Literarni Noviny*, 1, 1965,' *Svedectvi*, VII:25–6 (1965), 16.

[2] *Rude Pravo*, 19 January 1965; 'On the Activity and Problems of Radio,' *Zivot Strany*, 5 (1965), 282–6 and 'On the State, Activity and Tasks of Czechoslovak Television,' *Zivot Strany*, 5 (1965), 287–91.

[3] *Svoboda, The Press in Czechoslovakia, 1968* (Zurich, 1970), 43.

such as those telecast on the programs 'The Inquisitive Camera,' 'Face to Face,' and the discussion series introduced in the fall of 1966, 'Public Affairs.'[1]

THE PRESS

Of all the mass media the regime was most disturbed by the press, specifically the specialized press and journals. These served as a platform for the intellectuals and liberals, spearheading and continuously exploiting as well as fighting for the continuation of de-Stalinization. It was on the issue of the journals and the press that the regime most often came into conflict with the liberals, who not only struck back through this medium but also continued to publish in just the vein so often criticized by the regime. Moreover, as the press became more lively, its readership grew and with this its influence.

At the close of 1963 the party gave serious consideration to the problem which the press and journals presented for the continued orderly rule of the relatively stabilized leadership. At its December central committee plenum it worked out a policy statement on the press, published in the party organs in April 1964. It was most likely intended as the 'final word' on the matter, for it clearly, meticulously, and in minute detail enumerated the party's complaints and demands.[2] It stated that editors had a grave responsibility given the fact that cultural periodicals were 'instruments of the ideological influence of the party on a relatively broad strata of readers ... the broader the orientation of these periodicals, the greater the responsibility.' This was notice to such cultural journals as *Kulturny Zivot*, *Kulturni Tvorba*, and *Literarni Noviny*, specifically mentioned as being published in 278 000 copies, that if they wanted to broaden their content to include political matters they would have to bear the broadened responsibility. The party pointed out that 'there are political errors and ideological confusions which indicate that the requirements of the new tasks and the political responsibility of publishing activities which take the initiative in a socialist society are not sufficiently respected.' Attributing the problem to 'a narrow concept of the struggle against dogmatism,' the party explained that it

cannot consider it normal when cultural periodicals assume the role of autonomous interpreters of the political line of the party – especially when they concentrate their attention on important

Ibid. 41–4.   [2] *Rude Pravo*, 3 April 1964.

problems concerning the internal affairs of the party, with regard to which the highest party organs have taken a clear stand – and then carry on polemics with the approach of the party and with the interpretation of such problems in party documents.

The party cited a long list of articles which it considered revisionistic and in which the authors, according to the party document, rejected Marx, the class struggle, and all conflict with bourgeois ideology, elevating 'human problems' above all else. Thus cited were articles by Karel Minarik, Eugen Loebl, Vladimir Blazek, and Ivan Svitak, published in *Kulturny Zivot* and *Plamen*. Admitting that total unity of opinion would be impossible to achieve and would lead to formalism, the party reasoned that, nonetheless, this was no reason

> to give up efforts to establish uniform views and joint procedures on the basis of ideological unity conceived in the Leninist spirit. For that reason we cannot approve unrestrained discussions which not only are not oriented to unity ... but usually lead to a distraction of values without taking in consideration the level of the readers.

Other points upon which the article found the journals at fault were their distrust of the party, and their position on modern art and theatre, especially their 'intentional failure' to consider the ideological content or value of a work under review. While the party 'understood' the need for and was willing to encourage exchanges with 'progressive' artists in the West, it was disturbed by the fact that 'while the volume of information about culture in capitalist countries increases, the volume of information about Soviet culture is decreasing' or, if covered, presented one-sidedly. By way of example, the party document cited an interview of Hungarian Marxist philosopher Georgy Lukacs which had appeared without any explanation that Lukacs was a revisionist whose views were rejected by the Hungarian party.[1]

The party concluded on the basis of the foregoing, that 'individual interventions [censorship] directed against specific articles are necessary.' Such was the case for example, when the party 'had to influence from outside' in order to suppress a caricature *Plamen* was planning to publish which 'grossly disparaged' the state emblem. Another such example was an article *Tvar* wanted to publish which sought to 'misuse the name of an outstanding' poet and attributed to 'this honest comrade, the nonsensical and dirty bubbling of Ivan Svitak,' himself 'hiding

---

[1] Reference was to *Literarni Noviny*, 18 January 1964.

behind a pseudonym.' The party believed that the editorial boards, or certainly the party members who sat on them, should undertake such censorship rather than force the party to act from outside. Attacking Slovak communist intellectuals, in particular, the party document went so far as to admit that the cultural department of the Slovak party itself had demonstrated a 'lack of consistent and systematic approach to conceptual work.'

The party document left barely one journal or cultural institution unscathed. It did not, however, have the total effect the party intended and, although as already noted something of a slow-down did occur in the pace of criticism, most of the journals continued to publish outspoken pieces. *Kulturny Zivot*, the most vituperatively attacked journal, answered straightforwardly: 'Nothing would have been more convenient but also more irresponsible and immoral than to accept the critique with penitence and especially to accept it formally as it used to be done in similar cases in the past [when] sectarian methods prevailed in the management of the cultural front.'[1] Invoking Khrushchev, the editors concluded that they had become accustomed to 'criticizing and criticizing sharply,' and that they had no intention of burning 'two candles ... we prefer to burn our fingers by dealing with serious ideological problems.' This courageous rebuff set off a polemic between the journal and the party which ended with the accusation that the editors of *Kulturny Zivot* were succumbing to views of 'liberalistic anarchism' and 'find sustenance in a feeling of megalomania.'[2] A similar polemic followed a few months later between the *Literarni Noviny* editors and *Rude Pravo* on the topic of a proper interpretation of recent history and the behavior of certain communist artists. This polemic ended on the derisive comment in *Rude Pravo* that in the eyes of *Literarni Noviny* 'the responsibility of the individual was reduced to the sphere of personal ethics and pitted against the conditions of the time.'[3]

A debate of a different kind appeared later in the cultural press in which direct anti-communist views were actually printed. The occasion was the Mnacko–Hochhuth dialogue, prompted by Hochhuth's refusal to have his play *The Deputy* produced in Czechoslovakia and Mnacko's response that West Germany had published a distorted version of his book *Delayed Reportages*. The dialogue, on the topic of 'fundamental cultural and political questions between the East and

[1] *Kulturny Zivot*, 1 May 1964.   [2] *Bratislava Pravda*, 15 May 1964.
[3] *Rude Pravo*, 28 November 1964.

West' or, as Hochhuth defined it, 'the ability and freedom to revolt,' became a debate when joined by philosopher Miroslav Kusy and economist Eugen Loebl. The latter supported a number of Hochhuth's views (printed in *Kulturny Zivot*), arguing against blind partisanship. He also attacked, however, the tendency of placing all the blame on one individual, be it the Pope or Stalin.[1]

Despite these positive signs of a vigorous press, the party was still attempting to suppress certain articles and to restrain the journals. A certain loss of vigor could be noted in the summer of 1965, as attested to by the June 1965 Writers Conference and numerous articles (though many outspoken articles continued to appear). Juraj Spitzer, editor of *Kulturny Zivot*, subtly tried to explain that the party was clamping down. In answer to readers' questions on the difference between the intellectual climate of 1964 and that of 1965, Spitzer said that the years 1963 and 1964 had been very important 'for our whole life' but as for 1965 he quoted Russian poet Mayakovsky, ' "For the pen this is not an easy time." '[2] He implied that dogmatists were trying to restrain the press on the basis of the theory that all the negative aspects of Czechoslovak society had been done away with and were long since things of the past.

Spitzer's pessimism was soon borne out, for the party shifted from quiet censorship and exhortation to persecution and suppression. In the fall of 1965 the young writers' journal *Tvar* began to come under heavy criticism, and by the end of the year it and another journal, *Knizni Kultura*, edited by the liberal deputy Education and Culture Minister Josef Grohmann, were dissolved.[3] *Tvar* was attacked and termed anti-Marxist because of its criticism of Stalinist writers and its defense of persecuted writers and suppressed non-communist journals. It was also accused of exhibiting Catholic and spiritualist trends. This last was probably due to *Tvar's* publication of pieces by formerly persecuted writers such as Zahradnicek and Jaroslav Durych, as well as articles on such Christian thinkers as Josef Florian and Romano Guardini. *Prace* summed up the accusations against the journal with an article entitled 'Heidigger and Jaspers, the Spirit of Existentialism and Mysticism, on the Ginsberg Fashion, on the Literature of the Naked Man' which

---

[1] See *Kulturny Zivot*, 2 January, 12 February, and 19 March 1965.
[2] *Kulturny Zivot*, 2 July 1965.
[3] *Tvar* had been the heir to the liberal journal *Kveten*, suppressed in 1959. In its most liberal period *Kveten* had been edited by Jiri Sotola, a fact which *may* lie behind Sotola's criticism of *Tvar*.

claimed that *Tvar* used all the above to replace the revolutionary values which had been responsible for the '1948 victory.'[1]

The secretary of the Brno section of the Writers Union, Jan Trefulka, came to the defense of *Tvar*. He wrote that it was 'abnormal that magazines and authors who have a somewhat different view of an artistic work and its role in society from the Marxist one (in the narrow or outdated sense), or who adopt a non-Marxist point of view, are constantly threatened by strict reprisals.'[2] No defense was to any avail, however; *Tvar* had apparently stepped beyond the bounds of what the party was willing to tolerate, and the liberal intellectuals – divided among themselves over the issue – could not save it. According to a decision of the Czechoslovak Writers Union central committee, the publication of *Tvar* was to be shifted on 1 January 1966 from the union's press to its publishing house, at the time under conservative leadership. This move implied closer supervision and carried with it demands (from the party) for a change in the editorial board, ostensibly to cope with the journal's deficit. These conditions were refused by *Tvar*'s staff, causing, finally, the dissolution of the journal.

A new journal was to be created for young writers, but Jiri Lopatka, Vaclav Havel, and Jan Benes – all former editors of *Tvar* – had resigned from the union's youth commission in protest to the commission's approval of the new periodical.[3] An 'obituary' for *Tvar* was written by Jan Trefulka in which the closure was called a 'questionable' move politically and an 'abnormality' in the cultural scene reminiscent of the past.[4] Indeed reminiscent of the past, Jan Nedved, editor-in-chief of *Tvar*, was expelled from the party and severely criticized. Accusing him of disregarding the recommendations of 'higher party agencies,' *Zivot Strany* said that Nedved and his colleagues had 'radically changed the line, mission, and contents [of *Tvar*] in direct conflict with the interests of our socialist society.' *Tvar* thereby became 'the disseminator and propagator of bourgeois philosophies of various dubious idealistically mystically shaded trends.' Nedved, it was claimed, 'wanted to remain a party member but on the other hand he also wanted complete "freedom" permitting him to act and decide as

---

[1] *Prace*, 17 October 1965. For other criticism, see also: *Rude Pravo*, 5 and 6 October 1965; *Literarni Noviny*, 4 September 1965; *Plamen* 7:9 (1965); *Nova Mysl*, xix:12 (1965).
[2] *Literarni Noviny*, 16 October 1965. [3] See *Literarni Noviny*, 1 January 1966.
[4] *Ibid.*

he saw fit against the political line of the party.'[1] This the party could not – and did not – tolerate.

The closure in December 1965 of *Knizni Kultura* was a great deal less spectacular, mainly because this monthly of the Czechoslovak Center of Book Culture was in itself less spectacular. It was a journal of high literary standard but its flaw apparently was that it published too much literature written by formerly imprisoned or persecuted writers. Some observers believed that *Knizni Kultura* was merely a casualty of a struggle between party central committee ideology department chief Pavel Auersperg and deputy Education and Culture Minister Josef Grohmann who edited the journal. Grohmann was a liberal and had been brought into the ministry to head its literary department by Cisar, who had been dismissed from his position as minister in November 1965. Given the fact that the party was seeking a way effectively to control the cultural life of the country, it is possible that the personnel changes it made in 1965 – the appointment of Auersperg in place of Jaroslav Hes in January 1965, the appointment of United Nations delegation chief Jiri Hajek in place of Cisar in November, and the resumption of responsibility for ideology matters by Jiri Hendrych effected by his replacement of Vladimir Koucky as ideology commission chief in April 1965 – did have something to do with the decidedly stricter or more drastic measures applied.

Several new journals were created, two of which were to replace the suppressed journals, and they began to make their appearances in the first half of 1966. *Sesity pro Mladou Literaturu*, designed to replace *Tvar*, turned out to be a liberal if not radical journal, while *Impuls*, designed to replace *Knizni Kultura*, was a loyal mirror of its dogmatist editor Josef Burianek. Another new monthly of literary criticism, *Orientace*, appeared in mid-April, edited by liberal Milan Schulz; it generally abided by its declared policy of selecting works with an eye towards presenting differing viewpoints, guided 'by the simple fact, which is often overlooked, that literary works must be judged as works of art.'[2]

Still another periodical, though not a new one, began to reappear in late 1965. This was the weekly of the Slovak party central committee,

[1] Vaclav Uhlir, 'According to Leninist Principles,' *Zivot Strany*, 8 (1966), 17. Probably as a result of the *Tvar* affair, playwright Vaclav Havel was denied permission to attend the June 1966 PEN congress in New York. (*Literarni Noviny*, 9 July 1966.)

[2] 'Editorial,' *Orientace*, 1:1 (1966) 1.

Predvoj, created in 1957 but discontinued in 1963. Its reappearance in July 1965 was interpreted by some as an attempt by the regime to create a counterbalance in Slovakia to the outspoken *Kulturny Zivot*.[1] Although often critical of *Kulturny Zivot*, *Predvoj* was a lively journal which could not be characterized as dogmatic, at least not until the dogmatist Milan Lajciak became editor-in-chief in 1967.

The party did not, however, limit its efforts to the destruction and construction of journals, of dubious value given the persistence of the liberals. In 1965 and the first months of 1966 every literary journal, with the exception of those in Slovakia, underwent changes in its editorial boards. Most drastically affected by these changes was *Literarni Noviny*, which had become a particular strain on the party's patience. At its March 1966 committee plenum the Czechoslovak Writers Union agreed to place the control of its weekly under an editorial council to be chaired by conservative Bohuslav Brezovsky while the paper's editor Milan Jungmann would remain chief editor, subordinate to the council and responsible for the editorial offices. An investigation was to be undertaken into *Literarni Noviny*'s political writing, and a decision then would be taken on necessary changes, specifically of a personnel nature. Explaining this move, party presidium candidate Martin Vaculik (who was increasingly abandoning his earlier liberal positions) criticized the journal for printing articles by 'irresponsible' writers and journalists and said that the union had drawn the proper conclusions from this unsatisfactory situation and had effected a change 'in the system of direction' as well as personnel changes in the editorial board.[2] It was soon announced that the journal would be run by a triumvirate editorial board chaired by Brezovsky. His colleagues, however, were to be the reformed Stalinist Jan Otcenasek, and the liberal Milan Kundera.[3]

It would appear from the unusual combination of individuals made responsible for *Literarni Noviny*, in addition to the demotion of Jungmann, that the party was trying to tighten controls somewhat before the party congress due in May without, however, provoking the writers to outright defiance. Such a policy could be detected in editorials in *Zivot Strany*, such as one that criticized the cultural press

[1] *Reporter*, 15 May 1968.
[2] *Rude Pravo*, 27 March 1966. See chapter 19 below. His 'vacillation,' not a-typical of the party elite, continued even into 1969.
[3] The leading positions on this board were changed several times in the following months until the drastic stages of 1967 (see chapter 17 below).

for its 'biased' interpretation of the relation between human values and the class struggle, the lack of a clear Marxist concept of culture, its attempt to place art outside the influence of the party and ideology, and decreasing interest in a socialist culture. This editorial cited the April 1965 plenum of the party central committee which 'emphasized that our public is misled by articles describing life in western countries uncritically and repeating half-truths, often with an ill-concealed dislike of our socialist reality ... some of these tirades read like a well-paid advertisement for the western way of life.'[1] According to *Zivot Strany*, this even applied to such issues of international affairs as the Dominican Republic and South-east Asia. The editorial ended with a call for vigilance and communist partisanship, along with a democratic, critical attitude. The other side of this hard line was what slowly emerged as the party's new policy. Whether willing or unwilling to continue the albeit milder administrative measures of the more recent past, the party seemed to recognize that these methods had only a limited degree of efficacy, creating martyrs of 'revisionists' and supplying ammunition for the barrages of the liberals. The new tactic was first revealed by Hendrych in the same speech in which he warned the intellectuals not to deviate from the party line. He urged members of the Union of Theatrical and Film Artists to police themselves, to participate more in the activities of their union, and to intervene on attempts to publish views hostile to the party.[2]

The 'Theses' prepared for the party congress formally stated this line, revealing the party's basic attitude towards the communications media. It said that

the press, radio, and television must provide better help for developing a socialist way of thinking and for overcoming negative ideological–political influences ... each journalist must always bear in mind the social effect of the press, radio, and television ...

It is up to the journalists and in particular the communists in the press not to allow an abuse of the party and all society.[3]

The party congress passed a resolution adopting this policy of self-policing, presumably as a substitute for the now discredited 'administrative methods' of old.

Explaining it in a perhaps more palatable manner for the intellectuals, Jiri Hajek of *Plamen* tried to distinguish between 'liberalization,' which he defined as an attempt to 'equalize' the rights of opposition

---

[1] 'Disquieting Trends,' *Zivot Strany*, 1 (1966), 16–17.
[2] *Rude Pravo*, 1 December 1965.   [3] *Rude Pravo*, 23 December 1965.

and to permit varied opinions, and 'democratization,' which he defined as 'autonomy of culture' in which the artists would police themselves. It was not, therefore, a question of whether art should be guided by an 'official line,' for 'the active participation of communist writers and cultural workers in the forming of the party's cultural policy would diminish the necessity of direct administrative measures and simultaneously would expand the party's influence on culture.'[1] This 'active participation' was to be conducted through the mechanism of the artists' unions and social organizations.

The congress of the Slovak party reiterated this line but defended the intellectuals' rights to concern themselves with political affairs. The Slovak party declared its total rejection of the principle of administrative methods in favor of the policy of persuasion which called upon communists in their individual places of work to uphold and further the party's policies.[2] This policy conformed with the de-centralization of controls apparent in almost all the reforms of the period; its reaffirmation by the Slovaks and at the party's Thirteenth Congress was therefore not surprising. The long-awaited and to some degree feared resolution on ideological–cultural matters actually renounced direct intervention by the party in cultural affairs, assuring leading cultural workers autonomy, coupled, however, with responsibility to the party.[3]

Although liberal theory had prevailed, the whole idea of 'self-policing' or autonomy coupled with responsibility to the party was vague; its efficacy was wholly dependent upon the spirit with which it would be implemented. Indications that this 'spirit' would not be favorable to the liberals came with the presidium documents 'On Topical Questions of the Press and Other Mass Media of Ideological Activity' and with Novotny's hard-line speech to the October 1966 central committee plenum. The party criticized the 'bias of some radio and television programs' as well as shortcomings in the entire cultural sphere 'particularly in the cultural periodicals and in cultural journals in general.' These areas were charged with 'inconsistency' and 'narrow-mindedness' and 'the underestimation of the ideological struggle.' The party document clearly stated not only that 'all the shortcomings of the preceding years are far from eradicated' but also that 'particularly of late, some new shortcomings have begun to make themselves felt.' It closed with a warning that stronger measures would be taken against

[1] *Rude Pravo*, 1 April 1966.
[2] *Bratislava Pravda*, 13–15 May 1966 (see Dubcek, Bilak, and Mihalik speeches).
[3] *Rude Pravo*, 8 June 1966.

dissident party intellectuals, 'including cadre measures' against party members in the cultural sphere who continued to disregard 'frank critical warnings.'[1] Exactly what would constitute non-fulfillment of the party member/cultural worker's task remained unrevealed, perhaps as yet undecided.

The intellectuals had long been aware of the vulnerability of their achievements, and had sought some form of codification of their gains. They had hoped that by clearly defining in law the rights and duties of the censor, they could fix recognized limits for that body, by making it answerable to a court of law. Such a law would be a return in part to the pre-1948 situation in which the rule of law provided for the correction of false news, for the final responsibility of the editor, and for the right of the latter to withhold information on his sources. This law was abrogated after 1948 since which time censorship had been subject only to the will of the party.

At the Thirteenth Party Congress Novotny announced that there would indeed be a law on censorship, and in October 1966 this law was approved by the National Assembly, to be effective 1 January 1967.[2] The law was not, however what the intellectuals had hoped for, as most of their recommendations had been rejected in the regime's efforts to maintain and reassert its control of the cultural and mass media. On the negative side, the Press Law provided for a Central Administration for Publication (censor) which had the right to *prevent* publication of anything it considered a state, economic, or official secret. The censor was also to protect 'other interests of society,' defined as material the publication of which would violate the law, was 'biased against the policies and ideological line of the state' or material the publication of which would 'harm the interests of society as a whole.'[3] In regard to such material, however, the censor could not prevent or forbid publication; it was authorized merely to 'draw [*sic*] the attention of editor-in-chief, publisher, organizer or performer to the fact if any material which he intends to publish or otherwise disseminate is in conflict with other interests of society.'[4] Thus, technically, there was no pre-publication censorship on the grounds of harming the interests of society. The party presidium, however, issued a directive in August 1966 which placed this category too under pre-publication censorship.[5] On the

---

[1] 'On Topical Questions of Party Guidance of the Press and other Mass Media of Ideological Activity,' *Zivot Strany*, 18 (1966), 1–4.
[2] *Sbirka Zakonu* No. 8/1966.   [3] *Sbirka Zakonu* Decree No. 119/1966, Section 5.
[4] *Ibid*. Section 8.   [5] *Mlada Fronta*, 6 March 1968.

plus side – and this perhaps was the most important aspect of the law – the censor ruling preventing dissemination could be challenged in a regional court by the editor-in-chief, publisher, organizer or performer involved. The courts might also be the final judge of whether or not the publishing of specific material had constituted a criminal offense. According to the law, however, it was sufficient for the editor-in-chief or other so-accused official, in order to be cleared, to prove that at the time of publication he was justified in believing his report to be true. Moreover, in what represented a return to pre-1948 regulations, the editor or accused need not reveal his sources. The media were charged with the task of providing the public with complete and up-to-date information, i.e. they had the right to seek and receive prompt and thorough information.

The Press Law did indeed achieve legal protection against arbitrary, ill-defined and immutable censorship, and it did permit a certain degree of responsibility for the media themselves. This was in keeping with the self-policing method which gradually emerged as the party's policy. Nonetheless, the self-policing method had its drawbacks as well. Miroslav Galuska, a liberal intellectual, pointed out that self-policing could be more insidious than centrally imposed censorship since it tended to encourage opportunism and stifle rather than encourage boldness.[1] In essence, Galuska was trying to demonstrate that the law as it stood, with freedom very much a matter of personal responsibility, could not have favorable results in the climate of a police state. Any progressive elements of the law were entirely dependent upon most other aspects of society, i.e. the other reforms (for example, of the legal system). As with so many of the reforms the crux of the problem would be the spirit and nature of implementation or application of the law. An indication that this might not be as the liberals desired was the fact that censorship (the Central Administration for Publication) remained under the Ministry of Interior.

---

[1] *Kulturni Tvorba*, 1 December 1966. Galuska was editor of this weekly before the party took it over in August 1964.

12

IDEOLOGY AND THE PARTY

Transformation of the political institutions may well have been the most significant aspect of de-Stalinization in Czechoslovakia. Reforms in this area of society – together with the economic reforms – might have provided a major revision of Marxist–Leninist theory as well as a significant change in the organization and functioning of socialist society and the role of the Communist Party. Moreover, the genuine implementation and efficacy of the other reforms in Czechoslovak society – including those in the economic sphere – were to a large degree dependent upon the transformation of the political institutions. It was perhaps because of the deep significance of de-Stalinization in this realm that the sensitive questions of political changes were among the last to be faced by the party. The conservatives most likely had long been aware that this was the direction in which the liberals were going. The reforms of the mass organizations and the debates which accompanied them, as well as the economic reforms and the debates which accompanied them, often provoked demands for political changes and the recognition of the need for theoretical as well as practical adjustments within the political sphere. Most of the reforms raised the delicate question of the role of the party in a newly organized socialist society. Combined with or perhaps at the root of this issue lay the question of how to rule a socialist society given the unforeseen existence of conflicting 'group interests' within socialist society. The persistence of conflicts within society even after the advent of socialism could and was in the past explained by Stalin's theory of the intensification of the class struggle after the Communists' assumption of power. While this could justify the dictatorship of the proletariat as practised under Lenin and Stalin – the physical suppression or elimination of certain classes or groups – this theory was to exit with de-Stalinization. This much even Novotny had admitted in 1960 when Czechoslovakia was declared a socialist country, on the road to an all-people state and the transition to communism. Hostile classes no longer existed, but conflicts did. In some circles the Stalinist theory persisted as an explanation of this phenomenon, but liberal party intellectuals sought and began debating new explanations. These were by no means merely academic or purely theoretical discussions. They were intended as a basis for a practical

solution to what the liberals considered the shortcomings of Czechoslovak society. They believed it was not enough to explain and thereby
dismiss the latter with the simple injunction: remnants of the era of the
cult. Their very search, however, promised to threaten the pervasive,
all-powerful role of the party as much if not more than the reforms in
the other areas.

SOCIALIST SOCIETY

One of the earliest formulations of a theoretical approach to socialist
society based on conflicting interest groups appeared in *Pravny Obzor*
in January 1965 in an article by the Slovak legal scholar Michal Lakatos. Lakatos' premise was that the motive force of society is the conflict
generated between special interests, progress being the result of the
free confrontation of these conflicting interests. The Stalinist approach,
Lakatos argued, ignored the 'natural differences' among groups and
individuals, viewing them as vestiges of capitalism and its traditional
class conflict. In fact, socialist society might be differentiated according
to various relationships, such as the traditional Marxist distinction of a
class – i.e. the relationship to the production process (in socialist
society this would mean workers in the state sector, those in the cooperative sector, in the retail trades, etc.), or the relationship to the
division of labor, i.e. workers in industry, agriculture, physical labor,
mental labor. Moreover, distinctions or differentiation could also be
determined by the size of income, participation in the management of
society (management workers, members of the party, production
organizers), ethnic origins (Slovaks, Czechs, Hungarians, etc.), territorial divisions (Bohemia, Moravia, Central Slovakia, etc.), biological
origin (men and women), and so forth. In essence, Lakatos maintained
that the limited Marxist differentiation of society (relationship to the
means of production) was not sufficient for an analysis of socialist
society once owners had been eliminated and society was composed
entirely of the 'class' of non-owners.[1]

By the end of 1965 there were several signs that the party did not
entirely reject the above view of society. In November the party
theoretical journal published an article which argued that 'the more
mature the society, the more complicated the division of labor and the
relations between the various groups and classes.' Because of this
phenomenon it would become all the more necessary to take into

[1] Michal Lakatos, 'On Certain Problems of the Management of our Political
System,' *Pravny Obzor*, 48:1 (1965), 26–36.

consideration 'the social position of various classes and groups, their interests, education, style of life, etc.'[1] This was also admitted by Prague radio when it said that decisions must take into consideration the attitudes, interests, and needs of all groups and strata in society.[2] In December the *World Marxist Review* published an article along the same lines by the Czechoslovak legal expert Zdenek Mlynar. Mlynar recognized that the implications of the new economic system 'extend far beyond the purely economic sphere,' having an 'objective connection with the political regulation of social life.'[3] Socialist relations could not be regarded as merely relations of property but rather as 'the expression of the real and many-sided status' of the individuals in socialist society. Mlynar too rejected the tendency to assume an identification of the interests of society as a whole with the particular interest of 'various social groups, strata, working collectives, and individuals.' Because of this assumption, he said, any apparent conflict of interests had been exorcised as an anti-social remnant of capitalism. Mlynar recognized the legitimacy of contradictions between interests; contradictions which he called conflicts of a non-antagonistic nature. Such contradictions could exist even after the triumph of 'socialist relations (class and property relations)' because of the many-sided nature of man, he explained. Socialist relations were merely the formal framework within which a man worked, but other factors still existed for him. In the 'second stage' of socialist development, once the basic class contradictions were solved and the class struggle won, the masses should be united 'on the basis of the much more complex concrete social interests in the most diverse spheres of endeavor, on the one hand, and the particular interests associated with these spheres (economic and social, the division of labor, social and individual consumption, the political and ideological areas, relations between generations, etc.) on the other.' While contradictions might arise between short-term and long-term interests, Mlynar, like Lakatos, argued that the leading circles should seek the best way to harmonize these interests, using the contradictions as signals for the need to find better ways of uniting the specific group interests with the pre-defined aim of society.

One philosophy professor asserted that there is always tension

[1] Kamil Horn, 'Radio Propaganda From Abroad,' *Nova Mysl*, XIX:10 (1965), 1191–2.
[2] Prague radio, 12 November 1965.
[3] Zdenek Mlynar, 'Problems of Political Leadership and the New Economic System,' *World Marxist Review*, 12 (1965), 58–64.

between man and his political system, no matter who owns the means of production;[1] another professor argued on Prague radio that despite collective means of production, conflicts existed because of division of labor, different character of work, different place of people in the social organization of work, and different interests of people.[2] These discussions, conducted on the whole by and between party theoreticians, were not designed to contradict or revise Marx's strict class analysis of pre-socialist society nor directly to reject the idea of a harmonious classless communist society. Basically they were designed to deal with the intermediary stage, that of the all-people state, which, according to Mlynar, would be a 'comparatively long historical epoch' until reaching its higher, communist stage. It was irrelevant to the discussion at that time whether or not the conflicting 'strata' or interests would persist into *communist* society, when and whether or not the state would wither away. Perhaps the very absence of these issues from the discussion was an indication of the answer these intellectuals would have offered. The discussions were not, however, on the question of how to do away with the state (as asked in Yugoslavia), but how best the state might govern in a *socialist* society, thereby recognizing the necessity – even if unpleasant – of the existence of a state at this stage of development.

The party apparently was willing to go along with the new interpretation of society, although it was concerned that the recognition of the legitimacy of conflicting 'specific' interests might threaten the rationale of the dictatorship of the proletariat or, more pertinently, the leading role of the party. Thus the party 'Theses' of December 1965 recognized the persistence of classes even into socialist society, but characterized these as non-antagonistic classes *gradually drawing together*.[3] The 'Theses' admitted that socialist society was undergoing 'a complicated process of differentiation' in which differences of interests appeared which had to be taken into consideration. They asserted, however, that the interests of the workers' class were still primary and that to this class still fell the role of leading society, a role 'which cannot be implemented by any other class or social group.' Unwilling to admit of as much progress as the liberal intellectuals had, the party 'Theses' placed Czechoslovakia in what Mlynar had characterized as the first stage of socialist construction, the conflict between capitalism and socialism. Thus one could not yet begin the transformation of the dictatorship of the proletariat to the all-people state, for the

[1] Vladimir Blazek in *Literarni Noviny*, 20 November 1965.
[2] Prague radio, 11 March 1966 (Milos Kalab).   [3] *Rude Pravo*, 23 December 1965.

dictatorship of the proletariat was still completing its original task of 'overcoming – particularly in the ideological and moral fields – the influences surviving from capitalist society and stemming from the attack of imperialist forces from abroad.' In this sense the working class, through the state, was completing the historical tasks of the dictatorship of the proletariat. This basically Stalinist view was amplified by party cultural chief Pavel Auersperg who argued against moving too rapidly and against the idea that the working class would in the very near future cease to be a class and become, rather, a 'stratum.'[1] According to Auersperg, the dynamic of society is defined thus: 'Every individual, every collective, and every social group should be following truly socialist principles.' In this way the individual's interests would be identical with those of society as a whole. Conflicts existed, but they had to be solved, and solution could only be on the basis of socialist principles. Auersperg rejected as 'vulgar and simplified' the thesis that the very progress of socialist society might be based on just these conflicts and their free expression.

Despite the views of the conservatives reflected in the pre-congress 'Theses,' the Thirteenth Party Congress recognized the liberals' position. Novotny himself admitted to the congress that 'it is unavoidable that different sectional interests of various classes and groups, as well as different gradations of socialist consciousness still exist.'[2] Thus a congress resolution called for 'thorough knowledge of the interests and needs of the classes, strata, and groups of society,' assigning the party the job of harmonizing the 'various economic and social positions' created by different interest groups.[3]

DICTATORSHIP VERSUS DEMOCRACY

With this basic recognition that even socialist society was not homogeneous, party theoreticians turned to the question of how best to cope with this situation. This discussion inevitably placed in question Lenin's concept of the 'leading role of the party,' or at least the form in which Lenin's successors had applied this concept. As early as 1963 an article by Ondrej Kopcok had appeared in the Slovak party daily making an appeal for recognition of the term democratic in the guiding concept of democratic centralism. It pointed out that centralism, control from the top, which strongly resembled dictatorship, had resulted from a

[1] Pavel Auersperg, 'The Political and Social Changes in our Society,' *Nova Mysl*, XX:3 (1966), 3–7.
[2] *Rude Pravo*, 4 June 1966.   [3] *Rude Pravo*, 7 June 1966.

distortion of the Leninist concept of the party as the vanguard of the working class. Kopcok argued that the party had lost faith in the masses, turning to them only as objects of persuasion in support of the party-determined goals. He attributed this deformation of the concept of democratic centralism to Stalin's 'one-sided' interpretation of the dictatorship of the proletariat. Not only were the people ignored but a certain secretiveness set in, accompanied by 'dictate, command, administrative action, and even repression of the disobedient.' Thus a situation had been created in which 'the non-antagonistic contradiction between the party and the masses could easily assume antagonistic features and solution be sought in means harmful to socialism, as was the case in Hungary in 1956.'[1]

Kopcok's solution presaged later suggestions for a more democratic political life: an end to the cadre system and freedom of criticism at least for the organizations of the people. For Kopcok the leading role of the party consisted in 'giving validity' to the views of the people, basing its decisions on the experience and opinions of the people. Deriving whatever is rational from critical views, the party would be bolstered against 'one-sided views' by the fact that the people had participated in the decision-making, he maintained.

Michal Suchy of the CSAV Institute of Philosophy also championed the freedom of criticism, claiming that Stalinism had resulted from the suppression of just this institution.[2] There had been a distortion in the superstructure: necessary defensive measures against anti-revolutionaries and anti-Marxists in the first stage of socialism 'begin to work more or less independently.' These efforts against 'a contest of ideas' in turn 'hindered the development of scientific thought' so that immunity from criticism became not only the cause but the tool of the cult. According to Suchy, 'Once the principle is established that an exchange of views and mutual criticism are not allowed in a certain sphere (however limited it may be) rigidity of thought in this sphere . . . is inevitable.' Suchy used this theoretical argument in a plea for the removal not merely of the manifestations of the cult but of the conditions which gave rise to it, i.e. the prohibition of criticism. These early exponents of democracy refrained, however, from using the word opposition.

Julius Strinka, another Slovak, was one of the first and most important theoreticians to make a concrete proposal when he called for

---

[1] *Bratislava Pravda*, 8 July 1963.
[2] Michal Suchy, 'Freedom of Criticism and the Development of Marxist Theory,' *Otazky Marxistickej Filosofie*, 19:5 (1964), 409–14.

'institutionalized criticism' or opposition.[1] Strinka argued that a dialectical analysis of history must be applied to the present day as well,
i.e. society was constantly in motion, constantly producing the negation
of itself, and, therefore, present-day socialist society was not the final or
permanent form or prototype of socialist society. It was rather one of
the possible forms of the first stage of future, greater, and more far-
reaching social changes. The qualitative change of the existing structure
of socialism, the change that was part of the dialectic of history, could
not be limited to the economic sphere. To limit the qualitative change
of society to this sphere alone would be to risk its being submerged or
overshadowed by the continuation of the old society in the other spheres
specifically the sphere of political relations.

One aspect of the political sphere of present socialist society which
could and in fact did, according to Strinka, hamper the qualitative
changes in the economic sphere, was the lack of institutionalized
criticism. Strinka maintained that 'integrated power' and integrated
direction demanded 'integrated criticism.' It was not enough that there
was criticism; scattered, disintegrated criticism was dissipated and of
little use. Integrated, institutionalized criticism was needed, he maintained, as a corrective of possible mistakes of integrated power. This
corrective must, however, function objectively and be protected 'by
definite institutional guarantees' in order to be effective. But to be
effective criticism had to be 'responsible,' for 'scattered' or diffused
criticism assumed a certain anonymity, and if there were no clear
identification of responsibility, the sense of responsibility was also
dissipated. Only openly identifiable, integrated criticism could be
effective, for only such criticism was responsible and protected by
guarantees. By the same token non-integrated criticism 'cannot identify
responsibility or the degree of responsibility of this component of the
power apparatus or another, of this institution or another' and, therefore, could not serve as an effective social force. Only with clear identification of responsibility could the necessary implications follow,
i.e. correction of the fault. Only thus could there be any objective
guarantee for the criticism so that it could be effective. Such an
identification was almost impossible for non-integrated, scattered
criticism to achieve. It was, therefore, ineffectual and if ineffectual then
harmless. If, however, the importance of criticism were disparaged
then too the importance of responsibility was diminished: 'it is super-

[1] *Kulturny Zivot*, 26 November 1965. See also Strinka, 'Two Concepts of the
Dialectics of Socialism,' *Otazky Marxistickej Filosofie*, 18:1 (1963), 82–8.

fluous to point out the consequences of this for the moral state of society
. . . one question (is) whether a socialist society can afford to be content
with this form of movement.'

Citing the Yugoslav Marxist philosopher Korac, Strinka maintained
that the dialectic of society must be based on the concept that 'man is
not exclusively determined by existing conditions, but also by his own
projects.' This was basically the position presented by the Czech
philosopher Karel Kosik as well, whose important work *Dialektika
Konkretniho* of 1963 focused on the problem of alienation and man's
place in socialist society. Strinka maintained that society is not governed
or affected by abstract laws of development only, but even more so by
concrete social activity set in motion by man, with his particular
motives, interests, and attitudes. Like Kosik, Strinka called for a return
to Marx's 'anthropocentric' starting point; a return to the concept of
man as a 'free, authoritative being' participating in the historical
process. The existing contradictions could be overcome, socialist
society could develop with the dialectically necessary qualitative
changes, 'Only . . . if those conditions, institutionalized forms and
mechanisms are evolved in which the creative energy of the people as
well as the people's activity in the critical and practical fields which
helps to transform the present, will be able permanently to unfold to
the highest possible degree.'

Strinka went beyond the more amorphous demands for the freedom
to criticize, recognizing that the mere freedom to criticize, such as
Polish liberals apparently had won in 1956, would not be enough and
could too easily be swept away. He was demanding for the political
sphere what was being undertaken in other spheres – institutionalized
reforms. When applied to the political sphere, however, this was tantamount to advocating legalization and formalization of political opposition. Strinka's articles attracted a great deal of attention and might
well be considered some of the most important documents in the
efforts toward political reform. Strinka, a respected intellectual, was in
fact challenging the regime – serving notice that the intellectuals could
not be placated with the amorphous, perhaps arbitrary 'permission'
Novotny was willing to give them in lieu of genuine freedom.

Michal Lakatos saw the problem in much the same way as Strinka:
criticism (in Lakatos' words the 'clash of opinions') provided the motor
force in society, the 'dynamics of progress.'[1] As we have seen Lakatos

---

[1] Michal Lakatos, 'Some Problems of Socialist Democracy from the Viewpoint of
the Citizen's Position in our Society,' *Pravny Obzor*, 49:3 (1966), 213–23.

believed that society is highly differentiated and the goal of the ruling group is to harmonize the varying or conflicting interests. Lakatos maintained, however, that there is always a clash between 'the rulers and the ruled' since the former, in their effort to find harmony, in fact resort to manipulation, greater control, and discipline. Like Strinka, he maintained that 'socialist morality' was threatened by this, for 'those who govern can turn those ruled into a passive and apathetic nation that yields to any pressure exerted by the manipulators. If this pressure continues for a long time, it can influence the mentality of the citizens. The aim of subjecting society to the highest degree of manipulation is irreconcilable with socialist morality.'

The solution to this, according to Lakatos, was self-manipulation. By this he did not mean an elimination of central control (government) or manipulation, but control or manipulation through the public. The present conception of 'government of the people' tended to perpetuate non-public manipulation, he maintained, for citizen participation in government 'is often meaningless.' The solution, he argued, was a truly representative system of government in which the elected bodies 'really and not only formally contribute to the formation of the political line.' The legislature must be empowered to define and determine the principles of direction, thus placing manipulation under public control. The representative bodies must be truly representative, based upon free elections, so that all the different and varying strata or groups in society might be truly represented.[1]

For elections to be of any value, Lakatos argued, they must provide a real choice – not merely the right to elect the proposed candidate whose nomination has been approved from above. The electoral system must be organized to reflect and correspond to the real structure of society, with its group interests. In a traditional parliamentary system, political parties were the vehicle for the expression of group interests and self-government. In socialist society, the vehicles for social and other interests of citizens were the non-state social or mass organizations. The question arose, however, as to the degree that these organizations, as a starting point for democratic self-government, were representative and a platform for the partial interests of the citizens. These organizations, according to Lakatos, must cease to be mere 'conveyors' of policies from above, for if they failed to provide a platform for the partial interests, the representative bodies, in their turn would be mere conveyors of policies from above:

[1] *Svobodne Slovo*, 4 April 1966.

If the objective social interest, local or at the center, in any specific question, is to be objectively expressed, this requires the possibility of co-ordinating the different expressions of these interests and settling conflicts which exist among them by democratic means, i.e. this requires that the social forces which are connected with these interests [the social organizations], also be enabled to stimulate their social activity.[1]

Thus the harmonization of conflicting interests in society must be achieved not through manipulation from the center but by self-government, by permitting the different interests to be expressed through the participation of social organizations (themselves already democratized) in elections and in the legislative bodies.[2] 'This may lead to conflicts which also reach the floor of the representative body [but] what is decisive is the fact that the representative body is the real carrier of politics and not merely a formal representative.'[3] Thus the clash of opinions could serve its function as the motor force of society, freely and truly expressed through an effective channel.[4]

Lakatos took the issue of institutionalized criticism one step further, outlining the ways and means of bringing about such a thing as well as explaining its function and necessity. This was not a proposal for an opposition party or plurality of parties; it was rather a bid for 'one party pluralism.'[5] Though not clearly spelled out, the party would have the function of an all-over unifying body without being the instrument of state power, while the social organizations would play the role accorded political parties in a traditional parliamentary system. Lakatos did not, however, squarely face the issue of whether or not these organizations would be independent of the National Front. One might imply from his argument in favor of the freedom and independence to establish one's own platform that the social organizations would perforce be outside the National Front. The question was more than academic if opposition were to be of any significance, for an opposition outside the government or the possibility of an alternative alignment within a government coalition might well provide the best guarantee that criticism would have some chance of being effective.

---

[1] *Bratislava Pravda*, 1 April 1967.
[2] Michal Lakatos, 'Twenty Years of Building Socialist Democracy,' *Pravny Obzor*, 50:2 (1967), 110–18.
[3] *Svobodne Slovo*, 4 April 1966.   [4] Lakatos, *Pravny Obzor*, 48:1 (1965), 26–36.
[5] See Morton Schwartz, 'Towards One-Party Pluralism,' *Problems of Communism*, XVI:1 (1967), 21–7.

Mlynar also suggested that conflicting or different views should be represented in the 'state sphere' to assert in these organs the views and interests of the various social groups.[1] He too argued that the elected state organs should be the arena in which conflicting interests 'fight it out,' with the result that the best possible harmonization of social needs and individual interest would be constantly worked out anew. A basic task, according to Mlynar, was to determine 'the sphere of competence and functions of bodies of political leadership' so as to avoid the all-pervasive nature of the party, its mixing in day to day or purely local problems, duplicating functions, assuming responsibilities due to others, while neglecting the socio–political functions that should be their primary concern.[2] One must also 'develop political institutions in such a way as will give free scope to the initiative of the masses.'

With the all-people state, Mlynar claimed, self-government of the masses would be synonymous with the 'inner evolution' of the state itself. 'The function of the basic nuclei of government could increasingly be fulfilled by democratically constituted bodies of the various communities of working people, both territorial and production communities, while the higher state bodies should maintain democratic contact with these basic components of self-government.' In this way the state would evolve into a 'mass organization' as envisaged by Lenin. Although this concept was by no means clearly delineated by Mlynar, it would appear that he favored the direction taken in Yugoslavia of greater local self-government with a decreasing role for the higher state organs. Mlynar too would take the party out of the sphere of everyday interests and local politics, but unlike Lakatos he saw the party as protector of the overriding interests of society.

While Mlynar tended to see self-government in eventual terms of workers councils and territorial organizations, two Slovak intellectuals Miroslav Kusy and Juraj Suchy, pointed out another element to be taken into consideration – that of the difference in generations.[3] Agreeing that society as a whole changes and develops according to the 'convergence or divergence of many group interests,' Kusy and Suchy claimed that the interests and attitudes of the generations were of the greatest significance and one must eliminate any obstacles to their manifestation of free expression. The program of socialism must link all the social forces of all the generations, and to do so one must not only ensure free expression of these forces but the integration of the program

[1] *Praca*, 25 January 1966.   [2] Mlynar, *World Marxist Review*, 12 (1965), 60–3.
[3] *Bratislava Pravda*, 2 August 1967.

of these forces (specifically of the youth) into the program of society. Tolerance was not enough; genuine integration of a platform for the youth could only come if the youth were permitted to formulate such a platform themselves. Thus, free expression, integration of views, and participation of the youth in the formulation of policy were required if society were to be formed in such a way as to represent the 'temperament of their generation' as well as of the others.

A similar argument was raised for the workers by Ivan Bystrina. He argued that the trade unions must represent their members and not the government.[1] One must be willing to risk errors for the sake of defending the workers' interests. A way of avoiding errors, however, was by a 'truthful and objective' information policy. Thus, the

> decisive method of solution will obviously be a maximum of information (without the preliminary sifting), a maximum of democratic debate, and the development of the institutional and methodically functional richly differentiated system of representative state institutions and special interest social organizations combined with a system of legally anchored, solid rules, real (especially juridical) guarantees, and real mutual controls.

Mlynar too urged a stable legal system, above the subjectivism of everyday directives and expediences, providing protection for the interests of the individual as well as of the organization or institution.[2]

The idea of objective information and the obvious implication – the importance of public opinion – was expanded by an article in the Ministry of Defence weekly. As long as the party refused to admit of any possible discrepancy between its interests and those of various strata of society, it was claimed, there was no need or wish for any analysis or expression of public opinion. Though public opinion might be wrong, it might also be right, and, therefore, should be both permitted and taken into consideration by the party in its release of information.[3]

These partial solutions (representation of generational views, the importance of law and objective information) supplemented the more comprehensive solutions proposed by such people as Strinka, Mlynar, and Lakatos. There were, however, some who went more deeply into the problem, questioning the meaning of such concepts as democracy and freedom, at least for Czechoslovak society. The sociologist Miroslav Jodl went so far as to say that

[1] *Literarni Noviny*, 17 December 1966.
[2] Mlynar, *World Marxist Review*, 12 (1965), 63.
[3] *Obrana Lidu*, 25 February 1967.

among all the nations of the Soviet bloc, we are probably the most democratic, a nation with the strongest tradition of local autonomy, a nation which has known and appreciates fully the freedom of the press, the freedom of expression and of association . . . whose concept of democracy has always been connected with the social and socialist concept.[1]

Yet, Jodl asserted, the Czechoslovak concept of democracy tended to be based more upon the idea of equality than upon freedom of action. Devoted to the concept of democracy, Czechs tended to lack sufficient perseverance in pursuing it to its fullest, losing sight of the real meaning of democracy: rule from above balanced by control from below, with the freest possible selection of representatives. Czechoslovakia could only 'hold its own' in the challenge of the times if it 'succeeds in contributing to the establishment of a democratic, humanist, and scientific socialism.' In connection with this last point Eugen Loebl too called for a humanistic socialism, arguing that the unity of science and humanism – the 'godparents' of socialism – could only be achieved by 'determined effort.'[2] Jan Uher raised a similar basic issue when he defined freedom, at least in the political sphere, as 'the search for and the realization of the best alternatives, in other words, a selection from several possibilities.'[3] Thus Uher too maintained that freedom and democracy were active elements which 'can be effectively stimulated and guided only by democratically elected and qualified institutions.'

The party's official position on the way to govern socialist society, given the conceded existence of conflicting interests, was contained in the 'Theses.' While the socialist state still had to complete the task of the dictatorship of the proletariat, in this specific 'socialist' stage greater responsibilities must fall to the representative organs. These should 'democratically resolve the differences and eventual discrepancies between the partial interests of the people – group, local, work collectives' interests, and so on – and must correctly interpret and defend society's needs.' For this purpose the bonds between the people and the elected organs must be strengthened, a task which included the increased importance of the social organizations, whose function it would be 'to express diverse special interests and needs.' In this way the 'Theses' explained the changes in the mass organizations, including

[1] *Literarni Noviny*, 7 January 1967. See also Helena Peskova and Vaclav Veber, 'Notes on the History of the Personality Cult,' *Acta Universitatis Carolinae, Philosophica et Historica*, 1–2 (1966), 83–97.
[2] *Kulturny Zivot*, 16 September 1966. [3] *Kulturny Zivot*, 4 February 1966.

those of the trade unions, which were designed 'to increase further the effectiveness of democratic participation of the working people in management.'[1]

The discussions of integrated criticism, free and open debate, conflicts of interest, social groups or strata, objective information, legal protection, all implied or openly stated the need for a basic feature of democracy: opposition. If such a phenomenon were to be permitted as a necessary feature of socialist democracy, however, one would have to re-examine the Leninist concept of the leading role of the party and, perhaps, redefine it in view of the development of socialist society. At the Czechoslovak Writers Congress of June 1967, this issue was squarely faced by Ludvik Vaculik. In his speech to the congress, Vaculik clearly and directly attacked the leading role of the party as written into the Czechoslovak Constitution of 1960, calling this totalitarianism.[2] The fact that the Constitution designated the Communist Party as the leading party and the leading force in society created a dynasty of power. Since power's independent, invulnerable, unassailable position was anchored in the Constitution, it was permitted to perpetuate itself. Power was also totalitarian, for the Constitution concerned itself with the government and the rights of citizens with respect to the government, but in fact it was the party that directed the government and determined policy. The citizen, however, had no voice in or rights with regard to the party. In such a situation there was neither participation nor safety. There was no guarantee of civil rights, no objective control; not even the courts were free since the prosecutors were governed by the party, which could in fact determine all without recourse to the citizen or the elected organs.

Like Lakatos, Vaculik advocated a system wherein the rulers and the ruled would be as close as possible so that there was in effect self-government. He claimed that the pre-war Republic had had a high degree of progressive democracy. Not socialism but the power that claims to operate in the name of socialism, was responsible for the 'post-war failure.' Putting it bluntly, Vaculik said; 'not one human question has been solved in the course of the last 20 years,' no

[1] *Rude Pravo*, 23 December 1965.
[2] *IV. Sjezd Svazu Ceskoslovenskych Spisovatelu* (Praha, 1968), 141–51.

undemocratic system in the world could solve such problems as the feeling that political decisions are not subordinated to 'ethical criteria.' Vaculik proposed that the Constitution be changed to make power and the citizen equal. The National Assembly should propose changes to eliminate the purposely vague, rubber stamp nature of the Constitution. The possibility of willful interpretation of the Constitution must be minimized and guarantees created against the misuse of power by the ruling circles. Thus Vaculik took the argument for opposition one step further by challenging the constitutionally guaranteed favored position of the party. For this he was expelled from the party.[1]

The discussion on what should in fact be the role of the party had skirted this issue of the constitutionally guaranteed position of the party. Generally it had ranged from the proposals for institutional reform, such as the suggestions we have already seen, to attempts to redefine the methods and role of the party, to conservative demands for greater central control and discipline. The suggestions for 'integrated criticism,' e.g. opposition or a multi-'party' system, met with varying types of negative reactions. The moderate Josef Smrkovsky agreed that the clash of opinions, debate, and discussions were all quite valuable and valid concepts, but he claimed that they already existed within the party itself.[2] Any 'organized opposition' such as a second party would, he argued, have to be socialist since that was the social order the country wanted and for which it had fought. Yet, he concluded, a 'second Communist party' under another name hardly seemed realistic or expedient. In direct answer to Strinka, a letter to the editors of *Nova Mysl* rejected 'criticism for the sake of criticism,' claiming that criticism could only be within the party. Any 'oppositional ideological political movement' such as the author claimed Strinka proposed, would, the letter argued, be incompatible with the leading role of the party.[3] Using the simple argument of old, another party intellectual told a youth meeting that parties representing classes were necessary in bourgeois democracy, but in a one-class socialist society the party represented the interests of all, so against whom and for what purposes could an opposition operate.[4] Still another party retort ridiculed the idea that the period of the dictatorship of the proletariat was completed and that, therefore, it was possible to 'abandon the principle of one-party rule, calling back the old bourgeois parties or naming new

[1] See chapter 17.   [2] *Literarni Noviny*, 15 September 1967.
[3] Milos Marko, 'Responsible or Integrated Criticism,' *Nova Mysl*, XX:24 (1966), 2.
[4] *Smena*, 30 January 1966 (Michal Havran).

parties: Communist Party A, Communist Party B, and so on alphabetically until all interests and opinions were catered to.'[1]

Others were also not so willing to reject out of hand the idea that the dictatorship of the proletariat might be a passing stage, the ultimate disappearance of which would require reconsideration of the party's role. Two party theoreticians argued against the idea that the party should relinquish its direct management of society to the state and become a purely ideological center.[2] They argued that this would deprive the party of its ability to act in the name of the nation, thus depriving the world communist movement of unity of action. Until the advent of a world communist society, they maintained, the party must maintain its hegemony of political power in the socialist countries. The two theoreticians did argue, however, that 'hegemony of political power' did not justify the party's extending the period of the dictatorship of the proletariat until the advent of pure communism. In other words, the victory of socialism in Czechoslovakia, declared in 1960, brought an end to the justification of the dictatorship of one class since in effect classes had been eliminated. Given the world constellation of powers, however, the party must maintain its leading role. One might conclude that these two writers sought a form of rule for the party which would guarantee its leading position without permitting it dictatorial powers.

Some saw the party as the arbiter of the conflicting interests within society (a role Marx gave to the state) with the duty of determining the interests of society as a whole. Such a role would not necessarily rule out the existence of opposition, although one might certainly question the effectiveness of such an opposition if the party were guaranteed the final word. The more liberal Slovak, Miroslav Kusy, argued that although there was a need for the type of control on power provided by opposition groups, westerners, including many western communists, were naive in their assertions that the institutionalized, independent opposition groups of bourgeois democracy really served as a control on power.[3] Such opposition was a right extracted from the ruling class and merely an expression of the class struggle. In a classless society such as Czechoslovakia, Kusy asserted, such an opposition could only be artificially created. This did not mean, however, that there

---

[1] *Rude Pravo*, 26 February 1966 (Jiri Franek).
[2] *Predvoj*, 20 October 1966 (J. Sedliak and L. Tomasek, 'The Leading Role of the Party under the New Conditions').
[3] *Predvoj*, 24 February 1964 ('The Party and the Management of our Society').

should be no control of power, and socialism was in fact in the process of giving this control to all – not just to an institutionalized group – through the creation of the all-people's state, Kusy claimed. The institutionalized organ of the people's control over or guarantee against the misuse of power was the Communist Party. The party was the 'second echelon' of control, the people being the first. This role of the party, he continued, could only be effected through a process the party had already undertaken: the separation of the party from the executive power, the state. The party should replace its forms of power by political–ideological forms of leadership, so that it was no longer subordinate to the state power but independent and in a position to control it. This would be an advantage over bourgeois opposition, for in bourgeois society the opposition is subordinate to and dependent upon the ruling power. Kusy recognized the obvious flaw in his argument, that in fact he would set the party above the state and therefore *above* the elected organs of government, creating conditions even more conducive to dictatorship than when the party was indistinguishable from the government. His answer was that while the party would control the power (the government), the people would control the party. There would, therefore, have to be greater public discussion of and participation in the work of the party and the submission of the party line to the masses (though he did not specify if the use of the word 'submission' implied 'for approval'), as well as greater democracy and mutual controls within the party.

In March 1966 articles appeared in both party dailies which clearly spelled out certain functions deemed suitable for the party. Jan Svoboda in *Rude Pravo* described the party as a political organization which led but did not 'supersede,' nor assume the responsibility for the 'direct management of society in the individual, specific spheres.'[1] The function of the individual party member was to accept the party program, obey the party statutes, carry out party decisions, but also to take an active part in the formation as well as implementation of party policies. He was to explain party policies and win over the people to these policies, counter indifference and watch over and strengthen party unity. To increase individual responsibility and democracy within the party, the role of the local party organization was to be strengthened. This last point might well be explained more conservatively as a measure designed to cope with the decentralization of the new economic system. With regard to the economic system, however, Svoboda asserted

[1] *Rude Pravo*, 17 March 1966.

that the local party organization had only a political, not managerial–economic function.

To serve the people better, the party must know the people better. This, according to candidate presidium member Martin Vaculik, would entail greater use of sociological and psychological methods, e.g. public opinion polls.[1] It would also mean open discussions with the people, such as the 'Party Talks with Youth' campaign, freedom to criticize, and greater independence for the social organizations. Within the party there must be democracy and mutual respect between the *apparat* and the elected organs, the latter having a say in the formulation of policy.

Vaculik raised another issue connected with the role or power of the party: the cadre system. He argued that while the party must maintain control of the selection of cadres and have a say in personnel selection on all levels in all places, it should look first to the objective qualifications of the candidate. Political reliability might be a criterion insofar as it was considered part of the candidate's organizational and leadership abilities, in addition to his other qualifications. In the 'Party Talks with Youth' campaign this adjustment in the cadre system was explained thus: now that the bourgeoisie has been destroyed there is no longer a question of gaining key positions for the conduct of the class struggle. An executive, however, still needs more than specialized knowledge; he must also have leadership ability, the ability to guide his workers politically. He need not be a party member to inculcate pride of work but a leader in the economic production sphere must be a good socialist.[2] A *Nova Mysl* article also elaborated on this point, arguing that the cadre system was outdated, that party membership should not be the sole requirement for employment, and that similarly, it was not valid that only party members could lead.[3] However, the party journal continued, political reliability must accompany 'expertise,' for to lead was also a political function. The criteria therefore should be: first, socialist conscience; secondly, special qualifications for job; and thirdly, experience. Although party membership need not be a requirement, given equal qualifications on all other points, a party member should be given preference over a non-member. This was the position of the party as declared in the 'Theses.' Its intention was to raise the

[1] *Bratislava Pravda*, 16–17 March 1966.
[2] *Bratislava Pravda*, 30 January 1966.
[3] Vladimir Tuma, 'Cadre Work in the Leninist Spirit,' *Nova Mysl*, xx:16 (1966), 14–18.

level of management and performance without, however, impairing the leading role of the party.

The issue of employment criteria invariably evoked the basic problem of attitude towards non-communists. Was the Czechoslovak party willing to declare like the Hungarians 'who is not against us is with us?' Both theoretical journals of the party, *Nova Mysl* and the more conservative *Zivot Strany*, addressed themselves to this issue as early as March 1963. *Nova Mysl* admonished that one must not be indifferent to, look down upon, or underestimate non-communists, who in fact constitute the majority of the population.[1] In fact, there should be more contact with the non-communist masses, more honesty in the party's approach to them, and an effort to explain difficulties and shortcomings, so as to win support. The duty of the basic party organization should be to consult non-communists, invite them to meetings and hold public discussions. While this may not be Kadar's 'who is not against us is with us,' it was a step in this direction since the approach advocated by *Nova Mysl* entailed persuasion in the place of simple rejection or coercion. *Zivot Strany* advocated exactly the same policy two years later on the basis of an analysis still closer to the Hungarian. The journal stated:

reality proves that during the twenty years of our new Republic, millions of citizens have grown up in this country who, even if they are not party members, have an ardent attitude to socialism and the party, in which they see the shield of their life, and with justification. Thus the relation of communists cannot be other than a relationship between equal parties in the building of our society.[2]

Trouble did arise, however, when the liberals struck at the very principle behind the cadre system, the idea of class origin. This referred not only to the preference given to party members, but the preference to persons of working-class origin and children of workers, whether it be in education, housing, or employment, which had become akin to the worship of workers. This very principle was attacked as unsound, on the grounds that workers as such were not *necessarily* desirable entities.[3] A *Kulturny Zivot* article pointed out that many workers belonged to what Marx had called the lumpen-proletariat. Many of just this

[1] F. Hajek and A. Svarovska, 'Communists and Non-Communists,' *Nova Mysl*, XVII:3 (1963), 296–304.
[2] Josef Hojda, 'Communists and Non-Communists,' *Zivot Strany*, 12 (1965), 723–6.
[3] *Kulturny Zivot*, 16 November 1963 (Anton Rasla, 'For an Unprofaned Workers Class').

group tended to join revolutions and, thus, progressive movements gained from these fanatical but opportunistic supporters who 'demagogically boast of their working-class background and their disdain for education, who are prepared to toady and to inform on all and sundry.'

This argument played well into the regime's hands, for one of Novotny's tactics had long been to exploit worker distrust of the intellectual in hopes of preventing the kind of worker–intellectual alliance that had led to revolution in Hungary and near-revolution in Poland in 1956. The party promptly and strongly answered this 'attack' on 'working-class purity,' arguing that the liberals had not grasped that the lumpen-proletariat dies away with the destruction of the bourgeois state.[1]

The official answer of the party, as distinct from the suggestions and discussions of party members, on the broader issues, i.e. the role of the party in production, in government, or in society, reflected the continued influence of the conservatives. The party 'Theses' as can be seen in the statement on cadre policy, were particularly conservative, reflecting perhaps the realization of the conservatives and Novotny himself of the conflicts which threatened to mar the Thirteenth Party Congress as a result of ever-growing liberal demands. There is reason to believe that, in fact, disputes grew and intensified within the party between the time of the 'Theses' publication and the congress itself, with the liberals making certain gains. One Czech observer later said of the preparatory period for the congress:

> Any agile observer could sense that the conservative representatives in the party leadership would have to yield to certain alternative proposals for solving a number of very serious problems in Czechoslovak society ... Direct pressure was exercised with increasing frequency even on members of the central committee known to have a critical attitude

and the latter, such as Sik, were barely able to participate in the congress discussions.[2] The growing conflict could even be seen by the fact that Novotny and his supporters apparently felt the need to reiterate their position numerous times, especially on the point of the leading role of the party, which was being called into question in the course of the liberals' debates.

Thus the 'Theses' emphasized the political role of the party, warning

---

[1] Cited by Zagreb radio, 7 December 1963.
[2] Vojtech Menzl and Frantisek Ourednik, 'What Happened in January,' *Zivot Strany*, 17 (1968), 34; see also *Predvoj*, 29 February 1968.

against any limitation of the party to purely organizational functions. The party 'sums up the knowledge of the whole society and, therefore, is the main standard-bearer of creative political thought. It outlines the aim and prospects for further development in all fields of social life.' The 'Theses' did not, however, go into this question more deeply, refraining from any clear delineation between state and party powers except in the economic sphere. Here it recognized the inherent demand of the new economic system that the basic party organizations refrain from interfering in the day to day production and management tasks. On the other hand, the 'Theses' called for greater party activity at the local level to offset the decentralizing features of the reforms.

Early in 1966, party ideology chief Jiri Hendrych put the party's position on its own leading role in simpler terms. Recognizing that a greater role would be given to the social organizations, he asserted that the National Front would remain 'the alliance of all social forces in our society,' while the party's leadership of the National Front represented an 'essential premise' for the unity and educational efforts of the National Front.[1] He went even further than the 'Theses' in emphasizing the need for a strengthening of ideological work to offset the divisive factors in society, and clarified thus: 'The democratic character of direction cannot be isolated from the other aspect, from centralism. It is up to the party to determine the correct relation between centralism and democracy.' He did add, however, that the center should not duplicate the work of the state and economic institutions but should concern itself mainly with broad, long-range problems, so as not to restrict the sense of responsibility of those implementing party policy. This 'independence,' however, 'must not be interpreted to mean arbitrariness, indiscipline, or a 'free-hand.' One must not minimize the political role of the party nor expect 'autonomy' or limitation of party control in such areas as cultural activity.

Although the implementation of party influence and its leading role in various sectors assumes forms which change and develop, the principle itself of the party's leading role must not be weakened. All such half-baked views only play into the hands of enemy propaganda which, under the guise of talk about democracy, propagates liberalism and unlimited tolerance, puts the interests of groups above everything else, confronts the interests of social classes, strata and groups, tries to revive class antagonisms.[2]

---

[1] Jiri Hendrych, 'Before the Thirteenth Congress,' *Nova Mysl*, XX:1 (1966), 16–18.
[2] *Rude Pravo*, 9 January 1966 (Hendrych).

The above would suggest that the party was hard put to delineate the limits of the democratic solutions proposed, and particularly, to reconcile the recognized need for democratization in connection with the new economic sphere, with the obvious implications of this process for other spheres. This was particularly difficult since the party agreed – however reluctantly – to the liberals' analysis of the stratified nature of socialist society and the likelihood that this stage would last some time. While party leaders were willing to go a certain distance with the liberals' conclusions – that the differing strata or group interests, must be given greater voice – they were not willing to take this to the logical conclusion proposed by the liberals, i.e. integrated criticism, a certain measure of genuine democracy, and the right of opposition, for they were not willing to jeopardize the dictatorial position of the party.

In preparation for the Thirteenth Party Congress *Zivot Strany* called for greater party control and attempted to clarify a few points: 'Any attempt to deprive party organs of the power of control as some leading personalities seem to have in mind, is obviously absolutely nonsensical.'[1] Thus conservative voices asserted that the party not only had the right but the duty to control. It was the duty of the party to assure adherence to party policy in actual production conditions, control the implementation of the decisions of the superior organs of the party, and serve as a significant political influence on the economy. Lest there be any question as to how the party might exercise the control even with its withdrawal from the specialized tasks of the economic sphere, the reader was reminded that 'it is a matter of cadre work to appoint people and this is done primarily by party members ... control is really indispensable.' In addition to controlling, the party must lead, according to another conservative plea. Now more than ever the party had to be firm; it had to combat the 'misconceptions and false interpretations' of socialist democracy.[2] The party had to overcome certain negative aspects which had begun to appear, such as deviation from class views and positions, violation of democratic centralism, the 'considerable drop' in work discipline, declining authority 'at every level of management,' preferential treatment of local and group interests at the expense of the interests of society as a whole, and 'certain illusions, carelessness, and even political naivete in connection

[1] Vaclav Zima, 'Control, Knowledge of Strength, and Confidence,' *Zivot Strany*, 6 (1966), 21.
[2] Josef Valenta, 'What We Need,' *Zivot Strany*, 1 (1966), 5.

with the intentions of the capitalist world.' To overcome these features, the party had to cleanse itself of its opponents and fulfill its function as a 'voluntary fighting union of people who think alike.'

Just prior to and especially after the Thirteenth Party Congress, one of the biggest problems for Novotny was holding on to his supporters, the conservative *apparatchiks*, while implementing the reforms. He was intent upon proving to them that despite the new economic program, despite the changes in the mass organizations and the other reforms, despite the congress resolution to 'strengthen democratic methods of government' by revising the 'idea that the party decides every detail in advance and determines everything,' and particularly in view of the growing boldness of liberal demands, the party did not intend to relinquish its supremacy.[1] It was as a reassurance to the conservatives as well as a warning to the liberals that Novotny delivered his hard-line speech to the October 1966 party central committee plenum. 'In the first place we must refute the opinions and calculations of those who believe that the party's direction of the economic sphere will be relaxed under the conditions which we are in the process of creating through the application of the improved system of management,' Novotny exhorted.[2] Pointing to the dissident youth and intellectuals (and blaming the latter for the former), Novotny asserted the need for a 'firmer,' not weaker, hold on ideological activity. He called for the local party organization to counter attempts to elevate group interests over those of society, to enforce the party line, and to educate the people ideologically. The decentralizing effects of the various reforms placed greater responsibility on the local or basic party organizations, Novotny asserted, responsibility that carried with it a certain independence and entailed a need for higher standards in the selection of leaders at this level. By higher standards Novotny specified, however, not just technical skills but party-mindedness and worker background.

The year 1967 saw a number of conservative retorts to the liberals' challenge to the leading role of the party, and the official party line remained closest to Hendrych's dictum that groups with competing interests must be tolerated but that the essential directive activities of the party must remain unchallenged.[3] Nonetheless the need for the

---

[1] *Rude Pravo*, 7 June 1966.
[2] Antonin Novotny, 'Contemporary Problems of the Development of Socialist Society,' *Zivot Strany*, 21 (1966), 1–5.
[3] *Rude Pravo*, 14 February 1967 (Hendrych to central committee).

party to refrain from interference in the daily activities of production, to permit more enterprise independence, to limit the range of subjects handled by the central organs, and to make maximum use of non-party organizations was also recognized.[1] Of particular significance was the fact that the importance of winning over the people, the importance of persuasion, had become an essential feature of the leading role of the party as it evolved from these discussions.[2] This perhaps apparently innocuous difference in phraseology was fraught with ramifications, for it implied condemnation of the Stalinist method of control through 'administrative measures' and imposition of the party's will.

Of a more concrete nature, the party 'Statutes' were revised, defining more clearly the limitations on the role of the party in society.[3] The preamble of the new Statutes contained the definition of the role of the party as we have seen it defined above: the party is the leading political organization that determines the aims and purposes of all spheres of endeavor and guides the working people while *inducing* them to carry out the party's policies. At the same time, the party was to refrain from superseding the state agencies and economic and social organizations so as to prevent duplication of work and a confusion of responsibilities. The 'Statutes' codified the increase in the importance of the basic organizations and the expansion of their sphere of activity to the 'place of residence' as well as the place of work. Their work was to be streamlined in order to avoid anonymity and bureaucracy, and there was to be less direct intervention in the activities of the organization to which these local units were assigned.

With regard to the party itself, the 'Theses' had re-emphasized the need for democratic centralism as distinct from 'spontaneity' and 'social–democratic opportunism' – euphemisms for *lack* of strong central direction. Discipline was emphasized and the binding nature of the decisions of superior organs reiterated. The new 'Statutes,' nevertheless, provided for a certain albeit limited amount of inner-party democracy. There was to be greater responsibility placed on individual members and upon individual initiative. The period of candidacy for party membership was to be eliminated; members of the auditing and

---

[1] *Rude Pravo*, 15 February 1967 (Kolder to central committee).

[2] See interview with Hendrych, 'Unity and the Party and Society,' *Zivot Strany*, 6 (1967), 1–4 ; *Rude Pravo*, 20 July 1967 (Kolder and Hendrych to central committee); Frantisek Hubeny, 'The Dangers of Clashes of Ideas,' *Zivot Strany*, 4 (1967), 22–3.

[3] 'The Party Statutes,' *Zivot Strany*, 12 (1966), 49; *Rude Pravo*, 17 March 1966; Prague radio, 17 March 1966.

control commission of the basic organizations were to be permitted to attend party congresses and conferences as advisors. Regional and district committees were required to meet every two years and, to promote turnover, the terms of office for municipal, factory, and enterprise party committees were limited to two years. Two of the more significant changes were that party members were to be allowed to apply for repeal of party punishment, and basic party organizations would have to approve a decision from higher up to expel any of its members.

While these changes were made, the party decided that the discussions had indeed raised too many questions which defied immediate or unanimously acceptable solutions. In the fall of 1966 the party appointed a committee at the CSAV Institute of State and Law, under the chairmanship of Zdenek Mlynar, to prepare studies on the topic of 'The Development of the Political System in Socialist Society.' The group grew out of a symposium, organized by the Institute with the party legal commission in 1965, which had produced a report entitled 'Civilization at the Crossroads.' This study, headed by Dr Radovan Richta, produced the idea for a larger study, which was underwritten by the state budget for research in the fall of 1966. As Mlynar explained it, since the class struggle was no longer the motive force in Czechoslovak society, a new way had to be found to propel society towards communism: 'we want to formulate a hypothesis for the development of the political system, a hypothesis which would be the best and most effective means of assisting in a process which could be embodied in the introduction of the new economic system and also . . . correspond to our social development to date.'[1]

The committee was composed of thirty to forty persons mainly from the areas of state and law but also from the fields of sociology, political economics, administration, history, architecture, international relations, and international law. These fields together, according to Mlynar, would permit an approach of another field 'which of late has begun to be recognized in this country,' the field of political science.[2] The immediate task of the committee, to be completed by 1968-9, was to prepare a study providing the foundation for an analysis of the existing state and to formulate hypotheses for subsequent research. The latter

[1] See interviews with Mlynar and committee members, *Student*, 27 September 1967; *Rude Pravo*, 6 July 1967; Bratislava radio, 22 May 1967.
[2] In 1967 the party created an Institute of Political Science, chaired by Vaclav Slavik.

would be conducted over a period of five to seven years, and would provide the basis for reform of the political system.

The starting point for the entire study was explained as 'the necessity to analyze social reality as far as the division into social and common interest groups is concerned . . . to propose the best suitable institutional forms for the movements of society.' To do this, consideration was to be taken of the development of political systems, 'including the plurality of parties in the West . . . and the aspect of crisis in the classical liberal parliamentary system and the positive aspects of the so-called division of power and the control functions of the pluralistic political system.'[1] Of primary interest would be the question of substantive guarantees for the democratic formation of policy. According to the secretary of the commission, law lecturer Petr Pithart, lawyers working on the concept of 'socialist constitutionalism' were reviewing the 'discarded' problems of power within the state, the legal guarantees of civil rights and political freedoms, and the function of law.[2] Committee member Karel Bertelmann of the CSAV Institute of State and Law said that a new election law and a new law on the National Committees were being considered in order to provide greater citizen autonomy.[3] As Mlynar explained it, the present electoral system did not reflect the structure of socialist society, which was differentiated according to interests, not classes. The social organizations representing these interests should be in a position to play a political role 'as equal partners in decision-making . . . by backing unequivocally the standpoint of the group they represent . . . and exert pressure as a group.'[4] For this the present institutional structure would have to be changed.

The group was also to investigate worker self-management, the role of public opinion, social engineering and the sociological–psychological features which determine how a person arrives at a position of power, i.e. elites and cadre mobility. Committee member Mirsolav Jodl of the CSAV Sociological Institute said that the study would look into such things as a leader's life history, his social ties, and the psychological aspects of his political activity.[5] Political workshops were established to study the role of the party in socialist society, while the party's new Institute of Political Science undertook to study the work of the party, internal party development, and the role of the party in connection with the economic reforms and in socialist society generally.[6]

[1] *Student*, 27 September 1967. [2] *Rude Pravo*, 6 July 1967. [3] *Ibid.*
[4] *Student*, 27 September 1967. [5] *Rude Pravo*, 6 July 1967.
[6] *Student*, 27 September 1967.

The scope and composition of the committee were themselves a sign of the distance traveled by the party in considering its problems. The fact that the committee was created – by the party – was an indication that the liberals had gained enough power to force Novotny to recognize the need for well-thought-out decisions in this sphere. The conservatives undoubtedly hoped to delay and perhaps influence the work of the committee, but as long as the pressures which led to the establishment of the group – including the extreme suggestions of some for opposition parties and the growing unrest of intellectuals and students as well as the irksome problems of political control raised by the decentralizing effects of economic reform – continued, there was little the conservatives could do to impede progress indefinitely. On the other hand, the long-range nature of the committee's work may well have been a device sought by Novotny to provide a breathing spell, perhaps even a brake or stalling device, in the discussions and proposals which threatened the position of the party. The creation of the committee was, nonetheless, a clear and official admission that traditional Marxism–Leninism, insofar as it was understood and practiced in socialist Czechoslovakia, was not sufficient. Modern industrial Czechoslovak society had reached a stage for which there was apparently no ready answer in the official annals of Marxism–Leninism or in the experience of the CPSU. In essence, the party was admitting that a modicum of genuine democracy was needed if society were to progress further; but the only ruling communists who had even raised the question of democracy and socialism were the Yugoslavs, and they as yet had not found the answer.

13

ELECTED ORGANS OF GOVERNMENT

The deliberations over socialist democracy and the problem of how best to govern a socialist society led naturally to changes in the governmental organs. Like the changes with regard to the party, these were basically limited measures, more reluctant concessions than sweeping innovations, but they were first steps in the right direction. The regime basically satisfied itself with 'implementing' rather than changing the 1960 Constitution in its effort to liberalize and improve the role of the government. Although the issue of a new Constitution may have been discussed within the party central committee, only isolated voices could be heard publicly advocating a change in the Constitution.[1] Just, however, as the Leninist concept of the party was subject to criticism as a concept suitable to socialist society, so too the Stalinist or Soviet concept of the state was also to receive its share of revision. As a result of these discussions the regime was faced with the dual task of first removing the party from its integrated position of control of the government, i.e. give the government greater responsibility, *and* secondly of eliminating the all-pervasive, highly centralized method of government control, i.e. permit local elected organs and economic enterprises greater responsibility. Thus the party 'Theses' of December 1965 maintained that organs of the central government must concentrate their work 'in the first place' on the formation of long-term prospects and basic problems. The 'Theses' called for 'increased responsibility on the part of the state organs . . . rendering them accountable for their work;' and 'efficient division of work between the state and the economic organs at all levels . . . linked with an overall reduction of the over-grown state apparatus.' Novotny had earlier explained this new attitude towards the government when he revealed that one of the party's purposes agreed on at the September 1963 central committee plenum was the 'growth of the government's authority.'[2] Connected with this there would be an effort to improve the quality of governmental work so that the government could concentrate its main efforts on a 'consistent realization of the basic political–economic directives

[1] There were rumors to this effect in 1965–6, but they centered on constitutional changes to accommodate Slovak demands for federation (see below).
[2] *Rude Pravo*, 29 May 1964.

of the party and its organs.' With this more general task government officials, particularly ministers, were at the same time to be accorded greater independence of decision and responsibility for the implementation of decisions. Thus, while the government would refrain from its detailed interference in day to day affairs, its own responsibility and independence from interference by the party – at all levels – were also to be provided. Whatever the ideological pressures for this decision there was also a very real, pragmatic side to the issue: the economy. Even prior to the reforms it had been realized that two basic – and interconnected – problems responsible for the deterioration of the economy were over-centralization, over-interference of the government in the day to day affairs of the economy on all levels *and* inefficiency caused by the complicated, top-heavy bureaucracy as well as by the absence of clear lines of responsibility and authority.

To a large degree, measures providing for the implementation of this newly recognized principle were contained in the economic reforms, which provided for decentralization and the removal of both the party and the government from interference in day to day economic matters. To combat inefficiency, the government began to release large numbers of civil servants. By the end of October 1964 the 'anti-bureaucracy campaign' had abolished some 27000 administrative posts.[1] For the same purpose and to adjust the government to the needs of the new economic system as well as to the demands for greater independence and responsibility on the part of the government ministries, a reorganization of the government began on 3 November 1965. In this connection, it was specifically stated that the functions of the central organs were to be limited to the following: to prepare long-term plans, arrange incentive programs, study investment, develop foreign trade contracts, handle basic economic issues, and secure plan fulfillment.[2] The reorganization involved the dissolution of certain ministries, the creation of others and of central administrations, and personnel changes which raised generally younger, technically qualified men to top ministry positions.

THE NATIONAL ASSEMBLY

Responsibility of the government as a whole and the ministries as

[1] 'Current Developments,' *East Europe*, XIII:2 (1965), 30.
[2] 'Current Developments,' *East Europe*, XIII:12 (1965), 34–5; *Bratislava Pravda*, 11 November 1965 (Lenart).

individual units of the government was affected also by changes agreed on by the party with regard to the elected organs of government. The scope, responsibility, and independence of these organs were to be increased and this in itself was likely to lead to a state of affairs in which the government would be serving, increasingly, the decisions of the elected organs – as provided by the Constitution. In this case, it was stated, the government would serve the party only with regard to the most basic or general matters. While Novotny had explained the primary task of the government as the 'consistent realization of the basic political–economic directives of the party and its organs,' he was more explicit in adding: 'the main thing will be that, on the basis of the leading directives and resolutions of the party, the activity of the entire State set-up will be guided by the National Assembly plenum toward the decisive tasks and their realizations.'[1]

This in the past had been no more than rhetoric but in May 1964 a party decision outlined new tasks which were to fall within the jurisdiction of the National Assembly. In this decision the party admitted that the Twelfth Party Congress directive to improve the activity of the National Assembly had not been carried out. According to the new decision, the most important change for the National Assembly would be a strengthening of its control function with regard to all links of the state structure, from the ministries to the local organs of government. By this was meant consistent control of adherence to constitutionality and law (including control over the work of the Prosecutor's Office and the Supreme Court); control of the government; and control through Assembly committees of industrial management sectors. Through basic legal norms 'and other directives,' the Assembly might thus direct the activity of the whole system of elected and executive organs; assure completion of plans and goals, and play a more active role in the creation and revision of laws, implementing (perhaps) its constitutionally proclaimed role as the supreme organ of state power.[2]

The party decision pointed out that to fulfill this control function properly the Assembly's working methods would have to be improved. The Assembly should meet more regularly and frequently and for longer sessions to afford the opportunity for more discussion by the deputies of the questions submitted and thus greater opportunity to exercise control over the government. The National Assembly had been meeting twice a year, usually for only two or three days at a time.

[1] *Rude Pravo*, 29 May 1966.   [2] *Rude Pravo*, 20 May 1964, for the following also.

The Assembly was to inform the public more regularly and fully, and stimulate the public's interest in its activities. Ministers should appear to answer questions on bills and programs, instead of merely having the premier deliver a report on the government's work, as had been the practice. As we shall see below, this control activity was to extend to work of the Slovak National Council (SNC) and the National Committees as well.

The legislative function of the National Assembly was also to be strengthened, according to the decisions, in order to provide a unified legal code. In this way it was hoped to eliminate or avoid the practice of administrative measures, decrees, and directives, and to assure adherence to a unified system of legally passed laws. The procedure for passage of laws was also to be changed to replace the system whereby government-proposed bills (which had accounted for virtually all bills) were merely affirmed by the deputies who were rapporteurs for the Assembly committees. Henceforth, whosoever submitted a law would have to appear before the Assembly plenum to justify it. This not only would produce the demand for a greater responsibility on the part of the government office making the proposal but, perhaps more important, it would open the possibility for the appropriate Assembly committee to submit to the plenum its own standpoint on the proposed law. Significantly, however, no changes were recommended to limit the excessively exercised power of the Assembly's presidium to issue decrees when the Assembly was not in session.

The committees of the National Assembly were given a good deal of attention in the party's decision, which termed them the 'center of gravity of the work and creative activity of the National Assembly.' The committees were to take an increased role in working out programmatic questions in such areas as the economy, with increased control over the fulfillment of such programs. Specifically this meant that the committees were empowered to check the drafts of regulations through which a particular law was to be implemented, and make appropriate recommendations to the state organs concerned. An important element of this function was that the organs concerned would be obliged to discuss and answer the criticism raised by the committees, and if the criticism concerned a basic matter the committee itself might suggest a solution to the Assembly. All the above, i.e. the relationship of the Assembly committees to the departmental managerial organs, was to be defined and protected by law. At the same time, the control work of the committees was to be coordinated, insofar as possible, with the Peoples

Control Commissions and, in Slovakia, with the Slovak National Commissions.

Committee chairmen were to be full-time employees, and their deputies were to be freed from other responsibilities when called upon to fulfill their functions in Assembly organs. A longer time was to be devoted to the consideration of proposed bills, with the principles upon which the bills were based also taken into consideration. Committees were regularly to review the effect of important legislation and to evaluate the rules of implementation as well as their continued legality. In conjunction with the recognition of the importance of the National Assembly committees, the number of committees was to be increased, with the notable addition of a National Assembly committee for National Committees.

According to the Constitution, the National Committees were to be under the direction of the government. In 1966 when Rudolf Barak was in the process of demotion, a government commission for National Committees was created, possibly for the purpose of placing him in a somewhat meaningless job. This commission was indeed abolished after Barak's arrest and in January 1963 Siroky, still Premier, stated that the commission had been 'superfluous.'[1] Its place was taken by a central commission for the local economy which in turn was abolished by the government reorganization of November 1965. With the party 'decision' on this matter, clause 48 of the Constitution was interpreted broadly to provide the National Assembly control over the National Committee in accordance with the Assembly's general task of directing the activity of the entire system of representative organs. Novotny himself explained that the role of the National Assembly vis-a-vis the National Committees was to be strengthened, but, he said, at the same time 'the activity of the National Committees would continue to be directed by the government in harmony with the Constitution.'[2] This somewhat confusing statement, given the clarity of the party 'decision,' may have been intended to justify, temporarily, the continued existence of the government commission on local economy which was abolished only six months later.

In speaking of the control function of the National Assembly, e.g. supervision and control over implementation of laws, Novotny stated that in the distant future 'this will presuppose a gradual merger of the legislative and executive function in the supreme organs of our socialist state.' This was the only occasion upon which mention of any

[1] Cited in *Rude Pravo*, 24 March 1966.   [2] *Rude Pravo*, 29 May 1964.

such merger was made, and it does not appear to have had any basis in the party ideology of the time. There was already a precedent in Czechoslovakia for such a merger, however, in the form of the Slovak National Council which was both the executive and the legislature of the Slovak 'state within a state.' It is difficult to determine, however, if Novotny was indeed referring to the eventuality of such an arrangement for the Czechoslovak government. It may be that he saw in this concept the ultimate in the rule of the people through their elected organs, whereby only elected officials would be responsible for the direction of implementation as well as the instigation of plans and laws. Such a system recalls the original concept of the 'Soviet' and it may be that Novotny on this isolated occasion was thinking of reconciling the basically western parliamentary ideas introduced by the party decision with some aspect, even an outdated one, of the Soviet system. It should be noted in this connection that most or even all of the measures recommended by the party 'decision' were traditional 'checking' features of western-style parliaments, including the pre-1948 Czechoslovak parliament. In many cases the measures called for were actually already provided for in the Constitution and the 1960 rules of procedure and activities of the National Assembly, but the need to reiterate them and secure them by further legislation was admittedly necessitated by the fact that they had not been implemented and, in effect, had become defunct.[1]

With these changes, the National Assembly lost some of its character of a purely rubber stamp organization. From 1948 until September 1964 the National Assembly committees and plenum had unanimously passed every bill submitted to them. After September 1964 one began to detect signs of change and activity. The Assembly itself began to meet more frequently: for example, from May 1964 to February 1966 the Assembly met nine times instead of the four times it used to meet in the same period under the previous system. One intellectual commented in 1966 that debates in Assembly committees had become so 'lively and long,' and opposition on the part of Assembly deputies had increased to such an extent that there were 'rigorous conflicts and real duels.' He added that the university bill, health bill, and other draft laws 'drew so many suggestions and proposed amendments that the drafts had to be redrafted' by the government.[2] Prague radio reported

[1] For such an admission, see *ibid*.
[2] *Reporter*, 14 April 1966. An innovation of the health bill was that patients would be free to choose their own doctors, including doctors outside their communities (albeit within certain territorial limits).

the 'lively discussions' of the April 1965 session, saying that in some cases deputies had not been satisfied with draft bills and had returned them to the respective ministers for re-drafting.[1] The list of rejected bills also included the bill on authors' fees, the criminal code, and the bill on vehicle tax. One deputy demanded a government response to a question concerning the development of Prague, and several deputies criticized 'the shortcomings in the direction of the national economy.' According to another Prague radio report, deputies of the foreign affairs committee had requested to be better informed (by the government) on current international questions.[2] The agricultural committee returned a bill to the Finance Ministry for a change regarding agricultural taxes and twice returned a bill concerning the contribution of collective farmers to health insurance. The constitution and legal committee criticized a bill on the right of assembly because the bill demanded prior authorization for assembly.[3] In still another case the government's police law passed only after an amendment offered in the Assembly was accepted by a 115 to 87 vote. The amendment provided for parliamentary immunity.

While these instances of activity befitting an independent parliament were encouraging, they were nonetheless limited and by no means evidence of a return to democracy in Czechoslovakia. Rather they were signs of change, which tested the sincerity of the regime's pronouncements and reforms in connection with de-Stalinization. More than changes in the procedure and functions of the Assembly would have to be introduced in order to remove all the obstacles which stood in the way of an independent and effective parliament. Perhaps the biggest obstacle was one of the basic principles of the socialist Constitution: the Czechoslovak Communist Party as the leading force of the society and state. Such a principle could not but interfere with the freedom of the Assembly, for deputies were constitutionally required to respect the will of the party and were thereby limited insofar as they might oppose party-decreed policy. With or without this change, however, the Assembly reforms could only be meaningful if government ministries were accorded greater independence and responsibility (vis-a-vis the party), if the nature of election to the assembly were altered, if the whole structure of elected government were given greater authority and responsibility as distinct from party and police control, and if the rule of law were once again ensconced.

[1] Prague radio, 12 April 1965. [2] Prague radio, 9 February 1966.
[3] *Lidove Demokracie*, 3 February 1967.

THE NATIONAL COMMITTEES

The party 'Theses' envisaged several changes for the National Committees, which were gradually worked out at a conference of National Committees and party central committee plena in February and March 1966.[1] The National Committees were to have increased independence and authority as a result of certain economic, organizational, and legal adjustments. Local National Committees were to be given more responsibilities while higher National Committees would concentrate more on participation and increased authority in the formulation of the state, long-term, and regional plans. The National Committees would be subject to less intervention in their local work, and they would be given freedom to operate on their own initiative. To achieve these goals the Committees were to strive for 'a maximum of self-sufficiency,' through the rights to levy taxes, charge fees for local services, and share in enterprise profits, and by construction of profitable facilities. On the other hand, in keeping with the economic reforms, they themselves were to refrain from interfering in the day to day functioning of enterprises. They would, however, absorb the Peoples Control Commissions at the local level. According to the then Premier Lenart, the National Committees were to be 'full-blooded' political organs; at one and the same time organs of state power and social organizations, representing and reflecting the social structure of society. To fulfill this dual role, however, they must be truly representative. They must be given greater scope, confidence, responsibility, and independence.[2]

Financial self-sufficiency was to provide a guarantee of political autonomy, for the local Committees would be free to construct their own managerial and representative forms. It was also to provide greater efficiency, for the local Committees would be subject to the principles of the new economic system, which demanded cost-accounting and profitability. It was decided, therefore, to reduce drastically the percentage of Committee funds centrally allocated (at the time some fifty-nine per cent of their funds), and force them to be self-sufficient by eliminating the practice of balancing their budgets by appropriations from the next level (local from district, district from regional, or regional from government).

These reforms of the National Committees were approved by the party central committee in March 1966 and enacted into formal party

---

[1] *Rude Pravo*, 28 March 1966, carried the party decisions.
[2] *Rude Pravo*, 26 March 1966 (Lenart speech).

policy by a resolution of the Thirteenth Party Congress. The congress resolution placed only two limitations on the above liberalization: first, that the budgets of National Committees, from the lowest level up, be approved by the next higher National Committee; and secondly, special problems of the National Committees be dealt with by a control group in the Ministry of Interior. It was stipulated, however, that this 'control' by the Interior Ministry would not include intervention in the affairs of the Committees or modification of their powers. This measure was presumably designed to find a suitable organ of government to fulfill the government's prescribed responsibility for the National Committees, in conjunction with the National Assembly, in place of the disbanded government office for local economy.

ELECTORAL REFORM

In order for the reforms of the elected organs to be of real significance, there had to be corresponding reforms of the electoral system. There were actually two revisions of the election laws in the period under review – one which preceded the above reforms and one which more or less accompanied them though following them in time. The reform of 1964 introduced the principle of choice, albeit in a limited fashion, which was expanded only slightly by the changes of 1967. In addition to this principle the election laws together wrought a number of changes from the previous electoral system which had been based on the Electoral Law of 1960.[1]

With regard to the National Assembly, the reforms provided for four to eight deputies from each constituency instead of one, as under both the 1964 and 1960 laws. This represented an adjustment to the varied nature of socialist society, for multiple representatives from each constituency would 'better reflect the social and political structure of the population,' permitting closer and easier contact with deputies. This would mean the 'end of the era of the universal deputy,' for deputies were to specialize in one branch of administration or another.[2] It was difficult to foresee if this stated purpose for the change would indeed work out in practice, for the number of actual deputies in the Assembly was to remain the same: three hundred. Presumably, therefore, constituencies were to be significantly enlarged, so as to permit four to eight deputies from each, while staying within the limits of a

[1] *Sbirka Zakonu* No. 37/1960; No. 34/1964; No. 113/1967.
[2] *Prace*, 18 January 1968.

three hundred total. If this were the case, it was not entirely clear that there would indeed be increased contact with the constituents, although the division of labor among deputies of varied backgrounds might be achieved.

The selection of candidates and the final choice from among the candidates were the most important elements of the electoral reforms. According to the 1964 and 1967 laws, each component of the National Front would prepare a list of candidates for each constituency. From each constituency the lists, which could contain more names than positions available, would go through the regional election commission to the central election commission of the National Front. This commission was elected by the presidium of the National Assembly, while the regional election commissioners were elected by the regional National Committees. The central election commission of the National Front would then compile a National Front list and send this, along with the original lists of the National Front components, to the regional election commissions. The regional election commission would then organize meetings of voters in each locality to discuss *all* the lists. At these meetings 'the voters express their opinions on the candidates and in that way participate in their selection.'[1] The voters could not, however, suggest other candidates. The regional election commissions would then compile the final list, which was to be one-third to one-half larger than positions open, and it would decide on the order of appearance on the ballot for each constituency.

The crucial elements here were that the lists submitted for consideration both initially and to the nominating meetings might contain more names than positions, that voter participation was exercised at these meetings, and that the regional committees made the final decision as to the candidates and their order on the ballot. The element of choice was indeed an innovation of the 1964 bill, but the efficacy of this improvement could well be seriously limited by the other provisions. Neither the 1967 nor the 1964 bills explained *how* the voters would exercise their 'participation' rights at the nominating meetings, other than by publicly 'expressing' their opinions. Moreover, the voters were not permitted to discuss any but the proposed candidates since they could neither add nor substitute names to the already prepared lists. It was not entirely clear just how binding – if at all – the opinions of the voters expressed at these meetings were upon the regional election commissions, whose job it was to compile the final lists and the order

[1] *Sbirka Zakonu* No. 113/1967, Part VI, Section 26.

of appearance on the ballots. The reformers apparently realized this weakness, for the 1967 bill was slightly different on this point. It specified that the regional election commission would 'take account' of the views expressed at the voters' meetings. While this was indeed a weak guarantee that the voters' discussions would have a bearing on the compilation of the final lists, it did represent some attempt to supply the crucial link between the people and the choice, missing from the previous bill.

This problem was all the more important if one considered the other task of the regional election commission: to decide on the order of appearance on the ballot. One might argue that even if the element of choice were without any real guarantee at the level of the voters' meetings, nonetheless there remained some degree of choice on the final ballot where more names appeared than positions available. Here too, however, the choice was more limited than would appear, because of the election procedure. The voter voted for each person individually on the ballot by crossing out the names of the candidates *not* desired. Election, however, was assured not by the number of votes received, but by the position on the ballot, so long as the candidate received fifty per cent or more of the votes cast. Thus the candidate third on the list might receive only 50·1 per cent of the ballots cast, while number nine received ninety per cent, but number nine still might not be elected if the number of deputies required for the constituency and appearing before him on the ballot received the minimum of fifty per cent of the votes. Thus the order of appearance on the ballot was a crucial element, and this element was the prerogative of the regional election commission.

This is not to say that the reforms did not represent any progress. Admission, even in theory, of the necessity for choice was a change in principle, just as the idea of representatives from varying strata and parties to reflect the structure of society was a concession in principle. There was nothing in the 1967 bill which specifically denied the voters' choice; the latter merely was not properly guaranteed by the text of the law. There too, as in many of the reforms we have already seen, the interpretation upon which the law was applied would determine all. If the law were applied in the spirit in which it was devised – to provide the voters a choice – then the regional election commissions would indeed base their final lists upon the expressed desires of the voters (and if the other reforms within the society were effective the meetings themselves could be free and open discussions of the candidates).

While there was no mention of a secret vote at the nominating level, such was guaranteed by the law for the elections themselves. The secret ballot, however, had always been protected by law; it was lost in practice only because of a communist-inspired custom: the demonstrative casting of ballots. As long as this custom was continued or even permitted there remained the element of intimidation for those who wished to exercise their right to a secret ballot. This point had not gone unnoticed but the party central committee chief for elections indicated that no significant change was envisaged. He said: 'Elections are free in our country and, therefore, we must not deny anyone the possibility of casting a ballot in this or that manner. Thus any voter may do so, demonstratively or otherwise,'¹ It might have been more promising had he said '*secretly*,' or otherwise.

The 1967 reforms did, however, produce certain changes of a positive nature. For example, if the number of votes cast in a particular constituency should be less than fifty per cent of the eligible voters the election was to be declared null and void and a new election held within two weeks, this procedure to continue until a majority of the voters appeared for an election. While alternates were to be elected along with the deputies, they were to be those next on the list, not a separate list, thereby eliminating the need for by-elections. Moreover, a deputy might resign *without* providing a reason, whereas previously a deputy had had to prove his inability to carry on his functions. Recall of a deputy was to be decided by secret ballot, whereas previously it had been decided publicly. Another potentially significant procedural change was the separation, in time, of the National Committee elections from those for the National Assembly. Under the 1967 bill, elections to the National Assembly were to be held six months after the National Committee elections, rather than on the same day as formerly. Given the key role allotted the National Committees in the preparation of the National Assembly election lists, it was a progressive step to have them elected separately from and *before* the general elections. Thus the nature of the final ballot presented to the voters might well be determined or at least influenced by the nature of the regional National Committees they themselves had elected six months earlier.

¹ Cited in J. Frank, 'The New Election Laws,' RFE (1968), 4.

14

SLOVAKIA

Any reforms of the powers, responsibilities, or structure of government organs in Czechoslovakia had to include changes in the governmental organs of Slovakia and their relative power and responsibilities vis-à-vis Prague. Yet such reforms involved an almost entirely different set of principles and problems than the aforementioned changes in the government. The 'Slovak question' had plagued the pre-communist First Republic no less than it has the communist regime. It was then as later a source of instability, for then as later Prague was unwilling or unable to find an alternative to strong centralist control which alienated the three million Slovak 'partner–minority.' It was the Slovaks who formed the spearhead of the de-Stalinization movement, mainly because of the desire of Slovak communists to undo the injustices inflicted upon their party in the Stalinist era. Thus their demands centered on rehabilitations of the former victims and purges of those responsible – and in these demands they were successful. Starting with the removal of Karol Bacilek in April 1963, compromised Slovak communists were one by one purged from their leading positions, until, by 1966, not one Slovak communist held a post in the Slovak or Czechoslovak party presidiums or secretariats who had been in the Slovak politburo or secretariat in 1954 – the time of the purges of the 'bourgeois nationalists.' Along with these purges had come rehabilitations and, finally, a declaration by Novotny that there had indeed been no substance to the charges of 'bourgeois nationalism.'

The above demands, however, had been only part of very basic grievances on the part of the Slovaks with regard to their status in the Czechoslovak Republic, for the past injustices had been designed to deprive the Slovaks of any independent leadership, even communist, and to subordinate them to Prague. The admission of 'Stalinist' errors with regard to the past injustices led to a reappraisal of such national phenomena as the 1944 Slovak National Uprising and with the belated justification of such events as this and of their perpetrators, certain old Slovak nationalist ideas seemed also to be rehabilitated. In fact the purges and rehabilitations seemed to act as a spur to Slovak nationalism, which increased with the progress of de-Stalinization.

Political Reforms

The Czech–Slovak problem, and the friction, born of many socio–cultural–economic, even religious, differences between the two peoples, is not a phenomenon unique to the communist period. The problem had remained unsolved by the centralist First Republic and even the Czechoslovak Communist Party was admonished by the Comintern for its failure to adopt 'proper' policies with regard to the non-Czech minorities. Indeed there are those who maintain that the Czechoslovak party, like the Republic itself, was constantly in danger of splitting into national units before the war.[1]

With the dismemberment of Czechoslovakia in 1939 the Slovak party was cut off from its parent organization. For the first time there was an independent, albeit illegal, Slovak Communist Party, registered independently as a section of the Comintern, though theoretically still subordinate to the guidance of the Czechoslovak party leadership. The party formed an active underground which had very little guidance from outside, for the emissaries sent from the Czechoslovak party in exile in Moscow, such as Karol Bacilek and Viliam Siroky, were arrested upon arrival in Slovakia. Thus the leadership fell into the hands of Slovak communists who had remained in Slovakia. These men, such as Gustav Husak and Laco Novomesky, had been domestic leaders little exposed to Moscow; they had been leaders of the national-ist–communist intellectual circle of Slovakia, known as the 'Davists' in the interwar period. Their objective, as stated in the Slovak Party Program of 1 May 1941, was a Slovak Soviet Socialist Republic. There are conflicting reports as to how much support, if any, Stalin gave this goal. By the time of the Slovak National Uprising of August 1944, however, Moscow clearly was suspicious of the local nationalist movement, especially as the problem of the future of Czechoslovakia had already been worked out with the Benes government in exile. Siroky once claimed, however, that as late as 1944 Husak continued to advocate Slovak independence as a Soviet republic.[2]

In keeping with the policy of a united front against fascism, the Slovak communists in September 1943 joined forces with the other anti-fascist parties of Slovakia and participated in the creation of the Slovak National Council (SNC), which organized a Slovak uprising

[1] Paul Zinner, *Strategy and Tactics in Czechoslovakia, 1918–1948* (London, 1963), 36–7.
[2] Cited in Netik and Franko, 'Communism in Slovakia,' RFE (1960), 85.

against the Germans. Moscow opposed both the coalition with the other parties and the uprising, but its struggle to gain control of the Slovak party was generally to no avail until the Soviet army occupied Slovakia. Despite the failure of the uprising, Slovak rights had been given a boost by the fact that the Slovaks' name had been somewhat reclaimed; the active Slovak underground could lay claim to future rights as that part of Slovakia which had refused to collaborate with the Nazis. When the SNC came out from its underground existence with the uprising in 1944 it had assumed the exercise of the entire legislative, governmental, and executive power in Slovakia. It provided for a board of commissioners or cabinet, appointed by and responsible to the SNC, and subordinate to the SNC presidium which was composed of three communists and three democrats. Both Moscow and the Benes government were forced to recognize the fact that Slovakia had a governing body which insisted on acting as the Slovak spokesman in any future Czechoslovak government.[1]

The official government program (The Kosice Program), proclaimed upon the Benes government's return to Czechoslovakia in April 1945, pledged full equality as the basis of Czech–Slovak relations and recognized the SNC as the sole source of governmental power in Slovakia. It promised that matters governing the whole republic would be settled in close cooperation between the government and the SNC, and that the interests of the Slovaks in the central administration would be protected by proportionate representation in numbers as well as importance of posts accorded Slovaks. The program was something of a concession to the Slovaks and it is significant that Gottwald himself chose to announce the part relevant to the Slovaks, presenting the communists as it were as champions of the Slovak cause. Communist voting strength in Slovakia was not, however, as strong as hoped for in the May 1946 elections, and subsequently the communists apparently saw no reason to push for more than token Slovak rights. Conceptually, the Czech communists argued that the problem of Slovak nationalism was a socio–economic one; given socialist development, i.e. a significant improvement in the economic position of Slovakia and social reorganization, the nationalist demands and with them the entire problem would disappear. In June 1946 the relationship between the SNC and the central government was worked out in greater detail – to

[1] Edward Taborsky, 'Slovakia under Communist Rule', *Journal of Central European Affairs*, XIV (October 1954), 258–9; Taborsky, *Communism in Czechoslovakia* (Princeton, 1961), 332.

the detriment of the Slovaks. The Slovak Board of Commissioners was made responsible to the central government cabinet in Prague, in addition to the SNC presidium, in all matters such as appointments and approval of decisions.

The Slovak communists were not dissatisfied with the Kosice Program, though it has been said that Husak and other nationalist leaders were interested in more of a federal or dualistic concept not unlike the Austro–Hungarian administration. In August 1945, however, the Slovak party was characterized by a clash between 'centrists' and 'nationalists,' with the former apparently gaining a slight edge. It was nonetheless decided that the Slovak party would not yet formally amalgamate with the Prague party, mainly for tactical reasons connected with the elections of 1946. Thus the Slovak party remained organizationally independent until 1948, though completely subordinate to and guided by Prague through Prague-oriented Slovaks such as Siroky and Bacilek.

After their accession to full power in 1948, the communists regulated the positions of both Slovakia and the Slovak party. The relative positions of the governmental organs were settled, not without Slovak opposition, by the Constitution of May 1948.[1] This was a strongly centrist document which left the Slovak organs with little but formal powers. The powers of the SNC were strictly enumerated, with no residual powers such as had been permitted by earlier agreements. The powers that were permitted were restricted to ten fields of rather limited political importance such as elementary and secondary education, cultural affairs, public health, building operations, care of orphans, and so forth. Even in these areas the powers were restricted by the phrase 'save for matters within the scope of the uniform and economic plan.'[2]

While the SNC was designated the national organ of legislative power in Slovakia, and the Board of Commissioners designated the national organ of governmental and executive power, the Commissioners were accountable to the central government and the corresponding ministers in Prague, the latter maintaining the right to exercise their authority *directly* in Slovakia. This clause for all intents and purposes rendered the Slovak Commissioners superfluous. The SNC itself was summoned by the Premier and could be dissolved by him. Its laws had to be approved by the cabinet and signed by the Premier, as well as by the

[1] Karel Kaplan, *Utvareni Generalni Linie* (Praha, 1966), 37–9.
[2] Taborsky, *Communism in Czechoslovakia*, 336.

chairman of the SNC. Moreover, the National Assembly was responsible for determining the franchise conditions for SNC elections and was responsible for carrying them out.

The appointment of the Commissioners also underwent a tightening up from Prague. In 1946 cabinet approval was made a requirement, but with the 1948 Constitution, the cabinet received directly and totally the power to appoint – and recall – the Slovak Commissioners. In another sphere, the Slovaks had pressed for but not received, except briefly in 1946, a clause that would require the consent of a majority of the Slovak members of the National Assembly for the passage of any amendment to the Constitution affecting the status of Slovakia. Under the 1948 Constitution a three-fifths majority of the Assembly was required for any amendment to the constitution. As more than three-fifths of the members were Czechs, Slovak opposition alone would not be sufficient to prevent the Czechs from amending the Slovak status in any way they wished.[1]

The change in formal provisions was accompanied by a change in the operation of Slovak government. SNC meetings became less frequent and legislation was replaced by administrative decrees from Prague. The SNC under the 1948 Constitution was given less and less responsibility and the Board of Commissioners was left merely trivial matters to administer.

Taking over the Slovak party required fewer formalities. In July 1948, the Czechoslovak party presidium (then politburo) passed a resolution to the effect that a Slovak party central committee plenum would resolve (which it did two months later) that the Slovak party was no longer an independent party and would be re-integrated into the Czechoslovak party.[2] The party organization would, however, retain the designation Communist Party of Slovakia. The resolution also provided that the Slovak party central committee would be subordinate to the Czechoslovak party central committee, would abide by the latter's directives, and carry out the policy of the Czechoslovak party in Slovakia. Shortly thereafter began the purges of those Slovak leaders who might present a threat to this renewed subordination.

During the limited nod to de-Stalinization in 1956 the regime did introduce certain improvements in the authority and jurisdiction of the SNC. Specifically a constitutional law granted the SNC increased legislative power, eliminating the strict enumeration of categories in which the SNC could legislate, and giving the Commissioners the right

[1] *Ibid.*   [2] Kaplan, *Linie*, 103.

to supervise the work of the National Committees in Slovakia. The Commissioners' rights were limited, however, by the granting of the central government the right to designate the areas in which the Commissioners would have competence.[1] Moreover, those measures included in the changes of 1956 which might have been progressive, were more or less nullified four years later by the 1960 Socialist Constitution, which significantly reduced Slovak powers. The most significant curtailment was the abolition of the Board of Commissioners which was said to have 'outlived its [*sic*] time.' The new needs of the state it was explained, required

> a strengthening of the position of the all-state (central) planning and directing organs of the government, the State Planning Commission, and ministries. In relation to the Slovak national organs, this means that ... it is neither suitable nor possible to extend the planning and directing mechanisms in Slovakia which were represented by the Commissioners and Departments.[2]

Thus the 1960 Constitution deprived the SNC of its separate executive arm and combined within the SNC both legislative and executive powers. The Commissioners' Offices were abolished and SNC departments, corresponding in part to the committees of the National Assembly, were all that remained of them. These were to administer 'sections' of the SNC and 'must not be identified with the former Commissioner's offices, which have been abolished.'[3] Indeed there were only one half as many departments as there were Commissioners' Offices. With the abolition of the Board went the Slovak control of the National Committees in Slovakia, for the Commissioner's Offices had been the depository of this responsibility within Slovakia. This was explained by the increased importance of the National Committees and the desire to place them under the immediate direction of the central government.

In addition to these curbs on the executive powers of the Slovak organs, a serious restriction was placed on the SNC's legislative activity. Whereas under the 1956 amendment the National Assembly could annul a law of the SNC, the 1960 Constitution stipulated that the SNC might legislate only when authorized to do so by the National Assembly. The Assembly, nonetheless, retained its veto right.

[1] *Sbirka Zakonu* No. 33/1956.
[2] Eduard Kucera, 'The Application of the Leninist Principle of Nationality Policy to the Settlement of the Czech–Slovak Relationship,' *Pravnik*, XCIX:7 (1960), 635–6. [3] *Ibid.* 635.

Slovakia

The Constitution probably did no more than formalize the central controls that were already being exercised – that is, over and above the controls already formalized by the 1948 Constitution and the 1956 amendments. As Jozef Lenart, then a Slovak party secretary, himself admitted, however, 'many people saw in the 1960 changes a liquidation of the Slovak national organs.'[1] While this may have been merely an advanced stage of the process begun by Prague in the late 1940s to absorb both the state and party organizations of Slovakia, the whole issue became the subject of much discussion when de-Stalinization finally was introduced in Czechoslovakia.

THE PRESSURES

The campaign for the 'rehabilitation' of the Slovak National Uprising was directly connected with the early de-Stalinization demands for purges and rehabilitations. The Slovaks won their first victories in 1963, with the rehabilitations; and the Twentieth Anniversary of the uprising was accorded a major fete, graced by the presence not only of Novotny but also of Khrushchev, in August 1964. The major principle gained by this campaign was recognition of the fact that the uprising had been a Slovak undertaking, planned and executed by Slovaks not by Moscow or by Czech (or even Slovak) emigres in Moscow.[2] The Slovaks achieved open recognition of the fact that the uprising had been the work not merely of Slovak communists, but of non-communist Slovaks as well, i.e. *justification* of their policy at the time, the policy of coalition with the Slovak democrats.[3] Thus the Slovak party could with pride admit to nationalism without the 'bourgeois' label, returning to the original purpose of the uprising, i.e. to clear the name of the Slovaks, so as to obtain for them their rights as a national unit.

[1] Jozef Lenart, 'About Some Problems in the Development of Slovakia in Socialist Czechoslovakia,' *Nova Mysl*, XII:7 (1960), 749.
[2] See *Kulturny Zivot*, 11 March and 8 April 1966.
[3] The role of the western allies was also recognized. The survivors of a U.S.– British team dropped into Slovakia during the uprising were invited to the anniversary celebrations. Later it was claimed that the U.S. had wanted to send more help, but the communists (not stated if local or Moscow) refused. (*Lud*, 28 August 1966.) Similarly, Josef Smrkovsky admitted that the communists had refused General Patton permission to continue eastward in May 1944, for the Americans would then have been 'the liberators of Prague' and there might have been 'undesirable political consequences.' (*Rude Pravo*, 4 May 1965.) In the West the dispute centers on the U.S. 'need' to request permission, rather than the understandable communist refusal. See Herbert Feis, *Churchill, Roosevelt, Stalin* (Princeton, 1957).

The Hundred and Fiftieth Anniversary of the birth of Ludovit Stur one year later bared still more basic grievances, still more nationalist in character and broader in their meaning for Slovaks than the earlier rehabilitation of Slovak party leaders and policy. Stur had been condemned by the Marxists in Prague on the grounds that he was a reactionary nationalist of the nineteenth-century bourgeois variety. He had been condemned by Marx himself because the Stur movement had opposed the 1848 Hungarian revolution. This opposition had in fact been based upon the strong anti-Magyar sentiment of the Slovaks, who looked upon the Magyars, not the Austro–Hungarian empire itself, as the greatest obstacle to their freedom as a nation. The Slovaks strove for a redemption of Stur's memory not only because they resented the short shrift accorded the national hero by the Prague-oriented party historians, but also because there was much in Stur's arguments of a hundred years earlier that was still pertinent and useful for present demands. As one prominent Slovak, Pavol Stevcek, put it: 'It is typical for our tragic, or perhaps tragi-comic specific national conditions, up to the present, that we have failed to celebrate the greatest Slovak in a fitting manner (and this means primarily that we have failed to acknowledge him),' but celebrating him was not a question of historical justice but one of 'we ourselves, our character and the shape of our future as a nation or as a State.' Challenging the tendency to mere phrase-making, Stevcek called for a return not only to the words of Stur, but to 'the spirit of his concepts ... A return to confronting words and deeds, to evaluating our national history along the lines of our *sole fully developed concept*, that is, Stur's national concept.'[1] Another leading Slovak intellectual, Karol Rosenbaum, said: 'It will be good for us if we consider Stur's attitudes as our own, if we make them the foundation of our socialist life.'[2]

Marx's condemnation of Stur was an obstacle to any return to Stur's national concept or the foundation of socialist life upon Stur's attitude. This condemnation was, however, dismissed by Gustav Husak as a judgment arrived at without the aid of deep knowledge of the events and their specific conditions.[3] Husak argued that Marx had not been sympathetic to the smaller nationalities of the Hapsburg empire and, therefore, had been willing to see the Slavs and the Slovaks assimilated into a multi-national empire, to surrender their 'national freedom' for 'political freedom.' Husak called for a 'Marxist' reassessment based

[1] *Praca*, 24 October 1965. Emphasis mine.   [2] *Kulturny Zivot*, 29 October 1965.
[3] *Kulturny Zivot*, 8 October 1965.

on all the facts. Such a reassessment was offered in part by a non-Marxist, the Slovak historian Daniel Rapant. Although he attributed Marx's faulty judgment to the influence of German arrogance, he explained Stur's opposition to the Hungarian revolution in terms which might be acceptable to Marxists: the Hungarian revolution was not a struggle for internationalism and the emancipation of mankind from tyranny, it was tyranny itself, and it pursued its own parochial objectives. 'The issue was not freedom but nationality and in this guise the national, economic, political, and social principles of the ruling sections, of the Hungarians and the Germans, were involved.'[1] The Slovak communist intellectual Vladimir Minac maintained, however, that Marxist standards might not be the proper criteria for judging the development of Slovak history: 'to judge our movement, its progressive or reactionary nature, by so-called objective historical criteria is senseless,' for these criteria are reserved for great nations.[2] One cannot, he argued, apply the same criteria to an independent power and to a small emergent nation struggling to assert its individuality against the rule of Czechs, Magyars, and Germans.

Husak, however, was willing to use orthodox Marxist criteria; indeed he sought to justify nationalism within Marxist terms and theory, no doubt to justify his own nationalism. He maintained that nationalism within the Austro–Hungarian context was a progressive, not a conservative force, a revolutionary program which sought revolutionary solutions to the political and social problems of the people within a national framework, against the conservative forces of society, feudalism and oppression of smaller nations. Husak maintained, however, that the nationality problem had not yet disappeared. 'All experience leads to the conclusion that the co-existence of peoples in one state unavoidably creates the desire for a situation of equality of these peoples.' A man cannot be free if he has inferior political status, Husak argued, because such freedom would by nature be discriminatory: one man was privileged, the other was not, and these privileges were inevitably used against the non-privileged in the political, cultural, and economic spheres, creating resentment among the non-privileged. The only safeguard against this dialectical set of circumstances was the creation of state institutions to protect the small and weak against 'aggression, evil practices, and one-sided interpretations of equality,' against the privileged 'hegemonistic' efforts of the stronger ruling nation. Social and

[1] Daniel Rapant, 'Stur and his Circle,' *Slovenska Literatura*, XII:5 (1965), 439.
[2] *Kulturny Zivot*, 15, 22, and 29 October 1965.

economic measures were not sufficient; they merely raised the need or demand for greater democratization of the social and state structure. Equality, including political equality, must be institutionalized, and the implication of Husak's argument was that only political autonomy could guarantee the rights of the smaller nations.

At the center of this commemorative and often quoted discussion, lay Stur's principle of nationhood: 'a nation that maintains its independence is a member of mankind, but if it merges with another nation it is only a vein, and therefore, every noble nation must certainly choose the first alternative, if it can do so.'[1] While this would seem to be a proposal for independence it may be interpreted, as Husak did above, to mean political autonomy, or more specifically, federalization. The idea of federalization apparently was attracting a good deal of attention, for at the 10–12 November 1965 session of the National Assembly the Assembly president spoke out against the idea. He condemned federalization as a manifestation of 'narrow nationalism,' describing tendencies towards the federalist idea as incorrect and harmful 'both to the interests of the Slovak people and to the interests of a united socialist republic.'[2] Michal Chudik, chairman of the SNC, echoed these sentiments, presumably to demonstrate that the official organs of Slovakia were not interested in such an idea.[3] The party too tried to keep the Stur revival within limits, especially since no small amount of Hungarian–Slovak friction had been aroused by the revival of Stur. Slovak party first secretary Dubcek appeared at the commemorative celebrations in Bratislava on 29 October 1965, but although he acknowledged the progressive nature of the thinker, and Stur's interest in the workers and internationalism, Dubcek emphasized Stur's call for co-existence with the Czechs, neglecting to mention the federative nature of the Czech–Slovak union envisaged by Stur. Nonetheless, Stur *was* restored to public attention and the discussions provoked by the commemoration gave rise to a demanding set of proposals – and counter-proposals – over the following two years.

One of the major things attacked by the Slovak advocates of change was the purely economic–social approach to the problem, an approach which left the national–political–cultural–ethnographic issue open, along with the constitutional form of rapprochement. One Slovak explained that what was required was a clear, concrete theory of rapprochement, for the present approach was based on generalities

---

[1] *Praca*, 24 October 1965 (Stevcek). [2] Prague radio, 11 November 1965.
[3] *Rude Pravo*, 12 November 1965.

which 'when followed by the unfortunate practice of abolition or reduction of the authority of some national institutions' aroused 'justified fears' of a revival 'under a new socialist name, of the discredited theory and practice of the old Czechoslovakism.'[1] One scholar, Jan Mlynarik, looked to the former party leader Bohumil Smeral for such a concrete theory of rapprochement, praising what he called Smeral's 'federative ideal.'[2] Claiming that this idea was 'rooted in the real needs of the Slovak nation,' he criticized the party for letting the idea fall to the fascist Slovak nationalists, i.e. Hlinka, after the fall of Smeral in 1925. This positive reference to Smeral also constituted an implicit bid for 'rehabilitation' of this victim of the Comintern-ordered purges of the 1920s.

Slovak central committee candidate, economist Viktor Pavlenda, argued that even the 'economic approach' to the Slovak problem required a political counterpart, indeed a federative solution. He urged that Slovakia be considered a national–political area within the system of a single socialist economy, responsible for its own economic development and using its own resources. In his opinion political autonomy was the only assurance of responsible economic development, if for no other reason than that national equality and national initiative would stimulate economic success. Such equality, however, could not be merely proclaimed; it would have to be realized by the creation of equal political institutions.[3]

Rapant made a most provocative contribution to this discussion when, instead of limiting himself to the concept of federalization, he went so far as to call for genuine independence.[4] He maintained that Slovakia's existence as an independent nation had been more declarative than real, mainly because of the lack of any international guarantee for the existence of small nations. Common statehood with the Czechs had, therefore, been the most acceptable solution, but this need not be looked upon as a permanent solution. A neutralized Germany, accompanied by a neutralized Central Europe, plans which were already under consideration, he pointed out, would create a situation in which single independent national states could exist in Central Europe.

[1] Jan Uher in *Kulturny Zivot*, 23 December 1966.
[2] Jan Mlynarik, 'Dr Bohumil Smeral and the Slovak Nationality Question at the Beginning of the Communist Movement,' *Ceskoslovensky Casopis Historicky*, xv:5 (1967), 654ff.
[3] *Bratislava Pravda*, 9 and 26 October, 2, 9, and 16 November 1966.
[4] Daniel Rapant, 'The Slovaks in History,' *Slovenske Pohlady*, 83:4 (1967), 28–38; 'On Dualism,' *Slovenske Pohlady*, 83:11 (1967), 94–102.

Political Reforms

Rapant did not deny the need for a strong unified Warsaw Pact *until* the neutralization of Germany, but he urged that Slovakia be prepared for the day when it would obtain 'full national existence.' The best preparation, he claimed, consisted of increasing national solidarity and strengthening national consciousness. The Slovak nation was capable of great things if free, he asserted, and there was no reason that the Slovaks should not be able to work as arduously for themselves as they had for 'foreign interests' for a thousand years.

While Rapant's ideas may have been a welcomed expression of the inner sentiments of a large proportion of Slovaks, they were on the whole more hopeful than immediately pertinent and not considered a significant contribution. Serious discussion continued to revolve around how best to live with the Czechs, and, in this context, federalization versus centralism was the main issue. The Slovak party Institute of History in March 1967 organized a discussion on Czech–Slovak relations to debate this issue. One member of the party's Institute explained that while the national problem had been deferred until after the revolution, even today, in the post-revolutionary period, there were still traces of the 'centrist mania' in politics and in the 'underestimation of the creative potential and the advantages, for the whole state, of de-centralism.' The campaigns against 'bourgeois nationalism' and later against German revanchism (the latter fully justified) had wakened old memories, revitalized old prejudices and lack of understanding of the Slovak cause. At the same time there was a lack of information, and even mis-information about Slovakia which glossed over the problems and exaggerated the successes.[1]

Similar ideas were expressed by another participant, the historian Gosiorovsky, who praised the pre-Republic Pittsburg Agreement, especially the provision for a Czech–Slovak federation with two parliaments.[2] 'Czechoslovakism' both on the part of the government and on the part of the communists was to be explained by the lack of importance or power of the Slovaks and the belated grasping of the nationality problem on the part of the communists. Gosiorovsky urged that the basic principle for the solution of the relations of nations living together in one state be that 'each of these nations, if it is to develop

[1] 'A Discussion About Czech–Slovak Relations,' *Historicky Casopis*, xv:4 (1967), 559–62 (Z. Holotikova).
[2] *Ibid.* 565–7. The Pittsburgh Agreement was an agreement between T. G. Masaryk and Slovak emigres in the U.S. in 1918. Most generous to Slovakia, the Czechs denied that it was binding upon the First Republic.

successfully as an individual nation, should have within its ethnic territory its own national constitutional organization.' This principle, he explained, was advocated in the 1943–5 period, but the development in this direction 'was halted by the repression of the foremost representatives of the Slovak Communist Party, during the personality cult.' Therefore, he concluded, 'today we are plagued by the unsolved or unsatisfactorily solved constitutional relationship of two extraordinarily close yet individual nations.'

Of particular interest were the comments of Gustav Husak in this discussion, for by virtue of his earlier positions and martyrdom he was a focal point for Slovak demands. He too accepted the fact that the national question had suffered from lack of attention and 'deforming political pressures' from the communists as well as others.[1] However, the more serious problem at the contemporary stage, Husak claimed, was that the equality of the two nations was merely declarative, with no concrete constitutional provisions or guarantees of equal national life within the state, of the 'democratic right of a nation to full state and political life, to the assertion of national and state sovereignty, to a democratic autonomy in various spheres.' Lenin's principle of the 'democratic right of every nation to occupy a position of equality with all the other nations' was not in fact applied in the full sense, Husak argued, concluding that a realistic application of Marxist principles to the solution of the nationality problem depended upon 'the degree of democratization achieved in a given society, upon the position of the forces implementing these principles.' The cult, Siroky, and the Ninth (1950) Slovak Congress, had put an end to the progess made in the application of the above Marxist principles, and 'for thirteen years influenced everything the wrong way.' Until 1963 the nationality problem was conceived of as a purely economic matter; the national form of culture was in every way subordinated to the 'fight for progress and socialism,' as the Stalinist leadership conceived the latter, i.e. 'absolute state authority, power wielded by the central organs, the progressive bureaucratization of the whole of public life,' so that 'the democratic political rights of one nation (and of the citizen) were in fact negated.'

The issue was still pressing, according to Husak, and in a word to the liberals he said that the process released by the Twelfth Party Congress should also address itself to the nationality question, for the problems of socialist democracy in a modern multi-national state were

[1] *Ibid.* 568–72.

perforce connected with the solution of the nationalities problem and the problem of national autonomy. According to Husak, the present situation was merely a form of regional autonomy with varying authority of the regional organs. This was not a 'specific' solution but rather a copy of a solution applied in other socialist states. Husak herein rejected the application of the Soviet model to Czechoslovakia's nationalities problem, and he advocated a rethinking of the problem in keeping with the historical development of ideas and the actual practices from the Slovak National Uprising and the Kosice Program to the present.

The reformers were not, however, the only ones to speak out, nor did they go unopposed. Moreover, the Slovak party itself was hesitant officially to press for constitutional changes, but Michal Pecho, chief of the Slovak party central committee ideology department, admitted that the constitutional status of Slovakia was a constantly debated problem among Slovak communists.[1] He even went so far as to argue that despite the importance of the economic aspect of the nationality problem there were indeed other aspects of the problem. If it were purely an economic problem industrialization would have provided the solution, he conceded. If it were purely a social problem the end of classes would have solved it. If it were purely an ideological problem education and propaganda would have solved it. In fact, he admitted, one must have more than these partial solutions; one must have a 'political, institutional, and particularly constitutional solution.' However, recognizing the need for a political solution, Pecho, like Chudik, argued against federalization as distinct from democratic centralism. Whereas, Pecho pointed out, Engels had called federation 'a step backwards' unless the national question has not yet been settled, Lenin had asserted that 'very often a federation is merely a transitory stage on the way to real democratic centralism in a real democratic order, and hence, all the more so, in the Soviet organization of the state.' In the case of Czechoslovakia, Pecho believed that a federation would be a step backward while the basis for the necessary solution already existed in the Constitution and the government reforms regarding Slovakia. His conclusion, therefore, was that while there was room for 'nations' within the concept of the socialist state, and one should seek indepen-

[1] Michal Pecho, 'Reflections on the Nationality Problem,' *Nova Mysl*, xx:4 (1966), 3–7. Implying approval, Dubcek told the Slovak party congress that the revision of the verdict against the 'bourgeois nationalists' had evoked a sound ideological ferment. (*Bratislava Pravda*, 13 May 1966.)

dence and equality for the two cultures involved, it would be best first to give the already existing legal, political, and constitutional framework a chance before speaking of a constitutional change or federalization.

That this was the official party policy on the question was confirmed by Slovak party presidium member (and ideology chief) Vasil Bilak. Like Dubcek and Pecho, Bilak could be considered a Slovak nationalist, albeit a Ruthenian and more conservative; like the other two Slovak leaders he argued that the present Czech–Slovak model contained within it the means for solution to the problem.[1] Also citing Engels and Lenin on the subject of a federation as a step backwards, Bilak added that the Czechoslovak model had no analogy in history and represented in fact an original contribution to Marxist–Leninist theory. He explained that party policy was based on the principle that 'every nation is a permanent social reality and is and must be the subject of political, social–economic, and cultural development.' He added, however, that this principle should be reflected by a 'correct' institutional expression of the nationalities' interests. The sovereignty of every nation must be expressed through participation in the direction of national and mutual affairs, and this, he admitted, required fuller development of the Slovak national organs.

The above official arguments appeared liberal and most reasonable when contrasted with the responses of both Czech and Slovak conservatives. For these, it was not a question of how best to guarantee Slovak autonomy and fight centrism but rather how best to protect and preserve the present system and practices. Indeed some of them refused to recognize the existence of a nationality problem at all, except as a figment of certain Slovaks' imaginations, arguing that all that was needed was simply improved education and propaganda work on the part of the party. Like Novotny in most of his speeches, they would speak glowingly of the economic development of Slovakia since 1948 and the efforts made to integrate and yet respect Slovaks outside Slovakia.[2]

There were of course the more vulgar responses to Slovak demands, in which Slovaks were criticized for refusing to take advantage of the rights they had, accused of 'exaggerated national pride,' or told that in fact the present system favored the Slovaks since Slovakia was 'a state within a state.' One commentator explained the problem as tendencies

[1] *Rude Pravo*, 2 March 1966.
[2] See for example, Juraj Zvara, 'Better Relations Between our Nations and Nationalities and their Mutual Progress,' *Zivot Strany*, 16 (1966), 15–19.

to 'big power nationalism' and to 'local nationalism.'[1] The former, he explained, was the nationalism of a 'formerly oppressor nation' and stemmed from the economic and political heritage. It consisted of a tendency to centralization, an unwillingness to grasp specific, local problems, a lack of sensitivity to feelings of the oppressed, and jealousy of the efforts to improve the oppressed nation (e.g. the arguments that the industrialization of Slovakia was nothing but pampering). 'Local nationalism' was the nationalism of a formerly oppressed nation and it too stemmed from past habits. It was composed of a belief that the socialist order was nothing but a continuation of the past oppression, distrust of everything belonging to or originating in the larger nation, exaggerated demands for a build-up of the formerly oppressed nation, and disregard for the problems of others. The solution to this problem was that each nation combat the extreme within itself rather than pit itself against the opposite group.

This somewhat simplistic analysis of the problem came in response to an article airing Slovak readers' complaints over the small yet annoying aspects of the nationality problem:[2] the failure to refer to the nations as equal or the tendency to use the adjective Czech without heeding the Slovaks. For example, one would hear or read of a 'Czech' film, the 'Czech–German war games;' Jan Cikker was called a 'Czech' composer in propaganda for abroad, Vincent Hloznik a 'Czech' painter. Some complained that Slovak culture was neglected in factories, Slovak subjects were not given enough attention, and there were not enough Slovak papers. In response to such complaints, the party demanded a campaign to 'overcome little things,' and greater sensitivity to national feelings.[3]

On a somewhat higher level of importance there were complaints against 'symbolism' or 'tokenism,' i.e. the inclusion of Slovaks in the ruling body of organizations without permitting them any real influence. As one writer explained, the Czechoslovak Union of Artists had Slovaks in its central committee, but they had no influence; its headquarters were in Prague (as were the headquarters of all state-wide organizations), and the tendency was to handle problems of Czech artists in

[1] *Nova Svoboda*, 3 January 1967.　　[2] *Nova Svoboda*, 13 December 1966.
[3] *Rude Pravo*, 24 May 1967. In 1966 the teams *Spartak* and *Dynamo* had their pre-communist names, *Sparta* and *Slavia*, restored. This despite Bilak's comments: 'An undesirable psychosis, often bordering on animosity [between Czechs and Slovaks] may sometimes be observed at sports events.' (*Rude Pravo*, 2 March 1966.)

those state-wide forums leaving the Slovaks to settle those of the Slovaks.[1] If this were the practice, the writer asked, why then continue the farce of a state-wide organization, why not accord the Slovak organization equal status and independence? The still more serious problems of economic discrimination and of discrimination in cadre selection were also mentioned, and the party addressed itself to these problems in the 'Theses' for the Thirteenth Party Congress.

SLOVAK NATIONAL COUNCIL

As a result of the demands of the Slovaks in the 1963 and 1964 period and in connection with the reform of the government which began to take form in 1964, the regime also introduced certain reforms in the Slovak governing agencies. These reforms concerned the Slovak National Council, which as we have seen above had undergone a number of restricting changes culminating in the 1960 Constitution's almost total emasculation of the Slovak governing body. Though unwilling to admit that the 1960 Constitution itself was at fault, SNC chairman Chudik admitted that the functions and tasks of the SNC had been narrowed down with the reorganization of 1960, and the pertinent articles of the Constitution implemented only passively.[2] This situation was to be remedied by the party resolution of the Czechoslovak and Slovak parties' central committees of 7 May 1964 and the subsequent law on the role of the SNC.[3] The main failings that the resolution was designed to eliminate were: the insufficient implementation of the role and power of the SNC in planning and the budget; the 1960 reduction of the SNC's control functions; 'the failure to take advantage of the constitutional right [of the SNC] to take legislative action;' failure to grasp the correct relationship of the SNC to the National Committees in Slovakia and, particularly, in economic production units. The SNC was not to be merely a regional organ responsible for the affairs of a regional nature but also a national link in the state-wide political and economic management of the territory of Slovakia. It must, therefore, participate in the shaping and execution of state-wide policies.[4]

[1] Dusan Havlicek in *Kulturni Tvorba*, 10 March 1966. This was just one of numerous demands for separate organizations or federated groups.
[2] *Rude Pravo*, 4 June 1964.
[3] *Rude Pravo*, 7 May 1964; *Sbirka Zakonu* No. 124/1964 (*Rude Pravo*, 22 May 1964).
[4] This provision was also in the new National Assembly Law.

The basic step towards fulfillment of the role as defined above was the 'organic enlistment of the SNC in the entire process of the preparation and implementation of the state plan *and* control of its fulfillment as well as fulfillment of the budget estimates' for Slovakia.[1] To achieve this SNC measures would have to be as binding as measures of the central government for the National Committees and productive units and organizations in Slovakia. At the same time, there would have to be increased cooperation between the SNC president and the central government, the SNC commissions and the ministries, the SNC apparatus and the ministries. With the above principles two important items were returned to the SNC: the Board of Commissioners and control over the National Committees in Slovakia.

The SNC plenum would have the responsibility for the control of implementation of party and government decisions in Slovakia and its legislative functions were to be expanded. For example, whereas in the 1960 Constitution it was stipulated that the SNC could legislate only when specifically authorized to do so by the National Assembly, the new law called upon the National Assembly to authorize the SNC by law to carry out legislative adjustments of questions in Slovakia which require a specific adjustment. This still left the SNC legislatively subordinate to the National Assembly (which retained the right to rescind SNC laws) and greatly limited the SNC's power to initiate legislation, but it was probably the broadest adjustment that could be made within the 1960 constitutional framework. The role of the Slovak Planning Commission as the regional organ of the State Planning Commission was to be expanded in the working out, evaluating, and discussing of draft plans for that part of the economy which fell under the direction of the National Committees in Slovakia and for the regional budget. The SNC presidium would coordinate the disposition of the reserves allotted the Slovak Planning Commission by the State Planning Commission. Changes in the state plan for the Slovak region would be subject to prior consultation with the SNC presidium while the SNC presidium and the Commissioners of the SNC were to 'take part' in the preparation of nation-wide laws, legal norms, and important government decisions.

By virtue of the above and other technical measures provided by the new law, the SNC and particularly its presidium gained control over the National Committees in Slovakia, lost in 1960 when the Board of Commissioners was abolished and the National Committees directly

---

[1] *Rude Pravo*, 22 May 1964.

subordinated to the government. This measure must be seen in conjunction with the powers accorded the National Assembly with regard to the National Committees. Insofar as these powers were defined as financial control, they were themselves limited by the reforms of the National Committees. If the Committees were to be financially self-sufficient this former bond, be it to the government or regionally to the SNC, would be of limited value. Nevertheless, the task of control was re-established, and until the National Committees would achieve solvency, financial control might still be effective. Moreover, the control accorded the SNC over the National Committees was not financial only, for the presidium and the Commissioners were accorded supervisory power over the National Committees with regard to plan fulfillment, and SNC decisions were nonetheless binding.

The most important single change provided by the new law was the re-establishment of the Board of Commissioners without, however, changing the framework of the 1960 Constitution. To accommodate the latter the Commissions maintained their legislative and control functions corresponding to those of the National Assembly committees, but they were to combine with this the exclusive, managerial function corresponding to that of the ministries of the central government. Specifically, the Commissions were to take part in the drafting of the state plan; check on and ensure its implementation; develop closer working relations with the trade unions and mass organizations, and especially with the committees of the National Assembly. With regard to the last, joint sessions were recommended for the drafting of new legislation as well as for control functions.[1] At the same time, in accordance with the intensification of their executive function (which 'has been neglected in their previous activities') they were to assure the accomplishment of the tasks and laws of the state-wide government in Slovakia as well as of the SNC, handle problems specific to their spheres in Slovakia, and initiate legislation and proposals to the SNC and the central government. While the Commissions were appointed by and responsible to the SNC presidium, the party resolution (but not the law) stated that in their executive functions the Commissioners were responsible to the 'SNC, its presidium, and the government.'[2] It was not stated anywhere, however, just how much control the central organs would have over the decisions of the Commissions.

[1] The law also provided for 'delegations' of the SNC, which in fact corresponded more directly than the Commissions to the traditional tasks of parliamentary committees. [2] *Rude Pravo*, 7 May 1964.

The resolution provided for a return not only of the functions but also of the titles of the former Board of Commissioners by declaring that 'it will be useful to return to the traditional, historic title, Commissioners' office of the SNC,' because the former title, department of the SNC, did not 'take root,' nor did it 'sufficiently express the character or position of the formation of the SNC.'[1] At the same time, in what was also a return to the pre-1960 structure, the number of Commissions was more than doubled.

While these changes represented a positive step, restoring to the Slovak authorities at least those formal powers stripped from them by the 1960 Constitution, the important question was whether or not the Slovak organs would receive the *actual* powers stripped from them gradually since 1948. Regaining authority over the National Committees and regaining its executive arm or cabinet were significant even as gestures but the key to the reform was the constant reference in the party's resolution to the increased responsibility and authority for the SNC, both in Slovakia and in the shaping of all-state policies. This of itself did not eliminate the subordination of the SNC to the National Assembly or the Board's ambiguous responsibility to the government, but the scope of authority of the SNC and the Board was much more clearly spelled out by the new law. Practically speaking, at least, the reforms were an improvement; like the reformed National Assembly, the SNC began to be a much more active organization. Instead of the customary two sessions per year there were, for example, seven sessions from the time of the reforms until the beginning of 1966, and these sessions were livelier and more productive than previously.[2] In addition, at least formally, the Commissioners' Offices were not totally ignored, as before. When the government in Prague was reorganized in January 1967, for example, the Slovak Board of Commissioners underwent a similar reorganization to adjust itself, a measure which demonstrated at the very least that Prague was not treating the Slovak organs with the same indifference as it had in the past. Nonetheless the reforms might best be characterized as a stretching of the restrictive bonds of the Constitution. As such, reform in practice was still left to the realm of interpretation without a constitutionally based legal guarantee. For this reason many Slovak communists, as we have seen above, looked upon these measures as merely a first step on the road to constitutional reform. Indeed their pressures in this direction, the

[1] *Ibid.* The title 'Board of Commissioners' was not, however, reintroduced.
[2] Prague radio, 9 February 1966.

discussion and proposals we have seen above, did lead the Czechoslovak party to decide that a constitutional 'arrangement' should be
studied to provide necessary 'legal norms' with regard to the Slovak
national organs.[1]

[1] 'Tendencies of the Development of Nationality Relations and the Solution of the
Nationality Question in the CSSR,' *Nova Mysl*, XXI:12 (1967), 7–9.

15

LEGAL SYSTEM

Socialist democracy such as party liberals were trying to achieve was to affect another set of institutions of state rule in addition to the party and the governmental organs: the legal system. Most liberals believed that socialist democracy or the democratization of socialist political institutions could not be accomplished without the return of the rule of law for the protection of the rights and liberties of the citizen. This was by no means a casual or minor demand in the de-Stalinization drive, for the injustices of the system as it existed, the 'trials,' executions, imprisonments, and general miscarriage of justice of the Stalinist era were part and parcel of the grievances which had led to the demands for de-Stalinization. The party liberals sought not only rehabilitations and redress of past errors but also assurance that such things could not happen again.[1] They attempted to convince the conservative party leadership that although miscarriage of justice was synonymous with the cult of the personality it had not necessarily died with the cult, for it had been institutionally founded during the period of Stalinism. There would, therefore, have to be institutional changes in this area as well if de-Stalinization were to be thorough.

THE CRITICISM

On the premise that it would not be accurate to claim that there was no violation of socialist legality at the present, party and non-party intellectuals attempted to expose the existing defects of the legal system and the reasons for them.[2] At the very root of the problem, it was argued by some, stood Stalin's philosophy and Vyshinsky's theories of legal practice which had been copied in Czechoslovakia. Stalin's theory of the intensification of class war after the revolution had led to a violation of the principles of socialist legality, particularly

---

[1] See for example, Oldrich Prusa, 'The Leninist Course of Affirming Legality,' *Nova Mysl*, XVII:6 (1963), 661.

[2] For the following see: *ibid*; Ladislav Schubert, 'Dogmatism and the Science of Criminal Law,' *Pravny Obzor*, 47:1 (1964), 7; 'Legality in Criminal Law and Procedure,' *Pravnik*, CII:7 (1963), 583–99; Jan Stern, 'Investigation,' *Socialisticka Zakonnost*, 5 (1963), as cited in Otto Ulc, 'Czechoslovakia's Restive Jurists,' *East Europe*, XIII:12 (1965), 19–25.

with regard to police authorities, the prosecutor-general's office, and the courts, for there had been a concentration on searching out the class enemy, especially in the party and the government. Moreover, it was argued, Stalin's belief that the withering away of the state would not come through the weakening of the power of the state but rather by the maximum enforcement of the state's power, had led to ever-increasing repressive activity on the part of the state, especially since Stalin believed that the cornerstone of socialist legality was the protection of socialist property. These distortions were compounded by Vyshinsky's contribution to legal theory, i.e. the idea that the defendant was guilty until proven innocent, the possibility of conviction on the basis of 'maximum probability,' the acceptance of confessions and evidence from co-defendants, even as sufficient evidence for conviction.

Thus, it was argued, the very concept of socialist legality was 'greatly narrowed' by Stalin and Vyshinsky, being defined as a means of realizing the dictatorship of the proletariat. Basic principles such as legal security and various procedural norms which protect the rights of citizens were declared to be remnants of bourgeois society and unnecessary legal formalism. Expediency subjectively replaced legality, often in connection with a mechanical application of the class theory or class interest used to 'supplement' laws and other legal norms. Moreover, the courts allowed and even promoted advantages for those in power, the state, the party or party members, against ordinary or non-party citizens. All of these malpractices had discredited socialist legality, resulting in a decline in the confidence and respect for the organs of justice.[1] That the basic cause might be found in the Soviet system and the wholesale copying of it in Czechoslovakia was of little consolation, for

> the judges, the public prosecutors, the investigators and some counsels have learned to think in a certain manner, thus becoming the bearers of the negative effects of dogmatism in practical life; the difference between them and their predecessors is that they are just passive bearers of these negative effects. At the bottom of this way of thinking is distrust of man.[2]

The liberal legal scholars and jurists attacked the discriminatory theory of 'class origin' or 'class law' which was a regular feature of the Stalinist system. The Penal Code of 1961, for example, stated that the 'personality' of the defendant, defined as class and political character-

---

[1] Prusa, *Nova Mysl*, XVII:6 (1963), 667; 'To Help Effectively the Strengthening of Legality,' *Pravnik*, CII:7 (1963), 521–6.
[2] *Pravnik*, CII:7 (1963), 591.

istics, also determined the degree of threat to society arising from the offense committed.[1] It was argued, however, that class distinctions did not exist in a socialist society and, therefore, were 'untenable' as criteria if not clearly immoral at any stage of development. The principle that every crime is an expression of the class struggle was incorrect and equally reprehensible was the 'mechanical division of all culprits into nine categories, in accordance with their class background.'[2] Likewise rejected was the creation of a 'morally indefensible' category called 'former people' and the subjecting of this arbitrary category to purely arbitrary rulings.[3]

Another basic problem pointed out by critics was the position of the citizen vis-à-vis the collective, whether it be the state or a state enterprise or organization. Lakatos, for example, argued for a system wherein citizens could legally defend themselves against *all* social factors and the individual's legal security be ensured by an independent court. Currently, he said, the citizen was often helpless in a conflict with the state or economic (or other) organizations.[4]

Also a subject of criticism were the judges of the Czechoslovak legal system. Ladislav Mnacko in his critical book *Delayed Reportage* accused the judges of cowardice and corruption because of their cooperation with and contribution to the distortion of legality.[5] One lawyer accused judges of seeking merely to punish rather than to weigh evidence, especially the evidence in favor of the accused.[6] More important was the problem of judges' independence. While it was the party that interfered with the work of the courts and not necessarily the judges who sought the interference, many claimed that the judges were nonetheless responsible for having tolerated (and cooperated) with such interference. Judges were often fearful and, therefore, willing to leave decision-making to the political authorities. Others defended the judges on the grounds that resistance would have resulted in the judges themselves having been declared 'anti-state.'[7] Still others

---

[1] *Sbirka Zakonu* No. 140/1961, Part I, Chapter 2, Section 3.
[2] See 'The Sign of Cain,' *Socialisticka Zakonnost*, 2 (1964), as cited in Ulc, *East Europe*, XIII:12 (1965), 21; *Pravnik*, CII:7 (1963), 595 (Mlynar).
[3] Vojtech Hatala, 'The Personality Cult and some Noetic and Ethical Problems of our Criminal Law,' *Pravny Obzor*, 47:2 (1964), 72–3.
[4] *Kulturny Zivot*, 3 March 1967.
[5] Ladislav Mnacko, *Opozdene Reportaze* (Praha, 1964), 182–3.
[6] *Pravnik*, 7 (1963), 592 (Krizek).
[7] Jozef Brestansky, 'Violation of Procedural Rules and the Substantive Legal Consequences,' *Pravny Obzor*, 47:2 (1964), 77.

excused the judges' weakness by their lack of training and experience. This last must be understood in light of the fact that the party, over the years, had introduced certain changes in the judiciary which had led to a lowering of judges' qualifications: the increased use of lay rather than professional judges, and the creation of the institution of 'workers' law school' whereby the judiciary was gradually replaced by workers who had been given ten-months' cram courses. These inexperienced and barely qualified judges were thus dependent upon the party for their very jobs and for guidance in affairs almost entirely new to them.

One critic argued that judges could be independent only if they had the confidence of society, for without this 'the judge appears in some kind of moral weightless state which prevents him from fully grasping his own judicial responsibility and simultaneously enables him to reject responsibility for the guilt caused by someone else.'[1] Judges should be guaranteed absolute immunity for their legal actions, the argument continued, if they were to be expected to risk taking their responsibility seriously and insist upon objectively following rules of procedure. This comment presumably was a reference to the system introduced in 1957 whereby a law on disciplinary responsibility subjected judges of the lower courts to the disciplinary senates of the regional courts and the judges of the regional courts to the disciplinary senate of the Supreme Court. Combined with this was the law on the election (by the National Committees) of professional as well as lay judges for terms of three years, and the Soviet practice whereby the National Committee electing a judge could recall him for gross violation of his duties (recall requiring an opinion from the Ministry of Justice and a hearing). Moreover, judges had to submit periodic reports on their work to the appropriate National Committees.

The following suggestions emerged for an increase in the independence of judges: punitive measures against those who violated the constitutional guarantees of judges' independence; limitations on the power of prosecutors; abolition of 'work load' norms or quotas for judges; abolition of the nine-category class list for defendants; abolition of 'campaigns' against one offense or another whereby judges had to produce 'enough' convictions of a certain type; curtailment of press campaigns, which proclaimed guilt before the verdict; improvement of training and, by implication, the abolition of the workers' law school.

The investigatory organs were also criticized, in part because investi-

---

[1] Hatala, *Pravny Obzor*, 47:2 (1964), 373-4.

gators were by and large unqualified political appointees. One survey ascertained that in Central Slovakia only one investigator was a lawyer by training and the majority lacked even elementary education and practical experience.[1] Moreover, supervisors tended to evaluate investigators *not* on the quality of their work but on the number of suspects they delivered for trial and the number of resulting convictions. Investigatory methods were also reprehensible, according to many critics, and confessions were still overrated. The result was that prosecutors often sent indictments to court in which they themselves did not believe. Almost ten per cent of charges preferred by public prosecutors were returned by the courts during preliminary hearings – and that in a system wherein the courts themselves were not too fastidious about objective truth.[2] Suspects were often denied information as to their rights, and the failure to publish or provide information on legal proceedings and decisions left professionals as well as citizens in the dark as to precedents and possibilities.

A direct outgrowth of the above problems, it was pointed out, was the diminished or deformed role of the defense attorney. The defense counsel was considered of secondary importance, an institution that had to be tolerated as a minor part of criminal proceedings. Defendants were often told that they did not need counsel and indeed citizens often wondered if representation by counsel made any sense at all. 'The further natural consequences was that attorneys were disgusted and some of them preferred a passive form of defence.'[3] With regard to cases of 'crimes against the state' only attorneys from a specially prepared list were acceptable.[4] This general disregard for the defense counsel had also led to the practice of denying counsel access to his client or to matters concerning the case during the investigation. Attorneys were not permitted to attend the first examination of accused juveniles even though they had such a right under law. As one jurist explained, the 1961 Criminal Code permitted the defense attorney to participate in the investigation stage and pre-trial hearings, but this provision 'has remained a dead letter. I do not know of a single case in

[1] Julius Koval, 'Criminal Procedure,' *Pravny Obzor*, 47:2 (1964), 92; Jan Stepan, 'On Guarantees of Legality in Pre-Trial Proceedings,' *Socialisticka Zakonnost*, 5 (1964), cited in Ulc, *East Europe*, XIII:12 (1965), 22.
[2] Schubert, *Pravny Obzor*, 47:1 (1964), 14.
[3] *Pravnik*, CII:7 (1963), 592.
[4] The list was actually of lawyers eligible to argue before regional courts, but political trials were heard only by the regional (or military) courts.

which the defence counsel has been allowed to participate. Those who requested were briskly rejected.'[1]

There was also a problem of the lack of stability in the law: too many laws were passed, with too many amendments and too frequent changes; the smallest details in fulfillment of economic plans became law. Moreover, the law tended to be vague and therefore too malleable, often lacking specific clauses regarding punishment in case of violation. It was pointed out, for example, that the 1961 Penal Code dealt with the criminal offense of murder in one sentence. Preparation of bills usually lacked juridicial or sociological research; this had been the case regarding the bills on abortion, 'parasitism,' and 'hooliganism.'

THE RESPONSE

The regime responded to the pressures for reform by passing five new laws, which in some cases abrogated or amended laws only recently passed. These included in 1963 a new set of rules pertaining to attorneys-at-law; in 1965 a law on the organization of courts and the election of judges, and a new Civil Code; also in 1965 amendments to the Penal Code and the rules of criminal procedure; and in 1967 rules for administrative procedure.[2] The party congress 'Theses' stated that 'a precise delineation and safeguarding of the rights, freedom and obligations of the citizens is a prerequisite for each person being able to utilize the opportunities for his own development and for the application of his abilities and, at the same time, for the interest of society being respected.' While this declaration had for its purpose the re-injection of the rule of law, the party paper earlier addressed itself to the difficulty of such a venture and the reasons for changes. Stating that violations of 'socialist legality' would not die of themselves with the death of the cult, a party editorial explained that 'the law represents a complex, multilaterally transmitted reflection of social relations between people and of their needs and interests, which even in a basically united socialist society are internally conflicting and cannot all be equally satisfied at once and at the same time.'[3] Thus, just as in the areas of

[1] *Pravnik*, CII:7 (1963), 593.
[2] *Sbirka Zakonu* No. 57/1963 (on lawyers); Decree No. 36/1964 (courts and judges) which abrogated No. 62/1961 (courts) and No. 63/1961 (judges); No. 40/1964 (civil code); No. 56/1965 which amended No. 140/1961 (penal code); and No. 57/1965 which amended No. 14/1961 (criminal procedure) and No. 71/1967 which replaced No. 91/1960 (administrative procedure).
[3] *Rude Pravo*, 11 August 1965.

government and party work, elected organs, and the mass organizations, so also in the area of the administration of justice the recognition that socialist society is made up of strata and conflicting interests demanded adjustments and changes. The party, in this editorial, admitted that the basic tasks of reform in this area included the introduction of better-qualified people, an overcoming of past habits, including the notion that legality was mere 'formalism,' and the practice of 'decree-mania,' whereby all decisions were enacted into law and the issuance of a decree was considered synonymous with the solution of the problem at hand.

With the acceptance of the principle that the court was bound to ascertain the full truth 'with a guarantee of full exercise of the rights of the defense,'[1] the basic role of the defense lawyers was altered. Previously the primary duty of the attorney was described as 'protection of the interests of the citizens in consonance with the principle of material truth,' and the 'material truth' – usually based on a confession – was in fact expressed in the indictment.[2] According to the new law, the lawyer's fundamental duty was to provide aid to the citizens 'in accordance with the laws of the socialist republic and in consonance with the socialist conscience.'[3] While the phrase 'socialist conscience' could be restricting, Slovak law professor Eugen Husar presented a liberal interpretation of the law. He explained that it was the defense attorney's duty, for example, to plead for acquittal on grounds of lack of evidence if the defendant's guilt could not be clearly established – even if the lawyer was personally convinced of the defendant's guilt – for the new law specifically stated that the counsel must use all means of legal assistance permitted him by the law.[4]

Before investigating just how the performance of this new primary function was to be guaranteed, there is the issue of the lawyer himself: his qualifications and his selection. Admission to the bar was to require a matriculation diploma and a law degree from a faculty of law. Thus, while the workers' law schools were not specifically abolished the practice of crash courses such as given in these schools, and the admission of party appointees without proper educational background were in effect eliminated. In addition, the list of lawyers eligible to handle

[1] Vilem Marsilko, 'Respect for the Rule of Law,' *Czechoslovak Life*, 2 (1967), 12.
[2] *Sbirka Zakonu* No. 114/1951, Section 1.
[3] *Sbirka Zakonu* No. 57/1963, Section 1.
[4] Eugen Husar, 'The Defending Counsel in Socialist Society,' *Pravny Obzor*, 46:3 (1963), 221. This issue has been the subject of debate in the USSR.

cases of criminal offenses of a political nature was also abolished. Any lawyer could take such a case with the exception of cases tried before military tribunals. The accused was given greater opportunity to take a lawyer of his own selection, and he might reject a lawyer assigned him by the court.

One of the most significant improvements in the defense counsel's position and his role as protector of the citizen's rights may be found in the increased rights granted him in the investigatory–pre-trial stage. Previously the defense counsel obtained access to the investigation material only at the end of the investigation, just prior to the filing of the indictment, and the accused was only gradually acquainted with the results of the investigation.[1] With the new rules of criminal procedure, the defense attorney could be present from the beginning of the investigation; he could submit proposals in the name of the accused, he could participate directly in the investigation (e.g. in searches, examination of experts and of witnesses), and he could have access to all the files connected with the case. He also received the right to confer with his client in the absence of a third person if the client were in custody, except in certain specified instances. Waivers of the counsel's rights could not be granted in the case of juveniles, and in any case a waiver could be granted 'only for serious reasons which must be examined immediately by the prosecutor, at the counsel's request.'[2] As we have seen the right of the counsel to participate in the investigatory stage had already been introduced in 1961, but the previous law did not enumerate the rights of the counsel (particularly the right to consultation in the absence of a third party) nor did it provide protection against the customary waiver of these rights.[3]

The length of pre-trial custody was limited by law to two months. This could be extended another month by a senior prosecutor but permission to extend it further could be accorded only by the Prosecutor-General. A person taken into custody was to be given a preliminary hearing within forty-eight hours and informed of the decision to keep him in custody, as well as of the charges against him, including mention of which acts of the accused were considered criminal. If a

---

[1] *Rude Pravo*, 13 August 1965.
[2] CTK, 23 June 1965 (Justice Minister Neuman).
[3] The 1965 law had provided that the lawyer could speak with his client 'without interference' once the charges had been preferred, but it did not define 'without interference,' nor did it specify a time limit for preferring charges. (*Sbirka Zakonu* No. 64/1956.)

person were taken into custody a member of his family and the director of his place of work were to be notified without delay. An interesting innovation was the provision that a social (mass) organization might, in certain cases, put up bail.

The investigatory procedure and apparatus also underwent reforms as a result of new laws,[1] resulting in a division of labor within the national security apparatus. In cases of punishable offenses which could be investigated within one month and in which the citizen was not threatened with incarceration, the inquiry apparatus of the security organs had jurisdiction. More complicated or serious offenses (including crimes against the state), involving the threat of incarceration, were to be handled by an independent body of the security apparatus and the Prosecutor's Office. This body was to be composed exclusively of investigators in possession of a degree from a law faculty, and it was to be an entirely independent organization within the Interior Ministry.[2] Investigators were *not* to be subordinate to the chief of the operational bodies of the security apparatus; they were to be independent of the local security units, subordinate only to superior investigating bodies.

The law also defined, in detail, the rights and jurisdiction of the Prosecutor's Office with regard to investigations. While the Prosecutor's Office was to ensure the observance of legality in the activities of the investigatory organs (as well as the activities of the detecting apparatus), it was not to assume the duties of the investigators.[3] On the other hand, the Prosecutor was required to respond to appeals by citizens and organizations within a specified period of time, and citizens and organizations were given the right to demand that a higher prosecutor reconsider a case already submitted to a lower prosecutor. The possibility of private appeal to higher organs provided for a transfer of the matter from the original or local prosecuting agency, to higher, presumably more objective, bodies. The State Prosecutor could delay execution of an appealed decision until the matter was settled at the highest level.

In effect the new laws placed the Prosecutor's Office in a control position while transferring investigatory powers to the police, with the important proviso that the investigatory organs would have complete independence in their investigation, subject only to observance of the law. While observance of the law was to be determined by the Prosecutor's Office, the improvement in the appeal procedure was intended

---

[1] *Sbirka Zakonu* No. 60/1965; No. 57/1965.
[2] *Rude Pravo*, 13 August 1965; CTK, 23 June 1965.
[3] *Rude Pravo*, 1 July and 13 August 1965.

as something of a safeguard against the inherent dangers of the control system. It was an attempt to achieve a delicate but desired balance of the Prosecutor as protector of citizens' rights against excesses of the police while denying the Prosecutor the overwhelmingly powerful position it has under Soviet law whereby there did not, in fact, exist an independent investigatory body.

With regard to courtroom procedure, the principle that a defendant was to be considered innocent until proven guilty was reiterated, and the prosecutor in court proceedings was charged with the responsibility of ensuring that no one's personal freedom or rights be illegally restricted. In this connection a confession by the accused or testimony of a co-defendant would not free the court from the responsibility of establishing all the facts of the case. While the laws of 1956 and 1961 had excluded confessions as sufficient evidence, the lack of implementation necessitated reiteration and emphasis of the innovation, it was pointed out.[1]

In response to the criticism of the quality of judges, it was ruled that professional judges must have a degree from a law faculty.[2] Reforms in the system of judges' election followed those of the election to the National Assembly and the National Committees, in that there were to be more candidates than judgeships available. Nonetheless judges were still elected for a specific period (four years) and subject to recall and disciplinary review. Moreover, the powers of constitutional review remained within the National Assembly, rather than with a court, so that there was still no independent check on the constitutionality of the laws of the National Assembly. Further, the new law did not eliminate the duty of the judge to interpret the law according to the interests of the working people, that is, in favour of one class as distinct from another. Thus despite the fact that classes had ceased to exist, the criticized 'class law' was not specifically rescinded.

Commenting on the new laws, chief Prosecutor Bartuska said that they 'strongly underline the importance of a trial before a court of justice. No person can be found guilty except by a verdict of the court, pronounced after a proper court trial.'[3] Given the tendency to administrative measures and rigged trials instead of the rule of law such a declaration was indeed important. Equally important were the formal

---

[1] *Rude Pravo*, 1 July 1965; CTK, 23 June 1965; Marsilko, *Czechoslovak Life*, 2 (1967), 12.
[2] *Sbirka Zakonu* No. 36/1964, Part VI, Section 68.
[3] *Rude Pravo*, 1 July 1965.

steps taken to safeguard the spirit of this declaration. For example, the guarantee of court trial was meant to include cases of citizens versus enterprises instead of the prior preference for arbitration or 'administrative jurisdiction' within the enterprise. A citizen's dispute could now be taken to court much more easily.[1] Unlike the Civil Code of 1950 preference would no longer be given the enterprise in such cases. At the same time the new rules for administrative procedure were designed to increase control over administrative decisions from below and through the courts.[2] This was of particular importance considering the wide range of penalties, services, and activities under administrative (governmental) supervision in Czechoslovakia. Appeals against administrative decisions would no longer be decided upon by the same administrative organ which had issued the original decision under appeal, but rather by the next higher administrative body. The party involved in an administrative decision would have the right to review the documents of his case, unless an official secret were involved. Moreover, to prevent the previous indefinite delays, sometimes intentional, sometimes merely the result of bureaucracy, the new law required that an agency come to a decision within sixty days of the original request or pass the case on to higher organs. The new law provided that courts could review a decision of an administrative agency in specified areas, but the only areas specified by the end of 1967 were pension rights and censorship. Nonetheless the high number of complaints lodged in a number of administrative agencies in 1966 led jurists to demand the restoration of the pre-1952 administrative courts.[3] On the other hand, it was also pointed out that, while citizens needed legal protection against the administration, 'In view of the existing cadre situation, the courts can barely cope with problems of control. Control ought not, under any circumstances be entrusted to judges who are elected by the very organs whose decisions they may be called upon to review.'[4] Interior Minister Kudrna, however, made it quite clear that a return of administrative courts was not under consideration.[5]

In practical terms some of the reforms, or at least the atmosphere of the reforms, began to be felt as early as 1963. Law makers began to

---

[1] See chapter 7 above.

[2] *Sbirka Zakonu* No. 71/1967 replaced No. 14/1957.

[3] Josef Elias, 'Scientific Discussion of Juridical Control of Administration in the CSSR,' *Pravnik*, CVI:7 (1967), 632–51; Elias, 'Questions of State and Law in Preparation for the Thirteenth Party Congress,' *Pravnik*, CV:4 (1966), 308; *Prace*, 22 June 1967.

[4] Elias, *Pravnik*, CVI:7 (1967), 641.   [5] Prague radio, 31 July 1967.

make greater use of sociology and cybernetics in the drafting of legislation, law journals began to discuss and criticize individual court decisions, biological tests were introduced in paternity suits, a law was drafted determining the responsibility of state organs for damage caused by illegal decisions.[1] The party legal commission undertook consideration of a proposal for post-graduate law studies (which were required for many prior to 1948), and a proposal that a law degree be required for certain positions in the state apparatus. In connection with the effort to protect or extend citizens' rights, a law on travel documents removed the former provision that citizens do *not* have a right to travel papers; substituted was a list of specific reasons that such papers might be refused. In the case of refusal citizens had the right to appeal and to receive an explanation, although here too the pertinent agency and not the courts decided the appeal.[2] A sign that the new regulations were being implemented in a 'progressive' spirit was the increase in travel to the West: in 1963 47000 Czechoslovaks visited the West; this number jumped to 118000 in 1964, 154000 in 1965, 203000 in 1966 and 258000 in 1967.[3]

While in a number of cases the 1963 7 reforms merely reiterated principles and laws already on the books, there was reason for optimism. These reforms came about as the result of public criticism and persistent pressure within the party. They were designed to cope with reforms in other areas of society which together with the reforms of the legal system responded to a change in ideology: the realization that socialist society consisted of conflicting interests and strata, that the dictatorship of the proletariat was no longer a pertinent form of rule and guide to law. They came about because of the realization that even those relatively liberal features of the previous codes must be reiterated and adjusted and imbued with the liberal spirit of the reforms, since pre-

---

[1] Ulc, *East Europe*, XIII:12 (1965), 23; *Rude Pravo*, 19 October 1966; *Rude Pravo*, 11 August 1965.

[2] 'Current Developments,' *East Europe*, XIII:8 (1965), 44–5; *Praca*, 21 March 1965; Prague radio, 18 June 1965 (*Sbirka Zakonu* No. 63/1965). While passports were to be valid for five years, exit and re-entry permits and permissions to stay abroad were 'valid only for the time necessary for the citizen to realize the aim of his trip.' (*Praca*, 21 March 1965.) The procedure for obtaining passports was to be simplified by making it possible to apply at regional and district offices under the Interior Ministry. (*Zemedelske Noviny*, 22 October 1965.) In fact this last measure was not implemented, and in 1967 the regime announced it as if for the first time (*Rude Pravo*, 15 April 1967).

[3] 'Situation Report,' RFE, 10 October 1969.

viously they had been largely ignored. The reforms by no means solved all of the problems of socialist legality nor responded to all the criticism levied against the legal system by Czech and Slovak jurists, while certain serious restrictions on the independence and impartiality of the courts persisted. Moreover, socialist legality could be democratized only insofar as the legislative and electoral systems were democratized. Nonetheless, as with the reforms in the other areas, these reforms marked a step forward – how much of a step forward being dependent upon the spirit in which they would be implemented in conjunction with the other reforms.

16

PRESSURES FROM THE ECONOMISTS

The Czech and Slovak liberals sought to avoid the mistakes of the Polish liberals of 1956; they sought in a typically Czech way to provide a legal and institutional structure for their hard-won reforms and proposed changes so as to safeguard them from later reversal. The crucial point, however, lay in the implementation of these reforms, for with or without the admittedly required institutional changes the reforms would lose much if not all of their value if not implemented speedily and thoroughly – and in the spirit with which they had been sought. It was on this crucial point that a conflict arose leading to the final overthrow of Novotny, for the very reluctance with which he agreed to the formal reform measures was the measure of his desire to see these measures fail. It was due to his reluctance – and that of his fellow conservatives – that the implementation of the reforms was seriously impeded. In the course of 1967 the uneasy compromise that Novotny had made with the liberals in 1963 broke down. It became increasingly clear that further progress would only come if Novotny and his major supporters were removed.

Dissatisfaction with the pace of implementation and pressure for change came from several quarters, almost all of which fall into the very general category of intellectuals, most of whom, though not all, were within the party. These groups overlapped, just as, most pointed out, the reforms themselves overlapped: reforms in one area demanding reforms in another in order to be fully effective. While the economists argued that the economic reforms could not succeed without political and other reforms, these economic reforms did appear to be the most urgent and perhaps essential measures.

Full implementation of the new system, albeit qualified by the numerous 'transition' measures added to it in 1965–6, was to be introduced in January 1967. Certain organizational and personnel changes, apparently decided upon at the December 1966 plenum of the central committee, accompanied this beginning. At this plenum Novotny announced certain, albeit minor, adjustments which, given his remarks, reflected a greater emphasis on central control than had been expected even *with* the 'transition' measures. For example, the branch director was to be nominated by 'higher organs' instead of by the enterprise directors as previously. While representatives of the trade unions were to be given seats on branch directorates, these representatives would have to be approved by the party. Moreover, it was announced that branches should decide 'some basic questions in the work of production units,' a marked increase in the powers of these organizations at the expense of enterprise independence.[1] Novotny's own conservative attitude towards the new system was reflected in his defense of the old system and his criticism of those who exaggerated the evils of what he referred to as the 'so-called' administrative methods in the economic system. This attitude predominated in the regime's measures in connection with the introduction of the new system and in its approach to the problems encountered during this first year.

PROBLEMS WHICH HAD ARISEN

The major problems encountered during the first year of the new system centered on inflation and investment spending. The wholesale price reform which had been introduced earlier than scheduled was a source of serious problems. Hastily drawn up and the result of haggling and bargaining between producers and the central agencies, wholesale prices had been some 10 per cent higher than expected, mainly because of the effort to cushion enterprises for the 'shock' of transition to the new system. Thus, instead of an expected 19 per cent rise in wholesale prices, 1967 was ushered in with a 29 per cent rise in wholesale prices.[2] This increase was reflected but little in retail prices, thanks to government subsidies: retail prices rose only by the maximum planned 1·5 per cent.[3] As a result of the miscalculated wholesale price rise, however, profits also rose beyond expectations. In fact, almost every factory was able to make a profit.[4]

Aside from the fact that this almost 'guaranteed' profit released the enterprises from the pressure of the market, it had led to a number of inflationary developments. The rate of growth of industrial investments did decline somewhat, but not as much as expected. Indeed much of the decline registered was due to reduced housing construction (which was not planned).[5] Despite planned development, the structure of investments did not shift significantly to the consumer area or production for export. Moreover, the volume of uncompleted construction was not

[1] *Rude Pravo*, 23 December 1966.   [2] *Hospodarske Noviny*, 29 September 1967.
[3] *Rude Pravo*, 30 January 1967.   [4] *Reporter*, 3 November 1967.
[5] *Hospodarske Noviny*, 11 July 1967.

reduced as planned. Combined with this development in investments, material input, especially costs for labor, also increased, although labor productivity showed no increase.[1]

Thus the inflationary effect of the higher than expected wholesale prices was reinforced by the increase in purchasing power. As a result of the investment situation, employment rose beyond expectations during the first half of the year, although the rate was curbed by the end of the year.[2] The rise in income paid out was due principally to increases in nominal wages, as a result of the unexpected (and in a sense unearned) increase in profits. In May 1967 the regime had set wage increases for 3·2 to 3·4 per cent per year with productivity to increase by 4·5 to 5·0 per cent. At mid-year, however, industrial wages had risen by 5·0 per cent while productivity had risen by only 4·3 per cent. In the first half of 1967 personal income grew by 5300 million korunas and personal consumption expenditures showed an increase of 4400 million korunas over 1966.[3] As we have pointed out, consumer goods stocks did not increase. It was estimated that at the close of 1967 there would be a shortage of 6–8000 million korunas of consumer goods on the market.[4] Both the monopoly position of the enterprises and their profitable position had led to a situation wherein not only overall demand but also the structure of demand was ignored.

Difficulties were encountered in foreign trade as well. Exports to the West fell considerably short of the projected goals and were even one per cent lower than those of 1966, instead of the expected eleven per cent increase.[5] Combined with a slight rise in imports from the West, this development led to an increase in the balance of payment deficit. At the same time exactly the opposite occurred in trade relations with the socialist countries: exports increased and imports decreased, which was of little help in balancing off the deficits with the hard currency areas.[6]

REGIME RESPONSE

A communique after the September 1967 central committee plenum acknowledged the unexpected growth in enterprise profits and the

[1] See *Kulturni Tvorba*, 5 January 1967; *Rude Pravo*, 28 September 1967 (speech by Strougal).
[2] *Hospodarske Noviny*, 11 July 1967. [3] *Rude Pravo*, 28 September 1967 (Strougal).
[4] *Hospodarske Noviny*, 29 September 1967.
[5] *Rude Pravo*, 28 September 1967; 30 January 1968.
[6] Bratislava radio, 18 October 1967.

fact that it was a result more of higher wholesale prices than productivity. It pointed to the fact that consumer supplies were not meeting demand, and yet overall stocks had increased, together with the excessive number of investment projects under construction.[1] These problems were attributed to the fact that economic 'conditions and rules' had not yet created 'sufficiently strong economic pressure against ineffective areas of production.' The regime sought solutions based on the strengthening of 'operational economic instruments,' i.e. further use of old-style methods.

To handle the problem of the higher than expected prices, candidate presidium member Antonin Kapek suggested directive and administrative measures, should the situation of unearned profits continue.[2] *Rude Pravo* editor Sulc also suggested that the 'central agencies' take measures against such an inflationary situation. Although he preferred that these be economic rather than administrative measures, he did not rule out the use of the latter.[3] At its September 1967 plenum the central committee recognized the need for speedy introduction of the second, detailed, phase of the wholesale price reforms so as to correct the current price distortions. At the same time it urged stronger measures to control profits. The September plenum heard a number of suggestions for controlling prices and wages and for punishing plant managers responsible for 'unreasonable' profits. The trade unions and Peoples Control Commissions were called upon as agents of the state to supervise price formation in their enterprises and to 'support and enforce the prosecution of those violating price discipline.'

Towards the end of 1967 the regime announced the principles for the second phase of the wholesale price reforms; it continued to seek its solution to inflation through control. Price subsidies were to be continued, albeit reduced, so as to prevent a rise in retail prices. The assumption here was that the free retail price category would not be enlarged, i.e. it was to compose thirteen per cent of retail prices until 1970. In wholesale prices the limited price category was to be enlarged, at the expense of the fixed price category; no increase in the free price category was permitted.[4]

To handle the investment problem, the regime ruled that enterprises planning capital construction after January 1968 financed partly or entirely from their own resources must pay, in advance and into blocked accounts, at least one-half of their contribution to the project.

---

[1] *Rude Pravo*, 28 September 1967.   [2] *Rude Pravo*, 29 September 1967.
[3] *Rude Pravo*, 3 October 1967.   [4] *Rude Pravo*, 21 November 1967.

Investment in new enterprises was cut, and enterprises were ordered to increase their reserve funds. Credit was also made dearer: the rates on operational credits were raised from four per cent to six per cent and on investment credits from six to eight per cent, both to be restricted to the volume of 1966.[1]

With regard to wages, the regime was concerned about the wage–productivity ratio per worker and considered placing controls on workers' premiums (bonuses).[2] The trade unions were given the task of supervising the 'harmony' between wages and labor productivity. This they promised to do through 'disciplinary meetings' and adjustments of contracts to conform to the state-dictated ratio.[3]

In the area of foreign trade too the solution to the pressing problems did not consist of the introduction of any liberal or fundamental measures. The regime apparently did take under consideration the idea of breaking up the monopoly of the foreign trade enterprises in favor of affiliating them directly to production enterprises. Nonetheless, this measure was not acted on in 1967 and 'administrative, interventionist measures' were considered a very likely alternative in the solution of the foreign trade problem.[4] There was also no indication that the stiff import–credit policies were to be changed. Indeed Foreign Trade Minister Hamouz explained that Czechoslovakia would have even less means in 1968 for financing imports than she had had in 1967.[5]

OTHER RESPONSES

Ota Sik and the liberals had their own comments in response to these problems. Sik advised the party of three major requisites for a solution to the investments problem: the volume of industrial investments should be reduced in relation to national income; the demand for domestic investments should be reduced and related to the availability of resources; and the structure of investments should be changed in favor of those economic spheres which promised the highest effectiveness in foreign trade.[6] Liberals of Sik's school of thought generally agreed on the necessity of reducing investment construction and limiting the growth of stocks (except in consumer industries). Josef Goldmann, whose theory of growth pointed to the existence of cycles in socialist

[1] See *Praca*, 15 August 1967; *The Economist*, 22 July 1967.
[2] CTK, 21 August 1967.
[3] Bratislava radio, 25 September 1967.   [4] *Rude Pravo*, 27 September 1967.
[5] *Rude Pravo*, 28 September 1967.   [6] CTK, 7 May 1967.

as well as capitalist economies, analyzed the problem slightly differently, however.[1] Though it was desirable to cut back investments and limit stocks, he argued, this produced a tendency towards hoarding for the future in anticipation of future difficulties. Yet, maintained Goldmann and other liberal colleagues, this anticipating was important as an indicator of changes in the economic equilibrium of the growth rate, to be dealt with by economic instruments such as credits and not by administrative measures.

This problem, generally considered part of the inherited disproportion of the pre-reform economy, was studied from the point of view of its inflationary effect. According to two other economists, the high level of accumulation, unfinished or unneeded projects (often financed with as yet unearned funds) had in the past led to a disequilibrium between resources and demand. This disproportion had continued and had caused an inflation in the raw materials and investment goods market, as manifested in rising prices, extension of building targets, lower quality, and so forth. If this were fought administratively with a price freeze the 'suppressed' inflation would manifest itself by disproportions which, as Loebl had pointed out, would in turn necessitate further administrative measures. The market should, therefore, be allowed to function freely, even if this eventually would affect the consumer through retail price rises. Reduction of state subsidies, combined with stricter credit policies (i.e. shorter repayment period), especially with a clear indication that there would be no 'help' (reduced levies, other types of subsidies, etc.), could change the structure of the investment market. What was needed, however, was not merely an across-the-board reduction of the volume of investment goods, they maintained; one could not arbitrarily cut the demands of all to the same degree. There must be a structural cut in demand so as to favor investments in the consumer goods industry, services, export branches, and so forth.[2]

Only such a change in the structure of investment could prevent inflation on the consumer goods market, according to Goldmann and his colleague Flek. Restrictions on the growth of wages merely

[1] See Josef Goldmann, 'The Rate of Growth and the Recurring Fluctuations in the Economy of Some Socialist Countries,' *Planovane Hospodarstvi*, XVIII:9 (1964), 1–14; Josef Goldmann and Josef Flek, 'The Fluctuations of the Rate of Growth and the Dynamics of the Inventory Cycle,' *Planovane Hospodarstvi*, XX:9 (1967), 1–16.

[2] See Jiri Kosta and Anna Cervenkova in *Literarni Noviny*, 27 May 1967.

'suppressed' the inflation. Prescribed schedules regulating the relationship of labor productivity (measured according to gross production) to wages was a sign of a return to the old administrative methods. 'If this method of wage regulation were to prevail, it would practically mean the end of the new system,' still another liberal economist said.[1] The familiar argument was offered: high wages in fact meant 'expensive' labor which in itself should be incentive towards increased productivity and modernization (although this might not hamper the inflation spiral until production were reformed).[2]

By and large the liberals' arguments against the restrictive measures taken in 1967 were the same as their more basic criticism of the imposition of limitations on the economic levers already apparent in 1966, reviewed in chapters 4–7 above.[3] Sik could but return to his original arguments in favor of an unhindered market mechanism, explaining and re-explaining the need for flexible prices and wages, enterprise independence and an end to subsidies.[4] Selucky tried to clarify the relationship the plan was to have vis-a-vis the market under the new system. He pointed out that the intention had been for the market to operate as a corrective to the plan, and not the contrary, as was the regime's practice.[5]

Most of the critics recognized that the real problem was political.[6] Many of the arguments revolving around inflation and calling for administrative solutions were but signs of the opposition of conservatives to the introduction of the new system. One article, hinting at the still broader implications of the reforms and reflecting Sik's oft-repeated assertion that reforms of the base demand changes in the superstructure, said: 'unless economic measures are coordinated with political measures, the new system cannot be introduced. One cannot

[1] *Reporter*, 20 October 1967 (Cestmir Kozusnik).
[2] *Literarni Noviny*, 27 May 1967.
[3] See for example, *Kulturny Zivot*, 20 January 1967; *Kulturni Tvorba*, 5 January 1967; *Reporter*, 20 October 1967; Otakar Kraus, 'The Enterprises and the Supra-Enterprise Sphere,' *Nova Mysl*, XXI:14 (1967), 41–2; Alois Remes, 'Positions of Small Enterprises in the National Economy,' *Planovane Hospodarstvi*, XX:4 (1967), 23–4.
[4] See for example, Ota Sik, 'How to Overcome the Imbalance in our Economy' *Nova Mysl*, XXI:8 (1967), 20–5.
[5] Radoslav Selucky, 'The Plan and the Market,' *Plamen*, 9:4 (1967), 149–50.
[6] CTK, 7 May 1967 (Sik): *Politika* (Belgrade), 14 May 1967 (Sik); *Kulturni Tvorba*, 5 January 1967; *Reporter*, 20 October 1967; *Hospodarske Noviny*, 11 July 1967; *Literarni Noviny*, 27 May 1967.

envisage that after the introduction of the new economic system, people will begin to function as mere cells of the market mechanism.'[1]

WORKER REACTION

An additional problem, which could destroy whatever effect the greatly limited new system could have, was that of workers' opposition. Sik had indeed warned about this problem as early as his first proposals. Despite the rise in wages that so concerned the regime, workers tended to see only the ill-effects of the reforms: wage de-equalization, unemployment or at least job insecurity, greater demands for high quality work, and the possibility of rising prices.

Basically the greatest opposition of the workers came in the realm of security, whether with regard to their wages or their jobs themselves. One worker, reportedly expressing the feeling of many, said: 'I cannot help feeling that you have invented a system which deprives people of security.'[2] Just as managers complained about the insecurity of supplies and being without contracts, and therefore without a clear view of their commitments, so workers complained about the instability of their individual production programs, which were 'changed at least once a year now.'[3]

Another source of low morale was the wage problem and the introduction of penalties for poor work. Strikes had been reported in 1966 as workers opposed de-equalization, and this opposition apparently continued in 1967.[4] De-equalization of wages tended to benefit blue collar workers less than executives or engineers, etc. Many rank and file workers, therefore, questioned the socialist aspect of this measure. Workers naturally enough questioned the criteria to be used for determining which workers were to earn more and which less. In this connection the role of the trade unions remained problematic, for under the reforms the trade unions were to represent the interests of the workers (not the regime) yet their major function was to help ensure the introduction of the new system.[5] Distrust was reportedly widespread among workers, and the wage ceilings in particular had 'killed and is killing any initiative tending towards a better organization of labor.'[6] Even union leaders threatened to resign, however, over transfers of

[1] *Ibid.*
[2] *Reporter*, 3 November 1967.   [3] *Ibid.*
[4] Prague radio, 19 January 1967.   [5] See chapter 9 above.
[6] Bratislava radio, 25 September 1967.

production (plant closures) as job security became a major concern.[1] Liberal economists generally denied that there would be unemployment, arguing that workers would simply have to be retrained or would have to change locale.[2] The regime finally admitted this problem and introduced unemployment insurance up to sixty per cent of average net earnings.[3]

The most serious aspect of the workers' reaction to the new system was perhaps their indifference or outright opposition to it. Workers tended to look upon the reforms as merely another of the many reorganizations instigated in the past, usually to their disadvantage. 'How many pages have been filled with an explanation of the new system. For you, everything is progressive, new, useful. Yet I still don't know what is actually progressive and new, how it will affect my work, my income, the life of my family,' was the comment of one worker.[4] As for direct opposition, one journal 'preferred not to quote' the number of anonymous letters it had received 'demanding the punishment' of those who had introduced the reforms.[5] Ota Sik had recognized that worker support of and interest in the new system was crucial given the profit-sharing productivity mechanism involved. Never denying the existence of this problem, he blamed it on past mis-education and mistakes. His solution was two-fold: better propaganda and the speedy implementation of the new system so that the workers might quickly experience and, therefore, understand the progressive and advantageous nature of the reforms.[6]

[1] *Reporter*, 3 November 1967.
[2] See Radislav Selucky, 'Is there a Danger of Unemployment in the Country?,' *Priroda a Spolecnost*, 11 (1967), 1.
[3] *Prace*, 17 June 1967; *Lidove Demokracie*, 18 July 1967.
[4] *Reporter*, 3 November 1967.
[5] *Ibid.*
[6] See chapter 4 above and Sik, *Nova Mysl*, XXI:8 (1967), 22–3.

17

PRESSURES FROM THE CULTURAL WORLD

As in the economic field so also in the cultural, the year 1967 opened with tensions. At the October 1966 plenum of the central committee Novotny had already announced that steps would be taken to strengthen party control of the cultural community. At the party's December central committee plenum Novotny announced a measure which had been rumored many times in the past and which apparently had been under discussion for some time: the splitting of the Education and Culture Ministry. While this move need not have been a sign of conservatism (even though it marked a return to the organizational set-up of culture of the worst days of Stalinism), Novotny's pronouncements and subsequent appointments indicated that this was indeed an effort to increase controls. With the reorganization, the Minister of Education and Culture Jiri Hajek stayed on as Minister of Education, while the Director-General of Czechoslovak broadcasting Karel Hoffmann became Minister of Culture and Information. Although Hoffmann had permitted a certain liberalization at the radio, he had been looked upon as the 'party's postman' at the radio.[1] That he was selected because of his amenability to party wishes was suggested by Novotny's statement that the ministry was being created to provide a vehicle for greater day to day 'guidance' in the cultural sphere.[2] The Slovak counterpart of this new office, the Commission for Culture and Information, was filled by a still less progressive man, Stefan Brenac, formerly the Bratislava regional party secretary for ideology. The administrative changes were completed with the replacement of party ideology secretary Pavel Auersperg. While there had been mixed views as to the extent of Auersperg's 'flexibility,' on balance he had not been as conservative as his successor, Frantisek Havlicek, promised to be. Havlicek was clearly tinged with Stalinism, having been head of the party agit–prop department at the height of the Stalinist era in 1952.

Simultaneous with the above changes and illustrative of their intent, the party began harassing two outspoken liberal journals, *Literarni Noviny* and the Brno literary monthly *Host do Domu*. The

[1] See *Reporter*, 17 April 1968.   [2] CTK, 25 January 1967.

party organ took on *Literarni Noviny* in January when it claimed that the latter had refused to publish an article by Ladislav Stoll, who until de-Stalinization had been the party's extremist Stalinist boss in the cultural world. Polemics ensued between the journal and *Rude Pravo*, culminating in a *Rude Pravo* attack accusing *Literarni Noviny* of anarchism, inadmissible liberal attitudes, bribery, and pilfering of socialist property. The party organ warned that the party was not inclined to compromise on such matters and would 'demand responsibility.'[1]

The party conducted a still more vituperative dispute with *Host do Domu*, centered around another Stalinist, Frantisek Necasek, who had been a cultural advisor to Gottwald at the height of the Stalinist era. The polemics between the journal and the *Rude Pravo* were prompted by a dogmatic book review written by Necasek which included personal attacks and counter-accusations. *Rude Pravo* wound up challenging *Host do Domu* by saying in effect: if you are willing to publish the views of non-Marxists or identify yourselves with 'other than communist viewpoints,' you should not be surprised when this 'quite naturally clashes with *Rude Pravo*.'[2] There were numerous letters to the editors connected with the dispute, and another Brno journal, *Rovnost*, became involved after publishing a Brno party decision condemning *Host do Domu*. This in turn led to a lively public discussion in the House of Arts in Brno, which itself was attacked (for the frankness or 'hypocrisy' of the *Host do Domu* editor's contribution) by the conservative party journal *Zivot Strany*.[3] It is true that this whole conflict in itself demonstrated the degree to which Czechoslovak cultural life had been liberalized. In the pre-1963 days the party might simply have closed the journal or, as it even tried on certain occasions after 1963, replaced its editors. Nonetheless, it was an indication of the party's expressed intention to curb the liberals and, while creating new tension between the writers and the party, it was in fact a harbinger of much stronger measures to follow.

ACCUMULATION OF GRIEVANCES

During the first months of 1967 liberal writers took up the issue of the press. This issue had several aspects, from the long-existing complaints about the unavailability of the foreign press in Czechoslovakia to the lack of implementation of the positive elements of the 1966 Press Law.

[1] *Rude Pravo*, 13 March 1967.   [2] *Rude Pravo*, 9 March 1967.
[3] Vaclav Zima, 'A Strange Talk with *Host Do Domu*,' *Zivot Strany*, 10 (1967), 33–5.

Signs of the first complaints appeared in the last issue of *Kulturni Tvorba* of 1966. The journal had sponsored a television program in which the paucity of information from and about countries outside Czechoslovakia came under criticism. It then received a number of letters echoing this, demanding foreign newspapers (such as are available in Yugoslavia, according to one correspondent) both as healthy competition for domestic journalists as well as to provide greater information.[1] In May the regime announced that some fourteen foreign (non-communist) journals were to be regularly imported. They were, however, to be sold only for foreign currency.

As the year opened, an interesting diversion of views appeared in two leading journals, *Predvoj* and *Literarni Noviny*. In the latter, liberal writer Antonin Liehm pointed out the need for a revaluation and rebirth of the critical spirit which had been apparent in the press only two, three, and especially four years earlier. He quoted a fellow party member who had asked him what had happened to the 'spirit of freedom in every new issue.' Though he argued that now one could find in many papers things that once had been said only in *Literarni Noviny*, Liehm said that he had to admit that this 'spirit of freedom' was not always an easy matter. He asserted that the time had come once again for the press to stop to think and to supply this spirit once again.[2] Just a few weeks later *Predvoj* published an article saying that the time had come for 'normalization,' i.e. that the necessary elbow room had been won and one need no longer be 'courageous' in order for his works to be well received by the critics.[3]

There were still complaints, however, that journalists were denied information and that they faced lack of cooperation and understanding when they sought facts. Supplying examples of such problems, one journalist argued that in fact the new Press Law stated that

> state agencies and organizations, scientific and cultural institutions and economic organizations, are obliged to furnish information concerning their sphere of activity to editors-in-chief and to other editors, which they require for truthful, prompt and all-sided informing of the public, or to give them access to information of this type.[4]

The fact that information was not accessible would indicate, according to the author, that the Press Law was not in force. Writer Ladislav Mnacko expressed much the same skepticism about the efficacy of the

---

[1] *Kulturni Tvorba*, 22 December 1966.   [2] *Literarni Noviny*, 7 January 1967.
[3] *Predvoj*, 27 January 1967.   [4] *Mlada Fronta*, 6 April 1967.

new Press Law when he complained that although writers and journalists had fought many years for a law to control censorship, and although they had finally succeeded in 'legalizing' it, in fact the regime seemed to use it in the same 'illegal and anonymous means as before.' Thus a writer legally had the right to express his opinion on a political subject, but the regime could (and did) find some other law to prevent one from expressing himself freely, especially on matters of foreign policy.[1]

Although the above remarks concerned mainly the press, Mnacko was the object of a related form of renewed regime restriction on writers. His book *The Taste of Power* was denied publication in Czechoslovakia, though two (censored) installments were published by *Plamen*.[2] The novel was subsequently published in Austria – for which party disciplinary proceedings were brought against Mnacko.

The Czechoslovak new wave in films also had suffered from the censor, especially after the October 1966 plenum when Novotny served notice on the liberal film-makers. As we have seen, four outstanding avant-garde films: Chytilova's *Daisies*, Nemec's *The Feast and the Guests* and *Martyrs of Love*, and Masa's *Hotel for Foreigners* (all but the last written with Ester Krumbachova) had been banned by the end of 1966. In 1967 they were subjected to official criticism and two films, Nemec's *The Feast and the Guests* and Chytilova's *Daisies* were discussed by the National Assembly on 18 May 1967. Deputy Jaroslav Pruzinec, on behalf of twenty-one deputies, presented an interpolation to the Ministry of Culture and Information expressing strong disapproval of these two films, which he termed 'anti-social'.[3] Nemec had prepared the scenario for another film based on Kafka's *Metamorphosis*, but he did not receive permission to go ahead with production. Masa was also denied permission to work on another film. Vera Chytilova was denied a passport to attend the Oberhausen Film Festival in April 1967, while Nemec and Krumbachova received their passports only after some difficulty.

Still another source of dissatisfaction in the cultural world was the issue of rehabilitations of writers. A large number of writers received varying degrees of rehabilitation from 1963 to 1966 and even early 1967, but these were almost always incomplete rehabilitations. Thus as of 1967, certain of Capek's works could not be published, nor all of the works of the rehabilitated Frantisek Halas; and most of the works of

[1] *Frankfurter Allgemeine Zeitung*, 11 August 1967.
[2] *Plamen*, 8:8 (1966), 122–14; *Plamen*, 8:9 (1966), 114–28.
[3] Prague radio, 18 May 1967. See *Filmove a Televizni Noviny*, 8 (1968), 5.

Durych, Zahradnicek, Palivec, and Teige were not republished. While in 1967 the courts threw out or quashed the convictions of a number of non-communist writers sentenced in the 1950s, this judgment had by no means covered all those unjustly punished. Moreover, the re-habilitated writers still living were not compensated for past damages nor returned to their former positions.[1] Slovak writer Theo Florin demanded that the forthcoming Writers Congress grant the 1950s victim–writers full rehabilitation.[2]

Still another disturbing element, the Arab–Israeli war of June 1967, entered the scene just prior to the Writers Union Fourth Congress. It seemed to demonstrate to the writers just how much Novotny had succeeded in nullifying the most important aspects of gains made over the four years since the dramatic third congress. Many Czech and Slovak intellectuals were concerned by the impossibility of commenting on the war in any but the regime's prescribed way and by the anti-semitic tone – reminiscent of the 1950s purge period – that accompanied in word and deed the regime's policy on the war.

This issue brought an entirely new element into the drive for de-Stalinization, for until this time the struggle had concentrated on purely internal matters. It was only insofar as internal matters were concerned that relations with other countries were even subject to discussion, e.g. trade matters that affected the economy, or the pressures for greater contacts with the West, travel, and foreign press, which were all matters tied up with personal freedom. Even relations with Russia were the subject of debate only on the issue of trade and this only occasionally and by no means as a major point of the liberals. It was natural, of course, that there be a certain criticism of the Soviet Union as the liberals urged abandonment of the practice of copying the Soviet Union in all things. There too, however, it was not a question of a drive for independence nor did the element of foreign policy as such come up.[3]

---

[1] See for example, *Universita Karlova*, 4 April 1968 ('Secret Rehabilitations'), *Literarni Listy*, 23 May 1968 ('Rehabilitations on the Sly').

[2] *Kulturny Zivot*, 23 June 1967.

[3] There were only two occasions on which Czechoslovakia's international relations seemed to be an issue: the regime, for purely economic reasons, wanted to improve relations with West Germany after 1963 but was thwarted in part by pressure from Moscow on behalf of East Germany. This, however, was never an issue in the liberalization drive itself. A second case was the manner in which Novotny received the sudden news of Khrushchev's removal. Protesting to Brezhnev (by telephone), Novotny refused to criticize his deposed supporter, and, alone of the Eastern European leaders, did not attend the Moscow anniversary celebration a

The Israeli–Arab conflict, however, bridged the gap between de-Stalinization of domestic and foreign policy. Czechoslovak intellectuals, like the population at large, tended to identify with Israel as a small nation surrounded by much larger forces whose very existence, like that of Czechoslovakia in 1938, lay in the balance perhaps even as the political football of the powers. Mnacko expressed this identification more ironically when he said:

our population . . . is only told how a nation of two and a-half million people is about to destroy the Arab world. We too were once in a situation in which we were a 'deadly danger' and a 'threat' to a great power. It seems that small nations possess a perverse inclination to threaten the big nations with destruction. That this is so, is asserted today equally in the case of Vietnam as in that of Israel.[1]

That these were the sentiments of most of the intellectuals and probably the population at large was confirmed by the subsequent Writers Congress, by foreign press observers and certain regime hints.[2]

The two most outspoken and courageous literary journals *Kulturny Zivot* and *Literarni Noviny* maintained total silence on the issue.[3] While this in itself took some courage and perhaps helped to maintain their integrity, it was just this silencing of their real views which was problematic for the writers. Mnacko attacked this situation as being a result of the failure to complete de-Stalinization. He explained that many questions might now be discussed or truthfully written about in Czechoslovakia, 'but in such an important question of foreign policy as the Middle East crisis we are silenced.' Many writers reacted to this denigrating state of affairs with extreme pessimism, daring to refer to the problem only most obliquely.[4] According to Mnacko, some party members turned in their party cards; for his part he interpreted silence as cooperation and left the country for Israel in protest.

few weeks later. This 'split' with Russia did not, however, last long; nor did it attract much attention in Czechoslovakia.

[1] *Frankfurter Allgemeine Zeitung*, 11 August 1967.
[2] See below for the congress; *Frankfurter Allgemeine Zeitung*, 12 June 1967; 'Don't Take it out on the Jews,' *The Economist*, 2 September 1967; Bratislava radio, 22 June 1967.
[3] While *Literarni Noviny* wrote nothing on the war, on 10 June 1967 it did publish a map and two pictures which revealed its pro-Israel sentiments.
[4] See for example, Tazky on the Slovak Writers Congress: 'we are very much like the Security Council, which meets, but solves nothing; which only has words, words, words . . . and we don't have even them.' (*Kulturny Zivot*, 23 June 1967.)

The second aspect of this problem was the official anti-semitism which could but remind the intellectuals of the purge era and all that they had been struggling to eliminate. There were any number of signs of this official anti-semitism, from the enthusiastic way in which Novotny supported the Arabs and condemned Israel to the extent of the forbidding of the singing of a Yiddish song and the withdrawal from circulation of a series of stamps depicting Prague's Alte-Neue Synagogue. There were reports that the writer Arnost Lustig and film-makers Jan Nemec and Ester Krumbachova had had their works and activities further restricted because of the regime's anti-semitism.[1] Israeli diplomats were sharply critized in the press and a number of persons with Jewish names were arrested for various offenses. The use of the Jewish names was particularly reminiscent of the Slansky period when Jewish defendants whose names had been changed (or did not have particularly Jewish-sounding names) were publicized according to distinctly Jewish names. Thus in June 1967 *Rude Pravo*, writing critically of Israeli diplomats, was careful to add these persons' former Jewish names to their present Hebrew ones.[2] As Mnacko pointed out, the anti-semitic aspect of the Slansky trials had never been fully confronted, and, as a result, it looked as if this type of Stalinist repression could find its way back into Czechoslovak life. This was especially so, Mnacko maintained, given the fact that one of the men responsible for the 1950 events was still on the political scene and that other people responsible for these events were 'still armed.' It 'might be more comfortable for them to find a justification for themselves in a new wave of anti-semitism,' he said.[3]

This apparently ignoble silence imposed on the Czechoslovak intellectuals, together with all the aforementioned signs of a hardening of policy, may account for the pessimism expressed by various leading writers when interviewed prior to the Writers' Congress. Many seemed to believe that nothing more could be expected from the writers, that they had given up the fight, or as one writer put it, 'The silence only confirmed that we are "one-time action people," that we sail only when the wind is good.' This pessimism was particularly apparent in responses leading intellectuals gave to the question 'what will you do after

[1] A. Kratochvil, 'The Cultural Scene in Czechoslovakia: January–July 1967,' RFE (1967), 11; *Literarni Noviny*, 4 August 1967; *New York Times*, 6 September 1967, reported cancellation of the scheduled celebrations of the millennium of the Czech Jewish community.
[2] *Rude Pravo*, 14 and 15 June 1967.
[3] *Frankfurter Allgemeine Zeitung*, 11 August 1967.

congress?' Placing these responses in their context both of circumstances and the aforementioned remarks it would appear that Jiri Sotola was not merely being witty when he answered: 'Nothing that has anything to do with the Writers' Union,' or Juraj Spitzer: 'For a long time I'll keep away from unions,' or Ladislav Tazky: 'Probably I'll be disgusted for a long time to come.'[1]

The Slovak Writers Congress which lasted one unexciting day, 11 May, probably contributed to the writers' pessimism. The Slovak writers, apparently satisfied that they had over the past few years gained their major demands (the rehabilitations of Slovak nationalists) did not seem to consider it worth fighting – at the congress – the increased regime pressures. The outgoing chairman, Mihalik, did urge that the efforts of the union be directed towards creating conditions for the 'undisturbed' development of literature, and he *was* replaced by a moderate, the non-communist poet Miroslav Valek.[2] Nonetheless the Slovak writers, in strange contrast to their last congress which had in effect launched de-Stalinization in May 1963, accepted without comment a hard-line speech by Slovak party ideology chief Vasil Bilak. Spelling out the regime's by now quite clear policy, Bilak asserted that while the party might settle certain political problems by a compromise, it would not 'use this method in the ideological sphere. It could not look on passively while ideological chaos prevailed in one part of our cultural front.'[3]

THE FOURTH CONGRESS OF THE CZECHOSLOVAK WRITERS UNION

In spite of this pessimism or perhaps because of it the Fourth Writers Congress developed into one of the most important events of the de-Stalinization process. Most of the speeches at the congress were frank and highly critical of the regime on many counts, providing heated discussions and the intervention, by way of a second speech, from party representative Jiri Hendrych. In his first speech Hendrych delivered himself of a tirade against 'ideological diversion' and 'cultural reaction.'[4] The only surprising element of this speech was its unusually aggressive dogmatic tone, but there could have been few at the congress

[1] *Kulturny Zivot*, 23 June 1967. See also Florin, *ibid.*, and *Kulturny Zivot*, 30 June 1967 (Jiri Sotola, 'The (Continued) Presence of Yesterday').
[2] *Kulturny Zivot*, 12 May 1967.   [3] *Kulturny Zivot*, 19 May 1967.
[4] Unless otherwise stated, sources for the congress may be found in *IV. Sjezd. Svazu Ceskoslovenskych Spisovatelu* (Praha, 1968).

who expected anything but a hard line from the regime spokesman.

The writers had already in fact been given a hint of the difficulties the party had wished to impose at the congress when, prior to the congress, the party ideological department 'strongly criticized' their proposed resolution. Basically a liberal document, the approved resolution characterized the role of socialist culture as a stimulus in the process of democratization and the acquisition of greater human freedom. Culture was the 'significant standard of the whole society . . . nothing can be a more permanent indictment of political regimes than the absence of a great culture.' The resolution noted the break in the continuity of Czechoslovak literature after 1949, at which point the 'creative process was narrowed and limited to propagandistic functions and to an intolerable identification of ideology and culture in the vulgar utilitarian sense.' The resolution criticized the arbitrary rejection of certain periods of Czechoslovak literary history as well as the turning away from the sources of European (western) culture such as were rooted in antiquity, the Renaissance, or Christianity. It called for greater participation in foreign exchanges of literature and contact with emigre Czech and Slovak writers (so long as these were not working against the CSSR). Airing a major grievance, the resolution said that 'the congress of Czechoslovak writers does not agree with the contemporary practice of press supervision,' and urged a reform of the law which would limit censorship to matters of national defense and which would grant the individual writer the right to defend himself when accused of violating the law. A good many intellectuals did not consider this resolution liberal enough; they resented the party's interference in its formulation, which fact nullified whatever positive elements existed in it. The fact that the resolution itself provided that the minutes of the congress be released only for the internal use of the union was indicative of the contradictory nature certain writers saw in the resolution.

Union presidium member Milan Kundera, who opened the discussion with his comment that the party had critically participated in the drafting of the resolution, amplified certain points in the resolution as if to insert what he considered missing. Thus he was much more severe in his criticism of the post-1949 interference in art and blamed Czechoslovak society for placing obstacles in the way of literary progress, implying that under present conditions the obstacles could not be overcome. He looked upon even the partial gains of the past four years as something of a 'cultural miracle,' given the conditions of society. Later in the day, Alexandr Kliment supported this view when he argued that all the attributes of creative freedom were lacking in Czechoslovak society.[1] Echoes of this view were heard on the following day, including Ivan Klima's criticism of the Press Law and the lack of press freedom, and Antonin Liehm's attack on party cultural policy and the 'dictates of power and of the market place.'

The most shocking speech of the first day, however, was Pavel Kohout's blunt criticism of the regime's foreign policy towards Israel. He praised Israel's progressiveness and accomplishments ('In Israel they have made a garden out of the desert . . . Nearly the whole system of agriculture is organized in a socialist or communist manner'). He likened the situation of Israel in June 1967 to that of Czechoslovakia in 1938, and he argued the moral right of countries so small to defend themselves, if need be offensively. Generating much interest and excitement, Kohout also read the congress Soviet writer Solzhenitsyn's letter to the Soviet writers union condemning Soviet censorship. With this Hendrych angrily left the hall.

Conservative, or less courageous or semi- or former liberals, together with certain Slovaks, alarmed by the turn of events of the first day, prepared a letter of protest the following day. This letter, signed by hard-liner Jan Drda, and some-time liberals such as Jarmila Glazarova and Vladimir Minac, criticized the political nature of many of the contributions and urged the congress to stick to literary union matters. The more liberal of those signing, such as Arnost Lustig, signed theoretically because they were fearful that the introduction of such issues as the regime's Middle East policy or Solzhenitsyn's letter would provoke the regime into taking repressive measures against the union.[2] This was by no means the only opposition to the liberals expressed at the congress; in effect heated debates were the norm.[3] Despite these efforts, the second day's speeches were even more outspoken than the first, with the speeches of Prochazka, Havel, and Vaculik attracting the greatest attention. Havel, the young avant-garde playwright already persecuted by the regime, was most critical of the union and of 'moder-

[1] Goldstuecker implied the same thing when he spoke of the incompatibility of art and ideology, but his conciliatory references to the progressive policies of the party won him praise instead of condemnation from the party. See *Kulturni Tvorba*, 6 July 1967.

[2] Prague radio, 28 June 1967; *Vecernik*, 14 February 1968; *Kulturny Zivot*, 29 March 1968.

[3] See the attacks on liberals in speeches of Jiri Hajek, Ivan Skala, Jan Skacel, and Milan Lajciak.

ate' liberals, who, he said, were content to make 'daring' speeches once every four years – and nothing more. He urged the union to fight, actively and practically, for freedom, democracy, and humanism rather than bend to the commands of the party.

Vaculik probably went the furthest of all the liberals at the congress when he spelled out his demands for a democratic society. These included the demand for a new Constitution which would eliminate the monopoly of power granted the Communist Party by the 1960 Constitution. He delivered a reasoned but scathing condemnation of totalitarian government, leaving no question that he was referring to Czechoslovakia. He strongly attacked 'power' as a negative, self-perpetuating feature of totalitarianism, and he called upon artists to resist power – especially the recent 'threat' heard even at the congress to take away from the artists such things as their union, publishing house, and journals. Speaking of those who wield power he asked:

But are they really masters over everything? and what do they leave in the hands of others? Nothing? Then we do not need to be here, but they should say so, then it should be crystal clear that, in effect, it is a handful of people who want to decide on the existence of all this, about what is to be done, thought and felt.

Vaculik argued for the legal right for the artist to criticize and for genuine, guaranteed freedom – not a token benevolency towards art. He said that as a citizen, not just an artist, he feared for the lack of guarantees of basic civil rights. Vaculik called upon the union to seize the initiative and demand an improvement of the Constitution, to take the problem to the people and see to it that it be discussed on the floor of the National Assembly. A heated exchange between Vaculik and Hendrych ensued in which Vaculik accused the party central committee of having no idea of the true meaning of socialism and communism. The following day Hendrych took the podium for a second, unexpected, time, and in an official party 'standpoint' he criticized Vaculik by name. He condemned the misuse of freedom at the congress, which he said had confused freedom with anarchy and 'the empty right of the propagation of reactionary opinions and of opinions which history has condemned.' He condemned what he called the concealed and even open attacks on the party, the government, its internal and foreign policies, and socialism.

Party central committee candidate and liberal writer Jan Prochazka closed the congress, however, without heeding Hendrych. He even appeared, at least by implication, to question the latter's right to pass judgment. Prochazka affirmed that the struggle for the right of free expression would continue 'as long as there is a last writer in this world, a last ruler, because the writer will not subordinate himself to doctrines and dogmas.' He also affirmed the writers' loyalty to all who fight against oppression, persecution, the poison of racism and anti-semitism, against chauvinism and narrow-minded nationalism.

The party had its way, in that it refused to accept the writers' nominations for the union's new central committee, specifically those of Vaculik, Kohout, Klima, and Havel. The party-dictated composition of the central committee was then acclaimed by the party as 'a vote on the attitude of the body of writers toward the party,' which demonstrated 'that the majority of those present rejected the attempts politically to abuse the congress and that the party has the support of the majority of writers.'[1] The party could not, apparently, entirely impose its will, for no presidium or chairman was elected at the congress, although it did block the nomination of Prochazka as chairman.[2] The elections of a chairman and presidium were postponed until September.

The approximately one hundred and thirty Slovak participants – with only a few exceptions – were entirely silent at the congress. While there have been varying 'explanations' for this, it would appear that the Slovaks had agreed, despite the closing speech at their congress of their own union chairman, to pursue independence from the Czechoslovak group. While many Slovaks were simply taken by surprise (and therefore unprepared to contribute) by the nature of the Czech speeches, many did not wish to jeopardize their own interests by association with the outspoken Czechs at the congress. Only Novomensky, whose speech was read in his absence (due to illness), supported the Czech writers and attacked censorship. One Slovak was willing to speak against the Czech liberals, ten Slovak liberals signed the letter asking for non-political discussions, and those who apparently felt that they could do neither but were unwilling to join the Czechs, left the congress. Whatever the reason for the departure – or the silence – on the part of the Slovaks, this provided a sharp contrast to four years earlier when the Czechoslovak Writers Congress was mild diversion compared to the bold, outspoken meeting of the Slovaks. It also presaged a later split between the more 'nationalist'-minded and the more 'democratic'-minded Slovaks.[3]

---

[1] 'Literature after the Congress,' *Nova Mysl*, XXI:15 (1967), 10.
[2] *Literarni Listy*, 11 April 1968; *Reporter* 21 February 1968.
[3] In early 1968 a group resigned from *Kulturny Zivot*, going over to *Predvoj* which they converted into *Nove Slovo*, a rebirth of Husak's journal of 1945–8. Led by

In addition to controlling or blocking the elections within the union, the regime attempted to keep most of the proceedings out of print. Thus only the conservative speeches were published in any length and, later, only one liberal speech got through the censor, that of Prochazka. Novotny himself replied almost immediately in a speech to the party college on 30 June. He defended the party against the accusation heard at the congress that Czechoslovakia was passing through a 'second darkness.'[1] He angrily referred to the congress attacks on the policies of the party and the internal and foreign policies of the state, claiming that these writers advocated 'a class reconciliation with bourgeois ideology.' He accused the writers of being a help to reactionaries, and he served notice (again) that the party would permit no compromise regarding its class war on ideologies 'that oppose communist views . . . all those who do not accept this are on the other side.'

With this the party launched an attack on those it considered to be the primary offenders: Vaculik, Havel, Kohout, Klima, Liehm, and Prochazka, as well as on the union journal *Literarni Noviny*. Thus *Kulturni Tvorba* editorialized against the 'demagoguery' and 'anarchistic' dangers engendered by Kohout, Klima, Havel, and Vaculik at the congress. It deplored their attack on the internal and foreign policy of the state and the 'sick' atmosphere which they created.[2] *Zivot Strany* was still stronger in its condemnation, implying that outsiders ('such as [*Svedectvi* editor] Tigrid and emigres of his kind') had been influential in forming the policies of the writers preparatory to the congress, mentioning *Literarni Noviny* and *Host do Domu* as journals which had published dialogues prior to the congress (the implication being that they too shared the responsibility for the atmosphere of the meeting).[3] *Rude Pravo* polemized against the liberals by accusing Kohout of having failed to see that in comparing 1967 to 1938, Israel represented Nazi Germany, not Czechoslovakia. The article dismissed Liehm for asking the state to pay but to leave the artists alone, and countered Kundera's claim that, because of the party, the level of literature had fallen to that of propaganda in the 1950s, by saying that in the 1950s the writers themselves had 'spontaneously' limited the scope of their

Husak and Novomesky, they referred to themselves as 'Federalists,' arguing that *Kulturny Zivot* was losing sight of Slovak goals in its pursuit of democratization. See *Reporter*, 15 May 1968; *Kulturny Zivot*, 26 April, 3, 10, 17, and 24 May 1968.

[1] *Rude Pravo*, 1 July 1967. The period following the defeat at White Mountain in 1620 is called the period of darkness. The reference was to Vaculik's speech.
[2] *Kulturni Tvorba*, 6 July 1967.
[3] Lg, ' A Note on the Writers Congress,' *Zivot Strany*, 16 (1967), 11–12.

work. Vaculik's provocative speech was dismissed entirely as 'beyond any discussion.'[1]

AFTERMATH OF THE CONGRESS

The stage was set for some sort of party action and rumors circulated about party proceedings against the writers in question. Instead of immediate action against these persons, however, the regime moved first against another group of intellectuals. While this move had probably been in preparation for some time and scheduled more in connection with the regime's general crack-down than specifically with the congress, it was an ominous step in the midst of the new tensions. On 3 July the trial of three intellectuals opened in Prague: the young writer Jan Benes, film and television student/producer Karel Zamecnik, and emigre journalist Pavel Tigrid, *in absentia*. Jan Benes, who had already come in for regime criticism as one of the editors of *Tvar*, was prosecuted for publishing in the Paris-based Czech-language emigre magazine, *Svedectvi*. Tigrid, the editor of this journal, had long been a favorite target of the regime, mainly because of the success of *Svedectvi*. In the original indictment he was accused of treason, but as his Czechoslovak citizenship had been taken from him in 1959, this charge was dropped. He was, however, found guilty of setting up and directing a subversion and espionage ring operating inside Czechoslovakia. Benes was accused of having collaborated with him by sending abroad reports on domestic conditions, and the charges against Benes included subversion, fraud, and speculating. Zamecnik was merely accused of violating the interests of the Republic abroad; he was acquitted. After two weeks of trial the court sentenced Tigrid (*in absentia*) to fourteen years' punishment, and Benes to five years.

The trial itself was closed to foreign correspondents. At its conference at the end of July, the International Pen Club passed a resolution, with the support of the attending Czechoslovak delegation, calling for the release of Benes. At their congress Czechoslovak writers had criticized the arrests, but the September meeting of the Writers Union central committee nonetheless ruled to strike Benes' name from the list of candidates for membership in the union.

Two additional things happened that summer which further aggravated the already tense situation between the intellectuals and the regime. On 10 August the most widely read communist writer in

[1] *Rude Pravo*, 12 August 1967. For details of the congress and after see Dusan Hamsik, *Writers Against Rulers* (London, 1971).

Czechoslovakia, Ladislav Mnacko, arrived in Israel on a protest trip. Mnacko, who is not Jewish, did not defect, but he left no question as to the protest nature of his trip. He vowed in an interview published in the *Frankfurter Allgemeine Zeitung* that he would return to Czechoslovakia only when it reopened diplomatic relations with Israel.[1] He said that he regarded Prague's policy towards Israel as an unfair remnant of the spirit and methods of the 1950s, and proof that things had not, indeed could not, change significantly as long as those responsible for the injustices of the 1950s were still in power. Thus both the anti-semitism which prompted and accompanied Czechoslovakia's *active* anti-Israel policy and the censorship used regarding discussion of the issue convinced Mnacko that some other way must be sought to bring about a change – since silence would be tantamount to consent.

Mnacko's protest was a blow for the regime, for he had been an extremely active and loyal party member since his wartime days as a partisan in Moravia and Slovakia. He had been a rising party journalist in the 1950s, untouched by and, at least publicly, unopposed to the terror of those days. His 'conversion' came in 1956, though he was still not to be numbered among those liberals criticized by the regime. His first troubles apparently came in 1963 over his book *Delayed Reportage*, but even after its publication he was considered a loyal, non-dangerous liberal. In 1966, for example, he was accorded the title 'meritorious artist.' Only the publication abroad of his second anti-Stalinist book *The Taste of Power* brought him into a headlong clash with the regime. For the rank and file of the country and party, however, at the time of his departure, he was still a popular, not excessively radical writer. The regime was embarrassed by Mnacko's move and statement; it was most likely also annoyed by the attention these had attracted coming so soon as they did after the highly publicized Writers Congress and less publicized but nonetheless incriminating trial of Benes, Tigrid, and Zamecnik.

The regime reacted swiftly. On 16 August it deprived Mnacko of his Czechoslovak citizenship, expelled him from the Czechoslovak party, stripped him of his former awards (Klement Gottwald Prize for 1961) and his honorary title of 'meritorious artist.' It also sought to discredit him in the eyes of both the West and the domestic public by pointing to his earlier (pre-1956) dogmatic posture. By contrast to the severe regime action, the Slovak Writers Union did not expel Mnacko from its ranks, rather only from its central committee. The union statement

[1] *Frankfurter Allgemeine Zeitung*, 11 August 1967.

was basically without venom but rather seemed to regret that Mnacko had chosen the path he had.[1] Both literary journals, *Kulturny Zivot* and *Literarni Noviny*, gave the statement as little attention as possible (though ordered to publish it) and both refused to acknowledge or admit any association with the decision.[2]

Another only slightly less embarrassing occurrence was the publication in London of what purported to be a 'Manifesto' written by Czech writers, artists, and scientists.[3] This Manifesto accused the party of carrying on a 'fascist'-style witch hunt; it appealed to western intellectuals for moral support in the Czechoslovak struggle against regime persecution, intolerance, and censorship. While the regime (and Czechoslovak intellectuals) probably recognized almost immediately the non-authenticity of the document, the damage was done. The document *was* believable given the summer's events in Prague. Moreover, the interest generated abroad, especially by Mnacko's journey, made it incumbent upon the regime to respond to the document, which it did in abundance. This in turn led to discussion, both between East and West and inside Czechoslovakia, as to the contents of the Manifesto. Once again the regime found itself on the defensive, attention tensely concentrated on its battle with the intellectuals. The intellectuals too were probably embarrassed by the document but they did not seek to renounce or deny anything but its authenticity; with regard to its contents the Czechoslovak Writers Union said only that its own views had been made clear in the documents of its recent congress.[4]

The party was apparently still undecided exactly what to do about the increasingly uncomfortable situation which had arisen with the intellectuals. Any effect that the Benes trial might have had in restraining the intellectuals had most likely been mitigated by Mnacko's action; the Manifesto merely served to keep things seething. The indecision was illustrated by the 14 September meeting of the Czechoslovak Writers Union central committee which once again failed to reach an agreement on a chairman and presidium. The absence of a decision was a manifestation of party influence, but the fact that Prochazka (the union committee's candidate for chairman) was permitted

[1] Prague radio, 16 August 1967.
[2] See *Kulturny Zivot* and *Literarni Noviny*, 18 August 1967. The Mnacko affair and the question of Israel (with definite anti-semitic overtones) became part of the 1968 split between Slovak 'federalists' and Slovak 'democrats.' See p. 243, n. 3.
[3] *Sunday Times*, 3 September 1967. It was written by Czech historian Ivan Pfaff (*Lidove Demokracie*, 21 March 1968); see *Reporter*, 3 April 1968.
[4] *Literarni Noviny*, 8 September 1967.

to remain on the temporary directing board was a sign that the party had not yet laid down the law. Three hard-line speeches, two by Novotny and one by Hendrych in early September, demonstrated, however, that the regime was still concerned, particularly about the comments at the Writers Congress. Novotny reiterated the theory of the commanding role of the party and the traditional view: 'our democracy is a class democracy, our freedom is a class freedom.' For these reasons, Novotny argued, it was impossible in a socialist state to allow the propagation of views and ideologies harmful to socialism and alien to the party.[1] Referring more directly to the liberal pressures, he told a party presidium session in early September: 'We have permitted Sik to write and he even spoke at the Thirteenth Congress, he was allowed as the last speaker to give a stormy speech about democracy. Naturally when this was discussed at the congress, then even the writers caught on and all of them stormed – democracy, democracy.' Novotny also referred favorably in this speech to purges in other (presumably the Polish) parties.[2]

REGIME ACTION

Party action finally came at the central committee plenum of 26–27 September 1967. After Hendrych delivered a strong attack against a number of writers and *Literarni Noviny*, Prochazka was dismissed as a candidate of the central committee for 'political errors.' Party disciplinary proceedings were begun against him. Klima, Vaculik, and Liehm were expelled from the party for 'attitudes incompatible with party membership.' They were accused of being 'ideologically immature,' confused individuals who resorted to insidious and destructive methods. According to one accusation, they had lost their political and class bearing, had parted from the program and ideology of the party and, in the case of Vaculik, had directly called for resistance. They were accused of formulating a platform of political opposition; Vaculik was called an anarchist of long standing, while Klima and Liehm were said to be suffering from delusions of superiority. Hendrych revealed the real concern of the party when he linked these men and the Writers Congress with an anti-communist campaign timed, he intimated, to reach its climax with the Fiftieth Anniversary of the October Revolu-

[1] *Rude Pravo*, 2 September 1967.
[2] *Kulturny Zivot*, 5 July 1968; Vojtech Mencl and Frantisek Ourednik, 'What Happened in January,' *Zivot Strany*, 14 (1968), 23.

tion and directed from Paris. He said that Mnacko and 'his attack on the Republic added fuel to the fire, which was further fanned by the "so-called Manifesto." '[1]

At the same time the party moved against the Czechoslovak Writers Union itself. The union weekly, *Literarni Noviny* was transferred to the Ministry of Culture and Information, because it had become a 'platform for political oppositional points of view,'[2] and its editorial board was disbanded. In another step directed against the writers, the union's publishing house 'Ceskoslovensky Spisovatel' was stripped of its 'rights' to publish domestic authors, and the writers' union welfare fund was partially restricted.[3] These measures were clearly an effort to deprive the union of its power and autonomy, by subjecting most of its publishing rights to government supervision and making it dependent on the government in the delicate matter of welfare and material security. Organizationally the union was to be 'split' into smaller local groups: regional branches were to be formed in Pilsen and Usti Nad Labem with the regional party authorities entrusted with control over them. At the same time, an 'aktiv' of party writers was to be set up by the central committee's ideological commission 'to assist' party work in this sphere. In connection with this effort to improve party work itself in culture, the party changed the editorship of *Kulturni Tvorba* by replacing editor-in-chief Jaroslav Hes with the still more conservative Frantisek Kolar. It also made personnel changes in various publishing houses.

These organizational changes were clearly designed to weaken the union and its ability to operate as a unit, as well as to provide easier party control. It was apparently in conjunction with this that the party agreed to what had heretofore been a radical demand by Slovak writers for a separate union. The Slovaks' demand stemmed from their general desire for autonomy or greater independence within the Republic, but, in the case of the Writers Union, the party probably saw this as a temporarily useful concession. In view of the Slovaks' own peaceful congress in May and their abstention from comment at the Czecho-slovak congress in June, the regime had either worked out a *modus vivendi* with the Slovak writers or at least felt they could be trusted, insofar as the new plan would require. It would seem that, however

[1] *Rude Pravo*, 28 September 1967.   [2] *Ibid.*
[3] *Frankfurter Allgemeine Zeitung*, 2 October 1967; Tanjug, 2 October 1967. Hendrych said 'some' functions of the fund would be transferred to the Ministry of Culture and Information (*Rude Pravo*, 28 September 1967).

temporarily, Slovak writers had opted for national interests which the Slovak party had recently done much to protect, as against the broader political struggle for liberalization. Thus already at the 6 September meeting of the Czechoslovak Writers Union's central committee reference was made to the 'Czech part' and the Slovak Union Committee – a distinction made still clearer by Hendrych when he spoke of 'independent' branches in Prague and Bratislava.[1] The Czechoslovak Union itself was apparently to be some sort of nominal roof.

Such strong measures, although they have little in common with former terror methods, nonetheless demonstrated the party's fear of the threat posed by the writers, and the determination to ignore the reforms and changes it had itself agreed to introduce over the previous four years when its power seemed threatened. Although it was a sign of Novotny's regained strength and stability since the 1963–4 crisis that he could afford to take such steps, there were many in the central committee who opposed the steps against the writers. Even some relatively conservative central committee members who had spoken sharply against the writers in question, warned against a return to 'leftist sectarianism' and dogmatism and 'the trap' of 'anti-intellectualism.' One central committee member, dean of the Charles University Faculty of Philosophy, Jaroslav Kladiva, urged that the party's action remain a party matter, i.e. that the expelled writers not be ostracized or denied work (as was the custom in past purges). According to reports reaching the West, the party presidium itself was not unanimous in its decision against the writers. While Slovak Michal Chudik (SNC President) was a conservative on the issue, Dolansky, Cernik, and Kolder were more moderate; Lenart was said to have remained silent.[2]

THE RESULTS

The party's problems with the intellectuals by no means ended with these measures. The party placed in charge of *Literarni Noviny*, now under the Center for Book Culture of the Ministry of Culture and Information, conservative journalist Jan Zelenka. No editorial board was listed on the mast-head of the first issue, mainly because the former editors had all been dismissed or refused to cooperate. Almost all

[1] *Ibid.*
[2] See *Rude Pravo*, 3 and 4 October 1967; *Le Monde*, 10 October 1967. Smrkovsky later said that the presidium 'more or less pushed the central committee' into its decision. ('Democracy Does Not Come Overnight,' *My 1968*, V:4 (1968), 5.)

important Czech writers and almost all union members refused to cooperate with the 'new' journal, and none of the former forty-member staff agreed to contribute.[1] Even the designer of the mast-head opposed further use of his design.

In his first editorial the new editor tried to handle the whole matter humorously, insisting that he did not intend to produce a 'government issue' newspaper or to ignore 'progressive' trends. He did intend, how-ever, to overcome the 'negative' off-shoots of the 'progressive' changes introduced by the party over the past years, i.e. he intended to protect the progressive platform from 'leftist moods, and 'alien' ideological elements.'[2] That there were mixed feelings and no small amount of controversy over the transfer of the journal to the government was illustrated not only by numerous articles and letters but also by the drop in circulation, from the former 150000 copies per week to 60000 by December 1967.[3] *Rude Pravo* acknowledged this situation in an article hitting criticism at the party's September decision. Now that the party had taken on the intellectuals it tried through its journal to convince the public 'that there can be no question of a conflict between the party and art, or between the party and the intelligentsia . . . [the party does *not*] intend to suppress art' as some were contending.[4] The Yugo-slav party paper's correspondent in Prague was not as sure as the *Rude Pravo* writer. He wrote that 'not too many people in Prague, including the top political functionaries, are convinced that taking the journal away from the writers was a good measure;'[5] he quoted one (unnamed) central committee member as saying that nothing had been solved by any of the party measures.

The expelled writers Liehm, Klima, and Vaculik, and the demoted Prochazka did not appear in print for some time, though there were demands – in print – that they not be expelled from literature because of a political mistake.[6] The first to appear was Liehm, with a mid-November article published in the film and television journal – a symbol of the solidarity of that group of artists with the writers, especially for this particular writer who was also a film critic. Liehm was twice denied a passport after his expulsion from the party, once for an intended trip

[1] *Nedeljne Informativne Novine* (Belgrade), 10 December 1967; *Borba*, 24 November 1967.
[2] *Literarni Noviny*, 7 October 1967.
[3] *Nedeljne Informativne Novine*, 10 December 1967.
[4] *Rude Pravo*, 19 October 1967.   [5] *Borba*, 24 November 1967.
[6] See letters in *Literarni Noviny*, 25 November and 7 December 1967.

to Sweden and once to attend the Mannheim Film Festival. Pavel Kohout was also criticized at the September plenum, but no action was taken against him at the time. Upon his return from abroad in October, however, he was disciplined by a reprimand with warning.

Kohout's punishment apparently came as a result of statements he made at the 6 October party *aktiv* of communist writers and party representatives. He sharply criticized the party's measures against the writers and challenged the party representatives present, specifically Hendrych, to refute the allegedly 'false' statements made at the congress. He also accused Hendrych and Novotny of misleading the party.[1] The next *aktiv* which was held between Slovak union members and the Slovak party on 16 October, was equally if not more explosive. The Slovaks once again sounded like Slovaks and one after another such important writers as Stevcek, Novomesky, Kusy, and Chorvath condemned the party's recent actions. Novomesky called the expulsions 'wrong, very wrong' and warned that it was as harmful for the Slovak party as for the Czechs. Stevcek likened the present repressions to the aftermath of the 1956 Second Writers Congress – only now the regime had not even permitted publication of the congress speeches. Zora Jesenska went still further by quoting Vaculik to point out that this whole issue of the party and the intellectuals was one of power: the party had power, the writers did not. Yet, she asked in Vaculik's words, 'do they really rule everything?'[2]

The Slovak writers seemed to have realized their common stake with the Czech liberals. Two days after this meeting the Slovak union's committee met and unanimously approved a letter to Hendrych in which it emphatically asked for a 'normalization' of the situation in the Czechoslovak Writers Union and the solution of the problem of that union's press organ.[3] It also accepted for membership in the union a number of Slovak writers formerly condemned for such things as spiritualism, nationalism, and even fascism. This unilateral rehabilitation could only be interpreted in Prague as an act of defiance. The Slovaks apparently also decided to fulfill *Literarni Noviny*'s function until the Czechoslovak union received its journal back; *Kulturny Zivot* became the unofficial weekly organ for the union, printing, for example, a detached report of the meeting of the union central committee.

[1] 'Letter to the Central Committee of the CPCS,' *Svedectvi*, VIII-IX, 32-3 (1967), 106-9.
[2] 'Record of the *Aktiv* of Slovak Communist Writers,' *ibid.* 89-105.
[3] *Kulturny Zivot*, 3 November 1967.

The Czechoslovak union's central committee met on 26 October and finally succeeded in electing a presidium. This consisted of Drda, Goldstuecker, Jaris, Kriz, Lustig, Mihalik, Otcenasek, Pilar, Ptacnik, Smatlak, Sotola, Stevcek, Tazky, and Valek, i.e. a mixture of hard-liners, moderates and liberals, the last coming mainly from the Slovak ranks. Of greater significance was the failure to re-elect Pavel Kohout, Karel Kosik, Milan Kundera, and most important, Jan Prochazka. Prochazka was the only member of the interim committee not to be elected. Either the party succeeded in having its way on the question of Prochazka or the writers chose not to fight over him at this point given the difficulties his presence (much less chairmanship) might pose in the coming battle with the party to regain the rights of the union. The question of the chairmanship remained unsettled. The moderate Goldstuecker; who was acceptable to both the liberals and the party, had refused the position.[1]

The union central committee discussed the fate of *Literarni Noviny* and 'expressed its regrets that the Writers Union had lost its press organ.'[2] A sign that the split into regional branches was still in effect – at least the Czech–Slovak split – was evidenced by the announcement that the 'Czech section of the central committee of the union' met to elect its own commission. From this it would appear that although the Slovaks were now willing to support and help their Czech colleagues, they were not willing to make an issue of or renege on the split. Since the union as a whole was nearly impotent as a result of the party's measures, this meant that the writers as a group were without a direct voice in Prague.

The film-makers supported the writers, both in Slovakia and in Prague. The central committee of the Slovak Film and Television Artists Union passed a resolution on 21 October condemning the decisions against the writers, and sought to confront the regime with a united front.[3] The regime responded with more criticism of the contested films and more restrictions on the production of new films. The film artists, however, tended to maintain pressures on the regime by awarding the criticized films prize after prize and defending them at all available forums, as they had indeed by their letter to the Writers Congress, condemning such things as the attacks by Assembly deputy Pruzinec.[4]

The journalists too maintained their attacks on suppression of in-

---

[1] *Le Monde*, 10 October 1967.   [2] *Kulturny Zivot*, 3 November 1967.
[3] *Svedectvi*, VIII-IX, 32–3 (1967), 113–14.   [4] *IV. Sjezd* (Praha, 1968), 136–7.

formation and the misuse of the Press Law. An article even appeared in the Slovak party daily attacking 'the absence of a concept of journalistic information adequate to the existing trends of development and a truly democratic, humanistic model of socialism.'[1] These attacks were reiterated at the 19–20 October Czechoslovak Journalists Union Congress, but the congress nonetheless succumbed to regime pressures. Hendrych represented the party at this congress too and his opening speech was clearly designed to let the journalists know that the party had not and would not retreat on any issue. He reiterated Novotny's theory of 'class freedom' and 'class democracy.' He somewhat defensively supported the party's decisions on *Literarni Noviny* saying that the 'exceptional and distressing' measures had been necessitated by the fact that the paper had become a platform for political opposition.[2] The journalists apparently understood the implicit warning and inserted virtually this whole statement into its letter addressed to the party central committee.[3] Hendrych's defensive tone may have been a sign of the party's realization of the trouble it had stirred up by its harsh measures. This was further illustrated when, in addition to criticizing *Kulturny Zivot* and *Literarni Noviny*, Hendrych also warned against dogmatism.

[1] *Bratislava Pravda*, 4 October 1967.
[2] *Rude Pravo*, 20 October 1967.
[3] In 1968 the Journalists Union passed a resolution condemning its 1967 congress.

18

PRESSURES FROM THE SLOVAKS
AND THE YOUTH

TO AND FRO WITH THE SLOVAKS

In addition to the economic and cultural spheres, other areas of Czechoslovak society provided sources of growing pressures on the party to
fulfill its promises. Thus Slovak nationalism and youth unrest must also
be added to the picture of at least organized opposition to stiffening
regime policies. No small part of the growing discontent of the Slovaks
was the inherent disadvantage of Slovakia under the new economic
system. Measures had been added to the economic program – in
violation of its principle of unfettered development according to market
criteria – designed to guarantee what was known as territorial equalization. Nonetheless many Slovaks were still concerned that industrially
less developed Slovakia would suffer from her disadvantageous starting
point. Slovak party first secretary Dubcek, though a supporter of the
reforms, expressed this concern at the September 1967 central committee plenum.[1]

Dubcek's position, based on the principle that Slovakia's resources
could not be utilized without more rational organization of the
economy to offset the national tendency of growth in the already
developed areas which had the means for further investment, was
expressed by a number of Slovak economists. There was a definite
dissatisfied nationalist strain to these complaints, reflecting the thoughts
expressed a year earlier by Viktor Pavlenda urging consideration of
Slovakia as a national, political, and economic unit. Thus one Slovak
argued that the real solution to the problem caused by the economic
reforms would not, indeed could not, be one based on 'exceptions,
concessions, subsidies or tutorial interventions in one area alone.'[2]
Just as the new management system strove to change the centralistic
model of the economy, so the economic jurisdiction of the Slovak
government bodies must benefit from decentralization of controls. The
meaning of this formula as explained by another Slovak was 'that a

[1] *Rude Pravo*, 29 September 1967.
[2] Hvzdon Koctuch, 'The New System of Management in Slovakia's Economy,'
Slovenske Pohlady, 83:1 (1967), 35.

255

degree of independence is the key which can free the hands of the Slovak economy,'[1] and an optimal degree of Slovak independence was an essential condition for the development of the Czechoslovak economy as a whole.

The crux of the matter, for the Slovaks at any rate, was actually how much independence Slovakia would have within the Republic. Thus the question of federalization inserted itself more demandingly into the tensions of 1967. Slovaks strove to point out the fact that these matters had not yet been solved. Such efforts came, for example, from Slovak intellectual Roman Kalisky, who had been criticized by Novotny in the early days of de-Stalinization for his accusations that the regime had far from settled the nationality problem. In May 1967 he questioned the right of Czechoslovakia to the name 'Socialist Republic,' pointing out that among other deficiencies, the state still did not serve the interests of the two nations equally and equitably.[2] The non-communist Slovak historian Rapant also argued that Slovak independence was more declarative than real and demanded that full equality for both peoples be reflected in the construction until independence could be achieved.[3] It is of significance that this suggestion was published in the monthly of the Slovak Writers Union, manifesting that organization's own belief in and campaign for federalization.

This campaign seemed to be reflected in even small things designed perhaps to keep the issue omnipresent and to accustom the public to the idea. Thus the Slovak radio and party daily *Bratislava Pravda* tended to give more thorough coverage of Rumanian pronouncements than that given by Prague. Bratislava radio and the paper on at least three occasions included excerpts, omitted by Prague, of Rumanian statements on the right of every nation to independent development, responsibility to its own people, and equality in talks with others without majority decisions being binding upon the minority nation.[4] There is very little reason to believe that Slovak organs were trying to support Rumania's move away from Moscow. It would seem, rather, that these discrepancies in reporting between Prague and Bratislava were a manifestation of a Slovak effort to benefit from or exploit any

[1] Vladimir Minac, 'Slovakia and its Economic Life,' *Slovenske Pohlady*, 83:1 (1967), 36–8.
[2] *Kulturny Zivot*, 5 May 1967.
[3] Daniel Rapant, 'The Slovaks in History: Retrospective and Perspective,' *Slovenske Pohlady*, 83:4 (1967), 37.
[4] Bratislava radio, 7 May 1967; *Bratislava Pravda*, 8 May 1966, 23 August 1967.

tendency that would increase her independence vis-a-vis Prague. The words 'independence,' 'national sovereignty,' 'mutual equality' were of significance to the Slovaks, apparently even the Slovak party, regardless of who uttered them.

REGIME RESPONSE

While the regime was aware and even concerned by the growing Slovak demands, its response went far to aggravate rather than amelior- ate the situation. *Rude Pravo*, for example, accused the Slovaks of being guilty of many of the same injustices – vis-a-vis the minorities in Slovakia – of which they accused Prague. Novotny himself sought to defend regime policies towards the Slovaks, on the occasion of a Czechoslovakia–Soviet friendship rally. He condemned what he called signs of nationalism in Czechoslovakia, terming nationalism a reactionary movement to be consistently combated.[1] The party then presented a 'standpoint' of the presidium on the 'nationality question in the CSSR.' This statement was basically an attempt to placate the Slovaks by calling for fuller awareness of the nationalities problem, greater regard for nationalist 'self-confidence' (as feelings of national- ism were more innocuously termed), and expanded efforts to improve Slovakia's position within the new economic system. On the last point, however, Slovakia's primary economic sphere, agriculture, was emphasized, rather than industry as the Slovaks might have wished. Emphasizing the role of the *central* authorities in guaranteeing nation- ality rights, the statement nonetheless called for proportional represen- tation in the central organs, the *apparat*, and the mass organizations. While it started from the premise that a basis for solution to the nationalities problem existed within the framework of the present Con- stitution, the statement did call for a re-analysis of the provisions regarding the rights of the Slovak National Council and a study of the effectiveness of constitutional provisions in the area of nationality relations. It implied that new laws should be enacted to improve the situation.[2]

The conciliatory tone of this document was unmistakable, and there was even the promise to study the constitutional arrangement. Either this was not enough for the Slovaks or Novotny himself was not pleased with the loose interpretation it might be given. In August,

[1] *Rude Pravo*, 5 June 1967.
[2] 'Tendencies in the Development of National Relations and the Solution to the National Question in the CSSR,' *Nova Mysl*, xxi:12 (1967), 7–8.

Novotny journeyed to Slovakia, apparently to address himself to Slovak demands. Pointing out once again the achievements (mainly economic) of the communist regime in settling the nationality problem, he admitted that he felt this defense necessary to counter what he called 'unsavory statements' concerning Slovakia's disadvantaged position within the Republic. He argued that the present framework, both economic and political, was the best possible arrangement for serving Slovak interests. He dismissed the arguments for federalization with the oft-used quote from Lenin whereby federation was depicted as a merely temporary solution applicable only to countries which had not yet settled their nationalities problem. According to Novotny, Czechoslovakia did not fall into that category.[1]

This declaration, like the earlier 'standpoint' was not, however, sufficient to silence or satisfy the Slovaks. As we have seen, Dubcek himself raised the economic issue at the party's September plenum and still more radical demands for federalization appeared just when the regime was having its greatest scuffle with the intellectuals.[2] Rapant published another edition of his plan for Slovak independence within a system of neutralized Central European single-nation states in conjunction with a neutralized Germany. More difficult for the regime to dismiss, however, was an article urging consideration of Smeral's federalization proposals. The author, party historian Jan Mlynarik, referred positively to what he considered Smeral's position: that a federation of the Swiss type would be a minimum requirement for the satisfaction of the needs of the nationalities in the Czechoslovak Republic.[3] At approximately the same time the Slovak Academy of Sciences published contributions made at a conference it had organized some months previously.[4] In these contributions the idea of autonomy and Slovak independence returned repeatedly, as the regime was criticized for centralist policies. Favorable reference was made to the policies of the Slovak nationalists purged in the Stalinist era, i.e. the *Dav*-ist hopes for Slovak independence. Most speakers urged some form of ethnically and territorially delineated 'national–constitutional' organization to guarantee political as well as economic equality between nations.

[1] *Rude Pravo*, 28 August 1967 (26 August speech at Martin).
[2] See Michal Pecho in *Tvorba*, 7–15 October 1969, for Slovak frustration over Novotny's negative reaction to their demands.
[3] See chapter 14 above.
[4] 'A Discussion about Czech–Slovak Relations,' *Historicky Casopis*, XV:4 (1967), 559–72.

Dubcek added his weight to these pressures again in November when he published an article praising the Slovak Communist Party of the pre-purge years, its contribution to the struggle against the Nazis, its participation in the 1944 SNC, and its role in preparing the 1948 take-over. He praised the Kosice program and called for a 'critical' analysis of post-1948 nationality policies. He urged a 'healthy' rejection of the present system in favor of 'new roads of progress.'[1] Thus the challenge from the Slovaks was placed upon Novotny by the highest authority and representative of the party in Slovakia.

YOUTH BECOMES AN ISSUE

Youth problems, specifically the various proposals for a reorganization of CSM and defining a role for youth in society, were one of the sources of difficulty prior to the Thirteenth Party Congress. Although such things as the university reform did go through, Novotny had taken a firm stand on the proposals for recognizing CSM. In response to this the students had launched an agitation and persuasion campaign prior to the June CSM congress, centering on the issue of the expulsion of Jiri Mueller from CSM and the university. On 3 January 1967 the presidium of the CSM Prague-district university committee met and a majority supported Mueller's appeal. Shortly thereafter the full Prague university committee of CSM discussed the issue of Mueller. There too a majority supported Mueller with such Communist Party members as Zdenek Pinc, Jan Kavan, Vladimir Lastuvka, and Jana Kohnova (all 'Prague radicals') speaking in favor of Mueller despite the party's orders not to do so.[2] The committee responded a few weeks later by electing Kavan and Pinc to its presidium. The CSM central committee was not, however, so liberally inclined; it too held a hearing, which upheld the CSM Prague-city committees' decision against Mueller.[3]

In preparation for the June CSM Congress, the 'Prague radicals' prepared a 'Critique' of the CSM's conservative 'Standpoint,' contacting students wherever possible regarding the 'Critique,' their own proposals, and the Mueller case. Their program was basically that outlined by Mueller in 1965, opposing direct party control of CSM and urging that the party's leading role be expressed mainly in the sphere of ideology, with its practical role limited to the setting of examples and

[1] *Bratislava Pravda*, 18 November 1967.
[2] *Student*, 13 March 1968; *Literarni Listy*, 7 March 1968; and private interviews.
[3] *Ibid.*

discussion. They advocated a federalized CSM operating as an interest organization and permitting expression of the interests (and political views) of its various components.[1]

While the group's influence did not extend to Slovakia, the Slovak CSM Congress, attended by Dubcek, did discuss the idea of devoting greater attention to the various groups within society, by age and social group.[2] This was step one of the radicals' plan – without the split into a loose federation and without step two: political power. The battle for the national CSM Congress was engaged, however, at the Prague-city CSM conference at which the students hoped to influence the delegation selected for the congress. This conference was an important step for the students, for it marked their first official contact with the workers – who knew little of the students' plans and issue and had been prepared by the party to oppose their suggestions. Through vigorous efforts, the Prague students persuaded the meeting to select a committee to look into the issue of Mueller's expulsion. This was probably a major achievement given the party's specific instructions (to CSM party members) not to permit the Mueller issue even to be raised. A vote at the conference also thwarted a CSM attempt to reduce the student delegation by placing CSM functionaries in a number of places allotted to the students. Thus the ten-man Prague student delegation to the congress contained five well-known 'radicals' and at least one sympathizer.[3]

The 5–9 June 1967 Congress itself was outwardly a conservative affair. None of the radical students were permitted to give speeches, the idea of federation was absent from the agenda, and the proposed statutes reiterated and emphasized the role of the union as a reserve for the party, with the primary function of 'activating the youth politically,' in order to convince them of the correctness of communist ideas. The union was to remain under the party and continue to act as a transmission belt, with other duties, such as representing and tending to the *interests* of the youth, only secondary. Perhaps an achievement of the students' pre-congress efforts, the proposed statutes did at least introduce the idea of 'interests' into the description of the union. In his speech to the congress Novotny supported the fact that CSM would remain a 'unified' organization, and, to clarify questions that may have remained on other than the radicals' proposals, the union chairman rejected any adoption of or return to the 'petty-bourgeois Boy Scouts.'

[1] *Ibid.*   [2] *Smena*, 19 May 1967.
[3] *Student*, 13 March 1968; *Literarni Listy*, 7 March, 1968.

Moreover, there was to be a return to active youth participation in economic campaigns. CSM, for example, was given patronage over construction of a blast furnace at the East Slovak Iron Works, and other tasks. This decision hardly promised to reverse the growing trend away from CSM among the youth.[1]

Yet the Prague radicals were most active at this meeting too and succeeded in disrupting many of the closed sessions. Although they had to convince a hand-picked group of CSM delegates, they succeeded in gaining support from the floor on a number of their comments regarding the statutes. Significantly breaking unanimity, the group's insistence upon discussion of almost every clause prolonged the meeting by over half a day. Their actual successes were limited to perhaps only three things. The vote for re-election of Zavadil as chairman of the union was not unanimous; some seventy-five persons voted against and sixty-two abstained.[2] Although this nowhere near prevented Zavadil's re-election, it was an unprecedented split for CSM. The second achievement was official recognition of the district university committees which had in effect been merely an *ad hoc* concession to the students in 1963. The third success was a clause supporting CSM recognition of 'interest clubs' as basic CSM organizations. The clubs could be established at places of residence, work, schools, cultural or sports institutions, with the rights to their own names, symbols, rules, and bulletin, albeit in keeping with CSM statutes. While the union may have seen this move as a way to bring under CSM control the independent clubs which had been cropping up, it also provided for the possibility of creating interest groups as basic, sovereign, components of CSM.[3] An example of the way in which the radicals intended, and did, use this clause was the formation in September 1967 of the academic Club of the Friends of Art, chaired by Zdenek Pinc.

This club actually was a manifestation of the contact between the intellectuals and the students which developed over the summer. The students, for example, distributed typed copies of Ludvik Vaculik's speech to the Writers Congress and when, for example, the university committee's bulletin was closed down (periodically), the Writers Union

---

[1] *Mlada Fronta*, 6, 11, and 15 June 1967. Between the CSM congresses of 1963 and 1967 membership dropped from 1418783 to 1055000. (Prague radio, 9 June 1967; *Mlada Fronta*, 24 April 1963.)

[2] Private interviews.

[3] For official position on the clubs, see F. Moravicky, 'Clubs Outside the Law,' *Nedele*, 1 (xxi):20 (1967); *Smena*, 1 February 1967.

permitted them to use its internal bulletin. Pinc's club became the scene of discussions with such intellectuals as Prochazka, Vaculik, Kosik, and Pithart.

Kusy, along with Juraj Suchy, had taken up the students' issue in the pages of the Slovak party daily. The two Slovaks criticized the regime for going only halfway in the reforms concerning the youth.[1] They said youth were now allowed to express themselves (within limits)[2] in their dress and customs, and even in their avant-garde poetry clubs, and so on, but they were not permitted to formulate their own program and were forced to accept a program issued by the older generation. The youth should be permitted to determine their way of life in social-ism, as well as the aim towards which they as a generation wished to strive. If not, the program already chosen for society would remain a thing 'alien to them;' without the possibility of participating or contri-buting to the creation of society's program, youth withdraw altogether, the result being the current a-political attitude of the youth tending towards 'breaches of the peace and actual criminality.'

The youth which has no generational program of its own cannot have positive aims and thus, as a generation, it must disintegrate; one part takes over the generational program of the 'fathers' and becomes a conformist 'appenditure' offering at most passive resistance, while the other part sticks to itself ... slowly sinking into a position of criticism for criticism's sake, protesting against everything that exists.

This was not the first warning of the significance of neglect in the area of youth, but it came at a time when the party had its hands full, so to speak, with the still-faltering economy (and complaining econo-mists) as well as the recalcitrant intellectuals and troublesome Slovaks. The party's response was limited to disciplinary proceedings against those radical students who were party members, and harassment for the others (e.g. expulsion of Holecek from the university and his immediate drafting into the army). The magnitude of the problem became all too clear, however, at the end of October when a purely non-political demonstration became the spearhead for volatile student demands no different from those of the intellectuals. As we have seen, Czechoslovak students and young workers had on previous occasions

[1] *Bratislava Pravda*, 2 August 1967.
[2] One such limit was the 1966 Prague City Council announcement that 'unkempt youths' would be denied entrance to certain restaurants and events. They were also to be denied exit visas for travel abroad (Prague radio, 31 August 1966).

turned peaceful meetings into anti-regime platforms, but in the early winter of 1967 the atmosphere was such – and the regime reaction a reflection of this atmosphere – that the student outburst was to be of much significance.

The trouble started on the evening of 31 October 1967 when student residents of the Prague Technical College Strahov hostel were gathered in a meeting with *Mlada Fronta* officials to air their long-repeated complaints about poor (electricity and heat) conditions in the hostel. During this meeting the electricity failed once again, and the students decided to stage a candle-light march to Vaclavske Namesti in order to draw public attention to their complaint. The marchers grew to an estimated 1500. At the approach to the castle, on Neruda Street, they were stopped by police who used clubs and tear gas to disperse the students. The police then entered the Strahov campus and indiscriminantly beat up students they found there.[1]

The following day the rector of the Technical College met with student representatives and promised the requested repairs. At this point, however, it was too late. On 8 November the traditionally activist students of the Charles University Faculty of Philosophy held a five-hour meeting to protest the police brutality. This meeting passed a resolution sent to Education Minister Jiri Hajek and Interior Minister Kudrna, in addition to the party central committee, and the CSM, with the following demands: immunity of academic grounds; identification and punishment of the policemen responsible for the beatings; number tags for policemen to make them easily identifiable; prohibition of the use of chemical gas against citizens; a National Assembly hearing on the Strahov events; publication of the investigation results; accurate and extensive press reporting of the events. The students' resolution demanded completion of the investigation by 30 November, though they scheduled an interim meeting for 20 November to decide on further steps to be taken.[2] The CSM organization at the faculty held two meetings protesting the police entry into the Strahov campus,[3] and the party's university committee initially supported the students' demands at its meeting on 9 November. The committee nonetheless condemned demonstrations as a means for solving problems and termed the whole situation 'politically sensitive.'[4]

[1] For accounts of these events, see *Rude Pravo*, 14 November 1967; *Praca*, 2 November 1967; *Prace*, 3 November 1967; *Smena*, 19 November 1967.
[2] CTK, 9 November 1967; *Frankfurter Allgemeine Zeitung*, 9 November 1967.
[3] *Mlada Fronta*, 14 November 1967.   [4] *Student*, 15 November 1967.

This last point was acutely realized by the authorities. The rector of the college, for example, warned the students not to let themselves be used for 'other,' presumably political, purposes. Declaring that the police action had been necessary to restore order, he warned against construing the events as a conflict between the police and students.[1] Conservative *Kulturni Tvorba* editor Kolar said that a number of students 'attributed a political meaning and political aims' to the demonstration. He blamed this on the intellectuals, saying that 'it was not by chance' that some students referred to speeches from the Writers Congress. He claimed that the students were thoroughly familiar with western anti-communist propaganda, especially that of Radio Free Europe, and he saw signs of *Literarni Noviny*'s influence as well. While condemning the political aspect of the demonstration and the ammunition that complaints of police brutality gave the western press, he revealed that the rector of the college had demanded an investigation of the affair. Kolar concluded by describing the police as young workers merely doing their job.[2]

The regime banned a student demonstration scheduled for Czech Student Day, 17 November, but the scheduled meeting of the philosophy students did take place on 20 November. It was a nine-hour session which extended to the following day, attended by Charles University Rector Oldrich Stary, pro-rector Goldstuecker, dean of the Philosophy Faculty Jarislav Kladiva plus party, CSM, and government representatives as well as representatives from all the faculties. The students protested the police brutality and the unfair reporting of the press, accusing *Kulturni Tvorba* editor Kolar of trying to drive a wedge between students and workers. The students went so far as to announce that they intended to press charges against the journal, under provisions of the Press Law.[3]

Students demanded two seats on the investigating committee and some urged more demonstrations and that the students go to factories to explain their problems to the workers. They set up a committee chaired by Prague radical Jan Kavan to coordinate student affairs among the different faculties and to assist the state investigating committee. In what was apparently an effort to pacify the students, Goldstuecker explained that the country was in the process of an irreversible democratization and demonstrations could harm this

[1] *Ibid.*
[2] *Kulturni Tvorba*, 16 November 1967.
[3] *Frankfurter Allgemeine Zeitung*, 17 and 22 November 1967.

process – although there was certainly room for students' initiative. The meeting passed a resolution demanding a settlement by 15 December, postponing all demonstrations until that time. The students' grievances were contained in a second resolution which stated: 'the events at Strahov are the consequence of the unhealthy atmosphere in this state and they stem from the general political and economic situation . . . We insist on our right to react to abnormal political conditions in the form of public demonstrations.'[1] One student after the meeting expressed what may well have been the general feeling of students gathered there: 'We are Communists, but freedom is not the privilege of the West alone. Communists also have the right to it.'[2]

The repercussions of the Strahov events were not limited to Prague. At least one lively debate took place between students at a vocational college and leading politicians over the students' demands, as well as over the Mnacko case and the Fourth Writers Congress. Thus the originally innocuous student protest grew, to take its place alongside the other sensitive issues pressing on Novotny at the beginning of December. On the day of the students' deadline the party published the results of the investigation. While most of the students' demands were not granted, the government's report did find the police guilty of 'unduly harsh measures.' The Interior Ministry was instructed to look into the shortcomings uncovered by the investigation. Persons responsible for the conditions in the hostel were punished, although there were to be no criminal proceedings in connection with the demonstration.[3] There is every reason to believe that the damage caused by the student affair was almost immediate, for even as the students were making their demands Novotny was fighting for his position as a result of the growing pressures of the last months of 1967. The students were in daily touch with the liberals in the party, coordinating with them such things as their threat to demonstrate so as to serve but not endanger the liberals' efforts within the crucial party meetings in November and December.

[1] Cited in Paul Collins, 'Czechoslovakia at the Crossroads,' RFE (1967), 10.
[2] *Ibid.*
[3] *Rude Pravo*, 15 December 1967.

19

THE PRESSURES COME TO A HEAD

SECURITY FORCES

The student demonstrations introduced an element which until then had remained entirely outside the realm of the reforms: the police. Implied in almost all the demands since 1962 was the opposition to controls, interference in the everyday lives of the people, injustice and miscarriages of justice and all the issues of basic security connected with freedom. As a result, the police were in fact used less (as regards surveillance and intimidation of the population, for example). Nonetheless, aside from reforms in the judicial–legal system, there was no reform of the security organs as such. The border guards had been transferred from the Interior to the National Defense Ministry in January 1966, but there is reason to believe that they remained part of the same independent security net as before, linked with and subservient to Moscow.[1] This was evidenced by a number of incidents which occurred in 1967 when policies of the regime seemed to be countered or impeded in practice by police actions. The Yugoslav correspondent in Prague suggested that the security forces, particularly in 1967, were moving to fill a power–leadership vacuum left by the party, i.e. that they were taking matters into their own hands in view of the regime's declining authority.[2]

Certain of these actions were of embarrassment for Prague and complicated some of their foreign relations. For example, shootings of refugees escaping to and already on Austrian soil were the source of difficulties between the Prague and Austrian authorities, with the former finally apologizing. A *Rude Pravo* accusation that the Austrian police were placing East European tourists under surveillance was later apologized for by the paper. It has been suggested that only deliberately misleading information from the Czechoslovak security forces could have led to an accusation that even *Rude Pravo* was forced, probably by the Foreign Ministry, publicly to recant.[3] Another embarrassing case was the abduction of Czech-born U.S. citizen Kazan-Komarek when his Paris-bound Aeroflot flight was diverted to Prague on 31

[1] See Stanley Riveles, 'Security and Politics,' RFE (1967), 1–7.
[2] *Borba*, 18 November 1967. [3] Riveles, RFE (1967), 4.

October 1966. The Foreign Ministry intervened on behalf of the foreign (trade) policies of the regime. The result was that Kazan-Komarek, who admitted to having engaged in espionage fifteen years earlier, was given a *pro forma* trial and promptly released to the U.S.[1]

Of a more serious nature and undoubtedly a source of consternation for the already harassed regime, accused of a return to anti-semitic Stalinism by Mnacko in the press of the West and by others at home, was the death of American Jewish leader Charles Jordan. Jordan was deputy director of the Joint Distribution Committee; he was visiting certain East European capitals on his way to a conference in Israel. He disappeared on 15 August and after his wife demanded a search, his body was found in a shallow part of the Vltava River on 20 August. The regime tried to pass the case off as a suicide but, instead of allaying suspicions, conducted an immediate autopsy so that two doctors arriving from the West could learn nothing from their late investigations. The affair was a source of embarrassment for the Czechs in their relations with the U.S. – to say nothing of world public opinion. While there appeared many theories on the cause of Jordan's death and the authorities finally attributed it to hooligans or Arab students, the Prague regime reportedly implied to the U.S. that Moscow's orders had been involved.[2]

These actions, combined with the police brutality in dispersing Prague students on 31 October, may have prompted the party to look into police reforms. At the time, however, the police were just one more sign that de-Stalinization had run into snags and, as such, was an added problem weighing on Novotny when he faced the central committee in December. While Novotny controlled the party's security department (under Miroslav Mamula), the fact that the security forces as such remained under Soviet control prevented Novotny from benefiting from them during the following crisis. Thus, without Moscow's willingness to help Novotny, the latter, through Mamula, could only try to employ the army. These efforts, however, were thwarted by the presence of liberals in the highest party organizations of the army (specifically General Prchlik).[3]

THE FINAL CRISIS

It is difficult to say just which area provided the greatest pressures

[1] *Christian Science Monitor*, 7 May 1967.
[2] *The Economist*, 2 September 1967.   [3] See below, p. 272.

upon the regime, although the area of pressing economic problems, which continued because of the failure to implement the reforms, was perhaps the most urgent. There were of course other pressures, for party intellectuals did not let the leadership forget that it had agreed to consider political reforms. Thus even in the midst of the crisis a letter written by the head of the committee selected to map out political reforms, Zdenek Mlynar, appeared in *Literarni Noviny*. This letter reiterated the need for new forms to fit the emergence of socialist society, i.e. democratic forms.[1] A similar hint had already appeared in *Rude Pravo* itself two weeks earlier when a party school lecturer pointed out the need for an adjustment or updating of Marxist philosophy.[2] While these hints were only part of the general malaise among party intellectuals, Slovaks, and the youth, they exhibited the persistence of demands for concrete political–ideological changes. The party central committee plenum of 30–31 October addressed itself to this problem but in keeping with the tightened policy it was merely to reaffirm the party's leading role.[3]

The actual leadership crisis began at this plenum, however, despite or perhaps because of the conservative nature of Novotny's response on the issue of the party's leading role. The immediate cause of the struggle was an attempt by Hendrych to push through a resolution (on the leading role of the party) entirely different from the one prepared by the central committee.[4] This prompted a speech by Dubcek which was critical not only of this way of handling decisions but also of the resurgence of conservatism within the higher party circles. Dubcek urged that the party recognize the need for change, particularly in the concept and nature of the party's role. A number of speakers supported Dubcek's attack, including the South Moravian liberal first secretary Spacek, and Slavik, Kriegel, and Kadlec. Surprisingly Martin Vaculik supported Novotny by attacking Dubcek's speech.[5] Kolder, on behalf of Novotny, asked that the central committee continue the proceedings

[1] *Literarni Noviny*, 9 December 1967.
[2] *Rude Pravo*, 16 November 1967 (Miroslav Rydl).
[3] See *Rude Pravo*, 1 November 1967.
[4] This account of the crisis is based primarily on Mencl and Ourednik, 'What Happened in January,' *Zivot Strany*, 14–19 (1968), and supplementary private interviews.
[5] Vaculik later explained that he had seen the whole dispute as a personal vendetta possibly harmful to the party. (*Literarni Listy*, 14 March 1968.) At both this and the subsequent plena there were a number of surprising switches, some the result of personal preferences, loyalties, or feuds (as well as simple opportunism) rather than questions of principle.

without the presence of non-members of the central committee. In this smaller closed session Novotny took the floor and answered Dubcek in what amounted to accusing the Slovak leader of 'nationalism.'[1] This indelicacy raised the whole Slovak question and produced a tense situation of charges and counter-charges, the implications of which were that there should be a separation of party and state jobs, i.e. that Novotny should give up one of his leading positions. The meeting ended after sharp debates without any formal agreement. Another plenum was scheduled for 12 November, but this was postponed and in its stead a number of presidium sessions were held. According to some reports, Novotny made an attempt to place Michal Chudik in Dubcek's position, but he apparently was unable to gain enough support to oust the moderate–liberal Slovak leader. This was at least the second time Novotny tried to do this, another having been just prior to the Thirteenth Party Congress.[2]

The Yugoslavs were the ones to call attention to the struggle that went on in Prague all the month of November. A series of articles appeared in the Yugoslav press which claimed that the Czechoslovak party stood at a crossroads because of the need to find new tasks for the party given the new social conditions. One Yugoslav political writer after a trip to Prague explained that the pressures which made it incumbent upon Prague to find this new solution stemmed from the intellectuals and the economic situation specifically because of the closure of *Literarni Noviny* and the undue compromises on the economic reforms.[3] Still another source of tension, he said, was the demand among some party members for a 'second Marxist party.' Referring to the demands for political reform, he explained that there were three groups involved: those who advocated that the economic reforms be followed by political reforms; those who advocated that political reforms precede the economic reforms; and those who wanted no reform but a return to a 'strong-arm regime' which would reintroduce 'iron discipline.' The last were in favor of party control of all areas and facets of society and argued that *criticism* of the personality cult stood at the root of the problems experienced in the economy. This would appear to be a reference to the conservative idea, often espoused by Novotny until 1964, that it was the effort to decentralize the economy in 1958 which led to the economic slump – not, as the reformists argued, the failure to implement this decentralization. The Yugoslav

[1] See also *Bratislava Pravda*, 14 April 1968.   [2] *Ibid.*
[3] *Politika*, 12, 14 and 15 November 1967.

writer claimed that the party conservatives 'have no political feelings for the new processes taking place in Czechoslovak society today,' but he minimized their relative strength as a 'political force,' characterizing them rather as a 'political anachronism.'

It is to the second, 'political reforms-precede-economic' group that the Yugoslav attributed the two-party theory. While this extreme liberal group stood a great distance from the conservatives, according to the Yugoslav, there existed possibilities for solution. How successful such a solution would be depended, *Politika* concluded, on the 'outcome of the current confrontation of various opinions.'

A *Borba* article divided the party into a minority who wished a return to the rule of power, and the majority who believed that the party should abandon all prerogatives of power, dominating only the areas of politics and ideology.[1] *Borba* claimed that the latter group was called 'the liberals,' the former 'bureaucrats.' *Borba* saw the liberals as a majority. The writer also revealed that heated debates at the lower levels had preceded the stormy October plenum, and the Czechoslovak party was engaged in a great debate at all levels as to its role in society.

On 8 December Brezhnev arrived in Prague to try to help settle the dispute. He had been invited by Novotny without the knowledge of the central committee, a fact which central committee member Frantisek Vodslon sharply criticized in the subsequent plenum. Refraining from directly entering the dispute, Brezhnev nonetheless informally supported Novotny, presumably in the interests of preserving the *status quo* as distinct from the instability which change might bring. His conversations with individual presidium members swayed the vote within the presidium from outright opposition to Novotny to a draw of five voices to five, Chudik and Lenart going over to Novotny's side. If Brezhnev gained anything of significance by this intervention, however, it was probably a promise that Novotny would be permitted to stay in the post of the presidency even if a majority of the central committee voted him out of the leading party position. Brezhnev did not insist upon more, apparently believing that the party was in control of the situation and that a change of personnel would not mean any drastic chance in policy. An additional, more personal factor, may have been a certain dislike for Novotny on the part of Brezhnev as a result of their argument when Khrushchev was ousted in 1964.[2]

After another delay the critical plenum finally took place 19–21 December. After an introductory report by Lenart, Novotny took the

[1] *Borba*, 18 November 1967.   [2] See above p. 236, n. 3.

floor and engaged in a certain amount of self-criticism regarding his remarks in October 'particularly in respect of the work of the comrades in the leadership of the Slovak Communist Party.'[1] Basically, however, Novotny maintained his earlier position regarding the need for strong party discipline and control in the face of the capitalist ideological onslaught. He sought to postpone indefinitely the whole issue of the party's role, presumably preferring to avoid any decision since the climate at the time seemed favorable to a liberal rather than conservative decision. Novotny added still more fuel to the fire when he informed the central committee that the Brezhnev visit had included talks on 'some of our internal problems;' he did not provide any further information or details. Several volatile speeches followed despite efforts by Bohumil Lastovicka, who was presiding, to minimize the significance and direction the remarks had assumed. Ota Sik, however, brought the basic issue into the open when he delivered a penetrating analysis of the shortcomings in the party's work. Sik continued his bold attack with the suggestion that Novotny resign as party first secretary and that a commission be elected which would submit to this same plenum the names of at least two candidates for a new first secretary (to be followed by a *secret* ballot). He also suggested that the presidium be charged with drafting fundamental measures for the democratization of the party.

Thus the issue was in the open, and the plenum turned into a direct discussion of Sik's first proposal: the resignation of Novotny as first secretary. Among those who attacked Sik and defended Novotny were Lenart, Chudik, and Simunek while a larger number of persons, including Bilak, Indra, and Piller, in addition to such liberals as Vodslon and Slavik aligned themselves with Sik's position.[2] The evening after this heated debate, i.e. 20 December, the presidium met and, apparently, Novotny conceded that he no longer had sufficient support to stay in office. The following day he took the floor and announced that he would accept whatever decision the central committee would agree on with regard to his continuation in office. Dubcek, who was then in the chair, proposed that the plenum be adjourned until 3 January, at which time it should decide the issue. This proposal was

[1] Cited in Mencl and Ourednik, *Zivot Strany*, 17 September 1968.

[2] Hendrych too criticized Novotny, claiming that the latter had pressured him into his strong position against the intellectuals. (See *The New Leader*, 29 January 1968.) It is unlikely that many were convinced that this stand was anything more than opportunism.

opposed by many liberals, for example, Smrkovsky, who feared that Novotny might use strong-arm tactics to delay a vote if the decision were not made immediately. He called for Novotny's immediate resignation, and a heated debate ensued. In accordance with a procedure agreed upon by the plenum each member of the party secretariat and presidium was asked to deliver a detailed statement of his position. A clear majority favored a separation of the two top positions in the country. The plenum then elected a 'consultative' group of regional party representatives which, together with the presidium, was to draft proposals on the issue and present these at another plenum in the first days of January.

It was principally during this break that Novotny tried to bring certain army units to his defense. The plan, apparently, was to bring a tank brigade into Prague and, simultaneously, arrest a long list of liberals (including Dubcek, Smrkovsky, Vodslon). Generals Sejna (who later defected to the West) and Janko (who later committed suicide) were involved, together with Prosecutor-General Bartuska, party security chief Mamula, and Novotny, in this plan. They had prepared a letter from the Defense Ministry's party unit to the central committee supporting Novotny, but their efforts and plans were thwarted by obstructionist tactics on the part of communist units in the army itself – subordinate to Prchlik's Main Political Directorate of the Army.[1]

When the central committee resumed its meeting on 3 January it became clear that the presidium and consultative group had not come to any agreement and had no concrete proposals to present. The issue was, therefore, back in the hands of the central committee with Novotny still fighting for his position by requesting indefinite deferment of the question. Lenart supported Novotny in this tactic. The opposition was now firm, however, with a number of previously less anti-Novotny officials now on the side of the liberals. The list of persons wishing to speak lengthened and the plenum heard more and more criticism of Novotny, including a strong and unusually frank statement by Smrkovsky. By the end of the following day, 4 January, the consultative committee and presidium announced that it favored immediate solution of the problem, i.e. that Novotny's tactic had been defeated. That night the consultative committee argued over Novotny's

[1] For details, see *Rude Pravo*, 19 March 1968; *Zemedelske Noviny*, 30 March 1968; Bratislava television, 26 March 1968; *Obrana Lidu*, 24 February 1968; Pavel Tigrid, 'Czechoslovakia: A Post-Mortem,' *Survey*, 72 (1969), 146–7.

replacement, with Novotny rejecting such candidates as Smrkovsky or Sik and the committee rejecting such candidates as Lenart or Vaculik, now identified with Novotny. Only as a compromise did they agree upon Dubcek, partially, it has been said, because Novotny thought the central committee itself would reject a Slovak, thus putting the issue once again in dispute, and because, at the worst, Dubcek could probably be controlled.[1] The following morning, 5 January 1968, Novotny presented the presidium–consultative committee proposal that he be released from the office of first secretary and that Alexander Dubcek be elected in his place. Most of the remaining speakers supported this proposal, a vote took place, and the forty-six-year-old Slovak leader was unanimously elected.

Thus Novotny was replaced not as a result of a 'power struggle' nor of outside forces but rather as a victim of a movement forced on him four years earlier by many of the same people responsible for his demise in December 1967. Novotny had been a clever leader who had managed to weather many storms, including 1956 and Barak's threat to him. Once he opened the door to de-Stalinization, however, he was almost fated to fail: first, because he himself had been involved in the Prague trials; secondly, because he himself did not believe in the reforms nor fully grasp the necessity for them; and thirdly, because movements for change and implying progressive changes have a tendency to sweep away the old leaders along with the old institutions in favor of new persons of the new school of thought to implement the innovations.

Two things about his replacement were of particular significance: the manner in which he was replaced and the person who replaced him. As the replacement came in the name of liberalization or democratization it had to be effected democratically. Moreover, as the replacement was a result of specific pressures by specific forces, the new man as well as the method of change had to reflect these forces. Clearly he had to be a man who believed in the reforms, a liberal. He did not have to be a Slovak, but it is of great significance that he was, first, because of the important role the Slovaks had played in both the earlier and eventually the later pressures for change. Secondly, and more important, the fact that a Slovak was chosen at all, for the first time in the history of the Czechoslovak party, was indicative of the sincerity of the intentions of the liberals. Their main object had been to remove the obstacles, i.e. Novotny, to a program already accepted by a majority of the central

[1] *Ibid.* 148.

committee. When they named Dubcek to succeed Novotny they voted for a program, not a Slovak. That it was this particular man was more a sign of their practicalness. They chose a man who could bring the dissident Slovaks back, who believed in the economic reforms (so long as Slovakia could have control of her needs), and a man who had shown himself to be a friend of liberal intellectuals and reform philosophers, at least in Slovakia. Yet he was not a 'radical.' He had not attracted too much attention over the years but, rather, quietly permitted the Slovak party to follow a more liberal path. Though he was probably no friend of the dogmatists he had never attacked them openly – his election would not *ipso facto* alienate that segment of the party *except* insofar as he represented a program that was alien to them. In other words, Dubcek was a compromise, a moderate rather than a radical who could answer the needs of the majority of the party, hopefully without too sharply alienating the minority.[1]

Just how loyal Dubcek was to the liberal program was to be seen only later, just as the full significance of this change was also discovered by many only later. It would appear that the Russians, like many rank and file Czechoslovaks, saw these events as a mere personnel change rather than a significant change of line. This view was probably based on the realization that the conservative *apparatchik* Novotny was not an all-powerful personal dictator on whom a party could stand or fall; he himself had been but a link in a system which could have been continued by any number of others, such as Hendrych or Kolder. His major qualification had been his knowledge of and clever manipulation of the *apparat* through which he himself had come to power, but ultimately he was significant only insofar as he represented the major obstacle to the implementation of the reform program. Only later did the general public and still later the Russians grasp that this was not an issue of personalities but of policies, and that these policies could have extraordinary significance for the future of socialism.

[1] For later confirmation of this interpretation, see Josef Smrkovsky, *My 1968*, v:4 (1968), 5–8; *Kulturni Noviny*, 29 March 1968 (Ota Sik); Miroslav Kusy, 'The Czechoslovak Political Crisis,' *Nova Mysl*, xxii:11 (1968), 1315–28; 'Documents—Czechoslovakia,' *Survey*, 69 (1968), 22–3; Mencl and Ourednik, *Zivot Strany*, nos. 14–19 (1968).

20

AN END AND A BEGINNING

What began in Czechoslovakia as belated de-Stalinization rapidly and, perhaps, inevitably, became a drive for thorough reform of the existing institutions. These reforms in effect were to mean the abandonment of the Soviet model of socialism in favor of a more democratic Czech–Slovak one. A key element in the movement, however, was its party nature. While non-communists joined in, and in many instances non-communist or pre-communist measures were recommended and even introduced, none of this was within the specific context of anti-communism. It was not an attempt to undermine or overthrow the Communist Party but rather to find for it a proper, defensible, more genuinely and positively effective role in society. The movement within the party grew out of dissatisfaction on the part of both idealistic and the most pragmatic of communists, with the added element of national-istic communists, the Slovaks. All three groupings, and to be sure they overlapped, saw that the present system did not provide those attributes or conditions which they believed essential to a successful socialist society in Czechoslovakia. Basic injustices, some of which already admitted and remedied elsewhere in the socialist world, had continued; dictatorship both within the party and within the society as a whole had led to apathy, bureaucracy, mediocrity, and inefficiency as well as to out and out injustice; outdated, perhaps never correct, methods and theories had led the economy into stagnation. Not only technical but also education, legal, cultural, and even moral standards had fallen; whether for pragmatic or idealistic reasons, the society was suffering for these failures. Unrectified past injustices combined with the strict centralized rule from Prague aroused Slovak nationalist grievances in addition to the above. In the most pragmatic of terms the economy could not run efficiently nor the population be mobilized to labor frugally and fruitfully under the then present system; in the most idealistic terms, dictatorship, bureaucracy, 'administrative rule,' the cadre system, centralism, all these and more, were not compatible with socialism. The opponents of reform also fell into roughly two cate-gories: the pragmatists (or opportunists) who believed reform would deprive them of their positions and/or power; and the idealistic (or at least ideologists) who saw that the reforms would lead to a revision in the theory of the leading role of the party, be it in the economic, the cultural, or the purely political sphere. It was indeed this interconnected nature of the proposed reforms, all leading as it were to political reforms, that united the conservatives so long behind Novotny.

The nationalist element played an important but complicated role. It was the existence of a dissatisfied nation living within the confines of the state – and the party – which gave the reform movement a significant push. In the beginning this push may well have been the crucial element, while later, once the process got under way, it became but one of several. The dissatisfied nation struck out not just against the injustices suffered by the nation itself, but against all the injustices of the society. In the case of some Slovaks, it was because they believed that theirs were not purely national grievances but rather the result of broader, more general failures of the society. Thus, they felt, their own rights as a nation could be guaranteed best, if not exclusively, by a general reform. Other Slovaks sought only the satisfaction of their nationalist grievances and saw in the reform movement a tool for their goals – but no more. Uncommitted to the broader aspect of the issues, they were unwilling to jeopardize or place their nationalist aims second to those of general democratization when such seemed to be called for. This distinction became apparent as certain Slovak demands were granted, and it came into the open in the period during which the liberals were in power.

As a party movement, liberalization in the pre-1968 period was basically the result of a 'revolution from above.' Popular discontent was a factor which influenced the regime – both because of the pressures this dissatisfaction created (in the form of complaints and occasional work-stoppages and demonstrations) and because of the lack of support for and therefore effort in fulfilling regime programs, specifically in the area of labor productivity. But the population at large took little interest in this movement; the man-in-the-street tended to look upon the whole thing as party in-fighting likely to have little, perhaps even a negative, effect upon his life. The workers by and large failed to grasp the significance of the movement; they tended to see only that side of the economic reforms which might deprive them of security, and they evinced little interest in the rest of the reforms. The only non-party group which might be considered an exception to the above was the youth, in particular the students, who quite early in the process apparently grasped what was afoot in the party. Thus quite early they took an active role in the drive, making sure their grievances were heard among the more general ones, yet working towards the broader interests of a democratization of the entire society.

The reformers pressed for institutional changes principally so as to ensure both the stability and the efficacy of the reforms. They did not want 'adjustments,' *ad hoc* arrangements, dramatic gestures, or informal changes but thoroughgoing, legally bound, institutionally based changes which would provide or be provided with permanent machinery for steady implementation and legal protection. Thus they methodically undertook the more plodding, but ultimately more lasting, liberalization that could only come through a rebuilding of the society's institutions, from top to bottom, both in terms of function and mode of operation. The direction in which the reformers were working was to separate the institutions (be they social, cultural, economic, or even political) from direct party control so that they would cease to be mere instruments of the party and become active components of a democratic society. Such a change, however, had to be thorough if it were to be effective, for institutional changes in one area often could barely hope to succeed if unaccompanied by similar changes in other institutions. In a sense this was the inner logic of the reforms.

The Stalinist concept of the strong, highly centralized state and the Soviet version of the Leninist concept of the party were rejected. It was from these two concepts, broadly speaking, that the then present system of institutions, including those governing the economy, had come. Not many dwelled on the correctness or justice of these concepts or the legitimacy of their claims to be the proper interpretation of Marxism, nor on their specifically Soviet origin. Rightly or wrongly these concepts applied to an earlier stage of socialism, that of the dictatorship of the proletariat. Their relevance to an industrialized, classless (in the Marxist sense), but nonetheless stratified society was what was in question. The reformers strove to find new concepts, new ways to apply Marxism–Leninism in conformity with the new reality. The ways suggested were numerous and varied; they all revolved around greater democracy, a larger individual say and initiative in the governing of society, greater independence and responsibility for subordinate organs be they of the economic, political, or cultural sphere.

Not all the reforms suggested were particularly radical; not all, indeed few, of the changes actually introduced were 'solutions' or considered final. It might in fact be said that the 1963–7 period was one of preparation, a first stage, a break-through for a new way of thinking and the first steps in the direction of total transformation. The reformers won their battle, perhaps as early as the decision itself to de-Stalinize, but the fruits of their victory could not be reaped, the reforms implemented and expanded in keeping with the reformers' original intent and demands, until at least one serious obstacle was removed. That obstacle was the conservative leadership of the party grouped around and personified by Antonin Novotny. The reform program fought its way through the party, and a majority finally saw the necessity for the changes; it remained only to bring in a leadership willing to permit the process to continue its way through the implementation and expansion of the reforms and the mobilization of the masses necessary for their successful outcome.

Thus the first few months of 1968 saw, in addition to personnel changes, efforts by the party to win popular support for the promised new policy. The public slowly began to comprehend the possibilities of the situation and by March of 1968 the reform movement assumed an entirely new character. What had been almost a purely party affair became a public matter, and the people, with increasing confidence, began to exert pressure to ensure fulfillment of the party's promises. The 'focal point' shifted to the masses who through spontaneous popular actions forced the regime's hand on a number of measures, converting the 'revolution from above' into a mass movement. These actions led to further, significant personnel changes – most notably the resignation of Novotny from his post as President on 22 March and the naming of a new government – as well as a broadening and deepening of the nature of the reforms. While this change greatly accelerated and to some degree radicalized the liberalization process, it did not significantly alter the basically legalistic, methodical, institution-directed, socialist thrust of the democratization movement. Aside from the specifically Slovak aspect, the movement remained as before non-nationalistic, though interference from the Soviet Union did in time become an issue. It focused more and more on specific conditions in Czechoslovakia, i.e. the humanistic–democratic traditions, as the fears of certain other socialist countries threatened to put a stop to this creation of a new model for socialism. The movement clearly went beyond the measures envisaged by the liberal regime, which did indeed try to restrain the process, but it also created a degree of enthusiasm for socialism – albeit of a specific variety – probably unprecedented in Eastern Europe.

21

ECONOMIC REFORMS[1]

As the major part of the economic reforms had been worked out prior to 1968, discussions during the revival period sought mainly to ensure implementation of the reforms, to improve them or undo the restrictions placed upon them earlier, and to bring about the political reforms necessary for the introduction of market socialism. The two major innovations of the revival period in this area were, therefore, the establishment of enterprise councils to provide workers with a share in enterprise direction and a restructuring of the enterprise system to provide the till then thwarted enterprise with the independence necessary for the functioning of the new system. The party's new program, known as the Action Program and accepted by the central committee at its early April meeting, sought to ensure enterprise independence by changing the nature of the branch enterprise relationship. In response to the arguments of liberal economists, enterprise subordination to branch directorates was to be mitigated by the right of enterprises to associate, reassociate, and leave the branches or trusts to which they belonged. In this way the branch directorates would not have total power over the member enterprises. Since association would be genuinely voluntary the directorates would have to serve and represent their members rather than serve or represent the government as they had been doing under the revised system introduced in 1966. This right of an enterprise to choose its own 'organizational allegiance' was not, however, unlimited.[2] To prevent chaos or to prevent successful enterprises from regrouping at the expense of weaker enterprises, for example, it was decided that organizational changes would be permitted only when economically desirable, and Premier Cernik explained that this would be determined by the branch and central organs.[3]

This revised system in itself contained a large potential for a return to central control and limitation of enterprise autonomy, and it was in time abandoned. This was accomplished by eliminating the association system altogether, thereby eliminating even the possibility of the branch

---

[1] In this and the following chapters an effort will be made only to outline the revised content of the reform program and the official reactions. The confines of the epilogue does not permit deeper analysis.

[2] Action Program, *Rude Pravo*, 10 April 1968.   [3] Prague radio, 24 April 1968.

or trust acting as a governmental representative in any way limiting the freedom of the enterprise. Thus the draft enterprise bill prepared in 1968 (though never passed) called for three types of enterprises: social, public, and those based on shares.[1] The social enterprise was described as an 'autonomous unit' managed exclusively by its own direction, albeit within the framework of the government's general economic policy. It was also solely responsible for all its business transactions and obligations. The public enterprise, on the other hand, was neither autonomous nor self-supporting, belonging directly to the state. Such enterprises were to be limited, however, to certain national services as railways, water, roads, etc. The third type of enterprise amounted to private ownership in the form of small cooperatives in services (such as catering), handicrafts, and other limited occupations. A committee was set up under Eugen Loebl to prepare concrete proposals for such enterprises of which Loebl foresaw some 250000, designed, in part, to break the monopolies of large enterprises.[2] The draft law on enterprises said only that these firms were to be entirely independent cooperatives, founded upon permission from 'the relevant bodies.'

A reorganization of the government's economic organs was also undertaken to limit state interference in the function of the market and enterprise autonomy. Specifically the reform was to control the various economic ministries by placing them under a central economic policy board. Thus the National Economic Board, advocated by Ota Sik but headed by Lubomir Strougal, was created on 12 April as a supra-ministerial body.[3] It was to prepare the government's position on fundamental questions of the national economy, bearing responsibility for the macro-aspects of the economy. Sik explained this as a measure designed to prevent administrative monopolies by the ministries (formerly responsible for the enterprises in their spheres) and bureau-cratic delays.[4] A number of other supra-ministerial organs were reduced to ministries and modified, including the State Planning Commission and the Commission for Finance, Prices, and Wages. The number of ministries, however, was not reduced, though this was often urged.[5] On such specific issues as government interference in the functioning of the market by price-setting, it was eventually decided to enlarge the category of free prices to approximately twenty-three per cent of all

[1] See *Zemedelske Noviny*, 31 January 1969.   [2] *Mlada Fronta*, 19 June 1968.
[3] CTK, 12 April 1968 and Prague radio, 16 April 1968.
[4] Prague radio, 25 May 1968.
[5] See for example, *Bratislava Pravda*, 3 May 1968; *Rude Pravo*, 2 April 1968.

wholesale prices while reducing the category of fixed wholesale prices to approximately twenty-one per cent, with the limited price category to be approximately fifty-five per cent.[1] There was to be a gradual elimination of subsidies.

The general thrust of the revision of the reforms was to strengthen the role of the market and in this connection there were to be changes in the foreign trade sector. Convertibility of the koruna was to be striven for, and to this end the system of protectionist and restrictive surcharges, discounts, subsidies and so forth were gradually to be eliminated.[2] The issue of Czechoslovakia's trade with the West and the need for hard currency credits was raised again in this period, as part of the oft-heard demands to link Czechoslovakia with the world market and base foreign as well as domestic trade on market principles. It was argued, however, that continued concentration of trade on 'soft' currency areas – with whom trade was on a barter system – would only perpetuate Czechoslovakia's inability to compete on the world market, from the points of view of both quality and structure of production. On this basis trade orientation, or at the very least increased trade with the West, with the necessary accompanying hard currency credits, became an issue of the reform movement. This did not begin as an effort to gain economic independence or to disengage from CEMA or the Soviet Union. A modification of orientation was urged for purely economic reasons rather than political considerations, although the increasing interference of Czechoslovakia's conservative allies in the later months of the 'revival' did lead to a radicalization – and politization – of some of the trade suggestions. Nonetheless the liberal regime often reiterated its motives and its continued loyalty to CEMA. Even its suggestions for reforms in CEMA called for increased (not decreased) cooperation and an international division of labor between the socialist countries, focusing only on making CEMA itself market-oriented and profitable.[3] While the regime did indeed seek western credits it continually asserted its belief that such credits need not and would not carry with them political commitments of any kind.[4] Under consideration were a loan from the World Bank, credits from individual western firms, or credits from a Western European consortium.[5] As an alternative, Prague had also turned to the Soviet Union for a hard currency loan of some $400

[1] *Rude Pravo*, 21 June 1968.   [2] *Noviny Zahranicniho Obchodu*, 19 June 1968.
[3] Prague radio, 20 March and 24 April 1968.
[4] For example, Prague radio, 24 April 1968 (Cernik speech).
[5] Cernik interview, Reuters, 18 August 1968.

million, but the Soviet response was never entirely clarified.[1] Such a loan was indeed larger than any hard currency (gold) loan ever granted by the USSR to a bloc country, and it may indeed have been beyond Soviet capabilities. Yet there is no evidence that the Soviets exploited the possibility of extending such a loan as much as they might have if they had been as concerned about the Czechoslovak bid to the West as observers in the West tended to claim at the time.

It is certainly difficult to know how much the Soviets believed information fed them by conservatives in Prague concerning the 'radical' nature of the liberals' plans (such as alleged plans for neutrality, economic independence, alliance with West Germany and so forth). Indeed as the crisis between the USSR and Prague developed, there were numerous articles critical of Czechoslovak–Soviet economic relations and even isolated demands for neutrality.[2] Yet Soviet efforts in the economic sphere (both with regard to Czechoslovakia and the West, both prior and subsequent to the Prague Spring) as well as the demands presented at Cierna nad Tisou in the summer, do not provide anywhere near conclusive evidence that this was a major part of the Soviets' (or other East Europeans') concern over Czechoslovakia.[3]

A major innovation in the economic sphere during the revival was the formulation of instruments of worker participation in management. After much discussion and various proposals, the government announced on 29 June 1968 the establishment of enterprise councils to be carried out in three stages, beginning 1 July.[4] The theoretical basis for the councils, as formulated by Rudolf Slansky Jr, among others, was that the producers should be the 'owners' in the Marxist sense of the term. The producers and not the state *apparat* should control surplus value, and this would entail their control over distribution of profits, investments, appointment of managers and so forth.[5] The councils were not strictly speaking workers' councils such as existed in Czechoslovakia in 1945–8 or as in Yugoslavia. In fact Sik preferred a model closer to the western board of directors, with a minority of workers represented.[6] The proposal announced and undertaken in the summer, however, called for over fifty per cent of council members to be elected from among the employees of a given enterprise (in secret elections organized by the trade unions), and ten to thirty per cent of

[1] CTK, 15 May 1968.
[2] See chapter 23 below.
[3] See chapter 24 below for the reasons.
[4] CTK, 29 June 1968.
[5] *Prace*, 18 February 1969.
[6] Prague radio, 20 May 1968 (Sik speech to Czechoslovak Economic Association).

the members to be drawn from outside organizations such as the bank responsible for the enterprises' credits, scientific institutions, etc. The manager was also to sit on the council though he was named by and subject to recall by the council, subordinate to it for all major decisions (including his own salary and investment plans), and subject to it for annual assessment. In 'important enterprises' the state would also be represented, though by no more than twenty per cent of the members (while this was to apply to the public enterprise, the draft of the enterprise law published after the invasion called for a representative of the state in the social enterprises' councils as well).[1]

With the announcement on enterprise councils workers began electing such councils, often spontaneously, electing new managers without benefit of the party intervention intended to guide this first, experimental stage. Moreover, workers began defending their rights and wishes by strikes and threats to strike. Trade union leaders supported workers' rights to strike and even Dubcek refrained from rejecting such steps, although he warned that strikes should be seen as 'the maximum method of exerting pressure.'[2] A law was even urged by some to provide funds and protection for strikes.[3]

Conservatives continued their efforts to separate the workers from the reformers, specifically by pointing to the loss in benefits or job security the former would suffer from the reforms. Regime promises of increased welfare benefits, greater job mobility, and the actual reduction of the work week to forty hours were in part designed to counter these efforts. Most of all, however, it was the democratization process itself, whereby the worker actually experienced a greater role in the conduct of society, that led to the eventual union between the workers and the reformers. It was this which in large part made the reform movement in 1968 a mass movement, as distinct from the earlier period in which the workers had remained skeptical if not in outright opposition to the reforms.

[1] After the invasion a dispute arose between the above plan and a more conservative one proposed by the Czech National Council.
[2] *Rude Pravo*, 19 June 1968. See also chapter 22 below.
[3] Czechoslovak television, 21 May 1968.

22

SOCIAL ORGANIZATIONS AND CULTURAL LIFE

The Action Program accepted the view of society presented earlier by the liberals when it affirmed

It is impossible to overlook or deny the various needs and interests proper to individuals and social groups according to the jobs they hold, their qualifications, age, sex, nationality, and so forth. We have often made this mistake in the past. Socialism can only develop by *making considerations of the various interests of the people possible.*

To assure this possibility Dubcek called for 'an open confrontation of interests and standpoints, and *institutional guarantees of this expression of interests*, of their evaluation and solution.'[1] And Smrkovsky further explained that this might mean the existence of independent organizations.[2] Thus three principles seemed to be at stake: the freedom to associate or dissociate at will; internal freedom of these associations; and external freedom or a role in society.

Freedom to associate was guaranteed by the Action Program which denied the right of any one group or association to monopolization. Although this right was already provided by the Constitution, the government on 25 April 1968 expressed its willingness to respond to demands for a law specifically to protect this right. This clause and the preparation of a new law would, thus, permit groups of individuals to break off from existing organizations, and to establish their own independent groups. Internal freedom of social or mass organizations was to be assured mainly by the elimination of party interference, including the practice of placing party people in key positions. Thus a consistent rotation of functionaries was to be introduced. More controversially, however, internal freedom was to mean democratization of the organization, not only with regard to external elections but also to the expression of dissenting opinions – and the right to try to gain support for dissenting opinions. This last could well affect the external freedom of the organizations for it posed the problems of freedom of expression and the right to mobilize public opinion, raising the question

[1] *Rude Pravo*, 21 April 1968.
[2] *Rude Pravo*, 4 April 1968 (speech to central committee).

of rights to limit the activities of the organizations. It had long been argued that an organization could effectively express and represent its members' views only if permitted 'the right to influence public affairs,'[1] including, according to *Rude Pravo*, political affairs.[2] The conclusion was that an organization should be permitted to be an independent political agent, representing, as Dubcek pointed out, not only the social interests of its members but acting as its 'political representative.'[3] How it might do so was a question to be considered by the political reforms, but certain organizations and individuals began to put all the above new principles to test even before the new system was defined.

TRADE UNIONS

It took the trade union movement three months and a good deal of prodding from workers at the factory level to respond to the new situation. It was only after a conservative party functionary reported that in many plants events had gotten out of the control of union officials and of party representatives (including demands for 'trade unions without communists'), and after Dubcek's demand that unions serve the specific interests of the workers, that the presidium of ROH began to act.[4] There were personnel changes and, in time, efforts to democratize the union internally as well as efforts to redefine its role.

While the general reforms of the social organizations were to remove the party from interference in and direct control of these organizations, this measure of independence alone would not guarantee protection of the workers' interests. The Action Program did recognize that the trade unions were now to function primarily as defenders of the workers' interests rather than simply substitute for management or government organs. Yet it maintained the union's educative role of 'orienting workers and employees towards a positive solution of the problems of socialist construction.' Moreover, it recognized the tasks of the union only at the enterprise level, without mentioning broader powers for the trade unions to represent the workers politically or in society as a whole. Dubcek, among others, however, explained on numerous occasions that the unions were to play a double role, one vis-a-vis the workers' enterprise and one vis-a-vis the organs of state

[1] *Mlada Fronta*, 2 April 1968. [2] *Rude Pravo*, 16 February 1968.
[3] *Rude Pravo*, 30 June 1968.
[4] See *Prace*, 5 March 1968; Prague radio, 13 and 18 March 1968; *Rude Pravo*, 7 April 1968; *Rude Pravo*, 5 March 1968 (Dubcek).

power. Thus 'trade unions should once more become the important political force in the National Front which they were before February 1948,' he said.[1] Several ways were suggested for accomplishing this, including initiating policy suggestions to the party, operating as representatives of the workers vis-a-vis the enterprise councils, and even, according to ROH chairman Polacek, by way of strikes.[2]

The ROH statutes drafted at its June 1968 conference proclaimed the movement an independent organization serving as an interest organization, expressing the political goals of the workers, promoting their human and social rights, and defending the interests and needs of its members. The statutes declared the ROH a 'voluntary' organization, but it somewhat diluted the significance of this by inserting, also, the word 'unified.' A federation of the union into Czech and Slovak components was permitted, but efforts by workers in a number of cases to split off from their local ROH component and/or create a new trade union organization became the subject of controversy. The most notable example was that of the railway engineers who, failing to achieve their own union within ROH, tried to form at least an independent social-interest organization, and, later, their own independent union outside the ROH.[3] The regime, however, was reluctant to permit fragmentation of the trade union movement (the unity of which was one of the first communist goals) or competition for the existing unions. It therefore upheld the monopoly of the existing ROH affiliates and, in direct contradiction to the Action Program, stuck to the letter of existing repressive laws.[4] It proclaimed once again the principle of one factory one trade union, and the June ROH conference (which included a supporting speech by Dubcek) as well as the 11 June meeting of the party presidium, promised autonomy for union organizations but not the right to associate or dissociate at will along what was called 'narrow interests [which] split and weaken the strength of the trade unions.'[5] Although the party retreated on this important issue, one must not overlook the fact that this retreat came in June, i.e. during a period of serious outside pressures on the Czechoslovak

---

[1] *Bratislava Pravda*, 4 June 1968 (speech to central committee plenum).
[2] *Prace*, 20 June 1968.
[3] See *Literarni Listy*, 18 April 1968; *Reporter*, 25 December 1968; *Zitrek*, 11 December 1968.
[4] For example *Sbirka Zakonu* No. 68/1951.
[5] CTK, 18 June (speeches by ROH chairman Polacek and Dubcek) and 20 June 1968.

communists and growing internal concern even among certain liberals that the democratization process was getting out of hand.

On a related issue, however, that of the establishment of an agricultural union, the regime was not so conservative. There had long been demands for a union of agricultural workers or peasants, distinct from and in addition to the purely economic–administrative organization of farming enterprises. As early as the Cooperative Farmers Conference in February 1968 this proposal was taken under serious consideration. Before any official decision on the matter, however, farmers, particularly in the Czech lands, spontaneously began forming unions. With over a quarter of a million farmers joining this spontaneous action the regime was more or less forced to take notice.[1] It proposed a union of Cooperative Farmers, to be a social-interest organization, taking part in the National Front, and playing the same political role envisaged by Dubcek for all the social organizations. The Slovaks did not accept this concept, preferring a union organized by agricultural enterprise rather than a union of individual farmers, and limited more to the idea of an economic functional organization rather than a socio–political interest group. Thus two unions differing in concept were set up pending creation of a federal union.[2] Conservatives feared that the strong pre-war centrist agrarian party was in fact being reinstituted by this move. Nonetheless, Dubcek clearly expressed the union's tasks as 'not only defending the individual interests of the cooperative farmers in problems concerning compensation and so forth, but also politically representing the cooperative farmers in the National Front.'[3]

CSM

The youth took advantage of the shock caused in many circles by the Strahov affair and formed themselves into something of a spearhead of the 'revival.' The students' role changed somewhat from that of the 1963–7 period. When the struggle was mainly within the party, the students could but join in, without, however, playing a leadership role. They could try to awaken their own ranks and strive for inclusion of their demands in those of the party liberals. When, however, the liberals looked to the public for support in 1968 the students could then move into the foreground. As the most involved and organized group outside

---

[1] Prague radio, 10 June 1968.
[2] Bratislavia radio, 11 July 1968; *Rolnicke Noviny*, 6 and 17 July 1968.
[3] *Bratislava Pravda*, 4 June 1968 (to central committee plenum).

the party – one of the few if not the only non-party group to have early grasped the significance of the pre-1968 struggle – they were the natural leaders of the hitherto uninvolved masses. They formed a natural bridge between the latter and the party liberals with whom they had begun working earlier. They succeeded in forming an alliance with the workers through meetings and discussions in factories, despite the continued efforts by conservatives to set the workers against the students. Moreover, they presented demands far broader than specific youth or student complaints. This is not to say that there was no generation gap: indeed the young people were highly suspicious of almost all the 'liberals' because of their Stalinist pasts, or at the very least their passivity in the 1950s.[1] Nonetheless, the youth did not permit this basic distrust of their elders to dissipate the campaign for change.

The new regime was aware of the force which the youth constituted and advocated a mutually satisfactory institutional framework through which this force could be channelled – in favor rather than against the party.[2] At this time, however, the existing youth organization, CSM, was rapidly disintegrating as a result of groups spontaneously splitting off. The students of several faculties set up academic councils open to all students, and plans were laid for a national federation of students. CSM tried to avert this split by reinstating Mueller to their ranks (the regime released him from the army) and supporting an investigation of the Strahov affair. Interior Minister Kudrna offered self-criticism with regard to police behavior, but after student demands for his resignation he was dismissed on 15 March 1968.[3] CSM also conducted personnel changes and came up with a suggestion for federalization – a suggestion now considered conservative in view of the demands by various groups for independence from the union and a political role. In fact student demands included not only postponement of the national elections, a new election law, freedom of expression, rehabilitations and removal of conservatives from party and government offices, but also suggestions of student-selected candidates to the National Assembly.[4]

In addition to the independent student unions established in May 1968, young workers began efforts to establish a Union of Working Youth, Slovaks a Union of Slovak Agricultural Youth; Hungarians and

[1] See comments by student leader Holecek, Prague radio, 20 March 1968 (to massive youth rally).
[2] See comments by Dubcek, *Rude Pravo*, 23 February 1968.
[3] CTK, 11 March 1968 and Prague radio, 16 March 1968.
[4] Prague radio, 19 and 23 March 1968.

Poles demanded their own youth organizations, as did young soldiers and secondary school pupils. The youth committee of SVAZARM declared itself a preparatory committee for the re-institution of the Scout movement, which was indeed re-instituted as an independent organization.[1]

While such leaders as Goldstuecker, Cisar, and Smrkovsky were sympathetic to the students' demands for an independent organization,[2] the party refused to support the idea. The Action Program had recognized the need for a youth organization independent of party control, but the regime never clarified if this meant the abandoning of CSM subordination to the party as the latter's own youth movement. In the name of independence, however, it did oppose the creation of youth organizations affiliated with other parties.[3] As to other independent youth organizations, both Dubcek and Sik urged the youth to recognize the need for and strength in a unified movement, and at its 21–22 May meeting, the party presidium came out clearly against the splitting of CSM and the creation of independent groups.[4] Thus the party's position, in contradiction to the Action Program's stand on freedom of association, advocated the continuation of CSM's official monopolization of the youth movement. That this may, however, have been merely a verbal concession to outside pressures was indicated by the fact that the party did nothing concrete to save the disintegrating CSM, i.e. it did not in fact bring pressures against the new student unions.

OTHER ASSOCIATIONS AND CLUBS

Other mass organizations such as SVAZARM suffered from the trend of fragmentation, with groups splitting off to form independent associations. In addition to this, however, a number of new, controversial groups began to form as clubs, seeking to represent their members' interests in all spheres of public life, including the political realm. Among these could be found such clubs as the Union of Scientific Workers (founded in part by Goldstuecker, Sik, and Kosik), the Circle of Independent (non-party) Writers, and, more controversial, the KAN (club of committed non-party members) and K-231. This last consisted of persons condemned under paragraph 231 of the Penal

[1] *Mlada Fronta*, 3 April 1968.
[2] Prague radio, 3 February, 20 March, and 8 April 1968; *Rude Pravo*, 4 April 1968.
[3] *Rude Pravo*, 24 May 1968.   [4] *Ibid.* (see also *Rude Pravo*, 2 April 1968).

Code and strove mainly for speedy rehabilitations. It was especially opposed by party conservatives who claimed that it covered some 120000 persons and included many who had been legitimately prosecuted as fascists and anti-communists.[1] As pressures built, Dubcek himself admitted that the group included persons justly condemned for anti-state activities, and the club was refused registration.[2]

KAN was also considered particularly dangerous by the conservatives. Numbering among its founding members leading intellectuals, KAN specifically declared itself a political outlet for non-party people, committed to both socialism and the democratic tradition of Czechoslovakia. It also declared its intention of running candidates, and, shortly after its formation, it recommended the re-institution of the Social Democratic Party.[3] KAN groups were formed in a number of communities, among workers and intellectuals alike, and to all intents and purposes KAN began to operate as a political party. Indeed this was the problem with most of the new associations, which also included the League for Engaged Action, the Club of Critical Thought, and many others. As most of the groups proclaimed their right to serve as vehicles for participation in political life they could easily be seen as the cornerstones of political parties or at the very least components of a pluralistic system, fulfilling the role of an opposition. For this reason the groups were linked with the problems of political reform, and the regime delayed a final response on most of them. By 18 June only one of seventy requests for registration with the Interior Ministry had been granted – that of the Czechoslovak League for Human Rights (though its Slovak counterpart was denied a permit).[4] At the same time, the promised law guaranteeing freedom of association was not expected until the fall.

RELIGIOUS AND MINORITY GROUPS

The new regime declared its intentions of extending to the various religious and national minorities the same freedoms promised for all. Thus the process begun for at least certain religious groups in the pre-1968 period was seriously resumed, now on a much broader scale and, apparently, with greater sincerity. A sign of this sincerity was the

---

[1] *Reporter*, 12 June 1968.   [2] *Bratislava Pravda*, 4 June 1968.
[3] Prague radio, 16 and 24 April 1968.
[4] Prague radio, 8 and 18 June 1968. (In late May 1969 the Czech group's license was revoked.)

replacement of the Stalinist director of religious affairs in the Ministry of Culture, Karel Hruza, by sociologist Erika Kadlecova. Immediately thereafter various religious groups began pressing their demands, with the help of a number of the intellectuals' journals and even the radio, in keeping with the new atmosphere.

The Catholic Church, under the vigorous leadership of Bishop Tomasek, was the most active in placing demands, and the most successful. A number of bishops were reinstated, and persecuted clerics were released from prisons, in some cases rehabilitated, and rehabilitations were generally promised. The question of reopening the closed monastic orders was reconsidered and eventually (after the invasion) officially granted.[1] The regime's puppet Peace Movement of the Catholic clergy under the defrocked Josef Plojhar was abolished, and in its place the Work of Council Renewal was founded as a legitimate organization of the Catholic Church in Czechoslovakia.[2] Tomasek demanded, however, independence for the Church, i.e. the right to administer its own affairs, including its financial affairs.[3] A step in this direction was the regime's agreement to place religious education (still to be conducted only after school hours) under the auspices of the Church (and the various other denominations).[4] It also permitted an expansion of the Catholic press, i.e. a rejuvenation of Catholic journals and liberalization as well as expansion of the publishing house of the Catholic Peoples Party.

Of particular interest to the Church was the lifting of the *numerus clausus* on theology students and the promise to reopen the theological faculty in Olomouc with the possibility of a new faculty in Kosice. The outstanding issue of the return of Cardinal Beran to Czechoslovakia was not settled, being left as part of the general agreement sought by the Vatican with Prague. Talks concerning a renewal of Vatican–Prague relations were to begin at the end of the summer, but informal relations improved as early as the spring. Thus various Czech prelates were permitted frequent personal contact with Rome, while the Vatican instigated the reorganization of certain border dioceses in keeping with Czechoslovakia's borders.[5]

---

[1] *Lidove Demokracie*, 18 April 1968; *Katolicke Noviny* (Bratislava), 19 January 1969.

[2] 'The Velehrad Conference,' *Noviny Zivot*, 7–8 (July 1968), 179. After the invasion the Ministry of Interior turned down this organization's application for registration (*Obroda*, 20 November 1968).

[3] *Reporter*, 12 June 1968.

[4] *Lidove Demokracie*, 9 July 1968. [5] See *Reporter*, 12 June 1968.

Among other religious groups to benefit from the liberalization were the long suppressed Uniates (Catholic Church of the Old Slavonic Rite). This church, located principally in Ruthenia and including some 100000 faithful, was rehabilitated on 13 June when the government accepted an appeal by the Uniate clergy. This rehabilitation was not entirely smooth nor without political significance, for Uniate property (including churches now to be restored to them) had been given to the Orthodox Church in Slovakia – bitter enemy of the Uniates and affiliated with Moscow.[1] Another sect, the Old Catholic Church, was also rehabilitated, but a number of other sects, e.g. Mormons, Jehovah's Witnesses, etc. remained under ban. The Protestants benefited from the general improvement, especially the new regulations concerning religious education. Specifically the Protestant Church sought mainly to overcome the stigma of their collaboration with the communists and promised to support the democratization process.[2]

The Jews benefited as both a religious and national group in response to a list of demands placed upon the regime by the ninety-year-old Rabbi Feder.[3] While hard put to take advantage of such things as the right to supervise religious education (due to lack of qualified persons given the past regime's restrictions), the Jewish community was permitted once again and more fully to maintain contacts with international Jewish organizations. The cancelled millennium celebrations were re-scheduled (although they were again postponed because of the invasion), and rehabilitations of Jews persecuted in the 1950s were promised. Some of these actually materialized, insofar as Jews were permitted to resume positions in the areas of culture, education, foreign trade, and even the foreign office. While the party's Action Program specifically condemned anti-semitism, the conservatives continued to use this as a tactic against the liberals, playing on anti-Jewish sentiments in much the same way as they tried to exploit worker distrust of intellectuals, in hopes of discrediting and dissipating the liberal movement. This campaign was aided perhaps unwittingly by the rise of Slovak nationalism, traditionally anti-semitic, and the split among Slovaks over such issues as Israel and Mnacko.[4] Many papers, mass organizations, groups, and leading personalities condemned the out-

[1] For reports of clashes, see *Praca*, 12 June 1968.
[2] *Lidove Demokracie*, 12 and 20 April 1968. [3] *Literarni Listy*, 30 May 1968.
[4] See for example, Novomesky in *Rude Pravo*, 12 May 1968 or *Nove Slovo*, 30 May 1968 (Pavlenda).

bursts of anti-semitism, however, and numerous articles appeared on the topics of Jews and anti-semitism in Czechoslovakia.[1]

The Hungarian and Ukrainian minorities also began to make their demands felt, struggling particularly against Slovak nationalism in their efforts to have their rights recognized and institutionally guaranteed. Their demands were numerous but centered around the principle of self-government with genuine opportunities for social–cultural–political expression as well as education in their own languages. This drive saw the revitalization – and politization – of the Hungarian and Ukrainian cultural organizations. The Ukrainians went so far as demanding a Ukrainian National Council, and together with the Hungarians they sought amendments to the Constitution.[2] While conservatives and many Slovaks even among the reformers condemned these demands as chauvinist, separatist, and irredentist,[3] many liberals (including such Slovaks as Zora Jesenska) supported the minorities' demands.[4] The party's Action Program called for 'constitutional and legal guarantees of complete and genuine political and economic and cultural equality of rights,' and state organs at all levels which would accord the minorities the right to decide on matters concerning them 'in an independent and autonomous manner.' The Slovak party program, however, did not speak of such 'guarantees' and the Slovak party standpoint warned the Hungarian and Ukrainian cultural associations that they were to remain 'cultural–education' organs – only.[5] The issue was thus a complicated one, left presumably for settlement by the new constitution, though dependent upon the success of the democratization in its struggle with intolerance of various kinds.

CULTURAL LIFE

As in the earlier period the cultural scene was one of the focal points of the liberalization process, for it was the intellectuals who both

---

[1] See for example, *Kulturny Zivot*, 28 June and 12 July 1968; *Reporter*, 24 July 1968. The 'reappearance' of virulent anti-semitism was claimed by one person (Stary) to be one of the reasons for the '2,000 Words' document discussed below. (*Prace*, 29 June 1968.)

[2] For the standpoints of both nationalities' unions, see *Uj Szo*, 15 and 30 March 1968.

[3] See for example, *Kulturny Zivot*, 12 and 19 April 1968; *Bratislava Pravda*, 29 May 1968.

[4] *Uj Szo*, 12 April 1968; *Kulturny Zivot*, 5 April 1968.

[5] *Bratislava Pravda*, 30 May 1968.

expressed and initiated demands for change. The intellectuals were, therefore, among the most sensitive to each step forward or retreat in the process and, by nature of their work, most involved in the central question of democratization: freedom of expression. There was a long list of specific issues with which the intellectuals concerned themselves, e.g. rehabilitations, personnel changes, union autonomy with the possibility of the unions' playing a political role, federalization of the unions (with the side issue of the split within the Slovak ranks over federalization versus democratization), and even the question of independence for radio and television. The major issue for the intellectuals, however, was censorship and its ramifications as to freedom of speech.

One front of the battle against censorship concentrated on the availability and dissemination of information, since a well-informed public was considered essential to genuine democracy. While the 1966 Press Law had called upon organizations, institutions, etc., to provide the media with information, no sanctions had been written into the law and implementation had never been assured. The demands in this connection also included the possibility of receiving information from abroad, and an early 'major' accomplishment was the agreement between the Journalists Union and the censor (Central Administration for Publication) to permit delivery of foreign papers directly to editorial offices without prior censorship.

On the second front, the intellectuals demanded the right to free and unrestricted discussion. They demanded not a liberal cultural policy but *no* cultural policy, i.e. no government–party say whatsoever as to what might be printed or not, said or not, criticized or not, created or not.[1] They specifically demanded independence of all creative organs and the mass media. To this end a struggle for the total abolition of censorship was waged. The less radical, such as Goldstuecker, advocated the maintenance of pre-publication censorship regarding state secrets but no more than a non-binding pre-publication warning system for all other materials (i.e. material considered 'harmful to society').[2] Others, including Mlynar as well as Ludvik Vaculik, advocated the abolition of all and any type of pre-publication censorship, the former arguing that the Penal Code already covered violations of state secrets.[3] Political censorship was in fact suspended in early

---

[1] See for example, *Literarni Listy*, 1 March 1968 or television round-table, 29 February 1968.

[2] Prague radio, 21 February 1968.   [3] Prague radio, 28 February 1968.

March, and the campaign for a new law abolishing censorship was then waged openly in the now unrestrained media.

Of the new regime, the two most consistent spokesmen on behalf of the demands for freedom of expression were Smrkovsky and Josef Spacek. Both argued for a free flow of information and 'self-administration' for the arts and media.[1] The Action Program reflected this position, calling for a new law 'to preclude the possibility of advanced censorship,' guarantee the regular and thorough flow of information (including the publication of dissenting views) and expanded supplies of western sources. Dubcek in time asserted his belief that socialism could not develop 'without a high degree of public involvement, without freedom of speech, without democracy in the widest sense.'[2] He, therefore, advocated a new law and institutional guarantees for the contest of views and interests now admitted to exist in socialist society.

In June, Miroslav Galuska, by then Culture and Information Minister, was entrusted with the task of drawing up a new law (to be submitted in August) and the National Assembly passed an amendment to the Press Law eliminating preliminary censorship by 'state agencies' (which in effect meant no limitation on the party).[3] It was up to editors, publishers, etc., themselves to prevent publication of secrets, though the state compiled the list (over 400 pages long) of what constituted a secret. Post-publication censorship held the editor responsible, with the possibility of court appeal. Thus the unquestionably progressive step of abolishing pre-publication censorship still fell short of the law sought by the intellectuals.

The liberal regime had other problems with the intellectuals, for the latter acted both as the spur and the conscience of the liberalization. They took full advantage of the freedom promised, publishing and broadcasting without almost any regard for limitations or even 'self-censorship.' Radio and television took the lead in revealing details of the past, conducting critical discussions, and reporting fully any information available to them. While in the pre-1968 period there had been changes in these mass media, they now for the first time assumed a lead previously in the hands of the specialized press (of the intellectuals). In the early period only a certain segment of society understood or even knew about the efforts of party liberals and the struggle within the party. It is, therefore, not surprising that the discussions and

[1] Prague radio, 11 March 1968; *Rude Pravo*, 16 March 1968.
[2] *Rude Pravo*, 21 April 1968.
[3] This was pointed out in *Reporter*, 26 May 1968.

pressures had remained within the somewhat elitist circles of the intelligentsia and its organs. After January 1968, however, the movement spread to the masses as the people began slowly to grasp the significance of the change and the possibilities of the situation. As the initiative passed from a small group to the masses the major voice as well as stage for the new ideas passed from the specialized journals to the mass media. The successful activity of these media was itself probably the result of a process similar to that apparent in the earlier period. Liberals within the media, bolstered by the presence (now in majority) of liberals within the party, were strong enough to prevail. From this developed a process whereby the limits were constantly pushed outward, this time in large part due to pressures from below (the masses) to say or reveal more.

There were numerous signs that the party was concerned about the instability of a situation which was rapidly surpassing party control and direction. This concern was aggravated by the fears of less liberal party members and outright pressures from conservatives and certain of Czechoslovakia's allies. As early as the April plenum (which adopted the Action Program), Bilak, the new Slovak first secretary, attacked the media and urged discipline, calling it 'naive' to demand that the party give up its direction of the press.[1] By May liberals such as Smrkovsky, Cisar, and even Spacek found it necessary to caution the media, though they did not abandon their support of a free press.[2] Bohumil Simon, new candidate presidium member, on the other hand, did not dilute his open support of the media.[3] At the central committee plenum of 29 May – 2 June Dubcek found it necessary to call upon communists in the media to remember their responsibilities. He criticized the media for failing to respond quickly to 'anti-socialist' attacks from abroad and, while supporting freedom of expression, he warned that the media belonged to the state and could not be used to disseminate subjective views.[4] At the same meeting Cernik announced measures to control the media: the media were to present official information and views 'without polemical commentaries' and a 'program board' would supervise broadcasting.

While certain intellectuals, such as Svitak, had long warned that the

[1] Bratislava radio, 9 April 1968.
[2] See *Praca*, 20 April 1968 (Smrkovsky); Prague radio, 2 and 8 April 1968 (Cisar); *Rude Pravo*, 23 May 1968 (Spacek).
[3] *Rude Pravo*, 6 June 1968 (Simon to central committee).
[4] *Bratislava Pravda*, 4 June 1968.

regime was dragging its feet and liable to crack down, these measures, combined with cases of censorship particularly in connection with the clubs and the effort to revive the Social Democratic Party, aroused wide concern. The workers even joined and supported the intellectuals in their resistance to the apparent retreat. Committees were formed in various work centers in defence of freedom of the press and some even threatened to strike if the press were muzzled.[1] Many believed that a return to censorship would mean a return to the suppression of discussion and of the expression of conflicting views, with a resultant limitation of public participation in decision-making upon which the very 'hope of democracy' was based.[2] Moreover, references at the June plenum to 'anti-socialist' and 'anti-communist' forces were seen as ominous signs that conservatives were gaining strength in conjunction with the growing pressures from outside.

Concern culminated at the end of June with a declaration entitled '2,000 Words,' signed originally by a selected list of workers, artists, writers, scientists, farmers, sportsmen, and engineers and published in their respective journals on 27 June. It was a matter-of-fact document which contended that the democratization process had reached a crucial stage which demanded a concerted effort by the people to secure their rights. Demanding no more (and even less) than much that had already been demanded on many public platforms it was to have tragic significance. It was seen by some as a call for 'action from below,' which threatened the already weakening control of the party. Because its fear that the document might be so interpreted, particularly abroad, the regime committed what was later admitted to be a tactical error: it officially condemned the declaration both at an emergency presidium meeting and in the National Assembly. Many liberals, including National Front chairman Kriegel and Sik, defended the signatories of the declaration, while Spacek and others criticized the party's condemnation. The declaration became a cause celebre both at party meetings at all levels and in the media, with the public adding thousands of signatures to copies of '2,000 Words' displayed in the streets.

The '2,000 Words' was in a sense the intellectuals' supreme effort to bring about change in the pre-invasion period, but it also marked the beginning of the final stage of what proved to be irreversible pressures on Czechoslovakia from outside. All subsequent efforts concentrated on

---

[1] *Prace*, 13 June 1968; Prague radio, 24 May 1968.
[2] *Literarni Listy*, 30 May 1968.

resisting these pressures, and the intellectuals closed ranks behind the party leadership in this struggle. They, nonetheless, maintained their own battle for freedom of expression, especially as a return to censorship was a major part of the Soviet, East German, and Polish demands on Czechoslovakia. Thus they made every effort to comply with the responsible demands of the regime without, however, conceding their basic rights, and they continued to play a major role in trying to have the public fully informed. While it is difficult to know just what stand the party would finally have taken on this whole issue of the freedom of expression had it not been harassed for at least one-half of those eight months of 'revival' by outside and conservative pressures, there is reason to believe that leaders such as Dubcek, Spacek, Smrkovsky, and Sik were basically committed to the principle of a free public exchange of views. Much of the attitude the liberals took or might have taken on this question, however, was connected with the problem of political reform and just what form they envisaged for their socialist democracy.

23

POLITICAL REFORMS

The most important and numerous discussions of 1968 focused on the political reforms, for it was indeed the need for reforms in this sphere which finally brought the liberals to power. Among the many points which had to be settled were: the role of the party, inner-party life, separation of the party and the state, the possibility of an opposition, the legal and security systems, the status of Slovakia, and, finally, Czechoslovakia's position in the world.

While it had in fact been conceded by 1968 that the party should step out of everyday matters of the society, the exact role this would leave the party had to be determined. Should the party play a purely programmatic role, i.e. supply the overall goals of society – and no more; should it become an arbitrator of the conflicting interests within society, settling disputes (without forcing a false 'unity') through supplying a common denominator; or should it operate as one of many components in the political sphere, participating with or even competing with other components? The last of these possibilities would mean an elimination of the constitutional preference accorded the Communist Party.

One of the major principles advocated by party liberals centered on the idea of popular co-participation with the party in the direction of society. To assure this the party itself would have to respond to conflicting views, mediate, and win its leading position by revising its views to suit the interests of others. If this were the case, however, the party would clearly have to abandon its practice of dictating its views and forcing unity. The party would have to limit its role to merely 'leading,' through example, persuasion, and possibly, setting the all-over goals. This view was advocated, in one form or another, by almost all the new leaders including Dubcek, who repeatedly maintained the programmatic role of the party and the need constantly to re-earn the right to lead.

Although there were differences of opinion on just how and when the concept of the leading role of the party had been abused, the Action Program clearly stated that a distortion had set in because of the 'false thesis that the party is the instrument of the dictatorship of the proletariat.' The state and economic and social institutions were the instruments of the proletariat and, according to the Action Program, the party's leading role was not to interfere in or duplicate their functions.

The Program specifically stated that the party was not to command or 'rule over society' nor replace (or dominate) the social and political institutions, which in fact represented the varied interests and groups within society. Citing the 'programmatic nature of the party,' the Program said the party should play the role of arbitrator, seeking 'a method of satisfying various interests that will not threaten the long-term interests of society as a whole.' The Program did add, however, that in addition to the party's programmatic function it should co-ordinate 'the practical efforts of the people to ensure' implementation of the party's line – a caveat reminiscent of the traditional role of the party. The difference was the way in which the party was to carry out this last function. As the party was *not* to command and was to abandon its monopoly on power, it was to exercise its authority, as the liberals had suggested, by way of example and persuasion – without benefit of the cadre system, intimidation or coercion.

This remained the regime's position on the role of the party despite and throughout the ensuing conflicts and pressures. Nonetheless, it was later suggested, by Cisar, that the party abandon not only its monopoly on decision making but also its monopoly on ideology: as in the political sphere so too in the ideological the party should be prepared to compete with non-communist Marxist and even non-Marxist views.[1] Others too challenged the idea of a 'state ideology' protected by the Constitution, and in quest for specific methods by which to break the party's monopoly on power and prevent abuses some suggested that the party abandon its leading role.[2]

DEMOCRATIZATION OF THE PARTY

One way to control the power of the party, according to some, was to change the party itself, its *modus operandi*, perhaps its structure and composition. Thus, accompanied by discussions on the origins of the Leninist concept of the party and the present applicability of such a concept in Czechoslovakia, proposals were raised for an adjustment of the concept of democratic centralism to permit inner-party democracy.

[1] Pal Feher, 'Conversation with Cestmir Cisar,' *Elet es Irodalom* (Budapest), 4 May 1968.

[2] See for example, Bedrich Rattinger in *Reporter*, 14 February 1968.

One of the major issues raised was availability of information within the party, particularly the dissemination of information from above to lower organs so as to permit greater genuine participation of the lower organs in party decisions. Participation of this sort meant, however, discussions and the possibility of debates, disagreements, differing proposals. How far such discussions could go raised the question of factions, i.e. should dissenters be permitted to publicize their views, seek support, and pursue their positions even after the party's decision. Spacek, for one, suggested a Marxist journal for just this purpose of supplying a platform for conflicting or dissenting views of party members.[1] Sik and Smrkovsky were one with Spacek in the struggle for internal criticism and the free exchange of views within the party. Criticism was to include not only policies but also individuals. This would mean individual responsibility of officials for their acts, together, however, with the right to honorable resignation, peaceful changes of personnel, the possibility of making a mistake without paying with one's life. Thus it was recommended that Novotny be permitted a pension, and it was argued that a summary purge of conservatives (persons of dissenting views in 1968) would not contribute to party democracy.[2] By the same token, the masses of party members should be granted greater power vis-a-vis the *apparat* or presidium, specifically through their elected organs within the party. For this to be effective, however, elections within the party would have to be democratized, including secret balloting, and rotation of functions.

The party statutes drafted for the extraordinary congress (to be convened in the fall) reflected the above ideas more thoroughly than the Action Program. The statutes sought to provide a new democratic and humane framework for party activities, placing the emphasis more on rights of members and participation than on duties and discipline as had been the case in previous statutes.[3] Aside from the general liberal tone of the new document, specific guarantees were provided such as: the right of members to resign, the right of a member to be present at all proceedings against him, accessibility of information (both for party members and the public), limitation of terms of office and offices to be held simultaneously, secret balloting, greater authority for the elected organs (with the control and auditing commissions to form an independent party organ responsible only to the congress and

---

[1] *Rude Pravo*, 11 April 1968 (Spacek to central committee).
[2] *Bratislava Pravda*, 4 February 1968.
[3] For draft of 1968 statutes, see *Rude Pravo*, 10 August 1968.

groups electing them rather than to the presidium or *apparat*), and greater independence of basic party units.

The statutes specifically accorded dissenters from party decisions the right to persist in their views, to have their views recorded, and to request new discussion and revaluations of decisions already taken. In order to provide the necessary atmosphere of security for implementation of this clause the statutes stated that only 'ideological means' could be used to dissuade minority supporters. This progressive clause nonetheless contained a caveat vague enough to be a serious obstacle to freedom of expression if so desired: such protection would be accorded only 'as long as they [minority supporters] are not in fundamental conflict with the program and statutes of the party.' Moreover the statutes did not specify just how much and in what manner one might safely persist in or propagate a minority view. For example, nothing specific was said about publishing such views, even though they were to be contained in the record of the party. Another clause did say that members had a right freely to discuss and criticize both activities and personnel of the party at party meetings and in the party press. Nonetheless it was expressly forbidden to form an organized grouping (a faction) or to 'organize minority supporters outside the framework of the statutes.' While the terms were vague, they clearly maintained the Leninist ban on factions – despite the right to dissent.

The only structural change provided in the new rules was federation of the party, i.e. replacement of the regional organs by 'national' bodies. Organizational measures to eliminate the system of parallel party organizations for every area or organization of society were rejected at the time.[1] Presumably it was felt that such a move was premature, particularly given Soviet concern, as it was, that the party was losing its leading role.

THE SEPARATION OF PARTY AND STATE

While the separation of the top party and governmental functions at the January plenum was basically a device to divest Novotny of his power, the reformers strove to carry this division to its logical conclusion, i.e. a full separation of powers throughout the political structure. If, as the Action Program stated, the party was not the instrument of the proletariat, it had no authority or theoretical basis for its 'direct management,' specifically of the government or elected organs. Given

[1] *Vecerni Praha*, 1 August 1968 (Martin Vaculik interview).

the extended period of pre-communist socialist society, in which state organs continued to exist, it was argued, a system of separation of power (checks and balances) should be re-introduced.[1] The latter was intended as a safeguard against monopolization of power, providing mutual controls. Leaders such as Dubcek and Smrkovsky recognized that freedom of expression would not be enough, and that democracy could be promised only through a functioning system of effective institutions dividing the executive, judiciary, and legislature, independent of the party and 'open in every respect to control and criticism.'[2]

The Action Program and the statutes embodied the above principles. The statutes withdrew the party from the functioning of the government, including the elected organs, and banned concentration of party–government positions in the hands of individuals. Party decisions were to be binding upon communists in the government elected organs, and the communists themselves were to operate only as one group among many, struggling through persuasion to win the others over to their views. Moreover, in keeping with democratic parliamentary procedures all would have the right to publicize and seek support for their proposals, even those unfavorable to the party, in these organs.[3]

Specific proposals for the improvement of the elected organs, particularly the National Assembly, followed the lines of the pre-1968 proposals. The National Assembly's control function vis-a-vis the government was to be expanded and it was even urged that the government be elected by the National Assembly rather than selected by the President, and subject to no-confidence votes by the Assembly.[4] Thus the Action Program declared: 'the policy and management, and also the responsibility of the state, economic, and social organs and organizations are independent,' answerable only to the National Assembly. The only caveat was contained in a speech by Dubcek when he said that the government must ensure the needs of the Republic 'expressed in the policy of the Communist Party.'[5]

The effectivity of the proclaimed reforms depended not only upon the interpretation and implementation of the above caveat but also upon the method of the selection of people to the government and

[1] *Rude Pravo*, 2 April 1968 (Dubcek); *Reporter*, 6 March 1968; *Kulturny Zivot*, 5 January 1968.
[2] Josef Smrkovsky, 'Democracy Does Not Come Overnight,' *My 68*, v:4 (1968), 6.
[3] *Rude Pravo*, 2 April 1968 (Dubcek); 13 April 1968 (Smrkovsky).
[4] See for example, Prague radio, 2 February 1968 (Smrkovsky).
[5] *Rude Pravo*, 2 April 1968.

representative organs. It was this realization that prompted a ground-swell of pressures for a postponement of the approaching National Committee elections until a new electoral law could be worked out. The party eventually acquiesced to these pressures and the elections were postponed until the fall, providing time until then for preparation of a new law. Popular discussions then bared severe criticism of the whole electoral procedure, with suggestions including the idea of individuals presenting themselves for election without benefit of organization or party, genuinely secret ballots, genuine choice of candidates and their place on the ballot, delegate responsibility to constituents, the right honorably to resign, and even direct election of the President. Students objected that the 30 March National Assembly election of Svoboda as President violated the spirit of these suggestions, and some demonstrated for a 'second candidate,' Cisar. The party, however, defended its right, as the 'politically most significant sector of society,' to propose the candidates for head of state.[1]

THE NATIONAL FRONT AND THE POSSIBILITY OF OPPOSITION

In the discussions on electoral procedures a controversy developed over the institution of the National Front. Since 1959 the National Front had been directly subordinate to the party, no more than a transmission belt, just as its components themselves had been no more than transmission belts. In 1968 there were those who sought a strengthening of the Front in hopes of rendering it an effective check on concentrated power. Adherents of this view believed the Front had merely been deprived of its powers and should, therefore, be upgraded as a policy-making body. Its components too should be upgraded, becoming co-participators – along with the party – in the formulation of policy. Mlynar, for example, saw the National Front as the platform for the clash of opinion he found inherent in and healthy for socialist society.[2] Thus here too the party was merely to compete for power in the decision-making process, recognizing the independence of the other components of the Front, including the other political parties. With the upgrading of the National Front, these parties were to be rejuvenated. Indeed they underwent personnel changes to remove the regime's

[1] Prague radio, 8 April 1968 (Indra to a Prague party meeting).
[2] *Rude Pravo*, 5 April 1968 (to central committee).

puppets, and their ranks expanded.[1] As we have seen there was even a bid for the reinstitution of the old Social Democrats, who did in fact create a preparatory committee in May despite the Communist Party presidium's opposition.[2] Thus a certain plurality was urged and even granted within the framework of the National Front, according the Front components the right publicity to seek supporters for their views. Moreover, according to Front chairman Kriegel, the Front itself was eventually to replace the party as state policy maker.[3] Nonetheless Kriegel asserted that the Front was to respect its founding principles, i.e. anti-fascism, anti-racism, communism (and anti-anti-communism), and alliance with the USSR. While this could be seen as a restriction on the Front's policy-making abilities (especially given past tendencies to broad interpretation of such things as anti-fascism), Kriegel maintained that the party was *not* to be guaranteed a leading role in the Front. This, however, would require a change in the Constitution, which explicitly asserted the leading role of the Communist Party.

There were those, however, who saw the National Front itself as a serious limitation on democracy and on the expression of the people's will, for it eliminated the possibility of genuine alternatives to the ruling power. This argument was based on opposition to the single list, single-platform principle of the National Front, which ruled out meaningful pluralism. The idea of the National Front (with a unified list at elections) eliminated the idea of opposition and ruling parties; and thus eliminated the idea of a struggle for the power to rule – which was in fact the very raison d'etre of political parties. What indeed was a 'party' which could present neither its own candidates nor its own program for election to the places of power, asked political scientist Pithart.[4] Moreover, he explained, the democratic nature of a political struggle for power was based on the principle that the power thus acquired might also be lost. Effective pluralism demanded the possibility of presenting the voter alternatives to the ruling party, either in candidates or ideas, and the components of the National Front could hardly operate as a control on the concentration of power if they had no possibility of replacing that power. The Action Program in fact expressly ruled out the idea of opposition and ruling parties, and with it the possibility that a majority might choose anything but the continued rule of the Communist Party.

Not only did the regime's concept of the National Front prevent

[1] *Lidova Demokracie*, 12 April 1968.   [2] *Svobodne Slovo*, 7 June 1968.
[3] *Rude Pravo*, 19 June 1968.   [4] *Literarni Listy*, 18 April 1968.

genuine pluralism, Pithart argued, it also prevented effective representative government. For if the National Front, and the party, had the right to determine state policy, what indeed was the parliament supposed to do but continue to operate as a rubber stamp? This was all the more serious given the fact the National Front was *not* an elected organ; it consisted of organizations (and 'political parties') with overlapping membership, and presented only one list for elections anyway.[1] This last was also presented as an argument against reliance upon social–interest groups as a brake on power, for these groups were neither based on political convictions nor independent of political groupings nor competitors in the struggle for political power; they therefore could offer no political alternative.

The only genuine control on power and guarantee of democracy, it was argued by many, was the existence of competitors for power: an opposition. It was argued that an end of the communist monopoly on power would permit representation for the political wishes of the eighty per cent of the population who were not party members. It would also provide healthy competition for the party, forcing the latter to satisfy the peoples' wishes and preventing it from degenerating into dogmatism.[2]

Insofar as the basis upon which opposition parties might be formed it was generally accepted that pluralism should be within the framework of socialism, though Pithart suggested that the concept of socialism might be open to discussion. The major question was not, however, socialism or not but democratic socialism, and the role of the Communist Party in such a system. There were many who fully believed that the Communist Party *could* prove itself in free political competition – as long as this were within the general context of socialism.[3] This 'socialism' generally meant a society free of classes and class conflict or exploitation in the Marxist sense, so that political parties could not be instruments of one class against another. The basis of opposition, therefore, might be the varying and freely expressed 'moral–political and cultural' interests of the citizens.[4] The mutual ideal of socialism, however, would no longer be identified exclusively with a single party. As some saw it, there might be numerous Marxist parties, such as the Social Democratic Party; others foresaw a development of the clubs

[1] See also *Literarni Listy*, 22 March and 4 April 1968; *Kulturny Zivot*, 12 April 1968.
[2] See for example, *ibid.* or *Literarni Listy*, 16 May 1968.
[3] See for example, *Reporter*, 17 April 1968.   [4] *Literarni Listy*, 15 March 1968.

into political parties, while still others sought groupings 'beyond' parties, based on the division of labor.[1]

As early as March there were signs that even party liberals were opposed to a genuine competition for power, as evidenced even in the Action Program, despite the willingness to grant the components of the National Front greater independence and participation. Some, such as Goldstuecker, took the classical Marxist approach to political parties, rejecting them as class phenomena; others such as Husak opposed a large opposition party 'in the present situation.'[2] By May the leadership was clearly nervous about the rising demands (and tendencies) towards pluralism. On 27 June *Rude Pravo* revealed that 90 per cent of non-party members queried preferred a multi- to a one-party system, as did 55·5 per cent of party members interviewed. Spacek and Mlynar advocated party democratization and strengthening of the National Front organizations instead of additional parties, as did other liberals such as Sik and Klokoc, while a *Zivot Strany* article argued that if an opposition party were permitted it would surely become a spokesman for anti-communism.[3] It was in the context of this growing concern that the regime banned the reinstitution of the Social Democrats and Dubcek criticized K-231. On 24 May the Interior Ministry announced that 'organized activity purporting to be that of a political party' would be considered illegal. This was also the predominant sentiment at the May–June central committee plenum at which Bohumil Simon was but a voice in the wilderness supporting the idea that the party could successfully compete with other parties.[4]

While Dubcek championed the idea of greater popular participation and democratization of the party, his position that the party need constantly earn its leading role specifically excluded competition with other powers or the possibility of losing the leading role. He told the May–June plenum:

The basic difference between bourgeois parliamentarianism and socialist democracy is the fact that relations between the political

---

[1] *Ibid.*; also *Literarni Listy*, 4 April 1968; *Student*, 18 April 1968 (Svitak); Prague radio, 17 May 1968 (Mlynar).

[2] Goldstuecker interviews to ASHAI (Japan), 22 March and *Volkstimme* (Austria), 12 April 1968; Husak, Bratislava television, 19 March and Prague radio, 20 March 1968.

[3] See *Rude Pravo*, 23 May 1968; *Bratislava Pravda*, 13 June 1968; *Zemedelske Noviny*, 30 June 1968; Karel Vlk, 'To Unify the Progressive Forces in the Party,' *Zivot Strany*, 11 (1968), 36.

[4] *Rude Pravo*, 6 June 1968.

parties which preserve the foundations of the National Front must be relationships of partnership and cooperation, not relationships of struggle for the repartition of power in the state – a struggle which is typical of the bourgeois political system.[1]

He even went so far as to say that the confrontation of views now to be permitted within the National Front must be based on the common socialist program *guaranteed by the leading role of the party*, since the party's program was the scientifically based Marxist way, the only way of achieving socialism. Thus Dubcek not only ruled out the existence of other parties, and the idea of competition for power, he in effect returned to the idea of the infallibility of the party and the domination of the party in the National Front and, thereby, all policy matters.

The above was not necessarily Dubcek's final position regarding the leading role of the party, coming as it did in response to internal and external pressures. Subsequent to the June plenum Dubcek reiterated his position on opposition, but he did soften his comments as to the role of the party, returning to the idea that the party must *prove* that its program was the only valid one. Dubcek explained that by 'prove' he meant contend for majority support – but not against other genuine contenders.[2] In essence his position was that the party should demonstrate its right to the leading role rather than decree it; it should permit the expression of differing views and respond to them without, however, permitting them a formal framework which might threaten the party or operate as an alternative to the party. Moreover, since the party recognized only its own program as the valid one to socialism and rejected any possibility of abandoning its dominant role, it hardly made any difference if it gained a majority or not, or if it heeded the majority or not. The system suggested by Dubcek may have marked an improvement in attitude or methods, but it still failed to provide the guarantees necessary to a democracy.

LEGAL AND SECURITY ORGANS

With discussions on the control of power, and more specifically with the accusations against Novotny and the old regime, the purges and trials of the 1950s were brought into the open and discussed in great detail in the mass media. Exposes designed to help prevent a recurrence of such injustices appeared and even such cases as the death of Jan Masaryk were re-investigated, with the active role of the Russians in

[1] *Bratislava Pravda*, 4 June 1968. [2] *Rude Pravo*, 30 June and 1 July 1968.

Czechoslovak security organs cited on a number of occasions. These revelations led to public pressures for personnel changes and rehabilitations, both of which were gradually undertaken by the regime. Dubcek was hesitant to conduct purges, for he opposed compounding past illegalities with further illegal action.[1] Nonetheless, personnel changes were made in the Interior and Justice Ministries as well as the party security organs and, in response to demands for action against those responsible for the past, the party expelled Novotny from the central committee and suspended Bacilek, Koehler, P. David, Siroky, Urvalek, and Stefan Rais in June 1968.

Rehabilitation committees were set up at all levels and in numerous organizations and offices. The party began to reconsider, still once again, the charges against Slansky. Public demands, however, called for rehabilitation of thousands of non-communists as well as the persecuted party members, and a rehabilitation law was urged. Indeed work on a draft had begun as early as 1966 (to cover indemnity and legal action against the responsible organs or parties). After some delays in 1968, and a threat by Smrkovsky to bring a no-confidence vote against the Justice Ministry, a law was finally presented and passed, 25 June 1968.[2] With these actions and an amnesty declared by Svoboda in May, a large number of political prisoners were released, including Barak.

The regime was not entirely satisfied with this whole process, for the revelations clearly sullied the name of the party. While conservatives pointed this out as early as March and April, even liberal leaders including Dubcek and Smrkovsky began to warn that some persons had been legitimately tried in the past. They warned against becoming preoccupied with the past or 'witch-hunting.'[3] Specifically Dubcek explained that individuals, not the party, were responsible for the past, and he urged the central committee to dissociate the party from the Stalinists. It is in this connection too that one may view the actions against Novotny and the others at the May–June plenum.

The liberals consistently urged a return to the rule of law as the best safeguard against misuses of power, and they hoped thoroughly to change the legal–security apparatus so as to restore these as controls on power rather than abusers of power. Among their demands was the

[1] *Bratislava Pravda*, 4 June 1968.
[2] *Bratislava Pravda*, 30 April 1968 (Smrkovsky interview). The law was *Sbirka Zakonu* No. 82/1968.
[3] See *Mlada Fronta*, 5 April 1968; *Praca* 30 April 1968; *Rude Pravo*, 4 April 1968.

return to an independent judiciary, capable of acting as a check on the legislative branch of government and free of interference on the part of the executive branch or the party. It was recommended that the National Assembly create a security and defense committee to which the Prosecutor's Office would be responsible, to replace the control exercised by both the party and the Interior Ministry over this office. This suggestion was also urged in efforts to control the security organs and to remove them from the hands of the party central committee's eighth department. General Prchlik, the new, liberal, chief of the eighth department did much to hasten the dissolution of this department (though his own resulting dismissal was connected with Soviet pressures against him, as we shall see below). All security organs, including the Interior Ministry itself, were to be subject to the supervision (for legality) of a National Assembly security and defense committee. The suggestions also sought the removal of Soviet control (through 'advisors') of the Czechoslovak security system. This was to be a logical consequence of the removal of the party itself from security affairs, and the subordination of the latter to parliamentary control. There is much evidence, however, that the new regime did not succeed in gaining independence from the Soviets in this sphere during 1968.[1]

Two other elements of the security establishment which came under criticism were the army and the party's militia. Especially because of Novotny's efforts to use the army in the political crisis of December–January – and the subsequent flight westward of General Sejna and the suicide of General Janko, involved in these efforts – there were demands that the army too be freed of party control and subject to a National Assembly security and defense committee as well as a control commission in the party central committee. These suggestions would, of course, have meant a redefinition of the role of the Main Political Directorate, the party's instrument in the army.

More serious, at least in the eyes of the Soviet Union, were the suggestions to disband the party's militia on the grounds that it was an armed force of a political party – and the exclusive privilege of one party at that – which had outlived any purpose it might have had given the advance to a socialist society. The very least demanded was subordination of the militia to the same control organs advocated for the rest of the security apparatus. The maximum appeal was contained in a popular petition urging the party to disband the militia. The party

---

[1] For example the cooperation between the deputy Interior Minister responsible for the secret police, Salgovic, and the Soviets with regard to the invasion.

came to the defense of its militia, probably as a result of pressures from the Soviet Union (which took up the issue publicly)[1] and the thousands of people connected with this organization. Both Dubcek and Smrkovsky sought to present the militia as an integral part of Czechoslovakia's protection against external forces, which could never be used 'against the people.'[2] Even with this support the Bohemian militia sent a conservative statement to the Soviet Union at the end of June, thus supporting – and helping – Moscow's efforts against the liberal regime.[3]

SLOVAKIA

Slovak communists for the most part concentrated their efforts on securing a new constitutional arrangement for Slovakia, in many cases neglecting or minimizing other issues.[4] Demands ranged from suggestions for full Slovak independence to confederation or federation; some advocated a return to the promises of the Kosice Program, some sought more than had been promised then – specifically, a symmetrical rather than the current 'asymmetrical' organization of the two nationalities. The symmetrical model implied a new Constitution to provide for a Czech National Council and other Czech organs as counterparts to the Slovak organs, within a Czechoslovak federation.

The Action Program accepted the principle of the symmetrical model, although it did not say anything about the creation of Czech organs. It did, however, call for a constitutional law pending a new Constitution and, among other things, it barred simple majority decisions on matters concerning the status of Slovakia. The vagueness of the Action Program, combined with subsequent delays and comments from leading Czech reformers rejecting the idea of separate Czech organs, led to increased pressures by the Slovaks and controversies within the ranks of the supporters of the new regime.[5] In May, however, a government commission was formed, with a sub-committee on special problems headed by Husak, to draft a constitutional law on federation – to be presented to the National Assembly in time for the Fiftieth Anniversary of the Republic, 28 October 1968.

The law envisaged,[6] and in part accepted after the invasion, called

[1] *Pravda* (Moscow), 21 June 1968.
[2] *Prace*, 26 May 1968; Prague radio, 19 June 1968.   [3] *Rude Pravo*, 25 June 1968.
[4] See complaints to this effect in *Kulturny Zivot*, 5 April 1968.
[5] See *Predvoj*, 28 March–18 April 1968; *Kulturny Zivot*, 2 August 1968: *Reporter* 15 May 1968; *Rolnicky Noviny*, 20 April 1968; *Praca*, 22 April 1968.
[6] See *Mlada Fronta*, 14 April 1968 (Husak interview) for the following.

for the federalization of all political, social, governmental bodies, creating autonomous organs for both Czechs and Slovaks with federal parent units above them. Indeed a provisional Czech National Council was set up under Cestmir Cisar in July 1968 as a result of a law passed on 24 June 1968. Economic matters, as well as foreign policy, trade, and defense would be under the government, with 'national' secretaries in Slovakia and the Czech lands for each ministry existing in the Federal government. The Federal parliament was to consist of a house based on the one man one vote principle elected from the whole country, and a second house composed of equal representatives of the two nations. The federal arrangement would also mean an administrative reorganization, eliminating the regional National Committees, leaving the district National Committees directly subordinate to the appropriate National Council. These arrangements would leave the other nationalities and areas such as Moravia either downgraded or minus the administrative autonomy demanded by the minorities. Neither Husak nor the law passed after the invasion was sympathetic to the demands of the other nationalities or Moravians, promising the former only cultural rights.

It is difficult to know if the federalization law passed in October 1968 followed in its entirety the proposals of the commission, though its passage reflected the Soviet's efforts to woo the Slovaks. The final arrangement greatly favored the Federal organs with regard to legislation, introducing the pre-communist central Constitutional Court to supervise the rights and actions of the National Councils, although it did provide the councils with extensive executive powers. Implementation since 1968, however, has not greatly changed the centralist practices of pre-1968 Czechoslovakia.

FOREIGN POLICY

Foreign policy was not a significant issue in the reform movement campaign prior to 1968, and it is indeed difficult to determine just how the new regime's position on foreign affairs would have been affected had the Soviets refrained from interfering in the democratization process. From January till August the regime consistently and repeatedly affirmed its commitment to the Warsaw Pact and the socialist nations, but the nature of this commitment as well as other elements of foreign policy did undergo review, especially in the later stages of the 1968 revival.

Political Reforms

Liberals very early began to assert the need for mutual respect of sovereignty and equality within the socialist world to permit each nation to develop socialism according to its specific conditions. As with regard to inner-party affairs and inner Czechoslovak affairs, so with the international movement, one should not proclaim or decree a false unity but rather permit differing views and diversity.[1] Both Rumania and Italy were singled out for supporting this idea of a diversified movement based on a voluntary unity as distinct from a movement dominated by one party demanding a preferential position and line.[2] In a February speech Dubcek himself proclaimed the above view, albeit adding the familiar caveat of 'firm international solidarity.'[3] He also demonstrated his broadened outlook by supporting Rumania's reservations regarding the nuclear non-proliferation treaty at the Sofia Warsaw Pact meeting in early March. Demonstrating similar independence, Prague's delegate to the Budapest consultative meeting of communist parties, the conservative Koucky, demanded that his party be dissociated from the anti-Yugoslav aspects of the 1957 and 1960 international communist declaration.[4] This was not a particularly dangerous act given Moscow's renewed detente with Belgrade, but it was a unique action at the conference.

Dubcek spoke of another plank which was to characterize the liberals' policy: a return to Europe. This meant the recognition of Czechoslovakia as a part of Europe, and the pursuit of normal relations as well as cooperation with the European states, regardless of social systems. It was argued that improved relations with Western Europe would restrict, not aid, western anti-communist efforts, and especially recommended were improved relations with progressive (leftist) groups there.[5] This attitude was urged in connection with a resumption of the efforts begun some years earlier for a normalization of relations with West Germany. Voices could also be heard favoring an independent Czechoslovak foreign policy, albeit within the general framework of the existing alliances. Galuska, for example, mentioned the possibility of resuming diplomatic relations with Israel, while a Prague radio commentary spoke of reappraising Prague's attitude towards Biafra.[6]

While not the entire reason, the above-mentioned signs of independ-

---

[1] See for example, Jan Mentel, 'Obsolete Epistles,' as reproduced in *Nedeljne Informativne Novine*, 18 February 1968.
[2] Prague radio, 18 February 1968. [3] *Rude Pravo*, 23 February 1968.
[4] Prague radio, 1 March 1968. [5] *Rude Pravo*, 22 March 1968.
[6] Prague radio, 20 March 1968; 25 February 1968.

ence in foreign affairs contributed to the 23 March Dresden meeting designed to call the Czechs and Slovaks to account. Rumania understandably was not invited, and the meeting therefore could easily issue a communique referring to 'practical measures in the immediate future to consolidate the Warsaw Pact and its armed forces.'[1] Probably a reference to the oft-discussed strengthening of the Pact's political consultative committee to serve as an instrument of central control over the Pact states (and opposed by Rumania), it had an ominous sound to it when seen in connection with the talks there on Czechoslovakia's reforms. Dubcek himself implied that this statement referred only to military coordination,[2] but he had agreed to a harsh communique regarding Bonn and reaffirmed Czechoslovakia's continued allegiance to the Warsaw Pact. It does not appear, however, that Dubcek made any compromises with regard either to the reforms, or Germany, or the nature of the commitment to the Pact.

The Action Program, approved one week after the Dresden meeting, categorically declared that Czechoslovakia 'will formulate its own stand on basic issues of world policy,' though it would do so aware 'that our own stand is an active component of the revolutionary process in the world.' The Program followed this statement with an assertion of loyalty to its allies, noting that relations between them should be based upon 'mutual respect, sovereignty, equality of rights, mutual esteem,' and, last, 'international solidarity.' Specifically the Program proclaimed a 'more active European policy,' i.e. improved relations with Western Europe and 'realistic' forces in West Germany (though not at the expense of East Germany). The Program also responded to demands for a 'democratization' of foreign policy, i.e. greater dissemination of information, discussion, and consideration of popular wishes as well as public and government participation in the making of foreign policy decisions.

Subsequent to the Action Program outside pressures became so strong that one cannot clearly determine when Prague's statements were merely reactions to these pressures and when they were expressions of the policies envisaged by the reform movement. There was a certain radicalization of demands as outside pressures increased, and internal popular pressures made their mark as well. The idea of neutrality was raised but barely discussed seriously; it was dismissed by most as untenable and unrealistic.[3] On the other hand, the removal

---

[1] TASS, 24 March 1968.   [2] CTK, 26 March 1968.
[3] See for example, *Mlada Fronta*, 14 June 1968 or Hajek in *Vjesnik* (Zagreb), 25 May 1968.

of Soviet foreign policy advisors and guidelines was advocated,[1] and Dubcek's 'return to Europe' actively pursued, although Foreign Minister Hajek insisted that this was not at the expense of the socialist camp or Czechoslovakia's integral position therein.[2] While the regime made no official statements, the popular support for Israel and for Biafra did lead to reduction of Czechoslovak arms supplies to Egypt and to Nigeria pending review of policies. Reporting on Germany became more objective (drawing admonitions from East Germany), and relations with West Germany were improved to such a point that old-time communist Stanislav Budin said that he expected a Czechoslovak ambassador in Bonn within a year.[3]

The new objective and thorough reporting of the media included a number of topics and facts with which Prague's allies took issue. In addition to revelations (not particularly favorable to the Kremlin) on the anniversaries of the Cominform decision against Tito and the execution of Imre Nagy, there was also coverage critical of Poland's anti-semitic, anti-Zionist campaigns then in progress. These, plus the frank discussions of possible reforms of CEMA or the Warsaw Pact, could but irritate if not embarrass the allies. While there is no evidence that anyone in authority in Prague was seriously considering the abandonment of the Soviet alliance (military or economic) system, one may assume that the vagueness of the regime's formula of a 'Czechoslovak' foreign policy did raise certain doubts and apprehensions. One can only speculate as to whether or not popular demands would have led to efforts for genuine independence, but it is probably true that the mere existence of an atmosphere in which such demands might be heard was in itself a serious threat so far as Moscow and certain of her allies were concerned.

[1] *Bratislava Pravda*, 31 May 1968. [2] *Vjesnik*, 25 May 1968
[3] *Prace*, 17 April 1968.

24

INVASION

While Czechoslovakia's reforms did not lead her to demand genuine independence from the Soviet Union, the growing pressures upon her did prompt more and more frequent references to sovereignty, equality, and a 'Czechoslovak' road to socialism. The sources of these pressures, specifically Gomulka, Ulbricht, and the Kremlin, may well have believed that the reform movement would, eventually, lead Czechoslovakia out of the bloc. But subsequent actions – and revelations – suggest that what worried them most was this 'Czechoslovak road to socialism,' i.e. the threat it presented for socialism as the Soviets conceived it, both in Czechoslovakia and in the other countries of the Soviet bloc. Even East Germany's objections to Prague's relations with Bonn appear secondary when viewed in the perspective of East–West relations from the year 1964 to 1970. This issue was certainly used by both the East Germans and the Soviets in their accusations against Prague (*viz.* their efforts to link the reform movement with Bonn, revanchism, and the Sudeten Deutsche[1]), but the Soviets never brought to bear all the means at their disposal to forestall such relations. Rather it would seem that something much more serious was deemed to warrant a full-scale invasion, with all the disadvantages such an act involved for international communism and Moscow's efforts in that sphere. This was the threat to the continued rule of the party, the threat of pluralism, and the dangers of freedom of expression – all considered incompatible in Soviet eyes with the continuation or building of socialism. Thus Soviet and subsequent conservative Czechoslovak attacks focused on the abolition of censorship, the criticism of the militia (read security organs), and the tentatives towards pluralism, specifically the clubs, of the 1968 revival.

Early in 1968 the Czechs and Slovaks had presented their new program as an example for the development of socialism in an 'economically and culturally mature' country, as Dubcek put it, thereby constituting Czechoslovakia's positive contribution to international socialism.[2] Czechoslovakia's democratic traditions were seen as that specific element which could mark the solutions offered to the problems of the new phase

[1] *On Events In Czechoslovakia* (Moscow, 1968).
[2] *Rude Pravo*, 23 February 1968.

of development (i.e. the achievement of socialism prior to the transition to communism). It was Czechoslovakia which could wed socialism with democracy *and* provide an example for industrially advanced countries. What this implied about the Soviets (who had also achieved a socialist society) was usually left unsaid, though some did go so far as to explain that the Soviet system suited, perhaps, its lack of a parliamentary tradition[1] – but did not suit 'the specific national conditions' of Czechoslovakia, as Dubcek put it.[2] On closer examination these specific national conditions were found to be not only the democratic tradition but also a humanitarian tradition, together with a mature economy and culture and a high educational level of the people.[3] Goldstuecker, Smrkovsky, Cernik, Spacek, and Dubcek all admitted that Czechoslovakia was trying to do something new and hitherto untried, i.e. to link freedom or democracy with socialism, as befitted her national traditions.[4] These references to Czechoslovakia's traditions could but remind one of the arguments between the Comintern and the even then 'evolutionary' Czech communists in the 1920s, as well as Gottwald's 'Czechoslovak road' in 1945.

As outside pressures grew Prague began to limit its offer of a new model for socialism, for the March demonstrations in Warsaw and comments by the East Germans clearly indicated that a spread of the Czechoslovak model was feared rather than desired. Moreover Prague had to be careful lest she appear to be challenging the Soviet model and presenting an alternative for others to follow. Thus by the spring, leaders such as Smrkovsky, Cisar, and Cernik were expressing reassurances that the Czechoslovak model was not a generally valid model for export and probably could not be used elsewhere. In this way greater emphasis was gradually placed upon the purely national quality of the Czechoslovak experiment, despite the liability of being accused of nationalism or sectarianism. The need to focus on the purely domestic nature of the movement did not in fact contradict the spirit or intentions of the reformers, for they were indeed intent upon improving their own society without any desire to question or come into conflict with the goals of international communism – or to develop a 'national communism' outside the international movement.

[1] Petr Colotka, 'Democratic Socialism,' *Zivot*, 17 April 1968.
[2] *Rude Pravo*, 2 April 1968.
[3] See for example, *Rude Pravo*, 11 April and 7 June 1968.
[4] See *ibid*. and speeches and interviews in *Prace*, 15 June 1968; Prague radio, 20 March 1968; *Volkstimme*, 12 April 1968; Hamburg television, 17 March 1968.

These intentions were repeated innumerable times from January until August (and even after the invasion), but interference from outside merely increased with the fears of the conservative 'allies' that freedom of the press and pluralism were gaining ground in Czechoslovakia. The Dresden meeting was but the first formal attempt by the 'allies' to influence events in Czechoslovakia and, insofar as may be determined, Dubcek merely reiterated at that meeting as elsewhere both his loyalty to the Pact and his conviction that the reforms in his country did not and would not constitute a threat to socialism. While April was marked by warnings contained in speeches from Moscow and the beginnings of (mild) polemics between Czechoslovak media and East Germany, Poland and the Soviets,[1] it was in May that the crisis became most apparent.[2] May opened with Dubcek's 4 May talks in Moscow, presumably to explain matters further, especially with regard to economic relations and, as Dubcek admitted, Soviet fears of anti-socialist excesses in Prague.[3] Dubcek told Brezhnev that the best way to cement relations would be to follow the policy Brezhnev had adopted in December 1967, i.e. leave the Czechoslovaks to solve their own matters.[4] Nonetheless, following Dubcek's unexpected quick trip, a meeting took place in Moscow between the party leaders of East Germany, Poland, Bulgaria, Hungary, and the USSR. According to Prague radio (12 May), quoting *Borba*, the meeting was called at Ulbricht's request and Hungary was hesitant about attending.[5] Yet rather than solve anything, these visits marked the beginning of strong polemics against Czechoslovak liberals in the Soviet and East German media, and rumors of a Soviet military build-up on Czechoslovak borders. The polemics singled out Smrkovsky, Ludvik Vaculik, Prochazka, Havel, the idea of opposition parties, the clubs, attacks on the militia, western exploitation of events in Czechoslovakia (remarks about which were accompanied by an increase in Soviet criticism of Bonn), Czechoslovak

[1] See Kurt Hager's comments, *Neues Deutschland*, 27 March 1968. Biased East German reporting had begun to arouse Czechoslovak comment on Prague radio as early as 13 and 17 March 1968.

[2] See speeches by Brezhnev and Grishin (RFE, SR, 24 April 1968; Moscow radio, 22 April 1968) and *Pravda* (Moscow), 30 April 1968; *Lidove Demokracie*, 3 May 1968, answering *Izvestia*, 30 April 1968; *Praca*, 25 April 1968 and *Rude Pravo*, 11 April 1968, answering Grishin and Hager.

[3] Prague radio, 6 May 1968.

[4] *Rude Pravo*, 7 May 1968 (Dubcek interview).

[5] Indeed Hungarian treatment of Czechoslovak events had been much more fair than the others and even sympathetic.

media's critical references to other socialist countries, and the Czecho-slovak student movement (criticism of which may have been connected with fear of the effects on Polish and Soviet youth).[1] The major accusation focused on the growth of anti-socialist forces in Czechoslovakia and the threat to the leading role of the party.

The rumors regarding Soviet troops were not immediately denied and alleged remarks by Soviet officers Yepishev and Konev did little to relieve tensions. Visiting Czechoslovakia for Liberation Day celebrations, Konev urged Kladno workers to preserve the militant revolutionary traditions of the proletariat, adding that the Soviet Union would not permit anyone to destroy the fraternal ties between the two countries.[2] Yepishev, according to an officially denied account in *Le Monde*, told the CPSU central committee (and later Czech soldiers, according to Czech reports) that 'the Soviet army was ready to comply with its duty should loyal communists in Czechoslovakia request help in safeguarding socialism.'[3] On 10 May CTK announced that there were indeed troop movements along the Polish–Czechoslovak border in connection with Pact maneuvers. A few days earlier it had been announced that general staff exercises were scheduled for the summer or fall.[4] Amidst rumors of Pact plans to station Soviet and Polish troops in Czechoslovakia, and, apparently, pressures for some change in the Warsaw Pact designed to effect central control over developments in Czechoslovakia, Marshal Grechko led a delegation to Czechoslovakia on 17 May. A few days later Defence Minister Dzur announced the imminent beginning of Pact maneuvers in Czechoslovakia.[5] Grechko's statement: 'the solution of the internal problems of the Czechoslovak People's Army is the internal affair of Czechoslovakia,' together with official denials about the stationing of Soviet troops in Czechoslovakia were presumably designed to silence the rumors.[6]

Simultaneously with Grechko's trip, Kosygin arrived in Czechoslovakia, ostensibly to take a cure in Karlovy Vary. While little is known of Kosygin's talks in Prague, aside from the fact that they also dealt with economic matters, the major result appears to have been the let-up in Soviet polemics against Czechoslovakia. One may, however, view the conservative tone of the end of May–early June central committee

[1] See *Komsomolskaya Pravda*, 11 May and later, 21 June 1968.
[2] Moscow radio, 13 May 1968.   [3] See *Literarni Listy*, 9 and 30 May 1968.
[4] Czechoslovak television, 7 May 1968.   [5] Radio Bratislava, 21 May 1968.
[6] *Rude Pravo*, 19 May 1968; Prague radio, 21 May 1968 (Frantisek Kouril); 22 May 1968 (Vaclav Pleskot).

plenum (especially the remarks regarding the media) in connection with the preceding pressures and direct intervention of the Soviet Union – as well as with the increased activity of conservatives within Czechoslovakia. Indeed by the end of May the new regime seemed to be facing a serious political crisis as a result of both the concerted efforts inside and outside Czechoslovakia to limit the revival, and the reaction of liberals to these efforts and the party's apparent retreat.

By mid-June polemics had started again from Moscow and these became almost frenzied in response to the '2,000 Words' published at the end of the month. The reason for the resumption is not entirely clear, although it followed an official Soviet protest of a Czech publication of western claims that the Soviets had helped Sejna flee to the West.[1] It also followed trips to Moscow by both Smrkovsky (parliamentary delegation) and Strougal (economic delegation). The strong reaction to the '2,000 Words' warned of the growing power and audacity of 'anti-socialist' forces in Czechoslovakia and focused on the demands for an opposition party. Slightly less polemical but a clear indication of the basis for Soviet objections was a Moscow broadcast to Czechoslovakia on 4 July which said:

Communists realize that the specific ways of socialist construction in different countries can be quite distinctive. In spite of this, the socialist countries are linked by the unity of their principles, their common social, economic, and political bases. There is not and cannot be socialism without common ownership of production; there is not and cannot be socialism without participation of the masses in the direction of society and the state; there is not and cannot be socialism without the leading role of the Marxist–Leninist communist party imbued with the spirit of proletarian internationalism.

While these polemics were gaining momentum Dubcek led a delegation to Budapest, from 13 to 15 June, to sign a new friendship pact. There he was well received and the feeling in Czechoslovakia was that Hungary, together with Rumania and Yugoslavia, was sympathetic to developments in Czechoslovakia. This sympathy, however, did not and probably could not forestall the crisis which followed.

On 8 July the Czechoslovak presidium gave an official reply to letters received from the East German, Polish, Hungarian, Bulgarian, and

[1] See 'The Second Round of Open Polemics,' RFE, 28 June 1968, 2.

Soviet parties calling for a joint meeting in Warsaw on 7 July.[1] Prague's reply was that it welcomed discussions but preferred to conduct them on a bi-lateral basis (and including talks with Rumania and Yugoslavia), at an 'appropriate time' and in respect of mutual non-interference in internal affairs.[2] Another bid for a meeting was received from the five on 11 July and a similar answer sent on 13 July, but the meeting was already getting under way in Warsaw.[3] The party cabled the meeting not to discuss Czechoslovakia in its absence, but the convening first secretaries sent a formal letter to Prague on 15 July 1968.[4] Pointing to the undermining of the leading role of the party in Czechoslovakia and stating that a threat to socialism in one country is a threat to socialism in all the socialist countries, the Warsaw letter demanded of Prague: first, an attack on anti-socialist forces; secondly, a ban on all political organizations acting against socialism; thirdly, re-establishment of censorship; and fourthly, revival of democratic centralism. Some Czechs indicated that the letters had come in response to the '2,000 Words,' although this may have been merely an excuse to try to bring the intellectuals under control. Be that as it may, it may be assumed that the crisis was accelerated by the liberals' efforts to prevent intervention (the '2,000 Words' contained the pledge of armed popular support for the Dubcek regime should it be threatened from outside).

The Czechoslovak party presidium met on 16 July to discuss the Warsaw letter and in the following days issued its reply. The Dubcek regime maintained its firm line regarding non-interference and, although admitting to efforts of anti-socialist forces it denied that these posed a threat to socialism in Czechoslovakia. It also mentioned the continued divisive efforts of the 'dogmatic–sectarian' forces whose work in the past had indeed harmed the position of the party. Prague recognized the importance of maintaining the leading role of the party but argued that the only way to ensure this in Czechoslovakia was to implement the Action Program and thereby present a party deeply rooted in and responsive to the demands of Czechoslovakia itself. In closing, the Czechoslovak reply again urged bilateral talks, after saying that 'the common cause of socialism is not advanced by the holding of conferences at which the policy and activity of one of the fraternal

[1] CTK, 9 July 1968 (Cisar speech).
[2] Prague radio, 8 July 1968.
[3] *Rude Pravo*, 20 July 1968 (Dubcek speech to special July plenum).
[4] *Pravda* (Moscow), 18 July 1968.

parties is judged without the presence of their representatives.'[1] Dubcek's firm stand in the first weeks of July was an extraordinarily courageous and independent act. Whatever the indications of a retreat on the domestic scene and the genuine concern over the liberalization's getting out of hand, this most difficult stand was indicative of the degree of Dubcek's commitment to the reform movement and his belief in its necessity as well as its viability. This is particularly apparent when one bears in mind that at the same time as the above communications (and the continuing polemics), Warsaw Pact troops were still on Czechoslovak territory, their withdrawal clearly having been delayed since the close of the exercises on 30 June.[2] The Soviets suggested a meeting with the Czechoslovak presidium in the Soviet Union or Poland, but Dubcek refused to meet outside Czechoslovakia (or, reportedly, to hold any talks) as long as Pact troops remained in the country. On 22 July TASS announced that Moscow had agreed to talks in Czechoslovakia and on the same day Prague radio reported the beginning of the withdrawal of the Pact troops.

In the period following the Warsaw letter the media and the party joined ranks behind Dubcek, supporting him mainly through numerous articles and unanimous central committee acceptance of the presidium's reply to the letter,[3] although the conservatives and some fence-sitters in the party were not too cooperative.[4] Polemics continued from outside, and the withdrawal of Pact troops proceeded at such a slow pace that many troops were still in Czechoslovakia by the time of the Cierna nad Tisou and Bratislava conferences. One 'issue' which arose prior to the talks, presumably a chance occurrence exploited by the Soviets to extract a symbolic compromise prior to the negotiations, was the suggestions by General Prchlik for a reorganization of the Warsaw Pact. Although his suggestions varied little from earlier Rumanian proposals, Prchlik made some very pointed comments about sovereignty and the Soviets' role in the Pact.[5] The Soviets attacked Prchlik and his

[1] Robin Remington (ed.), *Winter in Prague* (Cambridge, Mass., 1969), 234–43 (document no. 36).
[2] See statements by Dzur, Prague radio, 11 July 1968; Prchlik, Prague radio, 11 July 1968; and Kudrna, *Lud*, 11 July 1968.
[3] See for example, *Obrana Lidu*, 27 July 1968; *Literarni Listy*, 25 July 1968; *Reporter*, 24 July 1968; *Prace* 20 July 1968 (Kotyk).
[4] Bilak, Svestka, and Kolder were said to have dragged their feet; the Slovak party central committee meeting heard more conservative comments than the Czechoslovak plenum. See *Bratislava Pravda*, 19 July 1968.
[5] Prague radio, 15 July 1968.

proposals on 23 July, and on 25 July the Czechoslovak presidium dissolved the central committee's eighth department – and with it Prchlik's job.[1] While dissolution of the eighth department was a progressive step, recommended by Prchlik himself, it bore the markings of a concession to the Soviets. Indeed subsequent disavowal by the presidium of Prchlik's Pact proposals and the ambiguity over his reassignment – as well as the public reaction to his removal – all testify to this.[2]

The Czechoslovak presidium went to the Cierna nad Tisou talks amidst an atmosphere of polemics, 'discoveries' of arms caches, and Soviet suggestions that the border with West Germany needed greater protection, and with Soviet troops still on Czechoslovak soil but, also, with the support of the public demonstrated in a widespread signature campaign. The Soviets came armed with accusations and quotations, and, reportedly, an exaggerated estimate of the strength of conservatives in the Czechoslovak party.[3] The discussions were stormy and emotional but instead of talk of troops, they centered on the questions of censorship, personnel changes, and 'anti-socialist' forces in Czechoslovakia. In the midst of the talks the Soviets reportedly became more cooperative, according to one account because letters from leading communists such as Tito, Ceausescu, and the Spanish party on behalf of eighteen European communist parties had alarmed the Soviets with regard to the forthcoming international conference.[4] There are many reports that Suslov changed positions on the issue of invasion and it is logical to assume that the reason was the conference he had so long been responsible for planning. Indeed a major factor in the Soviets' hesitation over invading undoubtedly devolved from the knowledge of what such a move would mean for their position in the international movement and their so laboriously planned conference scheduled for November 1968.

An agreement was worked out which it may be assumed each side interpreted as a victory; at the least that was how Dubcek and his colleagues interpreted it.[5] Prague pledged continued loyalty to the Warsaw Pact and CEMA, and promised to safeguard against 'anti-socialist' forces, prevent reinstitution of the Social Democratic Party,

---

[1] *Krasnaya Zvezda*, 23 July 1968; Prague radio, 25 July 1968.
[2] CTK, 27 July 1968; 15 August 1968 (Defense Ministry statement); Prague radio, 5 August 1968.
[3] The best accounts of the talks available to date are those of Pavel Tigrid: 'Czechoslovakia: A Post-Mortem,' *Survey*, 73 (1968), 159–64; and 'Czechoslovakia: A Post-Mortem, II,' *Survey*, 74–5 (1968), 113.
[4] Tigrid, *Survey*, 73 (1968), 162.   [5] Tigrid, *Survey*, 74–5 (1968), 112.

and maintain control over the clubs and the media. This was in exchange for an end to polemics, a possible loan, and no further interference in Czechoslovak affairs. Both the Warsaw letter and the stationing of Pact troops in Czechoslovakia were forgotten with the Soviet promise to withdraw all the troops and the Czechoslovak promise to meet the other 'allies' in Bratislava two days later. The Bratislava meeting too was stormy, primarily because Ulbricht presented an early version of the Brezhnev 'limited sovereignty' doctrine as the basis for the final communique. The final agreement, as promised by the Soviets, contained no direct references to Czechoslovak affairs.

The population was highly skeptical of the enthusiasm with which the party leaders presented the achievements of the talks, fearful of a secret agreement, although some did accept the regime's optimistic view, especially since Soviet troops did leave the country and polemics ceased.[1] However, efforts to fulfill the agreement by seeking voluntary censorship (including rumors of a conservative personnel switch in *Rude Pravo*), and other acts, e.g. curbing demonstrations, condemning Prchlik, and supporting the militia, all led to rising apprehensions.[2] Tito's and Ceausescu's visits to Prague bolstered public morale, but a visit by Ulbricht tended to counteract the positive effects even of the Czechoslovak–Rumanian treaty signed on 16 August. Ulbricht arrived for talks in Karlovy Vary on 13 August, one day before polemics resumed from Moscow. While it remains unclear just how much of a role Ulbricht's visit played in the Soviet decision to invade, Brezhnev is reported to have repeated to the 16 August CPSU politburo meeting Ulbricht's remarks in Dresden that 'if Czechoslovakia continues to follow the January line, all of us here will run a very serious risk which may well lead to our own downfall.'[3] It was this meeting, in possession of a report from Ulbricht's trip, which reportedly decided finally and unanimously upon the invasion – although the resumption of polemics on 14 August[4] suggests that the decision was assured some time earlier. The Soviets and their allies were conducting so many maneuvers throughout the summer, including the weeks prior to the invasion, that it is difficult to trace the date of the decision to invade to the beginning of one set of exercises or another. The replacement of Warsaw Pact

---

[1] *Zemedelske Noviny*, 6 August 1968.
[2] See *Rude Pravo*, 11 August (10 August presidium meeting); Prague radio, 15 August 1968.
[3] Tigrid, *Survey*, 74–5 (1968), 7–14.
[4] *Literatury Gazeta*, 14 August 1968. See also *Pravda*, 15 August 1968.

Chief-of-Staff Kazakov in August may have been the sign of the final decision. There is one thesis that Kazakov, as commander of the southern group of Pact forces in the 1950s (and thus involved in the intervention in Hungary in 1956) opposed the invasion because of the long-range damage this would do to the Pact. He and other military leaders are reported to have foreseen certain and long-range negative effects an invasion would have on the dependability of the Czechoslovak army as a key member of the Pact. A more dubious thesis holds (without referring to Kazakov's opinions regarding an invasion) that the new Chief-of-Staff, Schtemenko, was brought in as a senior, experienced Stalinist, to conduct the invasion.[1] Whatever the timing of the decision, the timing of the invasion itself was probably connected with the 9 September date scheduled for the Czechoslovak party congress, for it was at this congress that the reform regime planned legally to replace the conservatives in the central committee.

Brezhnev sent the Czechoslovak party a letter on 19 August outlining his renewed complaints of Czechoslovakia's failure to abide by the Cierna nad Tisou and Bratislava agreements – though no mention was contained therein of possible military action. Reportedly confident that the conservatives could gain control of the Czechoslovak civil and military institutions as well as support of the workers, the Soviets undertook the invasion of 20–21 August together with East Germany, Poland, Bulgaria, and Hungary.[2] The spontaneous, though unarmed, resistance of the Czechoslovak population, and the failure of the occupiers to form a quisling government demonstrated the lack of foundation to this confidence and the depth of the reform movement.

There is a striking continuity in the history of the Czechoslovak party and its relations with the international communist movement. In the 1920s the Comintern saw fit to intervene in Czech affairs, conducting high-level purges (known as the Bolshevization of the party) in efforts to elicit a less gradualist–reformist approach from the Czech communists. In 1947 the Cominform brought pressure to bear upon Gottwald

---

[1] See Malcolm Mackintosh, 'The Evolution of the Warsaw Pact,' *Adelphi Papers*, 58 (June 1969), 14–15; John Thomas, 'Soviet Foreign Policy and Conflict within Political and Military Leadership' (Research Analysis Corporation, 1970), pp. 7–10 (which cites J. Erickson in the *Royal United Service Institution Journal* (September 1969) as supporting the idea of Soviet military opposition to the invasion).

[2] Reportedly because of Soviet ambassador to Prague, Chervonenko's reports. (Tigrid, *Survey*, 74–5 (1968), 116.)

and his colleagues to abandon their parliamentary 'Czechoslovak road to socialism' and decisively take power in Prague (the February 1948 coup). In 1968 the Warsaw Pact (minus Rumania) intervened with force, with the same goal of putting a halt to the Czechs' democratic, permissive procedures and policies. This striking similarity should not limit us to perceiving events as specific – and inevitable – Czechoslovak phenomena, for the nuclei of reform movements exist in perhaps every communist party; indeed they have come to the fore in at least two previous cases: Poland and Hungary, 1956. What is specific to the Czechoslovak party is the nature of the difficulties the international movement has, almost continuously, encountered regarding the Czechoslovak party and particularly the Czech elements. It has not been that the Czechs were nationalistic and thus placed a longing for national independence before the interests of the movement, or anti-Russian to the extent of rejecting Moscow's leadership. As we have seen, prior to the interference from the Soviet Union, Poland, and East Germany the Czechoslovak movement was little concerned with its international position, foreign policy, or relations with the Soviet Union. It is true, as we have seen, that certain aspects of the reforms implicitly and even explicitly argued for independence, but these were mainly within the realm of establishing a viable economy, free of political encumberments, be they internal or external. The talk of a 'return to Europe' was intended in terms of economic–political–diplomatic contacts, not direct political alliance or even neutrality. It is true that many of the reforms, both economic and political, might eventually and perhaps inevitably, have led to a desire for independence of a political–economic nature, since the principle common to most of the reforms was decentralization of authority and a system based on the free expression and fulfillment of the real interests of the component parts. Indeed in the summer months of 1968, as Soviet pressures increased, there were voices raised in this direction of national independence. But this was neither the point nor the intended goal of the proposed reforms. Until August 1968 the cry for a Czechoslovak socialism was not intended or even widely interpreted domestically as anti-Russian.

While it was a movement which sought to find a model of socialism suitable to Czechoslovakia's needs, realities, and traditions, this desire was not born of nationalism or abhorrence for things Russian. It was, rather, born of problems and developments within Czechoslovak society for which the prevailing model, that of the Soviets', proved inadequate. We have seen just what this inadequacy was, both in the practical and theoretical spheres,[1] and we have also seen that there were but rare voices which emphasized the Russian source of the ruling model. There is nothing in either the actions or speeches of the reformers to indicate that they saw their own, new model as unobtainable within the framework of the Warsaw Pact–CEMA alliances. Nor did they suggest that their emerging model was valid – or even desirable – for others; it was not meant as a challenge to the Soviet model. It was, rather, Soviet, Polish, and East German fears of the nature of this model and its already apparent attraction for certain elements in their own countries, leading to their efforts to interfere in Czechoslovak affairs, which prompted the Prague reformers belatedly to insist upon full sovereignty *and* the purely Czechoslovak nature of their experiment.

Since these last elements – which may be construed as elements of national communism – came in *reaction* to Soviet actions, one cannot accept them as the *cause* of the Soviet actions. The Soviets made every effort publicly to create the impression that their fear was that Czechoslovakia was falling into the hands of persons who wished to take her out of the socialist alliance, defy the Soviet Union, and move towards the West. Indeed the Soviets contrived a number of facts (such as caches of West German arms) to create the impression that the bloc was in danger from West German exploitation of the weakening of socialism in Czechoslovakia. That these were not the genuine causes for the Soviets' fears was evidenced by the nature of the Soviets' demands in their talks with Dubcek in Dresden, Moscow, and Cierna nad Tisou. On the basis of the impression created by Soviet propaganda organs, it has been argued in the West that the Soviet military were influential in precipitating the invasion because of fears of what they saw as a weakened West German–Czechoslovak border and neutralist (or pro-western) inclinations on the part of Prague. Yet the Soviets did nothing after the invasion about placing their troops on this border (and indeed their desire to station troops in Czechoslovakia well pre-dated the Dubcek regime). Moreover, and, as pointed out, there is some evidence that important elements among the Soviet military were among those opposing the invasion, in the belief that Czechoslovakia was a more loyal link in the Warsaw Pact under Svoboda and Dubcek than she would be after an invasion.

The discussions of Dresden, Moscow, and Cierna nad Tisou, as well

---

[1] See above, chapters 12 and 20.

as the history of the Soviet concept of power, all point to a more complicated, ideologically influenced explanation for the invasion. In 1968, as in 1929 and 1947, Moscow's concerns focused on Czechoslovakia's traditional tendencies to democratic socialism, with all its implications for Eastern Europe and the Soviet Union. Like the Comintern and Cominform before them, Moscow, Warsaw, and Pankow were unwilling to accept or believe that this type of socialism could lead to and preserve communism. Specifically, the concept of the leading role of the party, as applied by the Soviets for some fifty years, had become so intricately connected with the concept of communist rule that Moscow could not conceive a communist party's remaining in power if it were to abandon its leading role. Moscow could not conceive of a communist state without the unchallenged, dictatorial–ubiquitous authority of the party; and if the communist party could not remain in power in any but the orthodox way, then indeed Czechoslovakia's alteration of the leading role of the party to permit a certain degree of pluralism and controls on central power constituted in Soviet eyes a danger to communist rule in Czechoslovakia. The implications of this danger were clear: pluralism in Prague – which could mean not only difficulties for Soviet dictation of policy for that country but also the inevitable dissolution of communist power and therefore of the communist regime – might well spread to other countries (as the Warsaw riots of March 1968 and troubles within the Soviet Komsomol seemed to indicate was already happening). The fall of the communist regime in Prague would mean the loss of Czechoslovakia as a reliable ally or even friendly neighbor. Here the international power motive returns but only as a consequence of a much more basic and immediate concern: the possibility of communism in a pluralistic–democratic socialist society. It was the democratic nature and content of the Czechoslovak experiment, rather than some fabricated 'neutralism' or pro-western tendency, which precipitated the invasion.

It is in this context that the Soviets elucidated their concept of limited sovereignty, i.e. the right of the socialist nations to determine what constitutes a danger to communism even within other socialist nations. While this may be a highly questionable and arbitrary concept, designed ultimately to preserve the Soviet empire, it conveys an important lesson for reform efforts within the context of communism. There are certain concepts which are so intricately wed to the Soviets' concept of rule that even non-nationalistic, pro-Russian, loyally socialist movements cannot infringe upon them.

This would seem to mean that future movements for democratically oriented reform must, perforce, be anti-Soviet, unless the Soviets' concept of rule itself undergoes reform. There is every reason to believe that the Czechoslovak reform movement believed it could realize its program within the context of communism and alliance with the Soviets. It was Moscow, not Prague, which said – perhaps proved – the contrary.

BIBLIOGRAPHY

The major part of this book is based on primary Czech and Slovak sources, principally newspapers and journals from the period 1963 to 1968. A detailed bibliography of the articles used comprises some one hundred pages which the author is willing to provide upon request. The following is a general and selected bibliography.

SELECTED PERIODICALS

Czech and Slovak publications

Acta Universitatis Carolinae, Aufbau und Frieden, Bratislava Pravda, Ceska Literatura, Ceskoslovensky Casopis Historicky, Czechoslovak Economic Papers, Czechoslovak Foreign Trade, Czechoslovak Life, Czechoslovak Sociological Society Bulletin, Dikobraz, Divadelni a Filmove Noviny, Divadlo, Ekonomicka Revue, Ekonomicke Casopis, Filmove a Televizni Noviny, Filosoficky Casopis, Finance a Uver, Historicky Casopis, Hospodarske Noviny, Host do Domu, Hudebni Rozhledy, Impuls, Knizni Kultura, Kulturni Noviny, Kulturni Tvorba, Kulturny Zivot, Lidova Demokracie, Literarni Listy, Literarni Noviny, Listy, Lud, Mezinarodni Vztahy, Mezinarodny Politika, Mlada Fronta, My, Nedele, Nova Mysl, Nova Svoboda, Nove Slovo, Noviny Zahranicniho Obchodu, Obrana Lidu, Orientace, Osvetova Prace, Otazky Marxistickej Filosofie, Plamen, Planovane Hospodarstvi, Pochoden, Politicka Ekonomie, Politika, Praca, Prace, Prace a Mzda, Pravnik, Pravnicke Studie, Pravny Obzor, Predvoj, Priroda a Spolecnost, Reporter, Rohac, Rolnicke Noviny, Rovnost, Rude Pravo, Sbornik Historicky, Sesity pro Mladou Literaturu, Slovansky Prehled, Slovenska Literatura, Slovenske Pohlady, Smena, Smer, Socialisticka Skola, Socialisticke Zemedelstvi, Statistika, Statisticke Prehledy, Student, Svet Sovetu, Svet Vedy, Svetove Literature, Technicke Noviny, Tribuna, Tvar, Ucitelske Noviny, Universita Karlova, Universum, Vecerni Praha, Vecernik, Veda a Zivot, Vlasta, Vychodoslovenske Noviny, Zemedelska Ekonomika, Zemedelske Noviny, Zitrek, Zivot Strany, and the Paris-based Czech journal *Svedectvi*.

Other Communist periodicals

Elet es Irodalom (Hungary), *Kommunist* (USSR), *Kommunist* (Yugoslavia), *Nedeljne Informativne Noviny* (Yugoslavia), *Polityka* (Poland), *World Marxist Review*.

Western periodicals

Primarily *East Europe, Problems of Communism, Survey*; occasionally *American Political Science Review, Canadian Journal of Economics and Political Science, Christian Century, Die Welt Woche, Die Zeit, The Economist, Encounter, Foreign Affairs, International Labor Review, Jews in Eastern Europe, Journal of Central*

Bibliography

European Affairs, Journal of Politics, New Leader, New Statesman, Orbis, Political Science Quarterly, Soviet Studies, Spectator, Studies in Soviet Thought, The World Today, World Politics.

The monitoring services of the BBC and RFE; the analyses published by RFE.

SELECTED BOOKS, ARTICLES AND PAMPHLETS

Alton, Thad P. and associates, *National Income and Product of Czechoslovakia in 1948–1949 and 1955–1956* (New York, 1962).

Antologie z Dejin Ceskoslovenske Filosofie, vol. 1 (Praha, 1963).

Apanasewicz, Nellie and Seymour Rosen, *Education in Czechoslovakia,* U.S. Department of Health, Education, and Welfare (Washington D.C., 1963).

Benes, Jan, *Situace* (Praha, 1963).

Do Vrabcu Jako Kdyz Streli (Praha, 1963).

Benes, Vaclav, Andrew Gyorgy, George Stambuk, *Eastern European Government and Politics* (New York, 1966).

Bob, Jozef, *Kritika 64* (Bratislava, 1965).

Brod, T. and E. Cejka, *Na Zapadni Fronte* (Praha, 1965).

Bromke, Adam, *The Communist States at the Crossroads* (New York, 1965).

Brown, J. F., *The New Eastern Europe* (London, 1966).

Brusek, Vratislav and Nicolas Spulber, *Czechoslovakia* (New York, 1957).

Burianek, Bohuslav, *Studium na Vysokych Skolach* (Praha, 1966).

Burianek, Frantisek, *Ceska Literatura 20 Stoleti* (Praha, 1968).

Z Dejin Ceske Literarni Kritiky (Praha, 1965).

Buzek, Anthony, *How The Communist Press Works* (London, 1964).

Cakajda, Eremias, Janovic, Provza, *Integrace Mezi Zemedelstvim a Prumyslem* (Praha, 1967).

Charim, Alexander, *Die Toten Gemeinden* (Wien, 1966).

The Constitution of the Czechoslovak Socialist Republic (Prague, 1960).

Dallin, Alexander, *Diversity in International Communism* (New York, 1963).

DAV (Bratislava, 1965).

Dejiny Komunisticke Strany Ceskoslovenska, vols. I–III (Praha, 1961, 1965, 1967).

Dejiny Slovenskej Literatury, vols. I–III (Bratislava, 1958, 1960, 1965).

Dvacet Let Rozvoje Ceskoslovenske Socialisticke Republiky (Praha, 1965).

Feiwel, George, *New Economic Patterns in Czechoslovakia* (New York, 1968).

Fischer-Galati, Stephen, *Eastern Europe in the Sixties* (New York, 1963).

Gamarnikov, Michael, *Economic Reforms in Eastern Europe* (Detroit, 1968).

Goldmann, Josef and Karel Kouba, *Hospodarsky Rust* (Praha, 1967).

Griffith, William, *Albania and the Sino–Soviet Dispute* (Cambridge, Mass., 1963).

Communism in Europe, vol. II (Cambridge, Mass., 1967).

Grzybowski, Kazimerz, *The Socialist Commonwealth of Nations* (New Haven, 1964).

Hamsik, Dusan, *Genius Prumernosti* (Praha, 1967).

Writers Against Rulers (London, 1971).

Havel, Vaclav, *The Memorandum* (London, 1966).

Zhradni Slavnost (Praha, 1964).

Hobza, J. and A. Nesvadba, *Prirucni Slovnicek k Nove Soustave Rizeni* (Praha, 1965).

Hromadka, J., Chysky, J., Witz, K., *Ceskoslovenske Pracovan Pravo* (Praha, 1957).

Bibliography

Ionescu, Ghita, *The Break-Up of the Soviet Empire in Eastern Europe* (Baltimore, 1965).

The Politics of the European Communist States (New York, 1967).

Jamgotch, Nish, *Soviet-East European Dialogue* (Stanford, Calif., 1968).

Jancar, Barbara Wolfe, 'The Twenty-Second Congress and the All-People's State in Czechoslovakia,' Unpublished doctoral dissertation (Columbia University, 1965).

Janza, Vladimir, *Uloha Cen v Nove Soustave Rizeni* (Praha, 1965).

Jenik, Ladislav, *New Trends in the Czechoslovak Economy* (Prague, 1966).

The Jewish Communities in Eastern Europe (New York, 1967).

Franz Kafka—Liblicka Konference 1963 (Praha, 1963).

Kaplan, Karel, *Utvareni Generalni Linie Vystavby Socialismu v Ceskoslovensku* (Praha, 1966).

Karvas, Peter, *Jazva* (Bratislava, 1963).

Kaser, Michael, *COMECON* (London, 1965).

Kobr, Jaroslav, *Organizace Prumysla a Prumyslovych Podniku v Nove Soustave Rizeni* (Praha, 1965).

Kohler, Heinz, *Economic Integration in the Soviet Bloc* (New York, 1965).

Kondelka, Miroslav, *Finance a Uver v Nove Soustave Rizeni* (Praha, 1965).

Kosik, Karel, *Dialektika Konkretniho* (Praha, 1963).

Kratochvilova, Zdenka, *The New Civil Code* (Prague, 1965).

Labedz, Leopold, *International Communism After Khrushchev* (Cambridge, Mass., 1965).

The Labour Code (Prague, 1966).

Lettrich, Jozef, *A History of Slovakia* (New York, 1954).

London, Artur, *Spanelsko, Spanelsko* (Praha, 1963).

London, Kurt, *Eastern Europe in Transition* (Baltimore, 1966).

Machonin, Pavel, *Socialni Struktura Socialisticke Spolecnosti* (Praha, 1966).

Machovec, Milan, *Tomas G. Masaryk* (Praha, 1968).

Main Reports and Documents Concerning the New System of Management of the National Economy in Czechoslovakia, Vols. 4–5 (Prague, 1965).

Mechura, A. and K. Fisch, *Vnitrni Obchod v Nove Soustave Rizeni* (Praha, 1965).

Michal, Jan, *Central Planning in Czechoslovakia* (Stanford, Calif., 1960).

Milkus, Josef, *Slovakia: A Political History 1918–1950* (Milwaukee, 1963).

Miller, Margaret, *Communist Economy Under Change* (London, 1963).

Mlynar, Zdenek, *Stat a Clovek* (Praha, 1964).

Mnacko, Ladislav, *Opozdene Reportaze* (Praha, 1964).

Taste of Power (London, 1967).

Montias, J. M., 'The Evolution of the Czech Economic Model,' Unpublished paper (Yale University, 1962).

'Uniformity and Diversity in the East European Future,' Unpublished paper (Yale University, 1964).

Nastin Dejin Ceskoslovenskeho Odboroveho Hnuti (Praha, 1963).

Novotny, Antonin, *Projevy a Stati*, vols. I–III (Praha, 1964).

Opavsky, J., Pesat, Z., Suchomal, M., *Kriticka Rocenka* (Praha, 1963).

O Stanovach Komunisticke Strany Ceskoslovenska (Praha, 1965).

Pelikan, Jiri (ed.), *Potlacena Zprava* (Wien, 1970).

Bibliography

Plevza, Viliam, *Davisti v Revolucnom Hnuti* (Bratislava, 1965).
Press Group of Soviet Journalists, *On Events in Czechoslovakia* (Moscow, 1968).
Prirucni Slovnik k Dejinam KSC, vols. I–II (Praha, 1964).
Prochazka, Jan, *Politika Pro Kazdeho* (Praha, 1968).
  Prestrelka (Praha, 1966).
  Svata Noc (Praha, 1966).
Pryor, Frederick, *The Communist Foreign Trade System* (Cambridge, Mass., 1963).
Richta, Radovan, *Civilizace Na Rozcesti* (Praha, 1969).
Rovensky, Dusan, *V Prednich Radach* (Praha, 1965).
Rothchild, Josef, *Communism in Eastern Europe* (New York, 1964).
Rozner, Jan, *Daviste a Jejich Doba* (Praha, 1966).
Sbirka Zakonu Ceskoslovenske Socialisticke Republiky (Praha, 1960–8).
Sbirka Zakonu Republiky Ceskoslovenske (Praha, 1948–59).
Selucky, Radoslav, *Ekonomicka–Moralka–Zivot* (Praha, 1963).
  Zapad je Zapad (Praha, 1965).
Selucky and Milada Selucka, *Clovek a Hospodarstvi* (Praha, 1967).
Seton-Watson, Hugh, *The East European Revolution* (London, 1952).
Seton-Watson, R. W., *A History of Czechs and Slovaks* (Hamden, Conn., 1965).
Sik, Ota, 'Das Neue Verhaltnis Zwischen Wirtschaftsplanung und Market–Mechanismus in der CSSR,' Unpublished paper (Goesing, Austria, 1965).
  Plan and Market Under Socialism (Prague, 1967).
  Problems of Socialist Commodity Relations (Prague, 1966).
Siracky, Andrej, *Sociologia* (Bratislava, 1966).
XII. Sjezd Komunisticke Strany Ceskoslovenska 4–8 Prosinec 1962 (Praha, 1962).
XII. Sjezd Komunisticke Strany Ceskoslovenska 4–8 Prosinec 1962, Neprednesene Diskuse Prispevky (Praha, 1962).
XIII. Sjezd Komunisticke Strany Ceskoslovenska 31 Kveten–4 Cerven 1966 (Praha, 1966).
XIII. Sjezd Komunisticke Strany Ceskoslovenska 31 Kveten–4 Cerven 1966, Neprednesene Diskuse Pripevky (Praha, 1966).
IV. Sjezd Svazu Ceskoslovenskych Spisovatelu (Praha, 1968).
Skilling, Gordon, *Communism: National and International* (Toronto, 1964).
Skvorecky, Josef, *Zbabelci* (Praha, 1963).
Slovnik Ceskych Spisovatelu (Praha, 1964).
Statisticka Rocenka Ceskoslovenske Socialisticke Republiky (Praha, 1960–8).
Statisticka Rocenka Republiky Ceskoslovenske (Praha, 1948–59).
Stoll, Ladislav, *Tricet Let Boju za Ceskou Socialistickou Poesii* (Praha, 1950).
Svoboda, The Press in Czechoslovakia, 1968 (Zurich, 1970).
Szanto, Ladislav, *Co Nam Treba* (Bratislava, 1964).
Szirmai, Z., *Law in Eastern Europe*, vols. 1–2 (Leyden, 1958).
Taborsky, Edward, *Communism in Czechoslovakia* (Princeton, 1961).
Tigrid, Pavel, *Le Printemps de Prague* (Paris, 1968).
  Kvadratura Kruhu (Paris, 1970).
Tolar, J., Prenosil, G., Lakatos, M., *Mistni Lidove Soudy* (Praha, 1965).
Toman, Josef, *Uvod do Zasad Nove Soustavy Planoviteho Rizeni* (Praha, 1965).
Tomasek, L., Litera, J., Vecera, J., *Strana a Dnesek* (Praha, 1967).
Turek, O., and Sokol, M., *Narodohspodarske Planovani v Nove Soustave Rizeni* (Praha, 1965).

Bibliography

Urban, G. R., *Talking to Eastern Europe* (Detroit, 1964).

Uredni List Ceskoslovenske Republiky (Praha, 1959).

Usneseni a Dokumenty Ustredniho Vyboru Komunisticke Strany Ceskoslovenska, Od XI Sjezdu do Celostatni Konference 1960 (Praha, 1960).

Usneseni a Dokumenty Ustredniho Vyboru Komunisticke Strany Ceskoslovenska, Od Celostatni Konference KSC 1960 do XII Sjezdu KSC, vols. I-II (Praha, 1962–3).

Usneseni a Dokumenty Ustredniho Vyboru Komunisticke Strany Ceskoslovenska, Od Listopadu 1962 do Konce Roku 1963 (Praha, 1964).

Usneseni a Dokumenty Ustredniho Vyboru Komunisticke Strany Ceskoslovenska, 1964 (Praha, 1965).

Vaculik, Ludvik, *Rusny Dum* (Praha, 1963).

Sekyra (Praha, 1966).

Vopicka, Edward, *Vnitropodnikove Rizeni v Nove Soustave Rizeni* (Praha, 1965).

Yearbook of the Czechoslovak Academy of Sciences 66 (Prague, 1968).

Zinner, Paul, *Communist Strategy and Tactics in Czechoslovakia 1918–1948* (London, 1963).

Zubek, Theodoric, *The Church of Silence in Slovakia* (Whiting, Ind., 1956).

INDEX

Action Program: adoption of, 279, 296; and anti-semitism, 292; censorship, 295; economic reform, 279; foreign policy, 314; freedom of association, 284; interest groups, 284, 300; national minorities, 293; possibility of opposition, 305, 307; role of party, 299–300, 302; separation of party and state, 302–3; 'Slovak Question,' 311; trade unions, 285–6; youth, 289; other references, 301, 321
administrative procedures: new rules on, 215, 215n, 220
Agrarian Party, 95, 287
agriculture, 11–15, 17, 47, 257; economic reforms, 51–2, 89–90; students and youth in, 29, 115; trade union for, 95, 287
Agriculture Production Administrations, 15
Albania, 18
Albee, Edward, 121
'all-people state,' 150, 153, 160, 166
Amnesty International, 131
'anarcho-syndicalism,' 96
anti-semitism: and Arab–Israeli conflict, 238, 246, 247n, 267, 292; Action Program on, 292; problem of (1968), 292–3, 293n, and purge trials (1949–54), 9–10, 108, 236, 238; and Slovak nationalism, 247n, 292; see also minorities and religious groups
Antonioni, Michelangelo, 126
Arab–Israeli conflict, 236–8, 241, 246, 247n, 315
army: Main Political Directorate, 272, 310; and the December 1967 political crisis, 267, 272, 310; and reforms, 310
arts, liberalization in, 120–32
Auersperg, Pavel, 120, 144, 154, 232
Austria, 83, 137, 235
Austro-Hungarian empire, 20, 196

Bacilek, Karol: demotion of, 32–3, 38, 189, 309; and Dubcek, 32–3, 46; on intellectuals and culture, 24; and Novotny, 8n, 32–3, 46; Prague-oriented Slovak first secretary, 21, 32n, 192; role of in Stalinist abuses, 8n, 10, 24, 32; and

Slovak communist underground (World War II), 190; at Twelfth Party Congress, 10
balance of payments, 11, 12, 13; see also credits, foreign trade
Barak, Rudolf: and Novotny, 9, 9n, 17–19, 273; released, 309; other references, 181
'Barak affair,' 7, 9n, 17–19, 181; and Albania, 18; Moscow's role in, 18–19
Barak Committee of Investigation of purge trials, 3, 9, 10, 17
Bares, Gustav, 42
Bartuska, Jan, 219, 272
Bastovansky, Stefan, 42
Beckett, Samuel, 121
Belohradska, Hana, 127
Benes, Eduard, 119n, 136
Benes government, 190, 191
Benes, Jan, 127, 131, 143, 245–7
Beran, Josef, 106–7, 291
Beria, L. P., 3
Berlin crisis (1961), 14
Bertelmann, Karel, 175
Biafra, 313, 315
Bilak, Vasil, 203, 204n, 239, 271, 296, 322n
Blazek, Vladimir, 140
Blazkova, Jaroslava, 127
'Bloody Hand,' the, 38n
Borba, 251, 270, 318
'bourgeois nationalists:' purges of, 9, 21, 32n, 34–5, 39–43, 189, 193, 200–1, 258; rehabilitations of, 32n, 33–5, 35–6n, 45, 49 195, 202n
Brabec, Jiri, 128n
Bratislava Conference (1968), 322, 324, 325
Bratislava Pravda, critical role of: on cadre system, 24, 167; on copying USSR, 28; on freedom of press and journalism, 36, 254; Hysko's speech to journalists' congress, 40–2, 45; and Novotny, 42, 44, 45; on party, 28, 154–5, 166–7; on 'Slovak Question' and rehabilitations, 35, 256–7; spokesman for intellectuals, 22; on youth, 262
Bratislava University, 52
Brenac, Stefan, 232

335

Index

Brezhnev, L. I.: in Czechoslovakia, 7, 48, 48n, 136–7, 270, 318; doctrine of limited sovereignty of, 321, 324, 328–9; and Dubcek, 318; and Novotny, 236–7n, 270–1, 318; and Ulbricht, 324; other references, 325
Brezovsky, Bohuslav, 145
Budin, Stanislav, 315
Bulgaria (including party), 8, 19, 318, 320–1, 325
Burianek, Josef, 144
Bystrina, Ivan, 161

cadre system, 17, 155, 167–9, 171, 275, 300; in education, 110–11, 117, 117n; in Hungary, 168; Novotny on, 11, 29, 172; Thirteenth Party Congress 'Theses' on, 167–8, 169, 205
Canada, 57
Capek, Karel, 129n, 135, 235
Catholic Church, 106–7, 107n, 290–1
Catholic Peoples Party, 291
Ceausescu, Nicolae, 323, 324
censorship: Action Program on, 295; and Czechoslovakia's 'allies,' 298, 316, 321, 323; of films, 126, 235; intellectuals against, 34, 148–9, 234–5, 240, 294–5, 298; of media, 37, 127, 135, 137–8, 140, 235, 296; and the regime, 140–2, 147, 148, 296; of specific topics, 238, 244, 246, 252, 297; types of, 37, 146, 147–8, 149, 294–5, 324; other references, 220, 241, 297; see also Press Law
Central Administration for Publication, 148–9, 294
Cepicka, Alexej, 3
Cernik, Oldrich, 85, 250, 279, 296, 317
Ceskoslovensky Spisovatel, 249
Charles University, 264; Faculty of Philosophy, 116n, 250, 263, 264
Chervonenko, Stepan, 325n
China, 7, 14
Chorvath, Michal, 35n, 252
Chudik, Michal, 47, 198, 205, 250, 269–71
Chytilova, Vera, 126, 235
Cierna nad Tisou Conference, 282, 322–5, 327
Cikker, Jan, 204
Circle of Independent Writers, 289
Cisar, Cestmir: as early liberal, 24, 45–6; and mass media in 1968, 296; Minister of Education and Culture, 47, 116n, 120, 123, 144; and Novotny, 120n; on party,

33n, 300; party secretary, 33, 38, 47; Provisional Czech National Council chairman, 312; and reforms in education, 111, 112–13, 116; and reforms in theatre, 123–4; and students, 116n, 289, 304; other references, 120n, 317
Civil Code (1950), 220; see also legal system
Civil Code (1965), 215–22; see also legal system
Clementis, Vladimir, 21, 23, 35–6, 39, 41, 42n, 44
'Club of Committed Thinking,' 136
Club of Critical Thought, 290
Club of the Friends of Art, 261–2
Cominform, 315, 325, 327
Comintern, 190, 199, 317, 325, 327
Commission for Finance, Prices, and Wages (State Price Commission, State Wage Commission), 15, 61, 114, 280
Commission for Technology (Commission for Scientific and Technical Development), 15, 61
Committee of Czechoslovak Women, 25
Committee for Socialist Culture, 25, 26
Constitution (1948), 192, 193, 195
Constitution (1960): adoption of, 5; and elected organs, 179, 181–3; and leading role of the party, 5, 163–4, 183, 242, 299, 305; and role of the government, 177; and Slovakia, 5, 194–5, 205–9
Constitutional Court, 312
Constitutional Law (1968), 311–12
consumer goods, 15–16; and economic reforms, 53, 79–81, 84, 225–8
Cooperative Farmers Conference, 287; see also agriculture, peasants, trade unions
Council for Mutual Economic Aid (CEMA), 14, 16, 29, 61, 88, 89; International Bank for Economic Cooperation, 88; and the reforms, 88–9, 281, 323, 327; suggestions for reforms in, 88–9, 281, 315
coup of 1948, 1, 328
courts and judges, 11, 92, 210–11, 222; administrative courts, 220; Constitutional Court, 312; criticism of, 163, 210–14, 215, 219; reform of, 212–22; see also legal system
Coward, Noel, 121
CPSU: letter to Prague, 320–1; Twentieth Party Congress, 41, 51; Twenty-Second Party Congress, 2, 3, 7, 17–19, 21, 22; Twenty-Third Party Congress, 130; other references, 176, 319; see also USSR

336

Index

Czechoslovak Writers (*cont.*)
reaction to and results of, 164, 242, 244–5, 247–54; and Slovak writers, 243, 249; speech of L. Vaculik, 163–4, 241–5, 248, 251–2, 261; other references, 265
Czechoslovak Youth Union (CSM): conference of Prague section (1967), 260; congress (1963), 36; congress (1967), 104, 106, 259–61; congress of Slovak section (1967), 260; membership in, 102, 261n, 288–9; and Novotny, 105–6, 259–60; and party, 101–6, 259–61, 287–9; reforms of (discussions of and demands for), 36, 94–5, 100–6, 259–61, 288–9; and Scouts, 103, 260; and students, 101–6, 117, 259–61, 263–5, 287–9

Daniel, Yuli, 130
Dav, 21, 35, 39–40, 45, 190
David, Pavol, 32, 309
decentralization of 1958, 5, 14–15, 17
defense counsel, 214–17; *see also* legal system
Dejmek, Kazimierz, 123
Dementyev, A., 25
democratic centralism, 15, 37, 154–5, 202; and the party, 154–5, 170–1, 173, 300–2
de-Stalinization of 1956, 1–4
dictatorship of the proletariat, 150, 153–5, 162, 211, 221; and leading role of party, 164–5, 277, 299–300, 302; and socialist society, 153, 154–63, 275, 277
District Agricultural Associations (DAA), 90
Dolansky, Jaromir, 47, 47n, 250
domestic trade and services: and economic reforms, 82, 86, 184, 228, 280
Dominican Republic, 146
Drda, Jan, 241, 253
Dresden meeting, 314, 318, 324, 327
Dubcek, Alexander: and Bacilek, 32–3, 46; and Brezhnev, 318; to Budapest, 320; at central committee plena of September, October, December 1967 and January 1968, 255, 258, 268–9, 271, 273–4; commitment to reform movement, 46, 255, 274, 322; and 'Czechoslovak Way,' 316–17, 327; and economic reforms, 74, 255, 258; and foreign policy, 313–15, 317, 318, 327; and freedom of expression, 284, 295–6, 298, 303; and interest groups, 284; and K-231, 290, 307; and mass organizations (trade unions, youth, etc.)

260, 284–7, 289; on National Front and opposition, 307–8; and Novotny, 32–3, 46, 259, 268–9, 271–3; and outside pressures and negotiations, 289, 298, 308, 314–15, 318, 322–3, 327; on party, 268, 299, 303, 307–9; and security organs, 309, 311; and Siroky, 32–3, 46; and Slovak party, 32–3, 38, 46, 74, 202n; and 'Slovak Question,' 46, 198, 203, 255, 258–9; on strikes, 283
Durrenmatt, Friedrich, 121
Durych, Jaroslav, 129, 142, 236
'Dynamo,' 204n
Dzur, Martin, 319

East Germany (including party), 87, 129–30, 236n, 298, 314–21, 325–7
economic crisis of 1960s, 7, 11–16, 19, 29, 38, 268–9
economic progress of 1950s, 4–5
economic reforms: 50–93, 223–31, 279–83; Action Program on, 279; debate on, 14–15, 50–3, 57, 64–6, 73–81, 269–70, 275–6; and domestic trade and services, 82, 86, 184, 228, 280; and Dubcek, 74, 255, 258; and educational system, 111, 114; and elected organs of government, 177–9, 184; and foreign trade, 53, 55, 60–1, 65–6, 74–5, 82–9, 225, 227–8, 236n, 281–2; and government, 15, 50–93, 223–31, 279–83; and legal system, 215; and levies, 60–1, 63, 67–71, 74–6, 90, 184; and management, 53, 56, 60–2, 97–8, 184, 223–4, 226, 279, 282–3; and Novotny, 4, 74, 83, 85, 172, 223–4, 269, 276; and party and the economy, 57, 62, 93, 150, 160, 163–76, 178, 224, 299–300; and political reforms, 93, 150, 156, 223, 229–31, 269, 279, 283; problems over implementation of, 223–31, 268–9; and Sik, 14, 51, 53–4, 56–7, 59–60, 64–6, 73–4, 76–7, 81, 84, 93, 227, 229–31, 280, 282; and 'Slovak Questions,' 69, 255–8; and theatre, 124; Thirteenth Party Congress 'Theses' on, 170; and trade unions, 95–100, 224, 226–7, 230–1; and Twelfth Party Congress, 15; and wages and salaries, 54–5, 61, 63, 67–8, 74, 76, 79–80, 90, 95, 97, 114, 225–31, 283; and workers, 52, 55–6, 76–7, 81, 99–100, 230–1, 276, 279, 282–3; other references, 26, 98, 133, 135, 150, 152, 171; *see also* agriculture, consumer goods, credits, currency,

338

Index

economic reforms (*cont.*)
industry, inflation, investments, labor productivity, planning, prices
educational system: cadre system in, 110–11, 117, 117n; criticism of, 40, 109, 111, 114; and national minorities, 293; organization and nature of, 102, 109–13; and party, 110–11, 116–19; reform in higher education, 116–19; reform in primary education, 111–15; reform in secondary education, 111–15; reform of 1960, 110; and religious education, 107, 109, 291–2
Egypt, 315; *see also* Arab–Israeli conflict
electoral laws, 175, 185–8, 304
Elixir, 104–5
Encyclopedia of Czech Writers, 128–9
Engels, Friedrich, 202–3
enterprise councils, 279, 282–3, 286
Euro-Vision, 137–8

Faltan, Samo, 34
farmers, *see* peasants
Feder, Richard, 292
'Federalists' (Slovak), 243–4n, 247n
federalization: Constitutional Law on, 311–12; debate on, 198–205; 1967 dispute over, 256–9; of the party, 302; other references, 20, 177n, 204, 205
Fellini, Federico, 126
Filip, Miroslav, 37
Film and Television Artists Union, 124, 126
film-makers, 253
films, liberalization in, 28, 124–6, 235
Five-Year Plan, Third, 11, 12, 15
Flek, Josef, 228
Florian, Josef, 142
Florin, Theo, 236
foreign aid, population's view of, 16
foreign policy, 236–7, 312–15, 317, 318, 327; *see also under individual countries*
foreign trade, 11–14; and economic reforms, 53, 55, 60–1, 65–6, 74–5, 82–9, 225, 227–8, 236n, 281–2; *see also* CEMA
Forman, Milos, 125
France, 29, 83
Frankfurter Allgemeine Zeitung, 246
Fric, Martin, 124

Galuska, Miroslav, 45n, 149, 149n, 295, 313
GATT, 87

Germany, neutralization of, 199–200, 258; *see also* East Germany, West Germany
Ginsberg, Allen, 101n, 128
Glazarova, Jarmila, 25, 241
Gleason, Jackie, 138
Goldmann, Josef, 81, 227–8
Goldstuecker, Eduard, 27, 289, 317; and Capek, 129n, 135; on censorship and the media, 294; and Czechoslovak Writers Union, 241n, 253 and Kafka, 27, 129–30; on possibility of opposition, 307; and students, 264–5, 289
Gomulka, Wladyslav, 316
Gosiorovsky, Milos, 200–1
Gottwald, Klement, 3, 17, 34n, 233; and 'Czechoslovak Way,' 317, 325; death of, 2, 32n; and 'Slovak Question,' 191
government: 'anti-bureaucracy' campaign of, 178; and economic reforms, 15, 50–93, 223–31, 279–83; and National Assembly, 178–80, 303; and National Committees, 181–5, 194, 206–7; and party, 5, 158–60, 163, 165–6, 169–83, 269, 302–5; reorganizations of, 178, 208; reshuffle of (1963) 47; and Slovak organs, 189, 191–5, 205–8; and socialist society, 153, 162, 177, 275, 277; Thirteenth Party Congress 'Theses' on, 162, 177; and trade unions, 99
government organs, elected: and economic reforms 177–9, 184; and electoral laws, 185–6, 188; and government, 178–80, 303, and legal system, 213, 215, 219, 222; local, 177, 184–5; and party, 163, 166, 179, 183–5, 303; other references, 10, 158, 159, 160, 185, 216; *see also* National Assembly, National Committees, electoral laws
Grechko, Andrei, 319
Grohmann, Josef, 142, 144
Grossmann, Jan, 122
Guardini, Romano, 142

Haba, Zdenek, 52–3
Hajek, Jiri (government official), 117–18, 144, 232, 263, 315
Hajek, Jiri (writer), 23, 23n, 146–7
Halas, Frantisek, 235
Haman, Ales, 127
Hamernik, Emilian, 99n
Hamouz, Frantisek, 227
Hasek, Jaroslav, 25
Havel, Vaclav, 122, 143, 144n, 241–4, 318
Havlicek, Frantisek, 232

Index

health bill, 182, 182n
Hendrych, Jiri: and 'bourgeois nationalism,' 45; and CSM, 102–3; at Czechoslovak Journalists Union Congress, 254; at Czechoslovak Theatrical and Film Artists Union Congress, 122–4, 146; and economic reforms, 56, 57; on interest groups, 170, 172; on leading role of party, 170, 172, 268; party positions of, 47, 123n, 144; at Twelfth Party Congress, 10; and writers, 23, 239–42, 248–9, 249n, 252, 254; other references, 46, 131, 250, 271n, 274
Hes, Jaroslav, 144, 249
Hlinka, Andrei, 199
Hloznik, Vincent, 204
Hochhuth, Rolf, 141–2
Hoffmann, Karel, 137, 232
Holdos, Ladislav, 42n
Holecek, Lubomir, 104n, 106, 262
Holland, 83
Horvath, Ivan, 42n
Hospodarske Noviny, 27, 52
Host do Domu, 232–3, 244
Hostovsky, Egon, 129
Hrubin, Frantisek, 4
Hruza, Karel, 291
Huebl, Milan, 128n
Hungary (including party): cadre system in, 168; de-Stalinization in, 7, 8, 19; and Prague 'spring,' 318, 318n, 320–1, 325; and 1956 revolution, 2, 22–3, 35, 155, 169, 325–6; other references, 2, 37, 107, 140
Husak, Gustav: demands for rehabilitation of, 22–3, 41; and federalization, 198, 201–2, 311–12; and non-Slovak minorities, 312; and *Nove Slovo*, 243–4n; and Novotny, 43–4; on possibility of opposition, 307; and Siroky, 190, 201; and 'Slovak Question,' 44, 192, 196–8, 201–2; other references, 42, 44–5, 190
Husar, Eugen, 216
Hysko, Miroslav, 28, 40–6

Ilichev, L., 20
Impuls, 144
Indra, Alois, 271
industry, 11–15, 51–2, 257; and economic reforms, 50–81, 279–80
inflation, 74, 77–81, 224–9
Innostranaya Literatura, 130
Institute of History, Slovak party, 200

Institute of Political Science, party, 174n, 175
intellectuals, 139, 170, 176, 210, 232–54, 258; and Arab–Israeli conflict, 236–8; and freedom of expression (censorship), 34, 148–9, 234–5, 240, 294–5, 298; members of party, 22, 120, 147–50, 210, 223, 268, 295–6; and Novotny, 19, 22–3, 29, 48, 106, 120, 157, 169; and Novotny's Kosice speech, 44; and Novotny's Ostrava speech, 30–1; Polish press on, 37; regime's desire to avoid alliance of with population or workers, 22, 26, 29, 106, 169; revolt of in 1956, 3–4; revolt of in 1963, 22–31, 34–7, 39–42, 44; and students, 2, 261–2, 264–5; and Twelfth Party Congress, 23; and '2,000 Words,' 297; and workers, 2, 22, 29, 44–5, 106, 169, 292, 297
interest groups: Action Program on, 284, 300; and dictatorship of proletariat, 153, 221, 277; Dubcek on, 284; and leading role of party, 153, 154, 170, 172, 277; and legal system, 215–16; and mass organizations as, 94–6, 99–100, 102–6, 161, 260–1, 285–7; Mlynar on, 152–4, 160, 175; and National Front, 304–6; in socialist society, 103, 150–4, 157–60, 174–5, 221, 277; Smrkovsky on, 164, 284; and Thirteenth Party Congress, 153, 154, 162; other references, 124, 160–1, 185
Inter-Vision, 137
invasion, by Warsaw Pact (minus Rumania), 316–29; other references, 283n, 291n, 311–12, 318
invasion, Soviet decision for: Soviet hesitations, 323–5, 327; and Suslov, 323; and Ulbricht, 324
investigatory organs, 213–14, 217–19, 310; *see also* legal system
investments, 12, 13; and economic reforms, 55, 59, 60–3, 68–9, 75, 79–80, 90, 224–9, 282–3
Ionescu, Eugene, 121
Israel, 107, 238, 244, 246, 267, 292, 313; *see also* Arab–Israeli conflict
Italy, 86; Communist Party of, 130, 313

Janko, Vladimir, 272, 310
Jaris, Milan, 253
Jasny, Vojtech, 125
Jehovah's Witnesses, 292
Jesenska, Zora, 34–5, 40, 252, 293

Index

345

Index